ESSENTIALS FOR design

MACROMEDIA® DREAMWEAVER® MX 2004

level two

Julian Rickards

Prentice Hall
Upper Saddle River, New Jersey 07458

A Cataloging-in-Publication record for this book
is available from the Library of Congress.

Publisher and Vice President: Natalie E. Anderson
Executive Editor, print: Stephanie Wall
Executive Editor, media: Jodi McPherson
Acquisitions Editor: Melissa Sabella
Editorial Assistants: Alana Meyers, Brian Hoehl, Sandra Bernales,
and Bambi Dawn Marchigano
Senior Media Project Manager: Cathleen Profitko
Senior Marketing Manager: Emily Knight
Marketing Manager: Sarah Davis

Marketing Assistant: Lisa Taylor
Senior Editorial Project Manager: Anne Garcia
Project Manager, Production: Vanessa Nuttry
Manufacturing Buyer: Vanessa Nuttry
Interior Design: Thistle Hill Publishing Services, LLC
Cover Design: Blair Brown
Cover Printer: Coral Graphics
Printer/Binder: Von Hoffman Press

Credits and acknowledgments borrowed from other sources and reproduced, with permission, in this textbook appear on the appropriate page within the text.

The fonts utilized in these training materials are the property of Against The Clock, Inc., and are supplied to the legitimate buyers of the Against The Clock training materials solely for use with the exercises and projects provided in the body of the materials. They may not be used for any other purpose, and under no circumstances may they be transferred to another individual, nor copied or distributed by any means whatsoever.

A portion of the images supplied in this book are copyright © PhotoDisc, Inc., 201 Fourth Ave., Seattle, WA 98121, or copyright ©PhotoSpin, 4030 Palos Verdes Dr. N., Suite 200, Rollings Hills Estates, CA. These images are the sole property of PhotoDisc or PhotoSpin and are used by Against The Clock with the permission of the owners. They may not be distributed, copied, transferred, or reproduced by any means whatsoever, other than for the completion of the exercises and projects contained in this book.

Against The Clock and the Against The Clock logo are trademarks of Against The Clock, Inc., registered in the United States and elsewhere. References to and instructional materials provided for any particular application program, operating system, hardware platform, or other commercially available product or products do not represent an endorsement of such product or products by Against The Clock, Inc.

Macromedia Flash, Generator, FreeHand, Dreamweaver, Fireworks, and Director are registered trademarks of Macromedia, Inc. Photoshop, PageMaker, Acrobat, Adobe Type Manager, Illustrator, InDesign, Premiere, and PostScript are trademarks of Adobe Systems Incorporated. QuarkXPress is a registered trademark of Quark, Inc. Macintosh is a trademark of Apple Computer, Inc. CorelDRAW!, procreate Painter, and WordPerfect are trademarks of Corel Corporation. FrontPage, Publisher, PowerPoint, Word, Excel, Office, Microsoft, MS-DOS, and Windows are either registered trademarks or trademarks of Microsoft Corporation.

Other product and company names mentioned herein may be the trademarks of their respective owners.

10 9 8 7 6 5 4 3 2 1

ISBN 0-13-146834-0

ABOUT THE SERIES EDITOR

Ellenn Behoriam is president and founder of Against The Clock, Inc. (ATC), one of the nation's leading content providers. Ellenn and her staff have successfully produced many of the graphic arts industry's most popular and well-received books and related series. These works include the *Electronic Cookbook, Workflow Reengineering, Teams and the Graphic Arts, Adobe Photoshop Creative Techniques, Adobe Illustrator Creative Techniques,* and *QuarkXPress 6: Creating Digital Documents,* the foundation for the QuarkXPress Trainer certification programs. The Against The Clock series, published in concert with Prentice Hall/Pearson Education, includes more than 26 titles that focus on applications for the graphic and computer arts industries.

Against The Clock also worked with Pearson to develop the *Companion for the Digital Artist* series. These titles focus on specific and fundamental creative concepts, including design, Web-site development, photography, typography, color theory, and copywriting. These concise and compact works provide core concepts and skills that supplement any application-specific education, regardless of which textbooks are used to teach program skills.

Under Ellenn's leadership and direction, ATC is currently developing more than 20 titles for the new *Essentials for Design* series. Her staff and long-established network of professional educators, printers, prepress experts, workflow engineers, and business leaders add significantly to ATC's ability to provide current, meaningful, and effective books, online tutorials, and business-to-business performance and workflow-enhancement programs.

ABOUT THE AUTHOR

Julian Rickards has been involved in various computer-related fields over the last dozen or so years, including computer instruction, technical illustration and Web design and is always willing to assist someone who is struggling with a project or concept. He is an advocate of Web standards and web accessibility and is a member of GAWDS.org. In his employment with the Ontario government, he oversees the database and archives of digital publications and is often called upon to assist with the development of the Internet and intranet Web sites. Julian hails from Canada, where he resides with his wonderfully supportive wife, Nanette, and two sons, Sebastian and Graeme.

ACKNOWLEDGMENTS

We would like to thank the professional writers, artists, editors, and educators who have worked long and hard on the *Essentials for Design* series.

And thanks to the dedicated teaching professionals: Kara Hardin; David McGill, Azusa Pacific University; Dan Workman; and Dean Bagley. Your insightful comments and expertise have certainly contributed to the success of the *Essentials for Design* series.

Thank you to Terry Sisk Graybill, copy editor and final link in the chain of production, for her help in making sure that we all said what we meant to say.

And a very special thank you to Erika Kendra, production designer, technical consultant, partner in crime, and friend.

And to Melissa Sabella, Anne Garcia, Jodi McPherson, and Vanessa Nuttry — we appreciate your patience as we begin this new venture together.

CONTENTS AT A GLANCE

TABLE OF CONTENTS

HOW TO USE THIS BOOK

Essentials courseware from Prentice Hall is anchored in the practical and professional needs of all types of students. The *Essentials* series presents a learning-by-doing approach that encourages you to grasp application-related concepts as you expand your skills through hands-on tutorials. As such, it consists of modular lessons that are built around a series of numbered step-by-step procedures that are clear, concise, and easy to review.

Essentials books are divided into projects. A project covers one area (or a few closely related areas) of application functionality. Each project consists of several lessons that are related to that topic. Each lesson presents a specific task or closely related set of tasks in a manageable chunk that is easy to assimilate and retain.

Each element in the *Essentials* book is designed to maximize your learning experience. A list of the *Essentials* project elements, and a description of how each element can help you, begins on the next page. To find out more about the rationale behind each book element and how to use each to your maximum benefit, take the following walk-through.

WALK-THROUGH

Project Objectives. Starting with an objective gives you short-term, attainable goals. Each project begins with a list of objectives that closely match the titles of the step-by-step tutorials. ▶

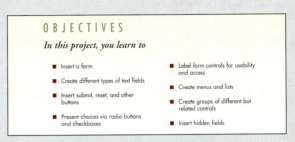

OBJECTIVES

In this project, you learn to

- Insert a form
- Create different types of text fields
- Insert submit, reset, and other buttons
- Present choices via radio buttons and checkboxes
- Label form controls for usability and access
- Create menus and lists
- Create groups of different but related controls
- Insert hidden fields

◀ Why Would I Do This? Introductory material at the beginning of each project provides an overview of why these tasks and procedures are important.

Visual Summary. A series of illustrations introduces the new tools, dialog boxes, and windows you explore in each project. ▼

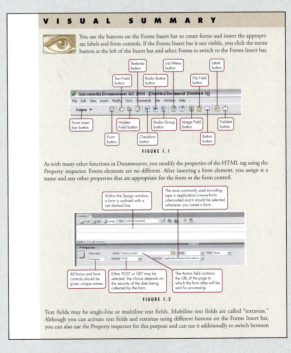

◀ Step-by-Step Tutorials. Hands-on tutorials let you learn by doing and include numbered, bold, step-by-step instructions.

FIGURE 1.9

If You Have Problems.   These short troubleshooting notes help you anticipate or solve common problems quickly and effectively.

To Extend Your Knowledge

CSS HACKS

Although the box model seems fairly simple to understand, unfortunately, Internet Explorer 5.x for Windows does not render the box model correctly. IE5.x takes the width measurement and then measures the margin, border, and padding inside the dimensions. According to IE5.x, the total width (and height) in the example given in the lesson lead-in would be 200 pixels with a 20-pixel margin, a 5-pixel border, a 10-pixel padding, allowing the content only 130 pixels space: 130 = 200-(2×20 pixels margin)-(2×5 pixels border)-(2×10 pixels margin). If you were designing only for IE5.x, you could easily fix this by changing the width to 270, but any other recent browser, including IE6 for Windows or IE5.2 for Macintosh, interpret the box model correctly, creating a discrepancy between the size of the element in IE5.x and the other browsers.

Commonly, designers deal with this by employing one of the many **CSS Hacks**, CSS tricks to fool different browsers into displaying various CSS properties correctly. All current browsers display many CSS properties and values correctly and consistently, such as background colors and fonts. However, some CSS properties are misinterpreted and others are not supported at all. Some misinterpretations may be corrected using hacks. Some CSS misinterpretations cannot be corrected so hacks are created to hide the misinterpreted CSS from the offending browser. Some CSS properties are not displayed at all by some browsers, so the designer must either accept the deficiency or use JavaScript to create the effect. IE7 is JavaScript by Dean Edwards (dean.edwards.name/IE7) created to fix some deficiencies in the Internet Explorer (5+) browsers.

To Extend Your Knowledge.   These provide extra tips, shortcuts, alternative ways to complete a process, and special hints about using the software.

CAREERS IN DESIGN

FORMS DESIGN AND USABILITY TESTING

You have learned to create static pages that, with the exception of links, have no features with which visitors may interact. Forms add a degree of interaction between the visitor and the Web page by allowing the visitor to enter information or make selections. Even without dynamic JavaScript effects, visitors know that by clicking the submit button, some effect will occur, such as sending an email, posting a question to a discussion forum, or purchasing a book. To ensure that your visitors can use the form as you would like them to use it, however, before you create the form, you must carefully evaluate the type of data that you want it to collect and the type of form controls that you might use.

Sometimes the best input method is not obvious. For example, credit-card numbers are often in the form of 1234 2345 3456 4567. With spaces, this credit-card number takes 19 characters. One possible issue is that people may not enter the spaces and may think, therefore, that they are expected to insert the 3-digit security number, as well; if they do so, the 19-digit number would be invalid. To avoid this problem, do you divide the credit card number into 4 input fields each containing 4 digits? Doing so means that after each field, the visitor must press Tab to move to the next field but, at the same time, this format makes clearer to visitors that they only need 16 numbers. Some developers add JavaScript to this type of form so after the fourth number is pressed, JavaScript moves the insertion point to the next field. If, however, a user looks at the credit card and not at the screen and presses Tab after the fourth number, JavaScript would already have moved the insertion point to the next field so the Tab would move one the insertion point one field further, leaving a field empty.

If you need to develop either a complex or a unique form, consider doing some usability testing in which people test your form and give their feedback. Usability testing can be expensive but it doesn't have to be. You can gather a group of friends or co-workers and have them test your form and provide feedback, either as written notes or in a group discussion afterwards. A Web site that depends on information collected by its forms must ensure that its forms are not an impediment to the success of the Web site.

Careers in Design.   These features offer advice, tips, and resources that will help you on your path to a successful career.

End-of-Project Exercises.   Extensive end-of-project exercises emphasize hands-on skill development. You'll find three levels of reinforcement: Skill Drill, Challenge, and Portfolio Builder.

Project 4   JavaScript Behaviors   **199**   LEVEL 2

SKILL DRILL

Skill Drills reinforce project skills. Each skill reinforced is the same, or nearly the same, as a skill presented in the lessons. Detailed instructions are provided in a step-by-step format. Work through these exercises in order.

1. Create a Double Rollover

In this Skill Drill, you set two images to swap when the mouse pointer moves over one. You could extend this technique to swap many images at the same time. However, that would mean that more and more images must preload, which would delay the loading of the Web page.

1. Open f1cars.html from the JavaScript site.

2. Click the photomontage image and, in the Property inspector, assign it the name `large`.

3. Click the Ferrari graphic link in the Document window.

4. Right/Control-click Swap Image in the Behaviors panel (not Swap Image Restore) and choose Edit Behavior.

5. Choose image "large" from the Images list, click the Browse button, choose images>ferrari_car.jpg, click Select/Choose, then click OK.

6. Click the Jaguar graphic link, edit the Swap Image behavior, choose the "large" image, assign the source to images>jaguar_car.jpg, click Select/Choose, then click OK.

7. Repeat Step 6 for the Mclaren, Toyota, and Williams graphic links, setting the "large" image swap image to mclaren_car.jpg, toyota_car.jpg, and williams_car.jpg, respectively.

8. Preview the page in your browser and notice that both the graphic text link and the large image swap images.

FIGURE 4.51

9. Return to Dreamweaver and close f1cars.html.

CHALLENGE EXERCISES

Challenge exercises expand on, or are somewhat related to, skills presented in the lessons. Each exercise provides a brief narrative introduction, followed by instructions in a numbered-step format that are not as detailed as those in the Skill Drill section. You can work through one or more exercises in any order.

1. Create a Multiple Choice Exam

In this challenge, you create three forms containing questions from a multiple-choice exam. The action URLs send the student to the next question. Hidden fields contain the answers to previous questions. Although using hidden fields this way may not be very secure, it is possible to **obfuscate** (make obscure or unclear) the answer using a **hash** (a process of encrypting text whereby the result cannot be reversed to reveal the original text, but two encryptions of the same text produce the same result, enabling comparison) of the answer so that the student cannot simply change the answer in the hidden field from A to B. This exam process, and the generation of the hash (which is an available function in PHP and other programming languages) would normally be done with a form-processing application. However, this exercise will provide you with an understanding as to the type of process one might apply to a form-processing application.

1. Open q1.html from the Casual University site, and click in the empty paragraph below the instructions.

2. Create a new form called `q1` with the Action set to `q2.html`, the Method set to POST, and the Enctype set to application/x-www-form-urlencoded.

3. In the form, type `1. Which text format displays using the largest text size?` and press Enter/Return. Create a radio button group with the name `q1`. Type `Heading 6`, `Heading 2`, `Paragraph`, and `Heading 1` as the labels and `a`, `b`, `c`, and `d` as the values. Lay out the radio button group using line breaks.

4. Press Enter/Return after the last answer and insert a hidden field with `studentID` as the name and `25D55AD283AA400AF464C76D713C07AD` as the value. This 32-character string is a hash of 12345678.

5. Create a submit button with `next` as the name and `Next Question` as the value.

6. Close, saving the changes.

7. Open q2.html. Use the same procedures as you did in Steps 2 to 6 with the following changes: set the form name as `q2` and the form's action to `q3.html`. The question is `2. Absolute links are necessary when linking:` and the answers are `a page to a named anchor`, `to a target window`, `to a page in another Web site`, and `alternate text`. Insert the same `studentID` hidden field plus another hidden field called `answer1` with a value of `8277E0910D750195B448797616E091AD`. When finished, close q2.html, saving your changes.

8. Open q3.html. Use the same procedures as in Step 7 with the following changes: set the form name is `q3` and the form's action to `results.html`. The question is `3. GIF and JPEG image formats:` and the answers are `are bitmapped graphics`, `are limited to 256 colors`, `can be animated`, and `are the storage formats of digital cameras`. Insert the same `studentID` and `answer1` hidden fields plus another hidden field called `answer2` with a value of `4A8A08F09D37B37956490384080B5F33`. When finished, close q3.html, saving your changes.

Portfolio Builder. At the end of every project, these exercises require creative solutions to problems that reinforce the topic of the project. ▶

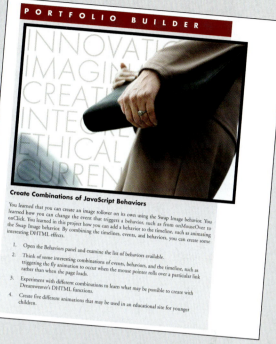

Integrating Projects. Integrating projects are designed to reflect real-world graphic-design jobs, drawing on the skills you have learned throughout this book.

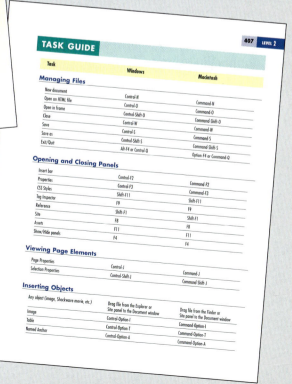

Task Guides. These charts, found at the end of each book, list alternative ways to complete common procedures and provide a handy reference tool. ▶

STUDENT INFORMATION AND RESOURCES

Companion Web Site (www.prenhall.com/essentials).   This text-specific Web site provides students with additional information and exercises to reinforce their learning. Features include: additional end-of-project reinforcement material, online Study Guide, easy access to *all* resource files, and much, much more!

Before completing the projects within this text, you need to download the Resource Files from the Prentice Hall Companion Web site. Check with your instructor for the best way to gain access to these files or simply follow these instructions:

1. From an open Web browser, go to http://www.prenhall.com/essentials.

2. Select your textbook or series to access the Companion Web site. We suggest you bookmark this page, as it has links to additional Prentice Hall resources that you may use in class.

3. Click the Student Resources link. All files in the Student Resources area are provided as .sea files for Macintosh users and .exe files for those using the Windows operating system. These files do not require any additional software to open.

4. Click the Start Here link for the platform you are using (Macintosh or Windows).

5. Once you have downloaded the proper file, double-click that file to begin the self-extraction process. You will be prompted to select a folder location specific for your book; you may extract the file to your hard drive or to a removable disk/drive.

    The Start Here file contains three folders:

    ■ **Fonts.**
    ■ **RF_Dreamweaver_L2.** You can place this folder on your hard drive, or on a removable disk/drive.
    ■ **Work_In_Progress.** You can place this folder on your hard drive, or on a removable disk/drive.

6. Locate the project files you need from the list of available resources and click the active link to download. There is a separate file for each project in this book (e.g., Project_01, Project_02, etc.).

7. Once you have downloaded the proper file, double-click that file to begin the self-extraction process. You will be prompted to select a folder location specific to your book. You should extract the project-specific folders into the RF_Dreamweaver_L2 folder that was extracted from the Start Here file.

Resource CD. If you are using a Resource CD, all the fonts and files you need are provided on the CD. Resource files are organized in project-specific folders (e.g., Project_01, Project_02, etc.), which are contained in the RF_Dreamweaver_L2 folder. You can either work directly from the CD, or copy the files onto your hard drive before beginning the exercises.

Before you begin working on the projects or lessons in this book, you should copy the Work_In_Progress folder from the Resource CD onto your hard drive or a removable disk/drive.

Fonts. You must install the ATC fonts to ensure that your exercises and projects will work as described in the book. Specific instructions for installing fonts are provided in the documentation that came with your computer.

If you have an older version (pre-2004) of the ATC fonts installed, replace them with the fonts in this folder.

Resource Files. Resource files are organized in project-specific folders, and are named to facilitate cross-platform compatibility. Words are separated by an underscore, and all file names include a lowercase three-letter extension. For example, if you are directed to open the file "graphics.eps" in Project 2, the file can be found in the RF_Dreamweaver_L2> Project_02 folder. We repeat these directions frequently in the early projects.

The Work In Progress Folder. This folder contains individual folders for each project in the book (e.g., WIP_01, WIP_02, etc.). When an exercise directs you to save a file, you should save it to the appropriate folder for the project on which you are working.

The exercises in this book frequently build upon work that you have already completed. At the end of each exercise, you will be directed to save your work and either close the file or continue to the next exercise. If you are directed to continue but your time is limited, you can stop at a logical point, save the file, and later return to the point at which you stopped. In this case, you will need to open the file from the appropriate WIP folder and continue working on the same file.

Typeface Conventions. Computer programming code appears in a monospace font that `looks like this`. In many cases, you only need to change or enter specific pieces of code; in these instances, the code you need to type or change appears in a second color and `looks like this`.

INSTRUCTOR'S RESOURCES

Instructor's Resource Center. This DVD-ROM includes the entire Instructor's Manual for each application in Microsoft Word format. Student data files and completed solutions files are also on this DVD-ROM. The Instructor's Manual contains a reference guide of these files for the instructor's convenience. PowerPoint slides with more information about each project are also available for classroom use.

Companion Web site (www.prenhall.com/essentials). Instructors will find all of the resources available on the Instructor's Resource CD-ROM available for download from the Companion Web site.

TestGen Software. TestGen is a test generator program that lets you view and easily edit test bank questions, transfer them to tests, and print the tests in a variety of formats suitable to your teaching situation. The program also offers many options for organizing and displaying test banks and tests. A built-in random number and text generator makes it ideal for creating multiple versions of tests. Powerful search and sort functions let you easily locate questions and arrange them in the order you prefer.

QuizMaster, also included in this package, enables students to take tests created with TestGen on a local area network. The QuizMaster utility built into TestGen lets instructors view student records and print a variety of reports. Building tests is easy with TestGen, and exams can be easily uploaded into WebCT, Blackboard, and CourseCompass.

Prentice Hall has formed close alliances with each of the leading online platform providers: WebCT, Blackboard, and our own Pearson CourseCompass.

OneKey.   OneKey lets you in on the best teaching and learning resources all in one place. OneKey for *Essentials for Design* is all your students need for out-of-class work, conveniently organized by chapter to reinforce and apply what they've  learned in class and from the text. OneKey is also all you need to plan and administer your course. All your instructor resources are in one place to maximize your effectiveness and minimize your time and effort. OneKey for convenience, simplicity, and success.

WebCT and Blackboard.   Each of these custom-built distance-learning courses features exercises, sample quizzes, and tests in a course-management system that provides class-administration tools as well as the ability to customize this material at the instructor's discretion.

CourseCompass.   CourseCompass is a dynamic, interactive online course management tool powered by  Blackboard. It lets professors create their own courses in 15 minutes or less with preloaded quality content that can include quizzes, tests, lecture materials, and interactive exercises.

Performance-Based Training and Assessment: Train & Assess IT. Prentice Hall offers performance-based training and assessment in one product — Train & Assess IT.

The Training component offers computer-based instruction that a student can use to preview, learn, and review graphic-design application skills. Delivered via Web or CD-ROM, Train IT offers interactive multimedia and computer-based training to augment classroom learning. Built-in prescriptive testing suggests a study path based not only on student test results but also on the specific textbook chosen for the course.

The Assessment component offers computer-based testing that shares the same user interface as Train IT and is used to evaluate a student's knowledge about specific topics in software, including Photoshop, InDesign, Illustrator, Flash, and Dreamweaver. It does this in a task-oriented, performance-based environment to demonstrate students' proficiency and comprehension of the topics. More extensive than the testing in Train IT, Assess IT offers more administrative features for the instructor and additional questions for the student. Assess IT also enables professors to test students out of a course, place students in appropriate courses, and evaluate skill sets.

INTRODUCTION

If you search the Internet for Web-design software, Macromedia's Dreamweaver appears often because of its power, sophistication, and support, not only from Macromedia but also from many user forums. It is therefore not surprising that Dreamweaver is the foremost application for Web design and development. Dreamweaver MX 2004 has great support for Cascading Style Sheets, server-side languages, and databases, such as PHP and MySQL, as well as for accessibility considerations.

Dreamweaver's WYSIWYG (What You See Is What You Get or visual) interface benefits new users who are learning Web design for the first time, graphic designers who are accustomed to creating their designs on screen, and hand-coders for whom some of the tasks are greatly simplified. Although Dreamweaver is primarily a WYSIWYG Web-design application, with the click of a button you can see and work with the code of the Web page you are building. In addition to its functions that enable you to create Web sites, Dreamweaver also has file- and site-management functions, enabling you to manage your Web sites directly from this application. These are only a few of the features that have made Dreamweaver so popular.

This book introduces you to the tools, utilities, and features of Dreamweaver, and gives you hands-on practice so you can apply your new skills to your own design projects. We define many of the terms and concepts that you need to understand when you work in the Web-design field, and explain how those ideas relate to Web-design projects.

Our goal is to show you how to use the software's features so you can implement your own creative ideas. You can apply the skills you learn throughout this book to any Web project, whether a small Web site, a corporate intranet, or a Web site of a large retailer.

We focus on intermediate to advanced concepts that are built upon the solid HTML structure learned in *Essentials for Design: Dreamweaver MX 2004 Level 1*. You learn how to create forms to collect information from your visitors, use advanced selectors to apply CSS for style and layout, create JavaScript behaviors and animations, build templates and child pages using Dreamweaver's template functions, prepare and manage your site on a Web server, and use PHP and MySQL to create dynamic and database-driven pages. The knowledge and skills learned in this book enable you to plan and build larger Web sites and more sophisticated Web pages. This book completes your knowledge and understanding of Web design and development and enables you to design and develop complete Web sites from concept to delivery.

PROJECT 1

Collecting Information with Forms

OBJECTIVES

In this project, you learn how to

- Insert a form

- Create different types of text fields

- Insert submit, reset, and other buttons

- Present choices via radio buttons and checkboxes

- Label form controls for usability and accessibility

- Create menus and lists

- Create groups of different but related controls

- Insert hidden fields

WHY WOULD I DO THIS?

Forms are a very important part of the World Wide Web. They are used on many Web sites to gather information from Web-site visitors. For example, you could use a simple form to gather login information, such as username and password. Web-based email, such as Hotmail and Yahoo!, is an example of a more complex use of a form. Forms can serve a wide variety of uses, such as asking questions for online surveys and polls, sending messages through *form mail* forms (email composed and sent via a form on a Web site), querying search engines, setting preferences, posting comments on other people's Web sites, adding/deleting/editing content to database-driven Web sites, and writing content for blogs. (*Blogs* are public online journals that are commonly used by the authors to discuss issues of interest to them. The term is a shortening of the phrase Web logs.)

Forms gather data that must be processed by a computer program (also known as a "Web application" or just "application"). These programs can be used to email the message to the recipient, display the results of the search query, process your purchase order, or post your article to your blog. In the past, these types of computer applications were called "CGI applications." (A *CGI application*, or Common Gateway Interface program, is a program that processes information passed to it, typically through a Web form.) CGI commonly refers to applications written in Perl, C++, and other formal programming languages. (*Perl*, an acronym for Practical Extraction and Reporting Language, is a powerful, free, open-source programming language especially designed for processing text. Perl files commonly use the extension .pl or .cgi. *C++* is a high-level programming language commonly used to develop Windows, Macintosh, and Linux/Unix applications.) However, more recently, form data processing is performed using ASP, PHP, and other more current Web programming languages. While you do not learn to create the processing application in this project, in *Project 8: Developing PHP and MySQL*, you learn to create a form-processing application using the PHP language.

Forms collect information using a variety of *form controls* (functions or features of forms that enable the forms developer to control the type of data, amount of data, and format of data collected by the form). The most common form control is a text field in which users can type text, such as a text field for their first name. Other form controls include checkboxes from which they can make multiple choices (like the toppings they would like on a hamburger), radio buttons that restrict them to selecting just one of the options presented (like the size of drink they want), and text areas that allow for large amounts of text (like the entire content of an email message).

It is important to know how to create and use forms and form controls. Whether or not you create the application that processes the collected data, you should understand how to create a form, know the differences between the form controls, and understand the options available in forms and form controls. In some cases, you may need to consult with the Web developer to determine how the data is to be handled, and you may need to consult with a specialist in surveys or data gathering to ensure the right questions are asked and asked properly.

V I S U A L   S U M M A R Y

You use the buttons on the Forms Insert bar to create forms and insert the appropriate labels and form controls. If the Forms Insert bar is not visible, you click the menu button at the left of the Insert bar and select Forms to switch to the Forms Insert bar.

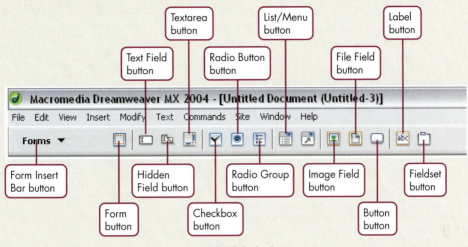

FIGURE 1.1

As with many other functions in Dreamweaver, you modify the properties of the HTML tag using the Property inspector. Forms elements are no different. After inserting a form element, you assign it a name and any other properties that are appropriate for the form or the form control.

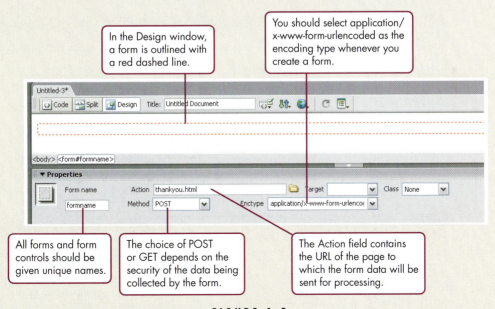

FIGURE 1.2

Text fields may be single-line or multiline text fields. Multiline text fields are called "textareas." Although you can activate text fields and textareas using different buttons on the Forms Insert bar, you can also use the Property inspector for this purpose and can use it additionally to switch between the two types of text fields. Password fields are similar to single-line text fields except that the text in the field is hidden.

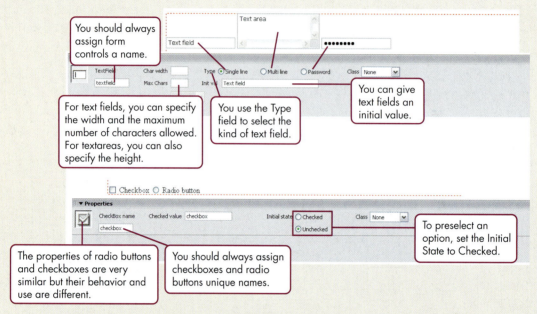

You should always assign form controls a name.

You can give text fields an initial value.

For text fields, you can specify the width and the maximum number of characters allowed. For textareas, you can also specify the height.

You use the Type field to select the kind of text field.

To preselect an option, set the Initial State to Checked.

The properties of radio buttons and checkboxes are very similar but their behavior and use are different.

You should always assign checkboxes and radio buttons unique names.

FIGURE 1.3

Menus are also form controls and are commonly used to enable a user to select a single option. Lists, which are similar to menus, allow users to make multiple selections. In addition to applying the list/menu properties in the Property inspector, you populate the list/menu with its values using a dialog box.

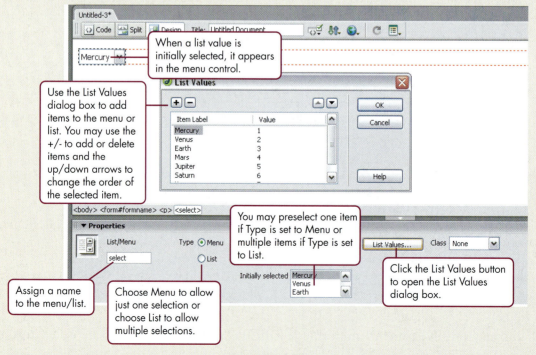

When a list value is initially selected, it appears in the menu control.

Use the List Values dialog box to add items to the menu or list. You may use the +/- to add or delete items and the up/down arrows to change the order of the selected item.

You may preselect one item if Type is set to Menu or multiple items if Type is set to List.

Click the List Values button to open the List Values dialog box.

Assign a name to the menu/list.

Choose Menu to allow just one selection or choose List to allow multiple selections.

FIGURE 1.4

LESSON 1   Creating Properties of Forms

Web forms are contained by opening and closing `<form>` tags. There are three primary options required for forms: the name of the form, the method of transmitting the data, and the encoding method for the data.

The name of the form is required for the processing application. If there is only one form on a page, the name of the form is not critical. If, however, there are multiple forms on a page or if the form is part of a series of forms for either a survey or an *e-commerce* (electronic commerce) site, it is important that the individual forms in the series have unique ids. (Electronic commerce can be between two businesses transmitting funds, goods, services, and/or data, or between a business and a customer.)

The `action` attribute specifies the URL of the form-processing application, such as `action="contact_me.php"`. You can use either a relative or an absolute path to the processing application. Some basic form-processing software can be *remotely hosted* (existing on another Web server), in which case, you would need to add `http://www.remote-host.com/` to the absolute path of the action URL. On some Web sites, you see the action URL with a cgi-bin folder, such as `action="/cgi-bin/formmail.pl"`. The cgi-bin folder is commonly below the root folder of the Web site for security reasons to prevent unauthorized access or use of any applications that may exist in the folder. The mailto: URL, such as `action="mailto:customer@domain.com"`, is a valid action URL but is rarely used and poorly supported by browsers. Its use occasionally opens a visitor's email software, which can be confusing.

The `method` attribute has two options, `post` and `get`. Search engines commonly use the get method — the data from the form are displayed in the URL sent to the search engine. For example, when searching Google.com for php editor, the get URL is http://www.google.com/search?q=php+editor&sourceid=firefox& start=0&start=0&ie=utf-8&oe=utf-8. The processing application then takes the *query string* (the portion of the action URL after the ?), processes it, and displays the results. It is just as easy to copy this URL from the browser's address bar as it is to bookmark the URL should you wish to return to a specific search later. The get option limits the number of characters that may be sent: a blog or news entry sent via the get method may exceed the character limit (which varies with operating system, Web-server software, and the processing application). The get option also may pose a security risk if sensitive information is revealed, such as credit card information. Furthermore, an unscrupulous user may create problems for the processing application by modifying a get URL, replacing part of it with other information. On the other hand, when you develop a form-processing application, you may want to use the get option to watch how the information is being sent so that you can adjust your programming code accordingly.

The post method does not display the query string but the data is formatted identically. The post method does not limit the amount of data sent and is more suitable for larger amounts of data. Furthermore, because the form data is not exposed in the URL, it is more secure and may also be *encrypted* (translated into a secret code) using the *HTTPS protocol* (also written as S-HTTP, a protocol for securely transmitting data between a browser and a server) that is used by e-commerce applications.

The `enctype` attribute specifies the type of data being transmitted. The `application/x-www-form-urlencoded` option transmits text. Using this option, spaces between words are replaced with + and certain reserved characters are replaced with hexadecimal codes for the characters. Line breaks are replaced with `%0D%0A`. The other option, `multipart/form-data`, is reserved for use when files are being *transmitted* (uploaded) via the form: the `method` attribute must be set to `post` when a file is being uploaded.

Create and Set the Form Properties

In this exercise, you prepare a basic form — the login form for returning customers. You learn to set up the form options using the Forms Insert bar and the Property inspector.

1 Define the Project_01>Forms folder as a site called `Forms`.

2 Open login.html and click in the empty cell between the header and footer cells.

3 Type `Login to Place Your Order` and format it as Heading 2.

4 Switch the Insert bar to Forms.

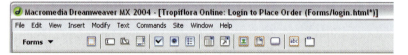

FIGURE 1.5

5 Click the first button on the left of the Forms Insert bar.

6 In the Property inspector, type `login` in the Form Name field, type `confirm-login.html` in the Action field, set the Method to `Get`, and set Enctype to `application/x-www-form-urlencoded`.

FIGURE 1.6

7 Save the changes but leave the file open for the next exercise.

To Extend Your Knowledge

FREE FORM-PROCESSING APPLICATIONS

Many of the common form-processing applications are available for free. HotScripts.com is an example of an archive that offers many programs for processing form mail. If you need to perform client-side form validation, you would search in the client-side languages, such as JavaScript or VBScript (supported only by Internet Explorer). If you need to perform server-side processing of form data and your needs are common (such as form mail), search in the languages you know your server supports, such as PHP, ASP, ASP.Net, or Perl. Generally, these programs are well documented: they come with instructions on how to install and configure them for your specific needs. Why go to the trouble of trying to learn a programming language when you can just download one and use it for free?

Not all scripts on HotScripts.com and other scripts archives are free: some are feature-limited trial versions; others are commercial; some are free for personal but not commercial use; and some are free, but to remove the script-author's Web-site link or logo, you must pay for the script. You must purchase complex or unique scripts either by downloading and paying for the script or by hiring a developer to create a script for your Web site.

LESSON 2 Creating Short-Text, Long-Text, and Password Form Controls

One of the most commonly used form controls is the text field. Most form controls use the **`<input>`** tag, which employs the **`type`** attribute to specify the type of input. For text fields, for example, you set **`type`** to text, such as **`type="text"`**. The **`size`** attribute specifies the width of the text field in characters; in Dreamweaver, this field is named the Char Width field. In Dreamweaver, the default width is approximately 24 characters, but if you don't specify a width, browsers use their own default widths for the text field. The **`maxlength`** attribute (the Max Chars field in Dreamweaver) specifies the number of characters allowed in the text field. If you don't specify a default number, the number of characters allowed is virtually unlimited, but the width of the field makes it difficult to use. If the size of the field is smaller than the maxlength, the field contents scroll to allow the user to enter as much text as the maxlength allows. However, if the size is larger than maxlength, white space appears to the right of the contents of the field.

All form controls require a name. Although generally the **`name`** attribute is deprecated in XHTML 1.0 and replaced by the **`id`** attribute, in the case of form controls, the **`name`** attribute is not deprecated. The form-processing application matches the submitted data to the applicable field using the **`name`** attribute. Regardless of whether the get or post method is selected for the **`<form>`** tag, the form-control name and its value are paired in the submitted data as name=value, such as **`firstname=Thomas&lastname=Denon`**. The **`id`** attribute can also be applied to the form controls for either CSS or JavaScript. Dreamweaver, however, does not provide an id option in the Property inspector for text fields, just a class option that may also be used by CSS and JavaScript.

The Property inspector also provides an Init Value field, which is equivalent to the **value** attribute in HTML. Any text you type into the Init Value field displays in the field. You may use this option to suggest to users what they may enter into the field or in what format. For example, you could set the initial value of a comments field to **Type your comments here**, or in a telephone field, you could set the initial value to **(555) 555-5555** to suggest the expected format. There is a useful JavaScript function that you can employ when using an initial value — as soon as the user types in the field, the initial value is erased, leaving only what the user types.

Create a Single-Line Text Field

In this exercise, you use two Dreamweaver options for the Text field: the Single Line option and the Password option. The Single Line option sets the **type** attribute of the **<input>** tag as **type="text"** and the Password option sets the **type** attribute as **type="password"**. The Multi Line option creates a different type of form control using a different HTML tag, the **<textarea>** tag, which you use in a later exercise.

1   In the open login.html page, click inside the form area, type **Customer Number:**, and press the Spacebar.

2   From the Forms Insert bar, click the Text Field button.

3   In the Property inspector, select Single Line from the Type options, type **customerNo** in the TextField Name field, type **15** in the Char Width field, type **8** in the Max Chars field, type **123-4567** in the Init Value field, and press Enter/Return.

FIGURE 1.7

4   Click to the right of the text field in the Document window, and press Enter/Return.

5   Type `Password:` then press the Spacebar.

6   Click the Text Field button in the Forms Insert bar.

7   Set the TextField name to `password`, the Char Width to `10`, Max Chars to `6`, and Type to Password; type `abcdef` in the Init Val field; and press Enter/Return.

Despite typing readable text in the Init Val field, the field in the form displays hidden characters.

FIGURE 1.8

8   Delete the text in the Init Val field and press Enter/Return to apply the change.

9   Close login.html, saving your changes.

To Extend Your Knowledge

SETTING DIMENSIONS USING CSS

You may wonder why the text, password, and other form controls use characters as the measurement for width. This measurement is a throwback to early Web browsers that used a monospaced font like Courier as the common font. With the width set to a specific number of characters, users could see exactly how much space they were allowed for that particular field. Most current browsers use proportionally spaced fonts, in which iii is narrower than MMM although both are three characters. However, you may use CSS to specify the width of form controls, such as in pixels, **ems** (the width of the letter M), or percentage of the container width. If you want to specify different widths for different form controls, you must apply unique ids to each control so that you may specify the width for just that control. If you want several controls to be the same width, you can apply the same CSS class to each and then they may all use the same width.

LESSON 3   Working with Multiline Text Areas

Unlike many of the form controls, the multiline text area does not use the `<input>` tag but, instead, uses the `<textarea>` tag. Dreamweaver puts both single-line and multiline form controls in the same Property inspector panel, despite the difference in tags. However, the `<textarea>` tag is a container tag requiring the closing `</textarea>` tag. Just like the single-line text control, `<textarea>` can be set with an initial value which is recorded in the Init Val (initial value) field in the Property inspector. The initial value, however, is written between the opening and closing `<textarea>` tags, such as, `<textarea>I would like to hear from you.</textarea>`, unlike any of the `<input>` form controls, which use the value attribute (which does not exist for this tag).

You set the width of the text area with the Char Width field in the Property inspector; this information is applied to the `cols` attribute. You set the height of the text area with the Num Lines field of the Property inspector; this information is applied to the `rows` attribute. The units of the width measurement are characters and the units of height are lines.

Developers commonly use the `<textarea>` tag to create an area in which users can enter large amounts of text. Dreamweaver's Property inspector offers the Wrap option with four possible values: Default, Off, Virtual, and Physical. However, the wrap attribute of the `<textarea>` tag is confusing for many reasons — it was never part of any HTML standard; some sources use Soft in place of Virtual and Hard in place of Physical; and current browsers treat Soft, Hard, Virtual, and Physical identically. Given the potential confusion and lack of validity, we recommend that you leave the setting at Default.

Create a Multiline Text Area

In this exercise, you create a basic form to which you add a text area.

1   **Open comments.html from the Forms site.**

2   **Click to the right of Comments (smaller black text) and press Enter/Return.**

3   **Click the Text Field button on the Forms Insert bar.**

4   **In the Property inspector, select Multi Line from the Type group of options.**

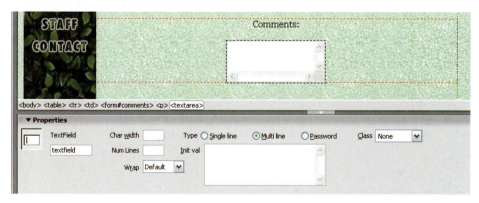

FIGURE 1.9

5   Press Control/Command-Z (Undo) twice, and then click the Textarea button on the Forms Insert bar.

Notice that the result is the same: the Textarea button simply preselects the Multi Line option.

6   Type **comments** in the Textarea Name field, set Char Width to 35, set Num Lines to 8, in the Init Val field, type `Type your comment here.`, and press Tab.

Don't press Enter/Return while the insertion point is in the Init Val field or you create a new line in the field.

FIGURE 1.10

7   Close comments.html, saving your changes.

To Extend Your Knowledge

FORM CONTROLS OUTSIDE THE WWW

Form controls were not first brought into being when HTML was created but existed long before. Examine any computer application on your computer and you will recognize many of these controls in Web pages. Menus, radio buttons, checkboxes, labels, single-line and multiline text fields, and password fields — all existed in computer applications before Sir Tim Berners-Lee wrote one character of HTML. If you are having trouble figuring out which controls to place in a Web form, try to think of an example in a computer application and use that as your inspiration.

LESSON 4 Using Submit, Reset, Image, and Other Buttons

The purpose of the submit button is to send data from the completed form to the processing application. The reset button resets the values of fields to their initial values. As with text and password form controls, you create buttons using the **`<input>`** tag with different types: for a submit button, **`type="submit"`**, and for a reset button, **`type="reset"`**. These types have special meaning to the browser, which submits or resets the data depending on which button the user clicks.

Two other attributes to use with these two buttons are the **`name`** and **`value`** attributes. When you select submit or reset from the Property inspector in Dreamweaver, the **`name`** attribute, by default, is set to that option. However, if the purpose of your form is to enable users to edit or delete items in their shopping carts, you might make the names of the buttons edit and delete and then you must program the form-processing application to pick up the name of the button selected and process the data appropriately.

You can use the **`value`** attribute to replace the text on the button. In Dreamweaver, you use the Label field in the Property inspector to enter the value-attribute content. For example, rather than Submit on a contact form, you might want to use Send Me Your Comments, and in place of Reset, you might want to use Clear the Form. The **`value`** attribute does not change the submit and reset buttons' functions — the **`type`** attribute specifies these buttons' functions to the browser.

If you want to provide edit and delete buttons on the form so users can edit their addresses when they move or delete items from their shopping carts, in both cases you must set the **`type`** attribute to **`submit`**, because these actions must be provided by the form-processing application. The names could be edit and delete and the values could be Edit This Address and Remove This Item. Therefore, if you want to provide a function that requires the form-processing application to act, you set the **`type`** to **`submit`** despite the name or value you assign to that button.

Dreamweaver also provides a None option which creates a generic button. You may assign it a name and value, but unlike the submit type, clicking it does not submit the form data to the action URL, nor does the browser perform a client-side action to the data as it does with the reset type. The purpose of the None type (in HTML, it is coded as **`type="button"`**) is to allow a Web developer to assign a JavaScript function to the button, which when clicked, triggers that JavaScript function.

The button labeled Image Field on the Forms Insert bar inserts an image form control. This form control also uses the **`<input>`** tag with the **`type`** attribute set to **`image`**. An image field behaves like a submit button and, commonly, an image field is simply graphic text, such as Place Your Order. Like all images, you should assign alternative text. Given that most image field buttons replace a plain submit button, the alternative text should be the same as the text that appears in the graphic. However, it is possible to use the image of a product as an image field that submits the customer's intention to purchase that product. A Web page with many product images could therefore enable customers to submit order requests using any of the product-image image fields.

In this exercise, you add both submit and reset buttons to your form. You preview the form in your browser, test the functionality of the buttons, and examine the query string sent to the action URL.

Add Submit and Reset Buttons

1   **Open login.html, click to the right of the password field, and press Enter/Return.**

2   **Click the Button button (third from the right end of the Forms Insert bar).**

By default, Dreamweaver creates a submit button.

3   **Click to the right of the Submit button and insert another button.**

4   **In the Property inspector, change the Label field to `Clear this form` and press Enter/Return. Change the Action to Reset form**

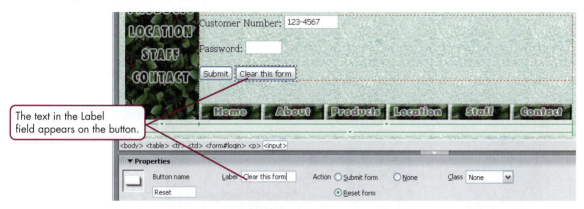

The text in the Label field appears on the button.

FIGURE 1.11

5   **Save the changes and preview this page in your browser.**

6   **Delete the Customer Number initial value, and type as much text as you can.**

The Max Chars property (maxlength attribute) prevents you from entering more than eight characters.

7   **Enter some text in the Password field.**

Both the Customer Number and Password fields limit the number of characters you may enter.

FIGURE 1.12

8 Click the Clear This Form button.

Both (all) fields are reset to their initial values.

9 Again insert a fictitious customer number and password in the form and click the Submit button.

This time, the confirm-login.html page opens in your browser because your browser has directed you to the action URL.

10 Click in the address bar of your browser, and press the End key to view the end of the URL.

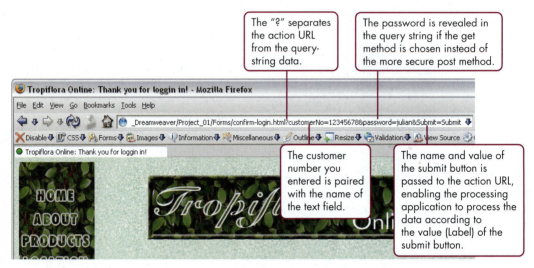

The "?" separates the action URL from the query-string data.

The password is revealed in the query string if the get method is chosen instead of the more secure post method.

The customer number you entered is paired with the name of the text field.

The name and value of the submit button is passed to the action URL, enabling the processing application to process the data according to the value (Label) of the submit button.

FIGURE 1.13

11 Close your browser, return to Dreamweaver, and close login-html.

To Extend Your Knowledge

THE VALUE OF THE RESET BUTTON

Jakob Nielsen of Useit.com, a Web-site usability specialist, questions the value of the reset button (useit.com/alertbox/20000416.html). He is not saying that the reset button does not do what it is supposed to do, but rather that users who don't want to complete the form, rather than resetting it, usually click a link or type a URL and move to another page. While a generalization, this does raise the question of the value of the reset button in some forms. For example, basic contact forms found on many Web sites may not need a reset button. Visitors who change their mind about submitting a message are likely to just move on. Armed with this knowledge, you may want to rethink whether or not you need a reset button on every form.

Remember also that you may want to provide a button that clears data from a database, such as Clear This Order. While it may seem similar in function to a reset button, the Clear This Order button may actually provide an action that should be processed by the form-processing application. For that reason, you should avoid button labels that could be confused with the functionality of the reset button.

LESSON 5 Creating Radio Button Form Controls

The radio-button form control is designed to provide users with mutually exclusive options, such as male or female. It is possible, however, to improperly create radio buttons so that they are not exclusive, for example, select three of your favorite sports. Because historically radio buttons have always been used to allow users to select just one option from a group, breaking this pattern risks alienating your visitors. A similar option, the checkbox, is meant to provide multiple options, any or all of which may be selected. Just as with the text, password, and button form controls, you create radio buttons using the **`<input>`** tag using the **`type`** attribute to identify the form control — **`type="radio"`**.

Radio buttons are commonly designed to work in a group, presenting options or answers to a common question. The individual radio buttons are related to each other through a common **`name`** attribute. For example, **`name="gender"`** would be common to both male and female radio buttons, and **`value="male"`** and **`value="female"`** would distinguish the two. By having a common **`name`** attribute, only one option from a group of radio buttons may be selected. However, if the **`name`** attribute for the female option were set to gender and the **`name`** attribute for the male option were set to sex, the two options would not be related, making it possible to select both male and female which, of course, is not possible.

Submit and reset buttons are unique in that whatever you apply to the **`value`** attribute appears in the button. (For buttons, this option is called the "Label field" in the Property inspector.) However, to identify the contents or purpose of the text, password, and radio button controls, the values of these **`<input>`** tags are not displayed in the Document window or in your browser: you must add additional text beside these controls to label them.

The **`value`** attribute of the text and password controls (applied using the Init Val field in the Property inspector) inserts initial or default text in the field. The radio button also has an Initial State option in the Property inspector, offering Checked and Unchecked options. Selecting the Checked option inserts the **`checked`** attribute in the **`<input>`** tag. The **`checked`** attribute is an unusual attribute in that there are no attribute values. If Checked is selected for the example of gender above, the **`<input>`** tag is written as **`<input type="radio" name="gender" value="female" checked>`**. Although HTML 4.01 and earlier versions allowed empty attribute values such as **`checked`**, in XHTML, all attributes must have attribute values: checked must be entered as **`checked="checked"`**. If a radio button is not to be checked, then the checked attribute is not included in the **`<input>`** tag at all.

Dreamweaver provides two methods of creating radio buttons: individually or in a group. In this lesson you learn both methods. Although using the radio group method is easier, there will be times when you may need to add more buttons after you have created a group. You also learn why you must use a common **`name`** attribute for all radio-button options.

Create Individual Radio Buttons

1   Open registration.html.

2   Click to the right of the Full Name text field and press Enter/Return. Type Gender: and press the Spacebar.

3 From the Forms Insert bar, select the Radio Button button.

FIGURE 1.14

4 In the Property inspector, type gender in the Radio Button name field, type male in the Checked Value field and leave the rest of the options at their defaults.

FIGURE 1.15

5 Click to the right of the radio button, type Male, and press the Spacebar.

6 Insert another radio button but type sex in the Radio Button name field and female in the Checked Value field. Click to the right of the radio button in the Document window and type Female.

7 Preview the page in your browser and select both Male and Female.

The name attributes for the Male and Female radio buttons are different, enabling both to be selected.

FIGURE 1.16

8 Return to Dreamweaver without closing your browser, change the name attribute of the Female radio button to gender, and preview and test the page in your browser again.

Now that both male and female radio buttons share the same name attribute, only one of the two may be selected.

9 Return to Dreamweaver, leaving the file open for the next exercise.

Create Multiple Radio Buttons

In this exercise, you learn to create a group of radio buttons using the Radio Group button from the Forms Insert bar. This function has a few beneficial features: it creates proper labels for the radio buttons, it applies the same name attribute for all radio buttons in the group, and it gives you the option of formatting the radio buttons with line breaks or table cells.

1   **Click to the right of the Street Address text field and press Enter/Return.**

2   **Type Dwelling Type: and press the Spacebar.**

3   **Click the Radio Group button in the Forms Insert bar.**

4   **In the Radio Group dialog box, type dwelling in the Name field. Under Label, click Radio and type Apartment. Press Tab and type apt in the Value column and press Tab. Type Row House and press Tab. Type rhouse.**

5   **Click the plus symbol (+) above Label to create a new row. Type Individual House and press Tab. Type ihouse.**

6   **Leave the Lay Out Using option set to Line Breaks and click OK.**

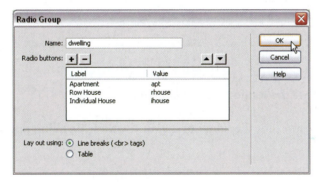

FIGURE 1.17

7   **To remove the line breaks, move the insertion point to the Apartment line, press the End key and then press Delete. Press End and then Delete twice more to bring all of the radio buttons onto the same line.**

8   **Preview the page in your browser and test the radio buttons.**

The Radio Group dialog box assigns the same name attribute to all radio buttons, ensuring that only one of the options can be selected.

9   **Return to Dreamweaver, leaving registration.html open for the next exercise.**

Add Another Radio Button to the Group

In this exercise, the option Condominium was forgotten and must be added to the group of radio buttons of dwelling types. You learn that the Radio Group dialog box is useful for creating a group of radio buttons but does not allow you to edit or add to the group. Instead, you must use the previously learned technique to add more radio buttons to a group.

1   **In registration.html, click anywhere in the group of radio buttons of dwelling types.**

2   **Click the Radio Group button from the Forms Insert bar.**

Notice that the settings are the same as the original default settings. This function does not pick up on the settings of the radio buttons in which the insertion point is positioned. This dialog box is only useful for creating a new group of radio buttons.

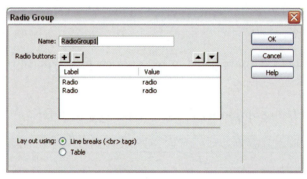

FIGURE 1.18

3   **Click Cancel to close the Radio Group dialog box.**

4   **Click the radio button (not the label) of any of the three dwelling options and note the Radio Button name.**

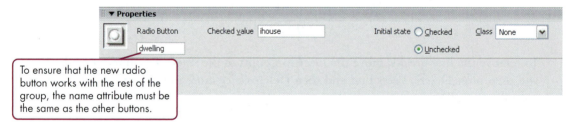

To ensure that the new radio button works with the rest of the group, the name attribute must be the same as the other buttons.

FIGURE 1.19

5   **Click to the right of Individual House.**

6   **Insert a new radio button (not a group, just an individual button). In the Property inspector, assign it the Radio Button name dwelling and the Checked Value condo.**

FIGURE 1.20

7   Click to the right of the newly created radio button in the Document window and type Condominium.

FIGURE 1.21

8   Preview the page in your browser to ensure that the new radio button works with the rest of the group.

9   Close your browser and return to Dreamweaver, leaving registration.html open for the next exercise.

To Extend Your Knowledge

THE OTHER OPTION

It is fairly common to see forms with several options for a particular question and the last option is Other with a text field to its right, expecting you to complete the Other text field if Other applies to you. This creates a difficult situation for the developer of the form-processing application — one that you should avoid whenever possible. For example, the radio button group might ask the visitor's profession and list options of Firefighter, Police, Retail, Management, and Other. If the listed professions were not applicable to most users of the form, more users would select Other than the identified professions. Among those who select Other, one person might type Actor in the Other text field where another might type Actress, listing essentially the same profession in two different ways (and spelling mistakes could create the same situation). Further, some might feel that they are in management in their government job and select Management, adding Government to the Other text field as well.

In all of these examples, it is virtually impossible to create a form-processing application that will handle this type of data easily. These types of situations require someone to review all entries to make sense of the data. On the other hand, it may be that Other is the best means to categorize data that does not fit within any of the listed options. Evaluate the form and try to anticipate the type of data you expect to collect before publishing the form on the Web site for visitors to complete.

LESSON 6 Working with Multiple-Choice Checkboxes

The checkbox form control shares the `<input>` tag with all of the other form controls discussed previously and, similarly, is differentiated from them using the **type** attribute, as in **type="checkbox"**. Checkboxes are similar to radio buttons in that a group of checkboxes pertaining to the same question should all have the same name attribute; the different options presented by the checkboxes are specified in their value attributes. Checkboxes also have the Checked/Unchecked options just as radio buttons do. However, unlike radio buttons, checkboxes are designed to allow multiple selections from a group.

Dreamweaver allows you to add radio buttons individually or as a group, but the group option is not available for checkboxes: you must create them individually. Therefore, you must remember to use the same name attribute so that the options relate to the same question or topic.

Create Checkboxes

1 In registration.html, click to the right of Condominium and press Enter/Return.

2 Type What type of plants are you looking to purchase? and press the Spacebar.

3 Click the Checkbox button from the Forms Insert bar.

FIGURE 1.22

4 Type plantType in the Checkbox Name field, type indoor in the Value field, and select Checked from the Initial State options.

5 Click to the right of the checkbox in the Document window and type Indoor followed by a space.

6 Create another checkbox with the Checkbox Name field set to plantType and the Value field set to outdoor. Leave Initial State set to Unchecked.

7 Click to the right of the new checkbox in the Document window, type Outdoor, and press Enter/Return.

8 Insert a submit button.

9   Save the page, leaving it open for the next exercise.

FIGURE 1.23

Compare Radio-Button and Checkbox Query-String Data

In this exercise, you learn how the radio-button and checkbox data is sent to the form-processing application. Only one option from a radio button group may be selected, therefore there will be only one name=value pair in the query string for the radio button. However, checkboxes allow multiple selections, so for each selected item from a checkbox group, there is a corresponding name=value pair.

1   Preview the open registration.html page in your browser.

2   Select your gender, leave Indoor selected, and click the Submit button.

3   Click in the address bar of your browser, press the End key, and examine the query string.

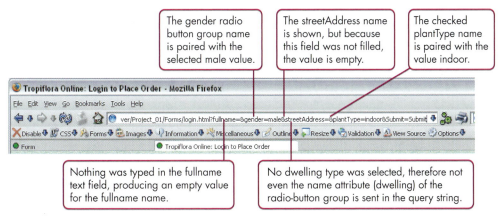

The gender radio button group name is paired with the selected male value.

The streetAddress name is shown, but because this field was not filled, the value is empty.

The checked plantType name is paired with the value indoor.

Nothing was typed in the fullname text field, producing an empty value for the fullname name.

No dwelling type was selected, therefore not even the name attribute (dwelling) of the radio-button group is sent in the query string.

FIGURE 1.24

4   Click the back button in your browser.

5   Select a different gender, select a dwelling type, select both Indoor and Outdoor plant types, and click Submit. Examine the query string again.

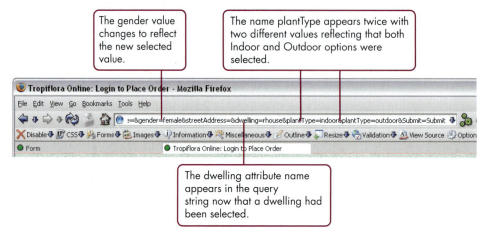

The gender value changes to reflect the new selected value.

The name plantType appears twice with two different values reflecting that both Indoor and Outdoor options were selected.

The dwelling attribute name appears in the query string now that a dwelling had been selected.

FIGURE 1.25

6   Close your browser and return to Dreamweaver, leaving registration.html open for the next exercise.

To Extend Your Knowledge

PROCESSING RADIO-BUTTON AND CHECKBOX OPTIONS

Processing radio-buttons options is not very difficult: only one option is selected for each group. Processing checkbox options is more difficult in that you must check for multiple instances of the same name, such as plantType=indoor and plantType=outdoor.

The usefulness of the checked option for radio buttons and checkboxes may not be clear. As you saw in the previous exercise, if none of the buttons for a radio-button group are selected, the name of the group is not passed in the query string. The same principle applies to checkboxes, too. On a purchase-order form, if there are shipping options for a product, one of them must be selected or the order cannot be shipped. The Web-site designer may choose to preselect the least expensive option, leaving it to the user to accept or change the option.

Another use for preselecting an option is when information has already been entered and the user is asked to modify or confirm the information. For example, an e-commerce application remembers (by requesting the data from its database) that Bob used his MasterCard to pay for his last purchase. The e-commerce application may create the Payment Method form and preselect the MasterCard option for him: Bob is then free to accept or change the preselected payment option.

While you might not be willing to preselect (assume) Male or Female as the gender of a new customer, there are other circumstances when preselecting an option improves the usability of the form for your visitors.

LESSON 7   Labeling Form Controls

There are two aspects to labeling forms: one obvious, the other not. In the previous exercises, you typed text beside a form control, such as a text field or radio button. It might seem logical to assume that the user would deduce the purpose of the control from the proximity of the text to the control that the text identifies. However, this relationship is not as clear to people who use screen readers. In the case of the Full Name field, the label is read before the text field is encountered, but in the case of the radio buttons and checkboxes, the labels commonly appear after the control. Using the **<label>** tag clarifies this situation for users of screen readers.

Using the **<label>** tag not only benefits people who use screen-reader software but also improves the usability of radio buttons and checkboxes for everyone. Without a **<label>** tag, to select either a radio button or checkbox option, you must click the radio button or checkbox. If you use the **<label>** tag, however, the width of the selectable area extends to include the label text. The user may click the label text to select the option, not just the control itself. If you click a label associated with a text field, the insertion point appears within the field.

There are two methods for applying the **<label>** tag: explicit and implicit. The **<label>** tag is a container tag that requires its closing **</label>** tag. The implicit method of applying the **<label>** tag is to enclose both the label text and the form control between the opening and closing **<label>** tags, as in **<label>Full Name: <input type="text" name="fullname"></label>**. The explicit method of applying the **<label>** tag separates the label text from the form control but using the **for** and **id** attributes, the relationship between the label text and the form control is explicitly stated. To apply this properly, the form control must be assigned an **id** and the **for** attribute of the **<label>** tag uses the same value as the **id** of the form control, not unlike the **usemap** attribute of the **<img>** tag and the **name** attribute of the **<map>** tag which relate the two. The following is an example of the explicit method of the **<label>** tag: **<label for="fullname">Full Name:</label> <input id="fullname" name="fullname" type="text">**.

Dreamweaver supports the implicit method with the Label button on the Forms Insert bar. You select the label text and the form control, click the Label button, and the **<label>** tag is created surrounding both the label text and the form control. Dreamweaver also automatically inserts the **<label>** tag when radio buttons are created using the Radio Button dialog box (activated by the Radio Control button of the Forms Insert bar), but the Radio and Checkbox buttons of the Forms Insert bar do not insert the **<label>** tag — you must apply these manually.

You can use tables to lay out forms, commonly with the labels in one column and the form controls in another column. You may have noticed that the Radio Button dialog box did provide a table layout option. We chose Line Breaks instead. When you use tables to lay out forms, by placing the label text in one cell and the form control in another cell, you cannot use the implicit label method as the **<label>** tag cannot cross the cell boundary. For this reason, you would need to use the explicit label method. However, Dreamweaver does not support the explicit method in the Design view. You must work in the Code view to apply the **for** attribute.

Create Implicit Labels

In this exercise, you create implicit labels to associate label text with the form controls. You learn that the Radio Button dialog box inserts the **`<label>`** tag when you create a radio-button group using that dialog box. You also see how the **`<label>`** tag improves the usability of radio-button and checkbox controls.

1   In the open registration.html page, click in the text label Row House, and notice that the **`<label>`** tag appears in the Tag selector.

FIGURE 1.26

2   Click Condominium and notice that there is no **`<label>`** tag in the Tag selector.

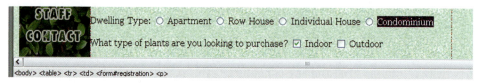

FIGURE 1.27

3   Preview the page in your browser and click the text Row House.

4   Click Condominium and then click the radio button for Condominium.

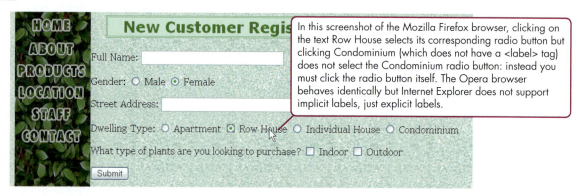

In this screenshot of the Mozilla Firefox browser, clicking on the text Row House selects its corresponding radio button but clicking Condominium (which does not have a <label> tag) does not select the Condominium radio button: instead you must click the radio button itself. The Opera browser behaves identically but Internet Explorer does not support implicit labels, just explicit labels.

FIGURE 1.28

5   Close your browser and return to Dreamweaver.

6   Drag to select Condominium and its radio button, and click the Label button from the Forms Insert bar.

The Document window switches to the Split view.

7   In the Design window at the bottom of the Document window, select Indoor and its checkbox, and click the Label button. Select Outdoor and its checkbox, and click the Label button. Select the text label Full Name and its text field, and apply the `<label>` tag. Apply the `<label>` tag to the Street Address and its text field.

8   Click the Design button to close the Code window.

9   Preview the page in your browser.

? If you have problems

Internet Explorer for Windows does not support the implicit method of applying the `<label>` tag, therefore, if you do not have access to any browser other than Internet Explorer, you won't experience the usability benefit of applying the `<label>` tag to the label text for radio buttons and checkboxes. If you have the opportunity to test this page with any of the Opera, Firefox, IE (Macintosh), or Safari (Macintosh) browsers, you will experience the benefit of implicit `<label>` tags to radio buttons and checkboxes.

10   Return to Dreamweaver but leave registration.html open for the next exercise.

Create Explicit Labels

In this exercise, you learn to apply explicit `<label>` tags to the male and female radio buttons. To do so, you must assign **id** attributes to the male and female radio buttons, apply the `<label>` tag to the Male and Female text labels, and add the **for** attribute to the `<label>` tags to explicitly relate the labels to their radio buttons.

1   In the open file, registration.html, Right/Control-click the radio button for Male, and select Edit Tag <input> from the contextual menu.

FIGURE 1.29

2   In the Tag Editor – Input dialog box, select the Style Sheet/Accessibility category, type `male` in the ID field, and click OK.

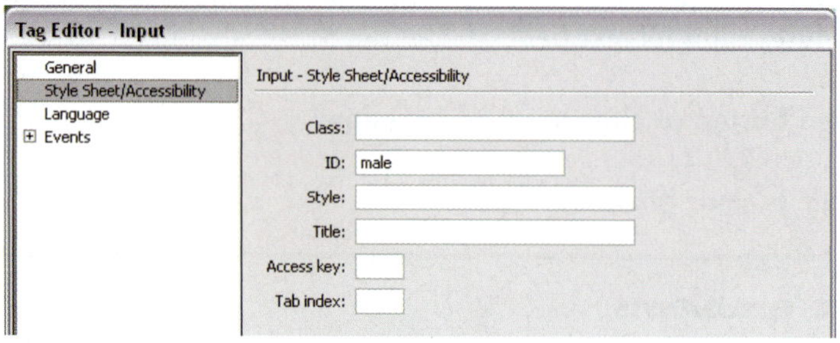

FIGURE 1.30

3   Select the text label Male and Right/Control-click the selected text.

4   Choose Wrap Tag from the contextual menu.

FIGURE 1.31

5   In the little editor window, press `l` (lowercase L) and press Enter/Return to accept `label`. Press the Spacebar, press `f`, and press Enter/Return to accept the `for` attribute. Type `male` and press Enter/Return.

FIGURE 1.32

6   Repeat Steps 1 to 5 for the female radio button, and then wrap the text Female with the `<label>` tag using the `for` attribute set to `female`.

7 **Preview the page in your browser, and click either the Male or Female text label.**

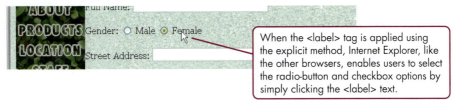

When the <label> tag is applied using the explicit method, Internet Explorer, like the other browsers, enables users to select the radio-button and checkbox options by simply clicking the <label> text.

FIGURE 1.33

8 **Close your browser and return to Dreamweaver.**

To Extend Your Knowledge

INNOVATIVE USES FOR JAVASCRIPT IN FORMS

Forms often contain JavaScript functions, and there are many scripts that increase the usability of forms.

Text fields, as you know, can have initial text. Although initial text is useful, in some circumstances, to explain what users should enter into that field, it requires that users delete the initial text before they add their own. JavaScript can be written to delete the initial-value text when the user clicks or tabs into the field.

When shipping and billing addresses are the same, clicking a checkbox with the label Same as Billing Address can be used to trigger a JavaScript function that completes the shipping-address fields with the same data as the billing-address fields.

JavaScript can be written to provide options based on previous selections. For example, if USA is selected as the country, a list of the states appears, whereas if Canada is selected as the country, a list of the provinces and territories appears. Peter-Paul Koch, an eminent JavaScript developer, has taken this principle to the extreme. His contact form changes quite significantly, depending on the purpose of sending him a message (www.quirksmode.org/contact.html). For example, if you select the subject Business from the list of possible subjects, a radio button appears with the options Nederland and Other.

Some forms contain both required and optional fields. Andy Clarke has created a form (with an accompanying tutorial) in which a JavaScript link hides the optional fields (stuffandnonsense.co.uk/archives/trimming_form_fields_3.html).

Finally, the granddaddy of all, validation: JavaScript is commonly used to validate the contents of a form to ensure that the email address is formatted correctly, the date is valid, and all of the required fields have been completed. These are just a few of the options available for JavaScript validation.

Despite the apparent benefits for usability that these JavaScript functions provide, keep in mind that if accessibility is a concern, many of these JavaScript functions may not be accessible to everyone. Some forms are so dependent on JavaScript that if people were to try to use the form with an older browser or a JavaScript-incapable or disabled browser, they would be presented with an empty page. Despite the benefits that JavaScript may provide sighted users with current browsers, be aware of your site's audience and what limitations may result if you use JavaScript.

LESSON 8 Selecting from Lists

Select lists, named that because they are based on the **<select>** tag, can provide alternatives to both the radio buttons and checkboxes: a select list can allow users to select just one item or multiple items. This is one of the few form controls that does not use the **<input>** tag.

There are two tags used to create select lists: the **<select>** tag, which, like the unordered list **<ul>** tag, surrounds the list of options, and the **<option>** tag which, like the list item **<li>** tag, appears as often as there are items in the list. The **<select>** tag has three attributes of importance: the **size** attribute, the **name** attribute, and the **multiple** attribute.

The **name** attribute acts identically to the **name** attribute for other form controls: it identifies, to the form-processing application, the type of data being collected, such as shippingMethod or favoriteAnimal. The **size** attribute does not set the width of the control but, instead, the height in single units, such as 1, 2, or 3. When the **size** is 1 or unspecified (which defaults to 1), the select list acts as a pop-up list. However, if the **size** is 2 or more, the select list displays as a scrolling list. There is no attribute that may be used to specify the width of the **<select>** tag — by default, it stretches to fit the width of the widest item in the option list. However, the width may be specified using CSS. The **multiple** attribute, like the checked attribute of radio buttons and checkboxes, has no attribute value. If **multiple** is inserted in the **<select>** tag, the user can select multiple items from the select list, whereas without it, the user can only select one item. In Dreamweaver, a menu allows you to select just one option whereas a list allows you to select multiple options.

The **<option>** tag has only two attributes: the **value** attribute and the **selected** attribute. The **<option>** tag is unique in that the closing tag **</option>** is not required in HTML (however, it is required in XHTML). Nevertheless, Dreamweaver does insert the closing tag **</option>**, which is good form.

The **<option>** tag is also unique in that the **value** attribute is optional, too. For example, **<option>Carrot** is valid and equivalent to **<option value="Carrot">Carrot </option>**. In this example, the value is the same as the text that is visible in the list. At other times, especially if the list is populated from a database system, you may need to display a product description but code the option with the product number, such as **<option value="PN2318L">Black & Decker: Left-handed Robertson Screwdriver </option>**. In this example, although the users would see Black & Decker: Left-handed Robertson Screwdriver, the value sent to the form-processing application would be PN2318L, the product number, and the form-processing application would act on this product number rather than the displayed text.

The **selected** attribute is similar to the **multiple** attribute of the **<select>** tag: it does not have an attribute value. The **<option>** tag with the **selected** attribute displays in the list, whether it is the first, middle, or last option in the list. If the **<select>** tag has the **multiple** attribute, multiple **<option>** tags may have the **selected** attribute.

Create a Menu

In this exercise, you create a select list from which only one option may be selected. You set one item to be initially selected and learn that you may go back and edit an existing select list.

1 In the open file, registration.html, click to the right of Outdoor and press Enter/Return.

2 Type How did you hear about Tropiflora Online? and press Enter/Return.

3 Click the List/Menu button on the Forms Insert bar.

FIGURE 1.34

4 Type hear in the List/Menu name field, and then click the List Values button.

FIGURE 1.35

5 Under Item Label, type Magazine, press Tab twice, type Search Engine, press Tab twice, and continue to create the following list (the last item is Got lost on Tallevast Road). Click OK when finished.

FIGURE 1.36

6 Click Magazine in the Initially Selected field, and notice that Magazine displays in the list in the Document window.

7 | **Control/Command-click Magazine to deselect it, and then click Yellow Pages.**

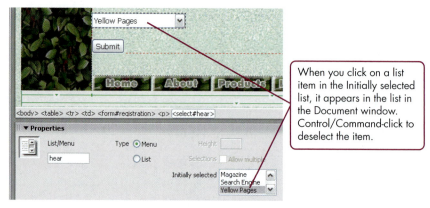

When you click on a list item in the Initially selected list, it appears in the list in the Document window. Control/Command-click to deselect the item.

FIGURE 1.37

8 | **Click the List Values button.**

Notice that unlike the Radio Button dialog box, in which you cannot edit a group of radio buttons, the List Values dialog box is filled with the existing options, allowing you to edit, delete, or add to the list.

9 | **Complete the Value column as shown in the following graphic and click OK.**

FIGURE 1.38

10 | **Preview the page in your browser.**

Notice that the browser window provides no evidence that the option values are different from the option labels. However, a form-processing application only uses the option values.

Firefox browser window

Selected Option in browser window and source code

Firefox source code window

Option values

FIGURE 1.39

11   Uncheck the plantType Indoor checkbox, click the Submit button, and examine the query string in your browser's address bar.

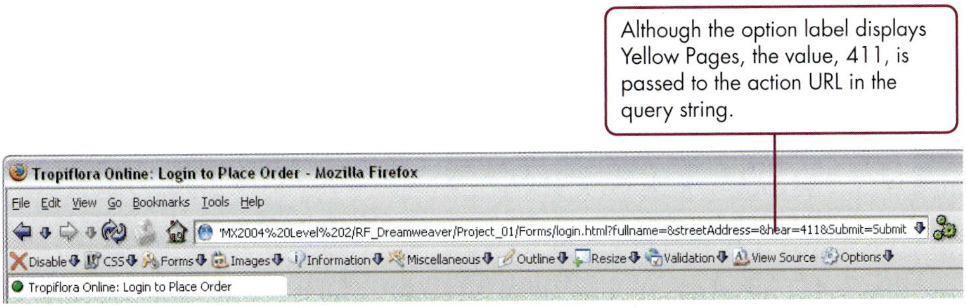

> Although the option label displays Yellow Pages, the value, 411, is passed to the action URL in the query string.

Tropiflora Online: Login to Place Order - Mozilla Firefox

File Edit View Go Bookmarks Tools Help

`MX2004%20Level%202/RF_Dreamweaver/Project_01/Forms/login.html?fullname=&streetAddress=&hear=411&Submit=Submit`

Disable   CSS   Forms   Images   Information   Miscellaneous   Outline   Resize   Validation   View Source   Options

Tropiflora Online: Login to Place Order

FIGURE 1.40

12   Close your browser and return to Dreamweaver, leaving registration.html open for the next exercise.

To Extend Your Knowledge

ADDING INSTRUCTIONS TO SELECT LISTS

Many Web designers add an another option to the top of a select list. This option contains information or instructions on how to use the list, such as Select your year of birth, Choose a shipping method, or just Country. We recommend that, in collaboration with the developer of the form-processing application, you create a dummy value for the option, enabling the developer to watch for it in the program. If this is a required option, the program must send the form back to the user to complete this option. For example, in a list of countries, the first option with the Select Your Country label may be coded as follows: `<option value="noCountry" selected>Select Your Country</option>` and the Web developer would make the program watch for a value of noCountry.

Create a List

Dreamweaver calls the multiple select option list a "list". In fact, the only difference between Dreamweaver's list and menu in code is that the `<select>` tag of the list contains the **multiple** attribute whereas the menu does not. Furthermore, the ability to apply the **size** attribute to the menu is not available from the Property inspector. What would you do to create a single select menu that is two or more lines in height? You would apply **size="2"** (or more) directly to the code either using the Code window or Right/Control-clicking the List/Menu control in the Design window and selecting Edit Tag `<select>`.

In this exercise, you create a list from which multiple items may be selected. You also preselect multiple items using Control/Command-click.

1   In the open file, registration.html, click to the right of the select list and press Enter/Return.

2   Type `Select the type of equipment you are interested in` and press Enter/Return.

3   Click the List/Menu button on the Forms Insert bar.

4 Type `equipment` in the List/Menu name field, and select List from the Type options.

5 Set the Height to **5** and enable the Allow Multiple option.

6 Click the List Values button; enter **Gloves**, **Tools**, **Chemicals**, **Clothing**, and **Books** in the Item Label column; and click OK.

FIGURE 1.41

7 Using the Initially Selected list, click Gloves and then Control/Command-click Chemicals.

8 Preview the page in your browser.

Notice that both Gloves and Chemicals are selected.

9 Click Tools, Control/Command-click Books, click the Submit button, and examine the query string.

> When multiple selections have been made, the control name is sent to the action URL as many times as there are selections, with each instance having a different value. When there are no values recorded to the <option> tag, the option labels are sent to the query string.

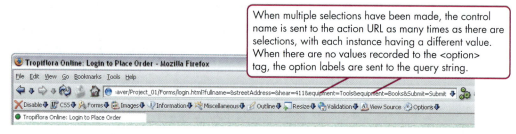

FIGURE 1.42

10 Close your browser, return to Dreamweaver, and close registration.html.

To Extend Your Knowledge

MULTIPLE SELECT LISTS ARE UNCOMMON

It is uncommon to encounter multiple select lists. Often, when they are used, the Web-page designer adds instructional text, such as "Control-click (Windows) or Command-click (Macintosh) to select multiple items." The other option is to avoid confusion altogether. Because multiple select lists are similar to checkboxes, which are more common and understood by a greater portion of the population, unless there is a compelling reason to use multiple select lists, you might consider using checkboxes, instead.

LESSON 9 Grouping Form Controls and Options

You have learned that the **<label>** tag benefits all users by extending the selectable area for checkboxes and radio buttons to include the area taken by the text labels. You learned that the **<label>** tag benefits screen-reader users by relating the label text to the form control. There are two other form options that provide similar benefits — the **<fieldset>**/**<legend>** pair of tags and the **<optgroup>** tag.

The **<fieldset>** tag is used to collect a group of controls. For example, a series of text fields, radio buttons, and checkboxes may be used to allow users to fill out the billing address for their orders. A virtually identical series of controls may be used to allow users to fill out the shipping address for their orders. To reduce the possibility of confusion, the billing-address controls may be enclosed in one **<fieldset>** tag and the shipping address controls may be enclosed in another **<fieldset>** tag, thereby creating, in code anyway, two groups of controls that are distinctly separated. The **<legend>** tag also plays a role: any text between the opening and closing **<legend>** tags appears above the group, thereby labeling the group. The **<fieldset>** tag also has a default presentation of creating a border around the group of controls enclosed within it.

The **<optgroup>** tag is used to group select-list options and assign names to groups. For example, UPS and FedEx both provide Regular and Express shipping services. Rather than list the four items as UPS-Regular, UPS-Express, FedEx-Regular and FedEx-Express, you may group the UPS shipping methods in one **<optgroup>** and the FedEx shipping methods in another **<optgroup>**. The **label** attribute of the **<optgroup>** tag identifies UPS or FedEx but these group names are not selectable.

Use the <fieldset> Tag to Group Controls

In this exercise, you surround a group of controls with the **<fieldset>** tag and label the group with the **<legend>** tag. You create three fieldset groups: the shipping address, the billing address, and the preferred shipper and method. You preview the page in your browser to view the default presentation of the **<fieldset>** and **<legend>** tags. Dreamweaver does not display the border that surrounds contents enclosed in the **<fieldset>** tag.

1   **Open addresses.html from the Forms site.**

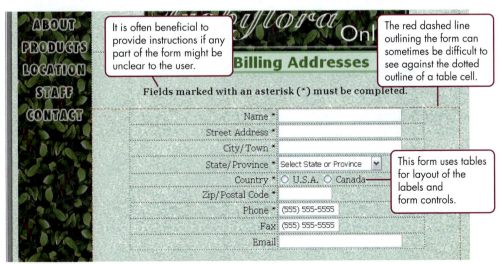

FIGURE 1.43

2 Click in the first table of the form, and then click the `<table>` tag to the right of the `<form>` tag in the Tag selector to select the table.

3 Click the Fieldset button (last button) on the Forms Insert bar.

When you click the Fieldset button, the Document window splits into the Split view.

FIGURE 1.44

4 Type `Shipping Address` in the Label field of the Fieldset dialog box and click OK.

FIGURE 1.45

5 Do not close the Code window. Click to the right of the selected table to deselect it.

6 Scroll down in the Design window. Using the same procedures as in Steps 2–4, select the second table, click the Fieldset button, and assign `Billing Address` as its label.

7 Deselect the second table. Select the third table (consisting of just two cells), click the Fieldset button, and assign `Shipping Preferences` as its label.

8 Scroll both the Code and Design windows so you can see the last fieldset in both.

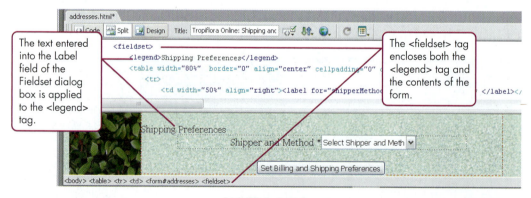

FIGURE 1.46

9   **Close the Code window, then preview the page in your browser.**

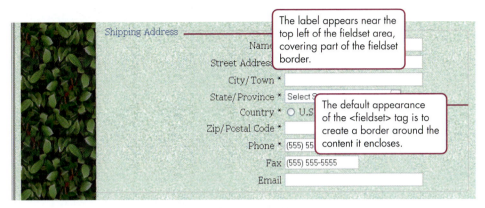

> The label appears near the top left of the fieldset area, covering part of the fieldset border.

> The default appearance of the <fieldset> tag is to create a border around the content it encloses.

FIGURE 1.47

10   **Return to Dreamweaver, leaving addresses.html open for the next exercise.**

Create Option Groups in a Select List

In this exercise, we use the **<optgroup>** tag to create groups of options. This increases the usability of select lists, especially if they are long lists. The **<optgroup>** tag adds an additional item to a list, or so it appears. When you assign the **<optgroup>** tag to a group of select-list options, you are prompted to name the group. The name is then applied to the **label** attribute of the **<optgroup>** tag. This name appears in the select list but it is not selectable: it is like a heading for a block of options.

You cannot apply the **<optgroup>** tag in the Design window. You must work in the Code window.

1   **In the open file, addresses.html, select the first select list of States and Provinces and switch to the Code view.**

2   **Click to the left of <option>Alabama, scroll down to Wyoming, and Shift-click to the right of Wyoming to select all states of the US.**

3   **Right/Control-click in the selected region, and select Insert Tag from the contextual menu.**

FIGURE 1.48

4 | Select HTML tags>Forms>optgroup, and click Insert.

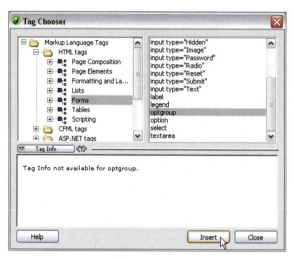

FIGURE 1.49

5 | Type **US States** in the Label field, click OK, and then click Close to close the Tag Chooser dialog box.

FIGURE 1.50

6 | In the Code window, click to the left of <option>Alberta, Shift-click to the right of Yukon Territories, and insert the <optgroup> tag using **Canadian Provinces** as the Label. Close the Tag Chooser dialog box and the Code window when finished.

7 | Apply Steps 1 to 6 to the second list of states and provinces.

8 | Select the third select list of Shipping Preferences.

9 | Select the two FedEx options (click to the left of the first <option> tag and Shift-click to the right of the second closing </option> tag), and insert the <optgroup> tag with the Label **FedEx**. Using the same procedures, assign **UPS** to the **label** attribute of the <optgroup> tag of the two UPS options and **USPS** to the two USPS options.

10   Given that the **label** attribute of the new **<optgroup>** tags identifies the FedEx, UPS, and USPS groups, delete **FedEx**, **UPS**, and **USPS** from the **<option>** label text (not the **<optgroup>** labels). For example, FedEx-Regular becomes just Regular.

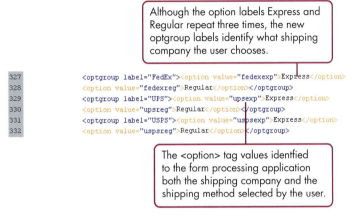

> Although the option labels Express and Regular repeat three times, the new optgroup labels identify what shipping company the user chooses.

```
327    <optgroup label="FedEx"><option value="fedexexp">Express</option>
328    <option value="fedexreg">Regular</option></optgroup>
329    <optgroup label="UPS"><option value="upsexp">Express</option>
330    <option value="upsreg">Regular</option></optgroup>
331    <optgroup label="USPS"><option value="uspsexp">Express</option>
332    <option value="uspsreg">Regular</option></optgroup>
```

> The <option> tag values identfied to the form processing application both the shipping company and the shipping method selected by the user.

FIGURE 1.51

11   Switch to the Design view, preview the page in your browser, and test the modified select lists.

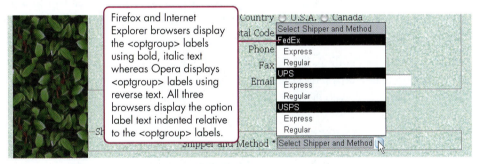

> Firefox and Internet Explorer browsers display the <optgroup> labels using bold, italic text whereas Opera displays <optgroup> labels using reverse text. All three browsers display the option label text indented relative to the <optgroup> labels.

FIGURE 1.52

12   Return to Dreamweaver, leaving addresses.html open for the next exercise.

Modify the Style of <fieldset> and <legend> Tags

In this exercise, you modify the default style of the **<fieldset>** and **<legend>** tags. Legend text is blue in Internet Explorer and black in Firefox and Opera, and is the size of paragraph text. To make the purpose of the group clearer to users, you change the color and size of the legend text. The **<fieldset>** tag, by default, creates a border around enclosed content: in Opera and Firefox, the border is a grooved style whereas in Internet Explorer, it is a thin, flat, solid, gray borderline. You modify the borderline style of the fieldset and, to match the fieldset line, you add a borderline to the legend.

1   In the open file, addresses.html, Right/Control-click in the CSS Styles panel and select New. (If the CSS Styles panel is not open, click the Design panel-group title, click the CSS Styles tab, and create a new CSS Style).

2   In the CSS Styles dialog box, set Tag as the Selector Type, type or select **legend** from the Tag list, ensure that Define in is set to This Document Only, and click OK.

3   In the Type category, set the Font to Verdana, Arial, Helvetica, sans-serif; Size to 1.2 ems; Weight to bold; and Color to #336600. Click OK.

FIGURE 1.53

4   Using the same procedure as in Step 2, create a new CSS style for the `fieldset` tag. From the Border category, leave Same for All checked; set Style to solid, Width to thick, and Color to #336600, and click OK.

As you noticed in Step 11 of the previous exercise, Dreamweaver does not display the fieldset border in the Design window.

5   To apply a similar border style to the legend text, Right/Control-click legend in the CSS styles panel and select Edit. In the Border category, leave Same for All checked, and set Style to solid, Width to thick, and Color to #336600.

6   In the Box category, uncheck Same for All in the Padding group, and set Top to 3 pixels, Right to 10 pixels, Bottom to 3 pixels, and Left to 10 pixels. Leaving Same for All checked for the Margin group, set Top to 0 pixels and click OK.

Did you notice that the Padding, Margin, Style, Width, and Color groups in the Box and Border categories of the CSS dialog box, respectively, were surrounded by the software equivalent to fieldsets and legends? Many features of Web design come from application design.

7   Preview the page in your browser.

8   Return to Dreamweaver leaving addresses.html open for the next exercise.

To Extend Your Knowledge

DO NOT REFER TO COLOR

One of the important practices of Web accessibility is to accommodate both the blind and the color blind. Many Web designers, when thinking about Web accessibility, forget that although the color blind can see, their eyes cannot distinguish some colors correctly. Some colors, such as red and green, can appear almost black. When designing forms, required fields are often colored to suggest to the user that those fields are required along with a statement, such as: "You must complete the fields shown in red." The color blind will have some degree of difficulty identifying the required fields and, of course, the blind will not be able to see the color at all. You must use some other method of identifying required fields, such as using an asterisk (a statement at the top of the form indicating the purpose of the asterisk is also useful). You may color the label text (and the instructions to match) as long as the color combination and contrast are usable by the color blind; just do not use the color as a criterion.

LESSON 10   Creating Hidden Fields

Hidden fields, as the name suggests, are not visible in the browser window but these fields do exist in code. They are commonly used to pass information from the form to the form-processing application. For example, when a customer orders from an e-commerce site, his or her customer number may be stored in a hidden field and passed to the e-commerce application via the query string.

A hidden field uses the `<input>` tag with the `type` attribute set to `hidden`. The `name` attribute may be used to identify the type of data carried by the `value` attribute, such as `name="customerID" value="123456"`. You may use as many hidden fields as necessary for your application, but understand that any sophisticated user can view the information in the hidden fields by simply looking at the code. Do not store a password or any other critical information in a hidden field. There are other more secure methods available, such as *cookies* (text that is passed between your browser and the Web server) and session variables. (*Session variables* are text that identifies you and may be passed as a cookie, stored in links, or in hidden fields. The session-variable text is just an identification code that is validated by the Web-server application and does not carry any recognizable information.)

Create a Hidden Field

In this exercise, you create a hidden field that contains an encrypted session variable to identify who you are and what database record you are updating through the use of the form.

1   **In the open file, addresses.html, click in the empty paragraph between the Shipping and Billing fieldsets.**

2   **Click the Hidden Field button on the Forms Insert bar (third from the left).**

3   **In the Property inspector, type `sid` in the HiddenField Name field (sid is a common short name for session id), type `c8b068f108ccbb25e6b43efd2dd13c66` in the Value field, and press Enter/Return.**

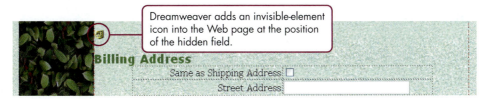

Dreamweaver adds an invisible-element icon into the Web page at the position of the hidden field.

FIGURE 1.54

4   Preview the page in your browser, and search the query string for the sid variable. (It is a long query string, so you will have to scroll to find it.)

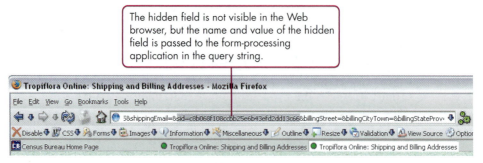

> The hidden field is not visible in the Web browser, but the name and value of the hidden field is passed to the form-processing application in the query string.

FIGURE 1.55

5   Close your browser, return to Dreamweaver, and close addresses.html.

To Extend Your Knowledge

SPAM, FORMMAIL APPLICATIONS, AND HIDDEN FIELDS

With the exception of the mailto: action URL, form-processing applications must be installed and run on a Web server, which is not something a free Web-hosting service (whether through your ISP or a third-party service, such as Tripod.com) will allow. However, many free Web-hosting services do recognize that their clients may wish to create some basic forms, such as a contact form with the data collected from their visitors emailed to them. Rather than providing you direct access to the application, these hosting services often provide you the action URL and some instructions on how to configure the form to send your visitors' data to you via email. This is not the same as a mailto: URL: the **formmail application** (an application that emails collected form data to the intended recipient) uses its own programming to email the data to you.

If you don't have access to the formmail application, how does it know to email your visitors' data to you? This is done using a hidden field in which the `name` and `value` are set using `name="email-address" value="you@domain.com"`. The formmail application then takes the data collected by the form and emails it to the email address in the `value` attribute.

In Project 6 of *Essential For Design: Dreamweaver MX 2004 Level 1*, you learned that forms are a good way to hide your email address from spammers, but not if you use hidden fields. These hidden fields are no more secure than an email link on a Web page. If you must hide your email address, you must have access to the formmail application and store your email address right in the application. Only someone with rights to access the files on your Web server (or your space in one) can extract your email address from the programming code. However, this is hacking and beyond the ability of spammers and their email-harvesting software, so you may be assured that storing your email address in the programming code will protect it. If you cannot afford anything but free Web space, recognize that your email address in a hidden form field may be harvested at some point. You may try another free hosting service; there are many.

CAREERS IN DESIGN

FORMS DESIGN AND USABILITY TESTING

You have learned to create static pages that, with the exception of links, have no features with which visitors may interact. Forms add a degree of interaction between the visitor and the Web page by allowing the visitor to enter information or make selections. Even without dynamic JavaScript effects, visitors know that by clicking the submit button, some effect will occur, such as sending an email, posting a question to a discussion forum, or purchasing a book. To ensure that your visitors can use the form as you would like them to use it, however, before you create the form, you must carefully evaluate the type of data that you want it to collect and the type of form controls that you might use.

Sometimes the best input method is not obvious. For example, credit-card numbers are often in the form of 1234 2345 3456 4567. With spaces, this credit-card number takes 19 characters. One possible issue is that people may not enter the spaces and may think, therefore, that they are expected to insert the 3-digit security number, as well; if they do so, the 19-digit number is invalid. To avoid this problem, do you divide the credit card number into 4 input fields each containing 4 digits? Doing so means that after each field, the visitor must press Tab to move to the next field but, at the same time, this format makes clearer to visitors that they only need 16 numbers. Some developers add JavaScript to this type of form so after the fourth number is pressed, JavaScript moves the insertion point to the next field. If, however, a user looks at the credit card and not at the screen and presses Tab after the fourth number, JavaScript would already have moved the insertion point to the next field so the Tab would move one the insertion point one field further, leaving a field empty.

If you need to develop either a complex or a unique form, consider doing some usability testing in which people test your form and give their feedback. Usability testing can be expensive but it doesn't have to be. You can gather a group of friends or co-workers and have them test your form and provide feedback, either as written notes or in a group discussion afterwards. A Web site that depends on information collected by its forms must ensure that its forms are not an impediment to the success of the Web site.

SUMMARY

In this project, you learned about forms and the many roles that forms play in Web applications. You explored form controls. You learned how to send form data to a form-processing application and the methods by which it may be sent. You learned how to insert single- and multiline text fields and password fields. You added submit and reset buttons, and learned how buttons may be used to trigger other actions, such as edit and delete. You explored the differences between radio buttons and checkboxes. You created menus and lists, and learned that they may be used in place of radio buttons and checkboxes. You learned why it is beneficial to everyone to properly label form controls. You grouped form controls into fieldsets and grouped options in select lists, and learned how both improve the usability of forms. You learned about hidden fields and how they may be used in a Web application. You learned that although, as a designer, you may assemble and design a Web form, that Web form is the gateway to a Web application that requires a programmer to create it so it can capture, analyze, and use the data.

KEY TERMS

application	e-commerce	Perl
blog	encrypted	query string
C++	form controls	radio button
CGI	formmail	scripts
checkbox	HTTPS / S-HTTP	session variables
cookies	menu	select list

CHECKING CONCEPTS AND TERMS

SCREEN ID

Identify the indicated areas from the list below:

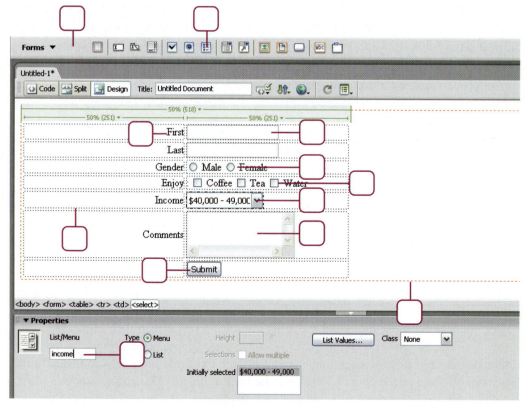

FIGURE 1.56

a. Forms Insert bar

b. Name of select list

c. Radio button

d. Label text

e. Radio group button

f. Text field

g. Checkbox

h. Button

i. Form outline

j. Layout table

k. Menu list

l. Textarea

MULTIPLE CHOICE

Circle the letter of the correct answer for each of the following:

1. Forms may be used to _____.
   a. pay bills online
   b. send an email
   c. apply for a credit card
   d. All of the above

2. The two controls that may be used to replace each other are _____.
   a. radio buttons and checkboxes
   b. checkboxes and multi select lists
   c. legends and labels
   d. optgroups and fieldsets

3. If the action URL is search.php, the value is 3F9J, and the name is XV9C, the correct query string is _____.
   a. `search.php?value=3F9J&name=XV9C`
   b. `search.php=XV9C+3F9J`
   c. `search.php?XV9C=3F9J`
   d. `search.php/value=3F9J+name=XV9C`

4. What attribute would you use to display the third option in a select list?
   a. `display="3"`
   b. `selected`
   c. `checked="checked"`
   d. `multiple`

5. Which button code would be best to display Modify and trigger an edit function?
   a. `<input type="edit"`
      `name="edit">Modify</input>`
   b. `<input type="submit"`
      `value="Modify" name="edit">`
   c. `<input type="button"`
      `label="Modify" id="edit">`
   d. `<input type="reset" name="Modify"`
      `action="edit">`

6. Why does the W3C recommend labeling form controls?
   a. The color blind have difficulty reading some text/background color combinations.
   b. Screen-reader software skips past unlabeled form controls.
   c. Labeled form controls improve the usability of the form.
   d. Label text displays in bold, increasing its readability.

7. In a select list of country names, which option would a Web application reject and request the user select a valid country?
   a. `<option>Select a country`
   b. `<option value="none">Select a`
      `country</option>`
   c. `<option value="notSelected"`
      `selected>Select a`
      `country</option>`
   d. All of the above

8. Which of the following is true?
   a. A group of radio buttons should allow only one item to be selected.
   b. A group of checkboxes can allow multiple items to be selected.
   c. The multi select list is uncommon and unfamiliar to most users.
   d. All of the above.

9. The <fieldset> and <legend> tags may be used to identify _____.

   a. a group of radio buttons

   b. a collection of a variety of form controls

   c. a group of related select-list options

   d. all of the above

10. The post method _____.

   a. sends the form data to the action URL

   b. encrypts the form data so a hacker can't snoop it

   c. emails the form data to your email address

   d. all of the above

DISCUSSION QUESTIONS

1. Online stores, from which you can purchase items, require a large amount of information to enable you to complete your purchase. What type of information would you need to collect from customers to enable them to complete their purchases? For each type of information, identify what type of form control you would use to simplify data entry for the customers.

2. HTML forms are the most important types of Web pages. Do you agree or disagree with this statement and why?

SKILL DRILL

Skill Drills reinforce project skills. Each skill reinforced is the same, or nearly the same, as a skill presented in the lessons. Detailed instructions are provided in a step-by-step format. Work through these exercises in order.

1. Create a Web Form to Sign in for an Online Exam

In this Skill Drill, you create a basic form that serves as the opening page for an online examination for the Web Design 301 course. (In Challenge Exercise 1, you add to this series of examination pages.)

1. Create a new site definition called **Casual University** from the Project_01>CasualU folder.

2. Open signin.html.

3. Click in the empty paragraph below the last sentence and create a **2**-row, **1**-column layout table with no width setting, **0** border thickness, **0** cell padding, **0** cell spacing, and no headers. With the table selected, set the table (not cell) alignment to center.

4. Insert casualu-logo.jpg from the images folder into the top cell, and assign **Casual University** as the alternate text.

5. Select the bottom cell and set the horizontal alignment to center. In the bottom cell, type **Web Design 301** and format it as Heading 1. Press Enter/Return, and type **Mid Term Exam**, and format it as Heading 2. Press Enter/Return and type **You are required to complete all fields in all pages of this examination.** Select this paragraph and apply bold to it. Click to the right of this paragraph and press Enter/Return.

6. Create a form where the name is signIn, the Method is POST, the Action is **q1.html**, and the Enctype is set to application/x-www-form-urlencoded.

7. In the form area, insert a **3**-row, **2**-column table with the width set to **60%**, border thickness set to **0**, cell padding set to **3**, cell spacing set to **0**, and headers set to none. Select the top four cells and set the cell width to **50%**. Select the top and middle left cells, and set the cell alignment to right.

8. In the top-left cell, type **Student Name**, and in the cell below, type **Student ID**. In the top-right cell, insert a text field named **studentName** that is **35** characters wide. In the middle-right cell, insert a password field named **studentID** that is **35** characters wide.

9. Merge the bottom two cells. Set the horizontal alignment of the merged cell to center. In the merged cell, insert a submit button with the name **signIn** and a Label **Sign Me In**.

10. Right/Control-click the studentName text field, and select Edit Tag <input>; in the Style Sheet/Accessibility category, ensure that the ID is **studentName** (add it, if it isn't). Using the same procedures, ensure the studentID text field has the ID of **studentID**.

11. Select Student Name in the left cell, Right/Control-click and wrap the selected text with the **<label>** tag, with the **for** attribute set to **studentName**. Using the same procedures, wrap Student ID with the **<label>** tag, setting the **for** attribute to **studentID**.

12. Close signin.html, saving your changes.

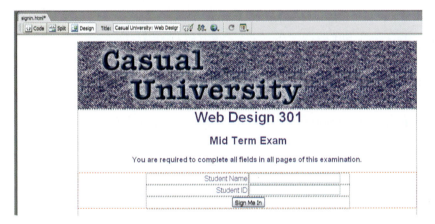

FIGURE 1.57

2. Create a Contact Form

A contact form is one of the most common means of contacting a company. It provides the employees some degree of protection against spam by hiding their email from direct access. A contact form can accommodate changing staff when a contact person changes position, department, or employers. A contact form can also help categorize the message based on the types of questions the customers/visitors have and the department they want to contact, making it easier for the company to respond.

In this exercise, you create a contact form that includes the basic Name and Email fields as well as lists of departments and types of questions the visitor might have.

1. Open contactus.html from the Forms site.

2. In the empty paragraph below the Contact Us heading, insert a form with the name **contactus**, Method set to POST, Action set to **thankyou.html**, and Enctype set to application/x-www-form-urlencoded.

3. In the form, insert a **7**-row, **2**-column table, with the width set to **100%**, border thickness set to **0**, cell padding set to **2**, cell spacing set to **0**, and headers set to none. Select the left column and set the horizontal alignment to right. Merge the bottom two cells and set the horizontal alignment to center.

4. In the top-left cell, type **Your Name:**, and in the right cell, insert a text field with a name of **contactName** and a width of **35**. In the left cell of the second row, type **Your Email:**, and in the right cell, insert a text field with a name of **contactEmail** and a width of **35**. In the left cell of the third row, insert one checkbox with a name of **ccSender**, a Checked Value of **yes**, and Initial State set to Checked. In the right cell, type **Send a copy of the message to you**.

5. In the left cell of the fourth row, type **Department:**. In the right cell, create a menu list named **department** with the following five items: **Select a department** (assign a value of **noDept**), **Sales**, **Service**, **Human Resources**, and **Web master** (no values for the last four items). Set Select a department as the Initially selected item.

6. In the left cell of the fifth row, type **Reason for Contacting Us:**. In the right cell, create a menu named **reason**. Using the chart below, create a list of items. When finished, set Choose a reason as the Initially Selected item.

Item Label	Value
Choose a reason	noReason
Order not arrived	notArrived
Order received broken	broken
Other	otherSales
Warranty enquiry	warranty
Schedule a repair	schedRepair
Order a part	partOrder
Other	otherService
Privacy and other Policies	policies
I would like a job	employment
Other	hrOther
Broken Web link	brokenLink
Other	webOther

The fact that there are multiple instances of an option labeled Other requires that they be distinguished using different values.

7. Switch to the Code view. Select from Order not arrived to otherSales. Right/Control-click in the selected region, select Insert tag, and insert the **\<optgroup\>** tag with a label of **Sales Department**. Select from Warranty enquiry to otherService, and insert the **\<optgroup\>** tag with the label **Service Department**. Select from Privacy to hrOther, and insert the **\<optgroup\>** tag with the label **Human Resources**. Select the last two options, and insert the **\<optgroup\>** tag with the label **Web Site**. Switch to the Design view when finished.

8. In the sixth left cell, type **Comments:**. In the right cell, insert a multiline text field with a name of **comments**, a Char Width of **35**, and a Num Lines of **10**.

9. Apply the **<label>** tag to all of the labels, assigning the **for** attribute the same value as the **id** attribute of the related form control. Right/Control-click a form control, select Edit tag, and check for an ID in the Style Sheet/Accessibility category of the Tag Editor dialog box. If an ID does not exist, create one that is identical to the control name (found in the General category of the Tag Editor dialog box). Select the form control's label text, and wrap it with the **<label>** tag, assigning it the **for** attribute identical to the ID attribute of the form control. Repeat these procedures for all six form controls.

10. In the bottom merged cell, insert an image field using the Forms>images>contactusform.gif graphic. Type **submit** in the ImageField field and **Send Your Message** in the Alt field.

11. Preview the page in your browser and click the image-field button.

    A thank you message is very respectful of your customers. It may contain a static message, like this one or, through the magic of the form-processing application, may contain a copy of the message they sent via the form.

12. Close your browser, return to Dreamweaver, and close contactus.html.

FIGURE 1.58

To Extend Your Knowledge

ONE LIST AFFECTS ANOTHER

This form uses optgroups to help the user select a reason that matches the department selected from the other list. However, this is a perfect example of a form in which JavaScript could be used so instead of optgroups, the selection of a department from the first list would hide all reasons except those that apply to the selected department.

3. Create a Marketing-Survey Form

In this exercise, you create a market-survey form using radio-button groups to provide the options while restricting the user to selecting just one from each group.

1. Create a new HTML page, title it **Market Survey**, and save it (but do not close it) as **survey.html** in the Forms site.

2. Type **Market Survey**, format it as Heading 1, and press Enter/Return.

3. Insert a form with the name **survey**, the Method set to POST, Action set to **market-survey.html**, and Enctype set to application/x-www-form-urlencoded.

4. Type **1. Select your age group** and press Enter/Return. Create a Radio Group called **age**. Create four radio buttons labeled **Under 25**, **25 to 34**, **35 to 44**, and **45 and older**. Make up your own values for the four radio buttons, keeping them short and without spaces. If necessary, use the plus button to add new rows, and the up and down arrows to sort the entries from youngest at the top to oldest at the bottom. Lay out the buttons using a table.

5. Click to the right of the radio-buttons table and press Enter/Return. Type **2. Select your family income.** and press Enter/Return. Create a radio-button group called **income** using **Less than $30,000**, **$30,000 to $45,000**, **$45,000 to $60,000**, and **Over $60,000**, and create your own values to match the labels. Lay out the buttons using a table.

6. Click to the right of the radio-buttons table and press Enter/Return. Type **3. Select your dwelling type.** and press Enter/Return. Create a radio-button group called **dwelling** using **Apartment**, **Row House — Rented**, **Row House — Owned**, **Condominium**, **Duplex**, and **House** as the labels, and create your own values. Lay out the buttons using a table.

7. Click to the right of the radio-buttons table and press Enter/Return. Type **4. Select your current profession.** and press Enter/Return. Create a radio-button group called **profession** using **Retail**, **Government**, **Health Services**, **Business Owner**, and **Other**, and create your own values. Lay out the buttons using a table.

8. In the last cell to the right of Other, click and press Enter/Return. Type **If you selected Other, please specify.** Insert a text field called **specifyOther** with a width of **25**.

9. Insert a submit button, and set it so that it displays **Thank You!** on the button.

10. Close survey.html, saving your changes.

4. Create a Book Wish-List Form

For the purpose of this exercise, pretend you have created an application in which you, your family, and your friends may add entries to a Book Wish-List database. If anyone is trying to think of a perfect birthday gift, all they need do is consult the database. In this exercise, you create the front-end form that will submit the book details to the database. As part of the form, you add the URL to the Web site of the book (if there is one), and insert a little JavaScript function with which you may test the book Web-site URL.

1. Create a new HTML page, title it **Book Wish List**, and save it as **wishlist.html** in the Forms site.

2. Type **Book Wish List** and format it as Heading 1. Press Enter/Return, type **Add a new entry**, and format it as Heading 2. Press Enter/Return and type **All fields marked with an asterisk must be filled.** Select this paragraph and apply bold. Press Enter/Return.

3. Create a form with the name **wishlist**, Action set to **wishlist.html**, Method set to POST, and Enctype set to application/x-www-form-urlencoded.

4. Create a **7**-row, **2**-column table with the width set to **60%**, the border thickness set to **0**, cell padding set to **2**, cell spacing set to **0**, and no headers. Select the left column of cells and set the horizontal alignment to right. Merge the two cells in the bottom row, and set the horizontal alignment to center.

5. In the left column type **Title***, **Author(s)***, **ISBN**, **Publisher***, **Publication Date***, and **Book Web Site**. In the right columns, insert text fields for the **title**, **author**, **ISBN**, and, **publisher** with appropriate names and widths. Create a text field for the book Web site and name it **bookURL**. (The name is important as it is used in a JavaScript function added in Step 8.)

6. To enable the user to insert the publication date, create two menus. The first menu is a list of the months of the year, so name it appropriately. Above **January**, insert **Month**, assign it an appropriate value, and then add the rest of the month names (with or without values, your choice). The second menu is a list of years starting with **Year**, then listing **2004** backwards to **2000**. Assign an appropriate name for this list and also an appropriate value for Year, the top item in the list.

7. In the merged cell, insert a submit button that displays **Add To Wish List**.

8. Open testurl.html, press Control/Command-A to select all of the content, copy it to the clipboard, and close testurl.html. Click to the right of the book Web-site text field, and paste the copied code.

9. Preview the page in your browser.

10. Complete the form as follows: **Speed Up Your Site** is the title, **Andrew B. King** is the author, **0-7357-1324-3** is the ISBN, **New Riders** is the publisher, **January 2003** is the publication date, and **http://www.websiteoptimization.com** is the book's Web site. Click the Test URL link and observe that the book's Web site opens in a pop-up window.

11. Close the pop-up window, close your browser, return to Dreamweaver, and close wishlist.html.

CHALLENGE

Challenge exercises expand on, or are somewhat related to, skills presented in the lessons. Each exercise provides a brief narrative introduction, followed by instructions in a numbered-step format that are not as detailed as those in the Skill Drill section. You can work through one or more exercises in any order.

1. Create a Multiple-Choice Exam

In this challenge, you create three forms containing questions from a multiple-choice exam. The action URLs send the student to the next question. Hidden fields contain the answers to previous questions. Although using hidden fields this way may not be very secure, it is possible to **obfuscate** (make obscure or unclear) the answer using a **hash** (a process of encrypting text whereby the result cannot be reversed to reveal the original text, but two encryptions of the same text produce the same result, enabling comparison) of the answer so that the student cannot simply change the answer in the hidden field from A to B. This exam process, and the generation of the hash (which is an available function in PHP and other programming languages) would normally be done with a form-processing application. However, this exercise will provide you with an understanding as to the type of process one might apply to a form-processing application.

1. Open q1.html from the Casual University site, and click in the empty paragraph below the instructions.

2. Create a new form called **q1** with the Action set to **q2.html**, the Method set to POST, and the Enctype set to application/x-www-form-urlencoded.

3. In the form, type **1. Which text format displays using the largest text size?** and press Enter/Return. Create a radio-button group with the name **q1**. Type **Heading 6**, **Heading 2**, **Paragraph**, and **Heading 1** as the labels, and **a**, **b**, **c**, and **d** as the values. Lay out the radio-button group using line breaks.

4. Press Enter/Return after the last answer and insert a hidden field with **studentID** as the name and **25D55AD283AA400AF464C76D713C07AD** as the value.

   This 32-character string is a hash of 12345678.

5. Create a submit button with **next** as the name and **Next Question** as the value.

6. Close, saving the changes.

7. Open q2.html. Use the same procedures as you did in Steps 2 to 6 with the following changes: set the form name as **q2** and the form's action to **q3.html**. The question is **2. Absolute links are necessary when linking:** and the answers are **a page to a named anchor**, **to a target window**, **to a page in another Web site**, and **alternate text**. Insert the same **studentID** hidden field plus another hidden field called **answer1** with a value of **8277E0910D750195B448797616E091AD**. When finished, close q2.html, saving your changes.

8. Open q3.html. Use the same procedures as in Step 7 with the following changes: set the form name as **q3** and the form's action to **results.html**. The question is **3. GIF and JPEG image formats:** and the answers are **are bitmapped graphics**, **are limited to 256 colors**, **can be animated**, and **are the storage formats of digital cameras**. Insert the same **studentID** and **answer1** hidden fields plus another hidden field called **answer2** with a value of **4A8A08F09D37B73795649038408B5F33**. When finished, close q3.html, saving your changes.

9. Open results.html. Below Results, insert a Definition List from the Text Insert bar. Type `1. Which text format displays using the largest text size?`, press Enter/Return, type `Heading 1`, and press Enter/Return. Type `2. Absolute links are necessary when linking:`, press Enter/Return, type `to a page in another Web site`, and press Enter/Return. Type `3. GIF and JPEG image formats:`, press Enter/Return, type `are bitmapped graphics`, and press Enter/Return twice.

10. Type `Congratulations! Perfect!`.

11. Insert the same three hidden fields as you did previously: `studentID`, `answer1`, and `answer2`. Create a fourth hidden field called `answer3` with a value of `0CC175B9C0F1B6A831C399E269772661`. Close, saving the changes.

12 Open signin.html and preview it in your browser. Sign in and answer the questions in the forms. When finished, close your browser, return to Dreamweaver, and close signin.html.

To Extend Your Knowledge

A HASH CALCULATOR

If you search for hash calculator using your favorite search engine, you will find a number of downloadable, free calculators that enable you to calculate different forms of hashes. You may also go to bfl.rctek.com/tools/?tool=hasher for an online version. When you compare the MD5 hash for a, d, and c (individually), you see that these values are equal to the values of the answer1, answer2, and answer3 hidden fields.

2. Create a Two-Form Page

When working with forms, one common programming technique is that when two or three forms are related to each other, all two or three forms are created within the same HTML page. The form data sent by the first form is used by the programming code to determine that the second form is to be displayed. For example, the first form could ask for your name. When the form is sent back to itself, the programming code sees that your name has been completed and sends you the second form (with the name stored in a hidden field). The second form asks you for your gender. When the form is sent back to itself, the programming code takes your name from the hidden field, your gender from the most recent form data and creates a suitable message for you.

In this exercise, you create both forms on the same page and insert some ***pseudo-code*** (programming-like code written in understandable English instructions to describe the process that will be used) that, on a Web server, might be used to populate the employee-details form with the information about the employees.

1. Open edit-student.html from the Casual University site, and click in the empty cell below the top graphic.

2. Type `Select a Student` and format it as Heading 1. Press Enter/Return.

3. Insert a form with a name of `selectStudent`, the Action set to `edit-students.html`, the Method to GET (for the time being so we can analyze the query string), and Enctype to application/x-www-form-urlencoded.

4. In the form, type **Select a student** and press Shift-Enter/Return. Insert a menu named **studentID** with the following five student names and values (student IDs): **Carole Brown** (**1234**), **Bruce Carter** (**2345**), **Jane Higgins** (**3456**), **Tommy Kettle** (**4567**), and finally, your own name and a four-digit number. Select both the label text (**Select a student**) and the menu control, and click the Label button to insert an implicit label.

5. Click to the right of the menu control and press Enter/Return. Insert a submit button with the name **submit** and a label of **Edit Student Record**.

6. In the empty paragraph below this form, type **Edit Student Record** and format it as Heading 1. Press Enter/Return and create another form named **editStudent**, set Action to **edit-student.html**, the Method to GET, and Enctype to application/x-www-form-urlencoded.

7. In the form, create a **9**-row, **2**-column layout table. In the left column, create the following labels: **Student ID**, **First Name**, **Last Name**, **Street Address**, **City/Town**, **State**, **Home Phone**, and **Birth Date**. In the right column, insert text fields for the first seven labels, and create three for Birth Date with the labels **Day**, **Month**, and **Year**. Merge the bottom row and insert a select button with the name **submit** and the label **Save Changes**.

8. Insert your name and particulars as the initial values for all of the fields.

9. In the empty paragraph below the second form, type **Student Record Updated** and format it as Heading 1.

10. Switch to the Code view and scroll to approximately line 17 where **<h1>Select a Student</h1>** appears. Open edit-student.php.txt, select lines 2 to 6, copy the text, switch to edit-student.html, and paste the text between the **<form>** and **<h1>** tags around line 17. Switch to edit-student.php.txt and select lines 10 to 17, copy them, switch back to edit-student.html, and paste them between the **<form>** and **<h1>** tags near line 34. Switch to edit-student.php.txt, copy lines 21 to 26, switch back to edit-student.html, and paste them between the last **<form>** and **<h1>** tags near line 86.

    Read the three inserted blocks of pseudo-code. The first block says that if there is no query string, the first form is displayed. The second block says that if the query string identifies that the Edit Student Record button is clicked and contains the studentID, the database will be queried using that studentID, and the second form is populated with the student's details and displayed. The third block says that if the Save Changes button was clicked, the database is updated with the new data and the third part of the page is displayed.

11. Preview the page in your browser. Select your name from the top form, click the Edit Student Record button, and examine the query string for submit=Edit+Student+Record and your studentID. Click the second submit button and examine the query string for submit=Save+Changes.

    In this situation, it is fine to have three Heading-1 blocks because only one displays at a time.

12. Close your browser, return to Dreamweaver, and close edit-student.html and edit-student.php.txt.

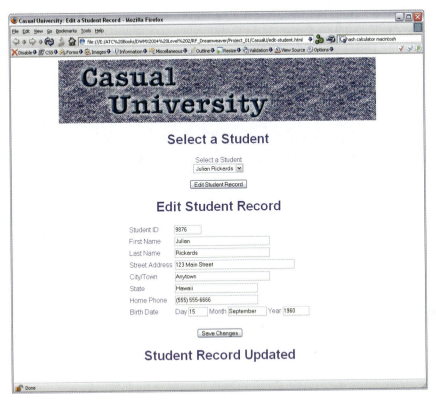

3. Using Image Buttons to Submit Orders

The image button is useful, not only for decorating the text of a submit button but also, on a shopping site, for submitting an item to the ***shopping cart*** (a term used to describe the shopping process used on an online store) for purchase. In this exercise, you complete the form that students may use to purchase books for their courses. In place of plain buttons, you use image buttons that are images of the book covers.

1. Open order-books.html from the Casual University site.

2. Click in the cell to the left of the description of the Dreamweaver book. Click the Image Field button from the Forms Insert bar, and insert ATC_DW_MX_Cover.JPG from the images folder. Type `Order this Dreamweaver book` in the alternate-text field. Copy the ISBN number from the right cell, and paste it into the name field of the Image Field button.

3. Repeat Step 2 and insert Image Field buttons for each of the books. Change the alternate text to reflect the book, and change the name of the field to reflect the ISBN number.

   The ISBN number is a unique identifier of each book and is used by the database system to manage the shopping cart as well as other business functions of the online store.

4. In the empty cell at the bottom of the table, insert a submit button with the name `submit` and the label `Checkout`.

5. Preview the page in your browser, click any of the book covers, and examine the query string.

Image field buttons appear twice in a query string because they indicate not only which image was clicked, but also the x and y position of the mouse pointer where it was clicked. In some other applications, the position of the mouse pointer is useful, but for this type of application, all that is needed is the identity (ISBN) of the selected book.

6. Close your browser, return to Dreamweaver, and close order-book.html.

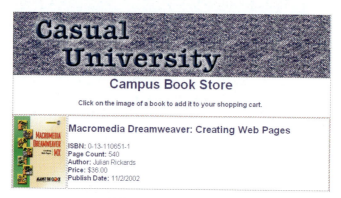

FIGURE 1.60

4. Hide Optional Fields Using JavaScript

You have read often in this project that JavaScript is commonly used to enhance the usability of forms. In this exercise, you create a form that has both required and optional fields. The JavaScript function in this page, when clicked, hides the optional fields and, when clicked again, reveals the optional fields. You don't need to insert or type any of the JavaScript: it is configured to act on certain classes and ids. When you create the optional fields in this form to enable JavaScript to work on them, you must assign them the class name optional. The JavaScript code looks for all instances of the class optional and hides or reveals them depending on how many times the link is clicked. The link to also is dynamically created using JavaScript. In Dreamweaver, the link is not visible because Dreamweaver does not run the JavaScript.

1. Open contactus.html from the Casual University site.

2. Click to the right of Contact Us and press Enter/Return.

3. Press Control/Command-B to apply bold, type **Labels with the asterisk (*) are required.**, press Control/Command-B to disable bold, and press Enter/Return.

4. Right/Control-click the empty paragraph, and select Edit Tag <p> from the contextual menu. From the Style Sheet/Accessibility category of the Tag Editor dialog box, type **hidedisplaylink** in the ID field (the spelling and letter case is important or the JavaScript won't be able to act on it).

❓ If you have problems

If you have problems Right/Control-clicking the empty paragraph, type some text, and then Right/Control-click and complete the rest of Step 4. Delete the text but not the paragraph tag when you are finished with Step 4.

5. Create a form with the name **contactus**, the action set to **thankyou.html**, the method set to POST, and Enctype set to application/x-www-form-urlencoded.

6. In the form, create a **6**-row, **2**-column layout table. In the left cells, insert the following field labels: **Full Name**, **Student ID**, **Email address**, **Subject ***, and **Comments ***. In the right columns, create appropriate text fields for each of these fields, except the Comments field. The Comments field should be a text area field, **35** characters wide and **10** lines high.

7. Merge the bottom two cells and insert a **submit** button with the label **Send us your comments**.

8. Click in Full Name and, using the Tag selector, click the **<tr>** tag. Right/Control-click the **<tr>** tag, select Edit tag, add **class="optional"** to the tag, and press Enter/Return. Repeat the process for the **<tr>** tag of the Student ID and Email address rows.

9. Preview this page in your browser.

    Notice the link that wasn't visible in Dreamweaver: the JavaScript function has been programmed to create this link and text dynamically.

10. Type information in all of the fields.

11. Click the link and notice that the optional fields are hidden (by hiding the table rows in which they exist), and the link-text changes, enabling you to reveal the optional fields.

    Notice that the contents of the fields are not erased when the fields are hidden and revealed again. The hiding processing does not erase the table rows and its contents; it hides them.

12. Close your browser, return to Dreamweaver, and close contactus.html.

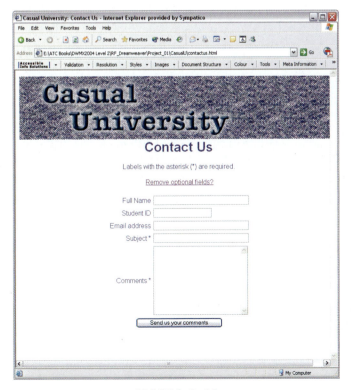

FIGURE 1.61

P O R T F O L I O   B U I L D E R

Create Forms to Process a Purchase

Online stores require a large amount of information to enable customers to complete their purchases. In this assignment, you're going to create a series of forms that collect and process customer and purchase information for an online bookstore.

Before you begin, write down the author and title of three books you own, and use these as the selected products from your online bookstore. Assume that the books you have chosen are stored in a shopping-cart database. Consider the following options when you create the forms:

1. The customer may be a new or returning customer. Given that you need information about the customer but don't want to ask returning customers to enter their personal information each time they visit your site, create the form or forms necessary to gather information from a new customer. Provide an option to allow returning customers to identify themselves without having to reenter this information.

2. A purchase-confirmation page allows customers to view their purchase selections and, if necessary, reconsider their selections. Create a form that displays their shopping-cart items and allows them to make some changes. Consider the type of changes you would allow customers to make to their orders and provide the appropriate options in the form.

3. Create a form that displays the customer's shipping information and provides shipping options.

4. Create a payment form allowing users to select how they will pay for their products. Do you only accept credit cards or would you also allow other payment methods? What type of information do you need from the customers and what information might customers need from the store for their selected payment option?

5. Create a page that displays their final invoice. This page is not a form but gathers information from the previous forms. Do not display sensitive information, such as credit-card information.

Working with Cascading Style Sheets

OBJECTIVES

In this project, you learn how to

- Use element selectors singly or grouped

- Apply styles using classes and ids

- Create style rules using contextual selectors

- Use pseudo-class selectors

- Create custom styles using the <span> tag

- Create and apply external style sheets

- Use design-time style sheets

- Create print and alternate style sheets

WHY WOULD I DO THIS?

Cascading style sheets (*CSS*) is a coding language that is part of the W3C Web technologies. Its purpose is to handle the presentation while leaving the document structure to (X)HTML. CSS version 1 was released in late 1996, just months before HTML 4.0. The current version is CSS2.1; CSS3 is in draft form. Despite the many years that CSS has been around and the intent that CSS be responsible for the presentation of Web pages, many designers use design software that does not make it easy to apply CSS. Dreamweaver MX 2004 is better than other Web-design software in its support for CSS, but even in Dreamweaver there are many options for applying CSS that cannot easily be chosen from a dialog box. In some ways, CSS may be considered a weak programming language because parts of it rely on relationships between HTML elements and these types of relationships cannot be easily offered through dialog boxes. In this project, you learn how CSS works and how you can make it work effectively for you.

The term Cascading Style Sheets requires some explanation. Style is obvious; CSS is used to add style, such as color, backgrounds, and borders, to Web pages. The word sheet indicates the most common methods of creating CSS — collecting all of the styles into a block or sheet. Style sheets can be embedded or external. Embedded style sheets appear in the `<head>` section of an HTML document between opening and closing `<style>` tags. External style sheets are separate files attached to all pages in a Web site. The word cascading refers to the fact that if you apply a style to the paragraph `p` element, the style applies or cascades to every paragraph on the page or in the Web site.

Two questions may occur to you when you think about CSS: what does CSS do and how may it be applied? The first question, to a certain extent, has been answered in earlier projects in this book and the previous book, *Essentials for Design: Dreamweaver MX 2004 Level 1*. Using CSS, you can add or change text styling, colors, backgrounds, bullet characters, and many other properties. CSS can also be used for layout, as we discuss in *Project 3: Using CSS for Layout*. How to apply CSS is a more difficult question to answer because applying CSS is more complex than the old HTML presentation methods which use presentation tags, such as the `<font>` tag, and presentation attributes, such as the `bgcolor` (background color) attribute. Applying CSS is the primary focus of this project.

You may wonder why you should learn CSS. Perhaps the most obvious reason is its power. Through one simple modification, you can change the paragraph typeface from Arial to Times, not just for the current paragraph, or even all paragraphs in the current page, but all pages in your site, whether 10, 100, or 100,000 pages. Another reason why CSS is so important is its versatility. For example, HTML allowed backgrounds (background colors or images) behind only a few elements: the body, tables, table rows, and table cells. Using CSS, you can apply backgrounds to any element on the page. Variety is another reason why CSS is important to learn. HTML does not allow you to create a custom bullet for lists, change line spacing, remove bold from headings, or remove underline from links. These are examples of commonly supported features of CSS that HTML cannot match. CSS can be written to apply certain combinations of styles just on the basis of relationships between HTML elements. For example `h2+p` tells CSS to apply a combination of styles to the first paragraph after a heading 2 whereas all other paragraphs after that one have a different style. CSS can help reduce *page weight* (the amount of bytes required to render a Web page) in two ways. It takes fewer bytes of CSS to define the style of a page than HTML presentation. For example, to change 10 paragraphs to Arial font, HTML would use `<font face="Arial"></font>` ten times ($26 \times 10 = 260$ characters) whereas **p {font-family: Arial}** uses only 22 characters and, unlike the `<font>` tag, additional paragraphs in the page do not need any additional characters. Redesign is another good reason to learn to use CSS. Property structured HTML determines the document structure and that does not change when there is a redesign of a Web site. However, the look and layout of the Web site may well change with a redesign and they are controlled with CSS. Of course, the design graphics may also require changing, such as background graphics.

Whenever you embark on a CSS-based design, you should start with a page with properly formatted content but with no style whatsoever — no text alignment, no colors, no background, nothing. This becomes your blank canvas on which you build your creative design. As a result, you build a Web page or Web site in which the structure is completely separate from the presentation: structure and presentation are the separate domains of HTML and CSS.

Web designers limit their creativity by not knowing and using CSS. However, just knowing the properties, such as background images or text color, is not sufficient. When you learn how CSS may be applied, what options are available to you, and how you may combine them, then you have learned to design using CSS.

V I S U A L   S U M M A R Y

This project focuses more on helping you understand how to apply CSS and less on the properties and values of CSS. However, you should be familiar with the CSS Styles dialog box with which you create the styles.

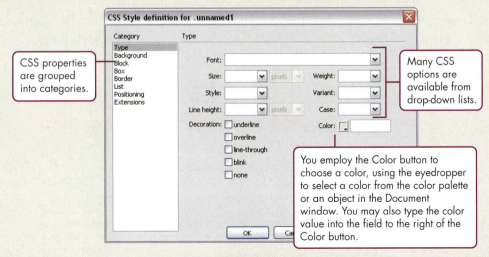

CSS properties are grouped into categories.

Many CSS options are available from drop-down lists.

You employ the Color button to choose a color, using the eyedropper to select a color from the color palette or an object in the Document window. You may also type the color value into the field to the right of the Color button.

FIGURE 2.1

However, before you assign a CSS property, you must identify the tag, class or other selector to which you are applying the style. You also must identify where the styles are to be stored: in the current document or in a style-sheet file.

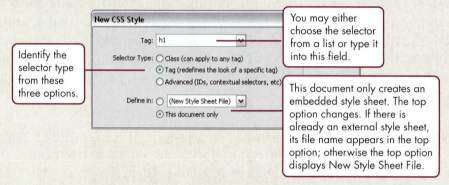

Identify the selector type from these three options.

You may either choose the selector from a list or type it into this field.

This document only creates an embedded style sheet. The top option changes. If there is already an external style sheet, its file name appears in the top option; otherwise the top option displays New Style Sheet File.

FIGURE 2.2

If you have an external style sheet, you must attach it to the Web pages so that the styles within it can be applied to the pages. The Link method is the most common method for attaching an external style sheet but the Import method is also useful.

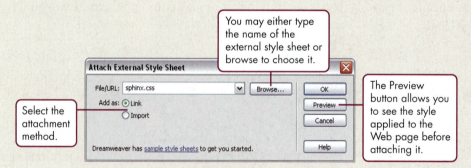

You may either type the name of the external style sheet or browse to choose it.

Select the attachment method.

The Preview button allows you to see the style applied to the Web page before attaching it.

FIGURE 2.3

The Design Time Style Sheet function allows you to hide or display selected style sheets during the design process. This is very beneficial when developing an alternate or print style sheet.

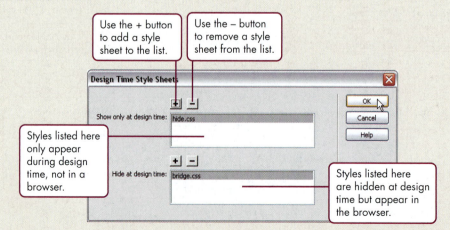

Use the + button to add a style sheet to the list.

Use the – button to remove a style sheet from the list.

Styles listed here only appear during design time, not in a browser.

Styles listed here are hidden at design time but appear in the browser.

FIGURE 2.4

LESSON 1 Using Element Selectors and Grouping

CSS, like any technology, has its own terminology. CSS uses ***properties*** (types of appearances) and ***values*** (options for the properties), such as the property `color` (used to change the color of text) and the value `red` (one of many possible values of the `color` property). In code, a property and its value are separated from each other using a colon (:), such as `color: red`. Some properties accept multiple values, such as font-family in which you can list multiple fonts in case the first font is not installed on a visitor's computer. For example, `font-family: Georgia, Times, "Times New Roman", serif`. Quotation marks are inserted around Times New Roman because the phrase as a whole identifies the font and the spaces would cause a problem.

A CSS property: value pair is called a "style declaration." You can group declarations; when you do so, you must separate declarations with semicolons (;), such as: `font-family: Arial; color: red`. Many CSS hand-coders add a semicolon after the last declaration — it is not necessary and it doesn't cause any problems, they just like to use it in case they should want to add another declaration and might forget to begin the next declaration with the semicolon. When you choose multiple properties in the CSS Style dialog box in Dreamweaver, it creates a grouped declaration. A ***style declaration block*** is a complete set of style declarations surrounded by curly braces, such as `{font-family: Arial; color: red}`. A declaration block can contain one or more declarations; it does not require multiple declarations to be considered a declaration block, but curly braces must surround it.

Despite the fact that a declaration block has been created, you don't know which text is red Arial because it is not identified in the declaration block. A ***selector*** is the HTML code to which the declaration block will be applied. The simplest form of selector is an ***element selector***: a single HTML tag, such as `p` or `h1`. Element selectors in CSS are the HTML tags without the angle brackets (`<p>` is the paragraph tag whereas `p` is the paragraph element). A ***style rule*** is the complete package of selector and declaration block, such as `p {font-family: Arial; color: red}` which styles all paragraph text as red Arial.

Just as declarations can be grouped, selectors can also be grouped, but the format is slightly different. Multiple selectors must be separated with commas, such as `h1, h2, h3`, which would apply the same style to text in any of these heading levels. Dreamweaver does not provide a click-and-point method of grouping selectors using its dialog boxes, but you can group them quite easily using the advanced selector option and typing the selector group in the Tag field.

Add Styles to Element Selectors

In this exercise, you add some basic styles to a Web page to learn the difference between single and grouped element selectors and single and grouped declarations.

1 Define the Project_02>My Travels folder as a site called My Travels. Do not click Done — leave the Site Definition dialog box open for the next step.

2 Click the first site in the list from a previous project, and click the Remove button. When asked to confirm the removal, click Yes. Repeat until you have removed all sites from the list (except the My Travels site you defined in Step 1). Click Done when finished.

3 Open index.html.

4 Right/Control-click in the CSS Styles panel (if it is not open, click the Design panel group title to expand it, then click the CSS Styles tab if it is not visible) and choose New. In the New CSS Style dialog box, set Selector Type to Tag, choose (or type) body in the Tag field, set Define in to This Document Only, and click OK.

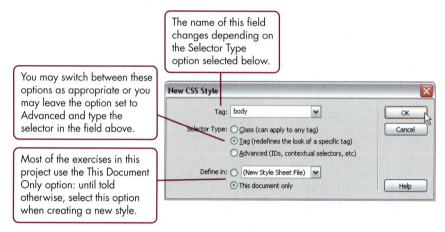

The name of this field changes depending on the Selector Type option selected below.

You may switch between these options as appropriate or you may leave the option set to Advanced and type the selector in the field above.

Most of the exercises in this project use the This Document Only option: until told otherwise, select this option when creating a new style.

FIGURE 2.5

5 In the Background category, set Background color to #969696 and click OK.

6 Right/Control-click in the CSS Styles panel and choose Go to Code.

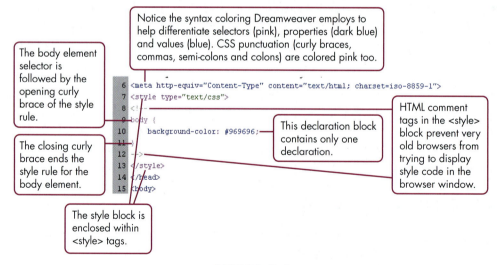

Notice the syntax coloring Dreamweaver employs to help differentiate selectors (pink), properties (dark blue) and values (blue). CSS punctuation (curly braces, commas, semi-colons and colons) are colored pink too.

The body element selector is followed by the opening curly brace of the style rule.

The closing curly brace ends the style rule for the body element.

The style block is enclosed within <style> tags.

This declaration block contains only one declaration.

HTML comment tags in the <style> block prevent very old browsers from trying to display style code in the browser window.

FIGURE 2.6

7 Right/Control-click body in the CSS Styles panel and choose Edit.

8   In the Box category, keep Same for All selected for both Padding and Margin, set both Padding and Margin to **0** pixels, and click OK.

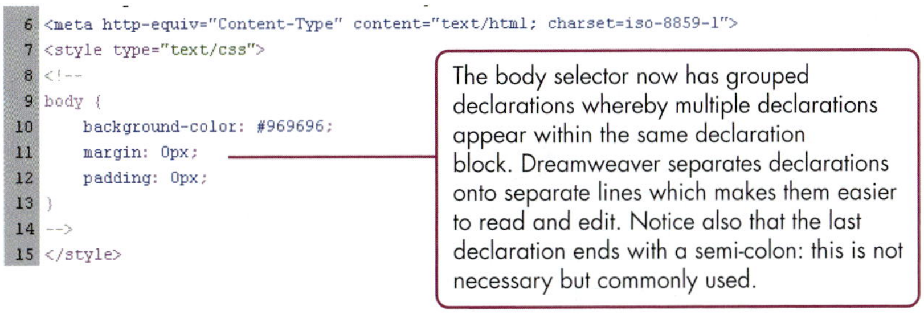

```
 6 <meta http-equiv="Content-Type" content="text/html; charset=iso-8859-1">
 7 <style type="text/css">
 8 <!--
 9 body {
10     background-color: #969696;
11     margin: 0px;
12     padding: 0px;
13 }
14 -->
15 </style>
```

The body selector now has grouped declarations whereby multiple declarations appear within the same declaration block. Dreamweaver separates declarations onto separate lines which makes them easier to read and edit. Notice also that the last declaration ends with a semi-colon: this is not necessary but commonly used.

FIGURE 2.7

9   Close the Code window.

10   Create a new style for the blockquote tag by Right/Control-clicking in the CSS Style panel, selecting New, selecting or typing `blockquote` in the Tag field, setting Selector Type to Tag, setting Define in to This Document Only, and clicking OK.

11   From the Type category, set Style to italic. From the Block category, set Text Align to center. Click OK.

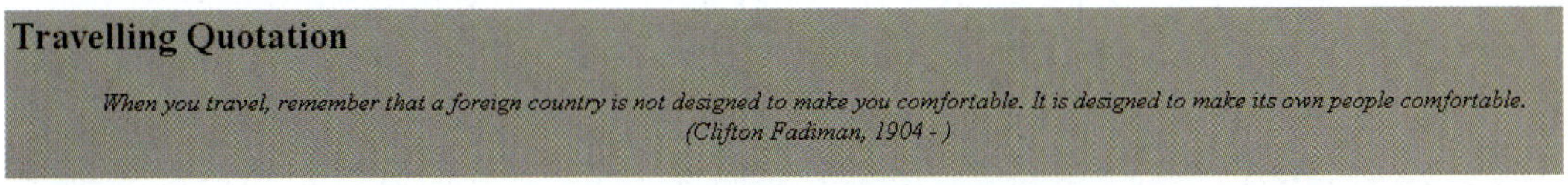

Travelling Quotation

When you travel, remember that a foreign country is not designed to make you comfortable. It is designed to make its own people comfortable.
(Clifton Fadiman, 1904 -)

FIGURE 2.8

12   Save the changes but leave index.html open for the next exercise.

Assign Common Styles to Multiple Selectors

In this exercise, you learn to group selectors. Dreamweaver does not provide any point-and-click tools to simplify this process, but it is not difficult. You simply choose the Advanced option from the Selector Type group of radio buttons and type the comma-separated list of selectors in the Selector field. When you are considering using grouped selectors, you must plan ahead, because although it is easy to create a group, if you decide that one member of the group should be removed, you must go into the code to remove it from the comma-separated list. You could consider creating the styles separately rather than grouping them, but that would increase the size of the CSS file and therefore the page weight.

1 Create a new CSS Style; choose Advanced from the Selector Type group; in the Selector field, type h1, h2, h3; and click OK.

Throughout the rest of this project, you will create styles for the Tag selector type, the Class selector type, and the Advanced selector type. Rather than switching between the types, use the Advanced selector type for all of them: the Advanced selector type allows all types of selectors. Also, until Lesson 6, set Define in to This Document Only.

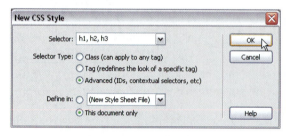

FIGURE 2.9

2 In the Type category of the CSS Style dialog box, set Color to #C4C4C4 and click Apply. In the Background category, set the Background Color to #969696 and click Apply. In the Block category, set Letter Spacing to 2 pixels and click Apply. In the Box category, uncheck Same for All for Padding; set Top Padding to 15 pixels, Right Padding to 0 pixels, Bottom Padding to 0 pixels, and Left Padding to 5 pixels; and click Apply. Set all margins to 0 pixels. In the Border category, uncheck all Same for All; set the Top Border to solid, 1 pixel, #000 (three zeros); and click OK.

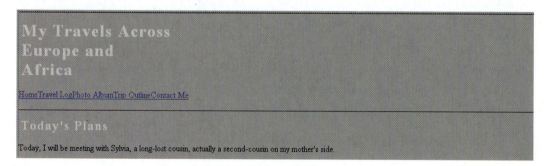

FIGURE 2.10

3 To remove the h1 selector from this group, Right/Control-click h1, h2, h3 in the CSS Styles panel and choose Go to Code.

4 In the Code window, delete h1, from the selector group and close the Code window.

The h1 selector is no longer part of the group: these style declarations will not apply to the h1 element.

```
18  h2, h3 {
19      color: #C4C4C4;
20      background-color: #969696;
21      letter-spacing: 2px;
22      margin: 0px;
23      padding-top: 15px;
24      padding-right: 0px;
25      padding-bottom: 0px;
26      padding-left: 5px;
```

FIGURE 2.11

? If you have problems

If the style of the Heading-1 block at the top of the page does not revert to its previous style, click the Refresh button in the Property inspector.

---

5 Create a new CSS Style for the h1 tag. In the Type category, set Color to #C4C4C4. In the Block category, set Text Align to right. In the Background category, set Background Color to #965156, Background Image to images>london-bridge.jpg, Background Repeat to no-repeat, Horizontal Position to left, and Vertical position to top. In the Box category, set Height to 200 pixels, set all paddings and margins to 0 pixels, and click OK.

FIGURE 2.12

6 Create a new CSS Style for the selector group p, li. In the Type category, set Line Height to 1.4 ems and click OK.

7 Scroll to the contact-form table at the bottom of the page, and click to the right of Name. Create a new CSS style for input, textarea. In the Box category, set Width to 200 pixels and click OK.

8 Create a new CSS Style for the textarea tag. In the Box category, set Height to 120 pixels and click OK.

FIGURE 2.13

9 Save the changes to index.html, leaving it open for the next exercise.

To Extend Your Knowledge

CSS SHORTHAND FORMATS

There are a number of CSS shorthand formats that Dreamweaver knows about and can apply. There are six font properties: `font-style` (normal or italic), `font-variant` (normal or small-cap), `font-weight` (normal or bold), `font-size` (various measurements), `line-height` (also referred to as "leading" in print publishing), and `font-family` (typeface). To specify all of them individually would take quite a bit of space. However, the `font` property, a shorthand CSS property, can be used to apply all of the individual font properties together. When this shorthand format is used, the values are separated by spaces, except `font-size` and `line-height`, which are separated with a forward slash (/). Comma-separated typeface names are also allowed. For example, to set a font property for the **p** element, you could use `p {font: italic small-cap bold 12pt/16pt Arial, Helvetica, sans-serif}`. To enable the shorthand formats, choose Edit>Preferences, choose the CSS Style category, and enable any or all shorthands you want Dreamweaver to use.

Another shorthand can be used to shorten hexadecimal color values. If all three colors (RGB) use pairs of hexadecimal numbers, they can be shortened to singles. For example, black is **#000000** which can be shortened to **#000** and white can be shortened to **#FFF**. The three pairs do not need to be identical: **#F07** is a valid shorthand of **#FF0077**, but you cannot shorten **#929292**.

LESSON 2   Using Class and ID Selectors

Element selectors are beneficial when you want to apply the same style to all instances of those selectors. At times, however, you may want to either single out one instance of an element or specify that some instances of an element be treated differently than others. In these situations, you would use classes or ids, so you need to understand the differences between them to be able to use them correctly. Classes are selectors that may be applied multiple times whereas ids may only be used once per page.

There are two types of classes and ids — regular and generic. *Regular classes* and *regular ids* are assigned to an element, such as **p.warning** or **tr#odd**, which mean the warning class of the paragraph element and the odd id of the table-row element. When you define the style for a regular class, such as **p.warning**, and try to assign the warning class to the **h2** element, the style does not transfer because it is assigned to the paragraph element. If you want to apply a class (for example, the warning class, which you may have designed as bold red text against a yellow background with an orange border) to multiple elements, you would use a generic class. A *generic class* style rule is defined without an element, for example, **.warning**. Therefore, the regular warning class of the paragraph element would appear in the style block as **p.warning {color: red; font-weight: bold; background-color; yellow; border: solid 2px #FFA500;}** whereas the generic warning class would differ only in that the selector would not have an element, such as **.warning**.

When creating a style rule for a class, whether generic or regular, you must precede the class name with a period and, if the class is a regular class, with the element selector. When creating a style rule for an id, the id name is preceded by the pound (#) symbol, such as **#odd**, and if it is a regular id, the element must precede the **#**, such as **tr#odd**. When assigning a class or an id in HTML, you use the class attribute, such as **class="warning"** or **id="odd"**. In Dreamweaver, you can use the Tag editor or Tag selector to assign a class or id to an element. However, if you create a **p.warning** regular class, the Tag selector does not allow you to assign the warning class to an h2 block because the class was defined as a regular class.

Because classes can be used multiple times, you may encounter a situation in which you want to apply two classes to the same element. For example, **.bgcolor1** may be a style rule for a background color and **.fgcolor1** may be a style rule for a foreground (text) color: you may apply both to the same paragraph by adding **class="bgcolor1 fgcolor1"** to the paragraph tag using the Tag editor or entering the code directly in the Code window. You may also use this principle to assign **class="bgcolor1 fgcolor2"** to one h2, **class="bgcolor2 fgcolor1"** to another h2, **class="bgcolor1 fgcolor2"** to a paragraph, and **class="bgcolor2 fgcolor2"** to another paragraph.

In contrast to classes, an id may only be used once per page, even if it is a generic id. For example, if you define a generic id called **#unique**, you may assign p with **id="unique"** or h1 with **id="unique"**, but once you have assigned it once in a page, you cannot use it again. Some older browsers display the styles from multiple uses of ids on a page, but current, standards-compliant browsers do not, just the first time. You also cannot assign two or more ids to the same element — that would be similar to saying that you have two different names or two different student IDs. However, you can assign both an id and a class (or multiple classes) to the same element, such as **id="footer" class="bgcolor1 fgcolor2"**.

Dreamweaver's New CSS Style dialog box offers a Class option for the Selector Type, but it accepts only generic classes, not regular classes. However, if you choose the Advanced Selector Type, you are free to create whatever type of class, id, or combination of selectors that may or may not be understood or supported by Dreamweaver.

Create and Apply CSS Style Classes

In this exercise, you create both regular and generic classes, and assign them to the Web page. You learn that a regular class is restricted to its element but a generic class may be applied to any element.

1   In the open file, index.html, create a new CSS Style, choose Class as the Selector Type, type **.right** in the Name field and click OK. From the Block category, set Text Align to right and click OK.

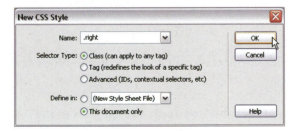

FIGURE 2.14

2   Scroll to the table below the heading Summary of Photographs. Click in the # Photos cell. Right/Control-click the `<th>` tag in the Tag selector, and choose Set Class>right from the pop-up menu. Right/Control-click in the `<td>` cell below, and apply the right class to the cell.

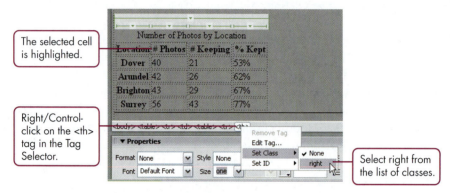

The selected cell is highlighted.

Right/Control-click on the `<th>` tag in the Tag Selector.

Select right from the list of classes.

FIGURE 2.15

3   Click again in the # Photos cell and then Shift-click in the 77% cell. Right/Control-click in the selected block of cells, and then choose CSS Styles>right from the contextual menu.

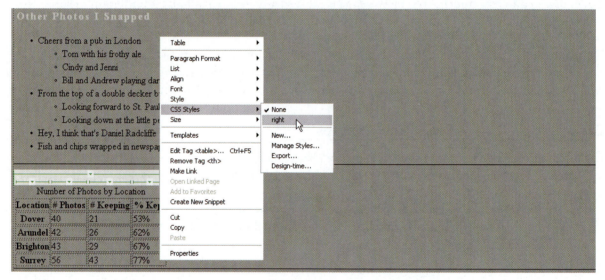

FIGURE 2.16

4   Create a new CSS Style generic class called `.left`. In the Block category, set Text Align to left and click OK.

5   Select the left column of the table and apply the left class to the selected cells.

6 Click in the caption above the table, and then click the `<caption>` tag in the Tag selector. In the Property inspector, choose left from the Style list to the right of the Format menu.

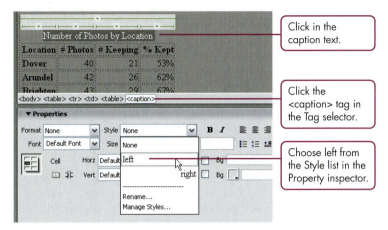

Click in the caption text.

Click the `<caption>` tag in the Tag selector.

Choose left from the Style list in the Property inspector.

FIGURE 2.17

7 Create a new CSS Style, choose Advanced from Selector Type, and type `p.first` in the Selector field. In the Box category, uncheck Same for All from both Padding and Margin, and then set Top to **0** pixels for both Padding and Margin. Click OK.

8 Click in the first paragraph below the Today's Plans heading and choose the style named first from the Style list in the Property inspector. Using the same methods, apply the first class to the first paragraph below the Recent Photos heading, and to the first paragraph below the Friends heading.

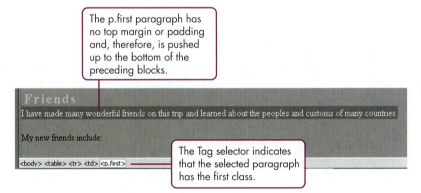

The p.first paragraph has no top margin or padding and, therefore, is pushed up to the bottom of the preceding blocks.

The Tag selector indicates that the selected paragraph has the first class.

FIGURE 2.18

? ## If you have problems

At times, the paragraphs tend to overlap each other. Press F5 to refresh the Design-view display.

9 Save your changes, but leave the file open for the next exercise.

Combine Multiple Classes

In this exercise, you create a CSS class and learn how to apply it to an element that already has a class. Dreamweaver does not support multiple classes from its interface. You must add any additional classes (you can apply more than two) to the code using either the Tag editor or the Code window. Dreamweaver does understand the multiple classes, however, and displays them correctly.

1   In the open file, index.html, click in the 53% cell in the table below the Summary of Photographs heading.

2   Create a new CSS Style using the Advanced Selector Type and naming the selector `td.highlight`. In the Type category, set Color to `#965156`; in the Background category, set Background Color to `#F0F0F0`; and click OK.

3   Right/Control-click in the 53% cell and choose CSS Styles>highlight.

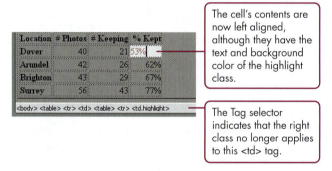

The cell's contents are now left aligned, although they have the text and background color of the highlight class.

The Tag selector indicates that the right class no longer applies to this <td> tag.

FIGURE 2.19

4   With the insertion point in the changed cell, Right/Control-click the `<td.highlight>` tag in the Tag selector, and choose Edit Tag. Type `right` between the quotation marks so that you end up with `class="highlight right"`. (The order of the classes doesn't matter; `right highlight` would be just as acceptable.) Press Enter/Return.

Add right to the class attribute.

FIGURE 2.20

5   Repeat Step 4 for the rest of the table-data cells in the right column so all of the cells have both the right and highlight classes.

6   Save your changes, leaving the file open for the next exercise.

Create and Apply Styles Using Ids

In this exercise, you create style rules that are based on id selectors. As you learned earlier, you cannot use a specific id more than once on a page, so before you create an id, you should think about whether or not you will need it again on the same page. If so, use a class instead. As you saw with classes, there are no limitations as to what style properties may be applied to a class; all style properties may be applied to ids, as well.

1 In the open file, index.html, create a new CSS Style for the Advanced Selector p#navbar. In the Type category, set Size to 1.2 ems, and Line Height to 2 ems. In the Background category, set Background Color to #000. In the Block category, set Text Align to center. In the Box category, set both Padding and Margin to 0 pixels (Same For All in both cases). Click OK.

2 Click in the paragraph below the photo of the London Bridge. Right/Control-click the <p> tag in the Tag selector, and set the ID to navbar.

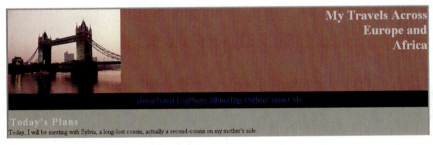

FIGURE 2.21

3 Create a new CSS Style for the Advanced Selector ul#places. In the List category, set the Bullet image to images>redball.gif. Click OK.

4 Create two similar styles as you did in Step 3. Make the first with the selector of ul#photos and the Bullet image as images>redsqare.gif; make the second with the selector of ul#friends and the Bullet image as images>reddiamd.gif.

5 Click in the list below the heading Places I Saw, Right/Control-click the <ul> tag in the Tag selector, and set the ID to places. Click in the list below the heading Friends, Right/Control-click the <ul> tag in the Tag selector, and set the ID to friends.

6 Click the first list item (Cheers from a pub in London) and set the ID of the <ul> tag to photos.

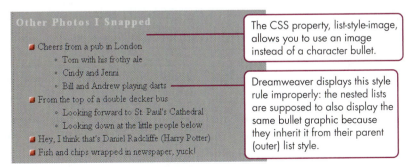

FIGURE 2.22

7 Save the changes to index.html and leave it open for the next lesson.

To Extend Your Knowledge

MANAGING CLASSES AND IDS

Classes and ids allow you to customize elements within a page. While this is desirable, it means that you must continuously modify the code of every new page to apply the custom classes and ids. It is not uncommon to see a page created by a beginner that is littered with classes. A style sheet with many classes and ids is quite difficult to manage. In later lessons in this project, you learn about inheritance that, with proper use, can greatly reduce the number of classes and ids on a page.

Another common mistake of beginning CSS designers is naming classes and ids based on the style that they create, such as boldred or italicyellow. What do you do when you redesign the site and decide that the elements with the boldred class no longer should be bold or red? It is best to use class and names that either describe their purpose or the contents within them, such as navbar, footer, header, datatable, and warning. In doing so, you do not limit yourself to the style described by the name of the class or id, or force yourself to rename all instances of boldred to italicyellow.

LESSON 3   Working with Selectors Based on Context

Although you hear more about the **_DOM_** (the Document Object Model, a hierarchical organization of HTML elements in a page, often shown as branching diagram) in JavaScript, it also applies to CSS. The following figure displays a Web page and its DOM. The second row of elements are children of the body element and adjacent to each other. The third row of elements are children of row-2 elements, descendents of the body element, and adjacent to each other, and so on with subsequent rows.

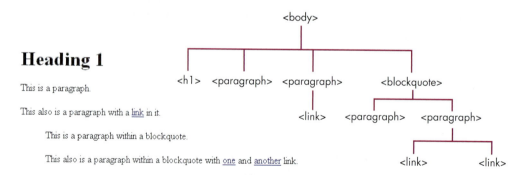

FIGURE 2.23

In most cases, styles you apply to elements are inherited by the descendents of that element. For example, if you set the font property to Arial using the body element selector, then the heading, paragraph, blockquote, and link text use that font. The exceptions to inheritance occur when the default appearance of an element conflicts with the new style setting: the default style takes precedence. For example, if you apply the `font-weight: normal` (which disables bold) using the body element selector, headings still appear bold. Also, if you use the body element selector to change the text color to red, link text still is blue. To override default appearances, you must apply the changed properties directly to the elements, such as `h1 {font-weight: normal;}` or `a {color: red;}`.

There are different methods of describing the relationships between elements on a page, and there are CSS selector methods that you can use to specify these relationships. There are descendent selectors, child selectors, and adjacent selectors. Descendent selectors are commonly supported, but child and adjacent selectors, despite being part of CSS2 (released in 1998), have less support.

The simplest selector based on inheritance, and the one with the most support, even in ***version 4 browsers*** (a term generally used to describe Netscape 4.x and Internet Explorer 4.x — Mozilla and Safari are still in their version 1 generations but are much more advanced than NN4 and IE4 ever were), is the descendent selector. You are a descendent of your parents as well as your great-great-great-great-grandparents. It does not matter how many generations there are, as long as there is a straight line of inheritance. All elements are descendents of the body element, but if you want to apply one color to links in paragraphs and another color to links in blockquotes, then you must create descendent selectors that account for these two situations. Descendent selectors are written with spaces between them, such as **blockquote p** and **p a**. To change the color of link text in blockquotes to red and the color of link text in paragraphs outside of blockquotes to green, the style rules would be written as: **p a {color: green;}** and **blockquote a {color: red;}**. In the second example, it is not necessary to specify the complete ancestry, such as **blockquote p a**, because **a** is a descendent of **blockquote**, however many layers may exist between them.

Children are the immediate descendents of their parents. To create a style rule for child selectors, you insert the > between selectors, such as **body>p** (or with spaces, such as **body > p**). The selector **body>p {text-style: italic;}** would make all paragraph text italic except paragraphs within the blockquote because those paragraphs are not children of the body element, just descendents.

Adjacent selectors are those that describe two elements that share the same parent and are immediately adjacent to each other. To define an adjacent selector, the plus (+) symbol is inserted between the elements. For example, **h1+p {text-decoration: underline;}** adds an underline to the first paragraph after the h1 element but not to any other paragraphs.

All of the previous discussions in this project about the application of CSS apply to selectors based on context. You may group descendent selectors, such as **blockquote a, p a**. You may specify adjacent classes, such as **p.warning+p.navbar**; descendent selectors to ids, such as **p#navbar a**; or any other combination of selectors.

There are some things you cannot do with style rules. You cannot create exceptions. If you want all paragraph text to be in the Times font except paragraphs within blockquotes, you can't exclude blockquotes. Instead, you must create a rule for all paragraphs, such as **p {font-family: Times;}** and then reverse blockquote paragraphs with **blockquote p {font-family: Arial;}**. You cannot create rules that apply to ancestors — for example, if you want paragraph text to be blue if the paragraph has a link in it, but to be red if the paragraph does not have a link in it (compare the first and second paragraphs following the h1 block in the preceding figure). The only way to achieve this is to use classes, and apply one class or another based on whether or not there is a link in the paragraph.

Observe Inheritance of the Font Property

In this exercise, you observe the effect of inheritance by creating a style rule for the body and seeing it applied to descendents of the body element. You observe that the default font property for the **<textarea>** tag is monospaced and does not take the font style applied to the body element. You must create a textarea element selector style to override its font.

1   In the open file, index.html, Right/Control-click the body style in the CSS Styles panel and choose Edit.

2   In the Type category, set Font to Arial, Helvetica, sans-serif and click OK.

3   Preview the page in your browser. Scroll down to the form and type in the large text area.

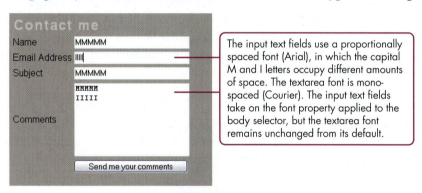

The input text fields use a proportionally spaced font (Arial), in which the capital M and I letters occupy different amounts of space. The textarea font is mono-spaced (Courier). The input text fields take on the font property applied to the body selector, but the textarea font remains unchanged from its default.

FIGURE 2.24

4   Return to Dreamweaver.

5   Edit the textarea style rule in the CSS Styles panel; set the font to Arial, Helvetica, sans-serif; and click OK.

6   Preview the page in your browser and type in the textarea.

7   Return to Dreamweaver, saving your changes to index.html and leaving it open for the next exercise.

Create Descendent Selectors

In this exercise, you create descendent selectors. You learn how powerful descendent selectors are and how they can reduce the number of classes used in a page. You apply a style to the links in the navbar paragraph, but the styles do not affect any other links because of the descendent selector. You create a style for a nested list. Using descendent selectors cleans up the styles and clears the problem of unwanted styles.

1   In the open file, index.html, create a new style for the selector p#navbar a. Set the Text color to #C4C4C4. In the Box category, uncheck Same for All for Padding, and set both left and right padding to 15 pixels. Click OK.

When you specify p#navbar a, only <a> tags in the navbar take on these properties. All other <a> tags remain unaffected.

FIGURE 2.25

2   Create a new style for the selector ul#photos ul. In the List category, set the Bullet image to images>redarrow.gif and click OK.

Using the descendent selector, ul#photos ul, only unordered lists nested within the ul with the id photos take on the arrow list image.

FIGURE 2.26

3   Create a new style for the table tag. In the Box category, set the width to 750 pixels, uncheck Same for All for Margins, and set both Left and Right margins to auto (choose from list) and both Top and Bottom to 10 pixels. Click OK.

The table selector applies to all tables in the page, including nested tables.

Location	# Photos	# Keeping	% Kept
Dover	40	21	53%
Arundel	42	26	62%
Brighton	43	29	67%
Surrey	56	43	77%

FIGURE 2.27

4 Create a new style for the selector `table table`. Set the Background color to `#E1E1E1`. In the Box category, set the width to `400` pixels and click OK.

Summary of Photographs			
Number of Photos by Location			

Location	# Photos	# Keeping	% Kept
Dover	40	21	53%
Arundel	42	26	62%
Brighton	43	29	67%
Surrey	56	43	77%

The selector table table selects any nested tables.

FIGURE 2.28

5 Save the changes to index.html, leaving it open for the next exercise.

Create Adjacent Selectors

In this exercise, you observe the usefulness of adjacent selectors. Unlike descendent selectors, adjacent selectors are less well supported by browsers: the Opera, Mozilla, and Safari browsers support this property, as does Dreamweaver, but Internet Explorer does not. You see that although you can replace classes created earlier with adjacent selectors, if the style for your Web-page design depends on the adjacent selectors working in current browsers, you may need to revert to using classes or ids to achieve the style you desire.

1 In the open file, index.html, scroll down to the form at the bottom of the page and click to the left of Name.

2 Create a new style using `form td` as the selector. In the Block category, set Text Align to right and Vertical Align to top. Click OK.

3 Create a new style using `form td+td` as the selector. In the Block category, set Text Align to left and click OK.

Contact me

All cell contents are initially right-aligned because of the style rule applied to the form td selector.

Name:
Email Address:
Subject:
Comments:

The right column of cells is left-aligned because of the style rule applied to the td+td selector.

Send me your comments

FIGURE 2.29

4 Right/Control-click the `p.first` selector in the CSS Styles panel and choose Delete. One by one, click each of the paragraphs immediately below the headings, Right/Control-click the `<p.first>` tag in the Tag selector, and set its class to none.

The paragraphs are no longer assigned the class of first and the p.first style rule no longer exists.

5   Create a new style using h2+p, h3+p as the selector. In the Box category, set all paddings and margins to 0 pixels and click OK.

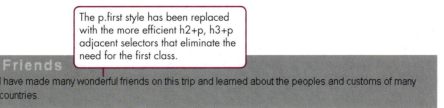

The p.first style has been replaced with the more efficient h2+p, h3+p adjacent selectors that eliminate the need for the first class.

Friends

I have made many wonderful friends on this trip and learned about the peoples and customs of many countries.

FIGURE 2.30

6   Preview the page in your browser.

If you have problems

The adjacent selector (element+element) is not supported by Internet Explorer but is supported by the Mozilla, Safari, and Opera browsers. If you have a style rule that uses adjacent selectors and want to retain that appearance in IE, you must create a class or an id and apply that class or id to the appropriate blocks in the document.

7   Return to Dreamweaver, leaving index.html open for the next exercise.

Use a Child Selector

A child element is also a descendent element but not all descendent elements are child elements. Because the child selector is not as well supported as the descendent element, you may have to resort to using either descendent or class/id selectors instead.

1   In the open file, index.html, create a new style using the selector body>table. In the Background category, set the background color to #DADADA. In the Border category, leaving Same for All checked, set Style to groove, Width to thick, and Color to #969696. Click OK.

2   Right/Control-click the table table selector and choose Edit. Apply a solid, 1 pixel, black border around all sides and click OK.

3   Preview the page in your browser. Scroll down to examine the other two tables.

Location	# Photos	# Keeping	% Kept
Dover	40	21	53%
Arundel	42	26	62%
Brighton	43	29	67%
Surrey	56	43	77%

Dreamweaver does not display any border style other than solid.

Both the background color and border of the outer table do not display in IE because it does not support child selectors. To create these styles, you must use a class or id.

FIGURE 2.31

4   Return to Dreamweaver.

5   Right/Control-click the body>table selector and choose Go to Code. Delete the selector `body>table` (not the style declaration block, just the selector) and type `table#body`. Close the Code window.

6   Click in the content of the page. Using the Tag selector, choose the left-most `<table>` tag, Right/Control-click the tag, and set its ID to body.

7   Save the changes but leave index.html open.

To Extend Your Knowledge

IE5, IE6, AND IE7

Internet Explorer is the most commonly used browser in the world — most browser statistics place its use at about 94%. The most recent version for Windows is IE6 whereas for the Macintosh, the latest version is IE5.2. Despite the difference in version numbers, these two browsers are similar in capabilities. However, both versions suffer from a number of weaknesses in support for some Web technologies, such as the abbreviation and acronym tags, `<abbr>` and `<acronym>`, respectively. IE also has weaker support for some CSS selectors (adjacent and child) and properties (width is sometimes miscalculated) than the Opera, Mozilla, and Safari browsers.

Although it is not known what the next version of Internet Explorer will bring (it will only be available for the next version of Windows, not for the Macintosh), Dean Edwards has been developing an advanced script in JavaScript, that he calls IE7, in which many of the deficiencies in IE5 and 6 for Windows are being resolved. At his Web site at dean.edwards.name/IE7/compatibility/ you can see which deficiencies he has been able to eliminate. The IE7 script is free to download and simple to install. With it in place, you are able to use more CSS selectors and properties without having to wonder if IE5/6 can support them. There are two caveats to using IE7: this code does not work if a user has disabled JavaScript, and the IE7 script is reported to slow the display of a Web page at times.

LESSON 4   Creating Pseudo-Class Selectors

You can deduce all of the preceding selectors from the document tree. You can examine HTML code of an unstyled page and identify which styles will apply and where based on the hierarchy of the elements of the page and the selectors in the style sheet. Pseudo-classes allow designers to create styles for conditions outside of the document tree.

There are seven pseudo-class selectors; some are dynamic and some are rigid. The most commonly used and understood pseudo-classes are used for links, where a visited link has a different color than an unvisited link, and an active link flashes red when clicked. These pseudo-classes are the `:link`, `:visited`, and `:active` pseudo-classes respectively. These three pseudo-classes replace the `link`, `alink`, and `vlink` attributes of the `<body>` tag. HTML only supported color changes for each of these attributes but CSS is not limited to just color — any CSS property can be used in these pseudo-classes. These three pseudo-classes are unique in that they only play a role for anchor tags.

The `:hover` pseudo-class does not have an HTML equivalent. You can use this pseudo-class to change the appearance of a link when the mouse moves over it, such as removing the underline or changing the text or background color. Although the `:hover` property can be applied to elements other than the anchor tag, Internet Explorer and version 4 browsers only support the `:hover` pseudo-classes when applied to anchor tags.

When you create a style rule for the a element selector, the rule applies consistently whether the link is visited, unvisited, or active, or the mouse pointer rolls over it. Occasionally, you may see a style sheet in which someone has specified **a:link, a:visited, a:hover, a:active {color: white;}**. It is simpler to simply use **a {color: white;}**. You can create a common style for all four states using the a element selector, such as **a {color: white; font-family: Arial; font-size: 1.2em}** and then use the pseudo-classes to create modifications of the default, such as **a:active {color: red;}**. If you are creating separate style rules for these pseudo-classes, they must be created in the following order whether you use some or all of these pseudo-classes: `:link`, `:visited`, `:hover`, and `:active`. Use LoVe HAte as a mnemonic to remember this order.

The `:focus` pseudo-class is commonly used in form fields to highlight the field in which the visitor is entering information. Many Web designers use the `:focus` pseudo-class to change the background (and sometimes, text) color of an input form control. Unfortunately, Internet Explorer does not support the `:focus` pseudo-class. There are no CSS workarounds for this deficiency — only JavaScript may be used to create a similar effect, one of the successes that Dean Edwards has had with his IE7 script.

The two static pseudo-classes are exceptions to the general rule of pseudo-classes in that you can infer them from the document tree; regardless, the W3C calls them "pseudo-classes." The `:first-child` pseudo-class is somewhat similar to the **>** child selector in that it applies to a child of the identified element, but it is different in that the first child may not always be the same. For example, if one table cell (td) contains an h2 block and then a p block, and another table cell contains two p blocks, **td:first-child** would apply the style rule to the h2 element in the first cell and to the first p element in the second cell. The `:lang` pseudo-class can be used to change the style based on the language specified. For example `:lang(fr) {text-style: italic;}` applies italic to any text in which the **lang="fr"** attribute (fr=French) is applied, such as **<p lang="fr">Bonjour!</p>**.

To Extend Your Knowledge

COMBINING PSEUDO-CLASSES

It is possible, although uncommon, to combine some pseudo-classes. Often you see different link properties for links in the body than for links in a navigation bar. Some designers take this a step further by combining pseudo-classes. For example, **a:hover {color: red;}** changes the link color to red when the mouse pointer rolls over it, and **a:visited {color: purple;}** sets the color of visited links to purple. However, you may want to have a different `:hover` color (or other property) for links that have been already visited. Therefore, you must combine `:visited` with `:hover`, such as **a:visited:hover {color: green;}**, which causes visited links to change to green when the mouse pointer rolls over them whereas unvisited links change to red when the mouse rolls over them.

As you may have guessed, Internet Explorer does not support this combination of pseudo-classes, but it is something to keep in mind.

Create Pseudo-Classes for Links

In this exercise, you create pseudo-classes for links in the page. You can combine pseudo-classes with any of the other selectors types, such as classes, ids, and any of the relational selectors.

1 In the open file, index.html, create a new style using the selector `a:visited`. In the Type category, set the Text color to `black` and click OK.

2 Create a new style using the selector `a:active`. In the Text category, set the Type color to `red` and click OK.

3 Create a new style using the selector `a:hover`. In the Type category, choose none from the Decoration group of radio buttons and click OK.

4 Create a new style using the selector `a:link`. In the Text category, set the Type color to `#965156` and click OK.

5 Preview the page in your browser. Move your mouse pointer over the links in the content section of the page (not the navigation bar). Click a link, then use the back button to return to this page. Return to Dreamweaver when finished.

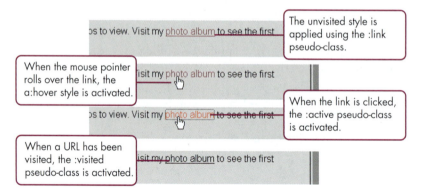

The unvisited style is applied using the :link pseudo-class.

When the mouse pointer rolls over the link, the a:hover style is activated.

When the link is clicked, the :active pseudo-class is activated.

When a URL has been visited, the :visited pseudo-class is activated.

FIGURE 2.32

6 Create a new style using the `p#navbar a:hover` selector. In the Type category, set the Text color to `black`. In the Background category, set the Background color to `#C4C4C4` and click OK.

7 Preview the page in your browser and roll your mouse pointer over the navigation-bar links. Return to Dreamweaver.

Both the background and text colors change when the mouse pointer rolls over the links in the p#navbar block.

Home   Travel Log   Photo Album   Trip Outline   Contact Me

FIGURE 2.33

8 Keep index.html open for the next exercise.

To Extend Your Knowledge

PADDING VS. MARGIN

The links in the navbar paragraph were separated from each other using left and right padding set at 15 pixels each, which means that the space between the e in Home and the T in Travel Log is 30 pixels. This space could have been created using either padding or margin. However, padding extends the content area of the element whereas margins are outside of the content area. If you apply a background to the element, the background extends into padding but does not extend into the margin. Therefore, the wide band of gray around the links in the navbar paragraph when the :hover pseudo-class is active is created because the padding extends around the links. If margin were used, only the background of the text would change to gray.

Add the :focus Pseudo-Class for the Form Text Fields

In this exercise, you use the :focus pseudo-class selector to change the text and background color of the input fields when the visitor is entering information into these fields. Just as JavaScript can improve the usability of forms, this pseudo-class can improve the usability of the input fields by clearly identifying to users which field they are working in.

1   **In the open file, index.html, create a new style using the selector `input:focus, textarea:focus`. In the Type category, set the Text color to `#FFF`. In the Background category, set the Background color to `#969696`. Click OK.**

2   **Preview the page in your browser. Type in one of the input fields, and then tab through the rest of them.**

Whether you are typing in an input (or textarea) field or you have simply tabbed to the fields, you have changed the focus to that field and, therefore, you have activated the :focus pseudo-class.

FIGURE 2.34

3   **Return to Dreamweaver but leave index.html open for the next exercise.**

To Extend Your Knowledge

SEPARATING PRESENTATION FROM BEHAVIOR

Much has been said about the separation of presentation from structure where structure is defined using HTML and presentation is created using CSS. Peter-Paul Koch and other advanced JavaScript developers are displeased with some of the CSS pseudo-classes, specifically, `:visited`, `:active`, `:hover`, and `:focus`. These CSS pseudo-classes border on creating behavioral effects that they feel should be in the domain of JavaScript. In his article, "Separating Behavior and Presentation" (digital-web.com/articles/separating_behavior_and_presentation/), Koch explains how CSS has moved into the arena of behavior and how one might evaluate which technology, CSS or JavaScript, should be used to create these types of behaviors. Peter-Paul Koch recognizes that `:hover` and other quasi-behavioral pseudo-classes can be used very simply and effectively to create very beneficial results. However, these pseudo-classes can and have been used to create more complex effects, such as Eric Meyer's Pure CSS Menus (meyerweb.com/eric/css/edge/menus/demo.html). Koch believes that effects at this level of complexity and sophistication should be the domain of JavaScript and not CSS. His articles, his Web site, and those of Simon Willison (simon.incutio.com) are very interesting reading.

LESSON 5   Working with the `<span>` and `<div>` Tags

The `<span>` and `<div>` tags have a special role, and unlike most other HTML tags, they serve no purpose in document structure. Their role is simply to be containers that deliver CSS styles. There are differences in their intended purposes, however. The `<span>` tag is meant to serve as an inline container whereas the `<div>` tag is intended to serve as a block container. A **block** fills the width of the browser window and separates itself from other blocks with white space. Paragraphs and headings are both block containers, but unlike div blocks, paragraphs and headings have a role in the structure of the document. An element is considered **inline** if it exists within a block, just as links or italicized words are contained within paragraphs.

Divs (a colloquial term used to refer to `<div>` tags and their contents) are commonly used to create CSS layouts whereas spans are less commonly used. The `<div>` tag does have the deprecated **align** attribute, but given that its current use is to provide a container for layout through CSS, using the presentational attribute **align** is contrary to using CSS for design. However, the `<div>` tag does support the class and id attributes with which CSS selectors can be applied. The `<span>` tag has very few attributes, including **class** and **id**, which, again, can be used for selection purpose in CSS style rules. We discuss the `<div>` tag in greater depth in Project 3.

Whenever you create a custom style in the Design view, Dreamweaver creates a class and a style rule for you using the **span** selector. The style is added to your style sheet. You can use it at any other time.

Create a Span Style

1   **In the open file, index.html, select Sylvia (in the first paragraph). Using the Property inspector, click the bold and italic buttons, and, using the Text Color color box, choose a dark red color, #990000.**

2 Click away from Sylvia, and then click in Sylvia again. Click the Split button to open the Code window.

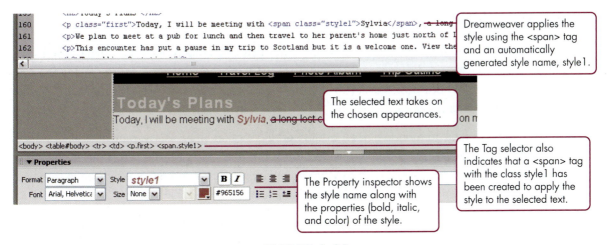

> Dreamweaver applies the style using the <span> tag and an automatically generated style name, style1.

> The selected text takes on the chosen appearances.

> The Tag selector also indicates that a <span> tag with the class style1 has been created to apply the style to the selected text.

> The Property inspector shows the style name along with the properties (bold, italic, and color) of the style.

FIGURE 2.35

3 Close the Code window. Select the word cousin from the same paragraph as Sylvia. Using the Style list in the Property inspector, choose style1 from the list.

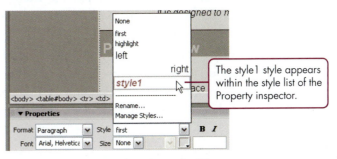

> The style1 style appears within the style list of the Property inspector.

FIGURE 2.36

4 In the CSS Styles panel, scroll down to the bottom of the list. Select another word from the same paragraph, Right/Control-click .style1 from the CSS Styles panel, and choose Apply.

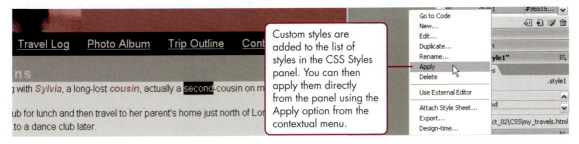

> Custom styles are added to the list of styles in the CSS Styles panel. You can then apply them directly from the panel using the Apply option from the contextual menu.

FIGURE 2.37

5 Save the changes to index.html, but leave it open.

To Extend Your Knowledge

SPANS CAN BE OVERUSED

You have learned how to use CSS classes and how styles based on inheritance and relationships can reduce the number of classes. You can apply the same thought process to styles that use the **<span>** tag as the delivery agent. Where possible, try to reduce your use of **<span>** styles and, instead, create styles based on document structure.

Span styles can be difficult to manage. They are generally applied when the document structure does not support their use, as if you randomly decided to change the style of some text. Even if you have given span styles meaningful names, such as warning or address, they can make it difficult to restyle a site later on. Try to keep span styles to the absolute minimum.

Be aware of conflicts with accessibility: if you are applying a span style to emphasize a word or phrase, remember that using span only adds visual style; the emphasis does not originate in the document structure. If you want to emphasize something, use **<strong>**, **<em>**, or both, and if you wish, add additional style.

The **<span>** tag can be used to add additional style to an element. For example, elements may have only one background image but your design may require two background images. Therefore, some designers add a **<span>** tag to deliver the second background image. For example, **<h1><span>Text</span></h1>** allows the designer to apply one background to the **h1** selector and another background to the **h1 span** selector. While this is an effective use of the **<span>** tag that does not damage the basic document structure (Heading 1 is still Heading 1), this technique does require a designer to add another tag to each **h1** element just so that the design remains intact.

LESSON 6 Using Inline, Embedded, and External Style Sheets

Styles can be created in any of the following formats: inline, embedded, or external. The properties and values are available to all forms of styles, but each method has its advantages and disadvantages.

An *inline style* is one in which the style rule is added as an attribute and attribute values to a tag. The style attribute is required and the attribute values are the CSS properties used anywhere else. For example, to change the color of the text in a paragraph to green, an inline style would be written as **<p style="color: green;">Text</p>**. Style declarations are formatted just as they are always formatted: the style property is separated from the style property value with a colon and style property:value pairs (declarations) are separated from each other with semicolons. However, curly braces are not allowed. Instead, a pair of quotation marks surrounds the style declaration block. One disadvantage of inline styles is that if you need to edit the style, you must edit right in the code of the tag. Secondly, if the style is required again, you either have to recreate it in the other location(s) or rebuild it as either an embedded or external style.

An *embedded style sheet* appears in the **<head>** section of an HTML document. Opening and closing **<style>** tags surround the style rules. The **<style>** tag requires one attribute, the **type** attribute, that is set to **text/css**, as in **<style type="text/css">**. Commonly, inside the **<style>** tags are comment tags **<!--** and **-->**. The purpose of the comment tags is to hide the style rules from old browsers (NN3, IE3, and earlier browsers), which would not understand the **<style>** tags and would, therefore, attempt to display the style rules in the browser window. Between the opening and closing comment tags are the style rules. Embedded styles have the advantage that you can apply them to any of the elements in the current page, but if you open another page on the site, the styles do not transfer.

An *external style sheet* exists in a separate file and is called into use by the Web page. The format of the style rules is identical to those in embedded style sheets with one minor exception: there is no need for the **<style>** or comment tags. However, in order to bring the style rules into use by the Web page, the **<link>** tag is commonly used. The **<link>** tag is an empty tag which has no closing </link> tag. There are three required attributes and attribute values: **type="text/css"**, **rel="stylesheet"**, and **src="style_sheet_file-name.css"**. The **type** attribute tells the browser the format of the information, the **rel** attribute identifies the relationship of the external file, and the **src** attribute identifies the URL of the external style sheet. The URL can be absolute or relative: absolute is recommended because the pages that depend on the style sheet can be found in different folders at different folder depths. An alternate method of calling an external style sheet uses the **@import** method. The **@import** method uses the **<style>** tag in the format of **<style type="text/css"> @import(style_sheet_filename.css); </style>**.

You can use any or all of these methods, as needed. Although it is rare to use inline styles, it is not uncommon to combine embedded and external style sheets, where the external style sheets have the styles for the whole Web site and an embedded style sheet provides either additions or modifications for the current page. You can use multiple external style sheets. Some designers divide their styles into logical blocks and save each block to a different file. For example, the navigation-bar styles may appear in one style sheet, the main-content styles may appear in another, and the styles that control layout may appear in yet another. Using CSS for layout is the topic of the next project in this book, *Project 3: Using CSS for Layout.* You must be aware of the order of the style sheets in the code. If two styles conflict, such as one color for h1 text in the embedded style sheet and another color for h1 text in the external style sheet, the last one to appear in code is the one that displays. Commonly, external style sheets are listed first followed by the embedded style sheet, so the embedded style sheet's rules take precedence if there is a conflict.

Using external style sheets is the primary method for reducing page weight. Exporting the style rules to an external style-sheet file reduces the number of bytes in the HTML page. Many professional CSS-based designers redesign a Web page by removing presentational HTML, rebuilding the appearance using CSS, and then exporting the styles to an external CSS file, thus losing as much as 80% of the HTML page weight. Of course, the CSS file takes space, but never as much as the lost HTML tags and attributes. There is another benefit to external style sheets — browsers cache external style-sheet files if they are used more than once. To *cache* is to store the file in the browser's temporary files from which the file may be recalled when needed again. This means that if a person visited a site, their browser would download the HTML document and the CSS file. If the person links to another page on the same site that uses the same CSS file, the browser does not download the CSS file again but recalls it from the cache. This further reduces the page weight to just the HTML document.

Dreamweaver does not create inline styles with the exception of layers, which we discuss in the next project. Even span styles are not inline styles. Span styles can be created on the fly but are stored in the style sheet, either embedded or external. When you create a style, you have the option of defining it in the current document or in a style-sheet file. Choosing current document creates an embedded style whereas choosing a style-sheet file creates an external style sheet.

Create an External Linked Style Sheet

In this exercise, we create a style that is stored in an external style sheet.

1   **In the open file, index.html, create a new style using the h1 selector. In the New CSS Style dialog box, set Define in to New Style Sheet and click OK.**

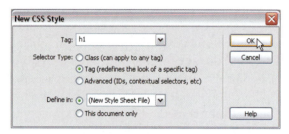

FIGURE 2.38

2   **In the Save Style Sheet File As dialog box, type test.css in the File Name field. Ensure that the My Travels folder is the current folder and click Save/Choose.**

3   **In the Type category, set the Text color to #FFF and click OK.**

4   **In the CSS Styles panel, scroll to the top of the list of styles, and click the –/down-arrow (Macintosh) beside <style> to collapse the list of style rules in the <style> block.**

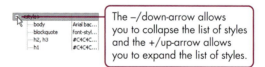

The –/down-arrow allows you to collapse the list of styles and the +/up-arrow allows you to expand the list of styles.

FIGURE 2.39

5   **Click the test.css tab (Windows)/Document title bar (Macintosh), and then close the external style-sheet file, saving your changes.**

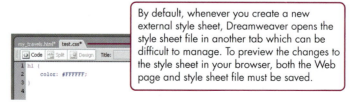

By default, whenever you create a new external style sheet, Dreamweaver opens the style sheet file in another tab which can be difficult to manage. To preview the changes to the style sheet in your browser, both the Web page and style sheet file must be saved.

FIGURE 2.40

6   Choose Edit>Preferences/Dreamweaver>Preferences (Macintosh), choose the CSS Styles category, remove the check from Open CSS Files When Modified, and click OK.

Preferences

Category	CSS Styles
General	
Accessibility	**When creating CSS styles:**
Code Coloring	Use shorthand for: ☐ Font
Code Format	
Code Hints	☐ Background
Code Rewriting	
CSS Styles	☐ Margin and padding
File Types / Editors	
Fonts	☐ Border and border width
Highlighting	
Invisible Elements	☐ List-Style
Layers	
Layout Mode	**When editing CSS styles:**
New Document	Use shorthand: ⦿ If original used shorthand
Office Copy/Paste	
Panels	○ According to settings above
Preview in Browser	
Site	☐ Open CSS files when modified
Status Bar	
Validator	

FIGURE 2.41

7   Save the changes to index.html, leaving it open for the next exercise.

Export an Embedded Style Sheet

In this exercise, you export all of the style rules you have created to an external style sheet. In the process of exporting, Dreamweaver also creates a link to the external style sheet so you don't have to attach the style sheet as an additional step.

1   In the open file, index.html, Right/Control-click <style> in the CSS Styles panel and choose Export.

2   Type `bridge.css` in the File Name field and click Save.

3   Again Right/Control-click <style> in the CSS Styles panel and choose Delete.

4   Right/Control-click test.css in the CSS Styles panel and choose Delete.

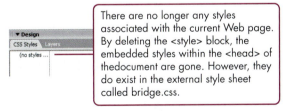

There are no longer any styles associated with the current Web page. By deleting the <style> block, the embedded styles within the <head> of thedocument are gone. However, they do exist in the external style sheet called bridge.css.

FIGURE 2.42

5   Save the changes to index.html, leaving it open for the next exercise.

Attach an External Style Sheet

In this exercise, you attach a style sheet with the link method and examine the `<link>` tag.

1 In the open file, index.html, Right/Control-click in the CSS Styles panel and select Attach Style Sheet. In the Attach External Style Sheet dialog box, choose Link from the Add as options, either Browse to choose or type `bridge.css` in the File/URL field, and click OK/Choose.

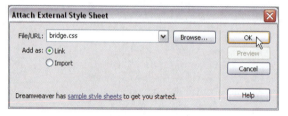

FIGURE 2.43

2 Again, Right/Control-click in the CSS Styles panel and choose Attach Style Sheet. In the Attach External Style Sheet dialog box, choose Add as Import, type or Browse to choose `test.css`, and click OK/Choose.

3 In the CSS Styles panel, click the +/up arrow to the left of <style>. Also, open the Code window.

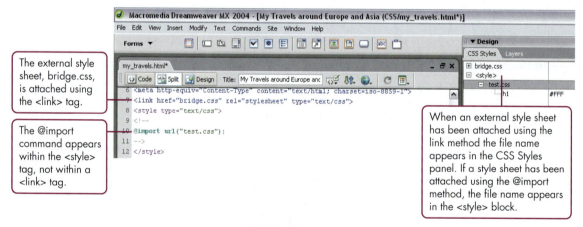

FIGURE 2.44

4 Right/Control-click <style> in the CSS Styles panel and choose Delete.

When an external style sheet has been deleted from the CSS Styles panel, the file still exists but is no longer attached to the current Web page. However, if the styles are embedded in the current page, deleting <style> deletes all of the style definitions. Although you can use Undo to recover the deleted style rules from the `<style>` block, be careful when considering that option.

5 Close the Code window and close index.html.

To Extend Your Knowledge

@IMPORT HIDES STYLES FROM NN4

Netscape Navigator 4.x is notorious for its poor support for CSS. You may wonder why this particular browser is picked on so much — why not IE3, Mosaic (the precursor to both Netscape and Internet Explorer), or Opera 2? The problem is twofold. For a long time, NN4 was the browser of choice for many individuals and corporations, so many, many visitors used this browser. Even today, 4% of all visitors use this browser. Secondly, NN4 has inconsistent support for CSS: some properties are supported, some are not, some display improperly, and some crash the browser. For these reasons, efforts are made to prevent NN4 browsers from seeing the styles. If successful, visitors using this browser do not see the styles but at least they can read the content and see inline images (another reason for creating proper document structure with HTML).

NN4 does not understand the `@import` method of attaching a style sheet and, therefore, those styles are hidden from it. Some designers use multiple style sheets, putting the styles that don't work in NN4 into an imported style sheet and the rest in linked style sheets. All other current browsers support the `@import` method of attaching an external style sheet, so they can use all of the styles — those attached using the `@import` method and those attached using the link method.

Create a Consistent Design

In this exercise, you attach the bridge.css style sheet to all other pages on your site. Where necessary, you apply classes to elements so that the style rules that need classes apply.

| **1** | Open contact_me.html. |

| **2** | Right/Control-click in the CSS Styles panel and choose Attach Style Sheet. Using Link as the Add as option, choose bridge.css, and click OK/Choose. |

| **3** | Click in the navigation-bar paragraph. From the Tag selector, select the \<p\> tag, then Right/Control-click on the \<p\> tag and set the ID to navbar. |

| **4** | Close, saving your changes. |

| **5** | Repeat Steps 2 to 4 for photo_album.html, travel_log.html, switcher.html, and trip_outline.html. |

| **6** | Open index.html. |

7   **Scroll down to the Contact Me heading and the form below it. Select both the heading and the form, and delete them.**

The form was beneficial to have in this page to help develop the style rules for forms. However, now that the bridge.css style-sheet file has been attached to contact_me.html, the form in index.html is no longer needed. The link in the navigation bar provides access to the contact form.

8   **Preview this page in your browser. Click any of the links in the navigation-bar paragraph, and note the consistent look of the Web pages in this site.**

9   **Close your browser and return to Dreamweaver, leaving index.html open for the next lesson.**

LESSON 7   Using Design-Time Style Sheets

Dreamweaver has an innovative feature called "design-time style sheets" that allows you to enable or disable style sheets when you are creating or designing Web pages. The style sheets are no different than any other style sheet — this option is purely a Dreamweaver feature. Design-time style sheets can have several beneficial roles as you develop a Web site. Some CSS properties and values are not well supported by Dreamweaver. You have seen some of these although none of them are very critical. Dreamweaver has great difficulty with some CSS properties, making it difficult to create new pages with the style sheet enabled. The design-time feature allows you to disable those properties and develop the pages without hindrance. You can use design-time style sheets when developing alternate style sheets. By hiding the primary style sheet, you prevent it from interfering with the alternate. At times, part of a Web page, such as the navigation bar, is created using a server-side language that, of course, doesn't run in Dreamweaver. Therefore, this may create a hole in the page where this dynamic content would appear. You can create a design-time style sheet to hide this empty area.

The design-time style-sheet feature works by allowing you to choose which style sheets you want to have active when designing or working with a page and which style sheets you want to disable. Unlike the earlier suggestion, you cannot enable or disable individual style rules, but if you make a copy of the primary style sheet, you can delete the rules that cause a problem, and then, using the design-time feature, disable the primary style sheet and enable the less-problematic duplicate.

Design-time is not a Web technology but purely a Dreamweaver feature. There is nothing in the HTML code that indicates how Dreamweaver manages this feature: it is managed from within the site-definition settings. Therefore, Dreamweaver is not creating any custom or special code that will cause any problems with your browser. Furthermore, because there is no HTML code controlling the design-time style sheets, the browser sees the intended production style sheets, not any that are used during design-time.

The Design Time dialog box enables you to choose which style sheets you want to show when designing and which style sheets you want to hide when designing. Notice the reference to multiple style sheets. When you plan to use design-time style sheets, you create a style sheet that has the properties you want to see when this style sheet is active or one that has properties that reverse other properties that are causing problems.

Create and Apply a Design-Time Style Sheet

In this exercise, you want to hide the navigation bar and the contact form during Web-page development. You create a design-time style sheet that hides those parts of the Web page and see that the properties in the design-time style sheet are active only in Dreamweaver.

1 In the open file, index.html, create a new style for the selector form, p#navbar, but choose New Style Sheet File from the Define in option, and click OK. Type hide.css in the File name field and click Save.

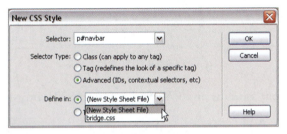

FIGURE 2.45

2 From the Block category, choose none from the Display list and click OK.

3 Preview the page in your browser.

FIGURE 2.46

4 Return to Dreamweaver.

5 Right/Control-click hide.css in the CSS Styles panel and choose Delete.

6 Right/Control-click in the CSS Styles panel and choose Design-time. Click the + button above Show Only at Design Time, choose hide.css, and click OK/Choose. Click the + above Hide at Design Time, choose bridge.css, and click OK/Choose. Click OK to close the Design Time Style Sheets dialog box.

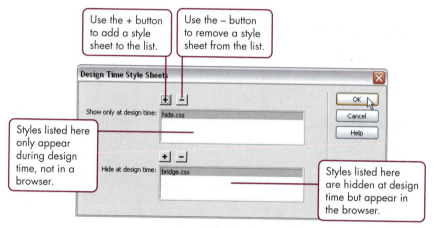

FIGURE 2.47

7 Examine the Document window and CSS Styles panel in Dreamweaver.

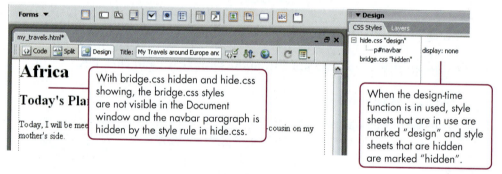

FIGURE 2.48

8 Preview the page in your browser.

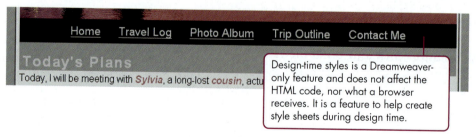

FIGURE 2.49

9 Return to Dreamweaver.

10 Right/Control-click in the CSS Styles panel, choose Design-time, and click both – buttons to remove both hide.css and bridge.css from their fields in the dialog box. Click OK when finished. Leave index.html open for the next lesson.

To Extend Your Knowledge

PROS AND CONS OF DESIGN-TIME STYLE SHEETS

The design-time style-sheet function is a useful feature of Dreamweaver. You can hide CSS properties that cause problems for Dreamweaver, you can hide dynamic content, and you can hide the current style sheet while you are developing a new look or design for the Web site.

Although this feature is beneficial, it is not perfect. If you want to use this feature for all pages in a site, you must enable it for all pages individually. Macromedia Contribute is software designed for Web-content contributors. Design-time style sheets would be beneficial for users of Contribute in that areas of a Web page that contributors are not authorized to modify could be hidden. However, Contribute 2 does not support design-time style sheets. As long as you understand the limitations, you may find design-time style sheets quite useful at times.

LESSON 8   Working with Print Style Sheets

Many news-related Web sites provide a link to a printable version of the current Web page, sometimes using an icon of a printer. The printable version commonly does not have colors or background images and sometimes, navigation bars are not present. Creating printable versions of your Web pages using this method involves creating a duplicate of every Web page either through server-side programming or manually. Style sheets have more uses than just styling content on a computer screen; they can also be developed for printers, televisions, and handheld devices, such as cell phones and *PDAs* (portable digital assistants, such as the Palm® devices). If a visitor decides to print a page that has a print style sheet attached, the browser displays the Web page on the printer using the print style sheet. This process is automatic and eliminates the need to create printable versions of the page. As long as the Web page is attached to the print style sheet, the browser uses the style rules in the print style sheet to style the printout.

There are no differences in the format of print and screen style sheets, although some screen options don't make sense for printing, such as the `:hover` pseudo-class. There also is one change that you should apply to the `<link>` tag to tell the browser not to display a print style sheet on screen, but only use it when printing. The default format of the tag is `<link rel="stylesheet" href="filename.css" type="text/css">`. The `media` attribute, not normally added by Dreamweaver, specifies for what type of device the style sheet is intended: `media="screen"` is for computer screens, `media="print"` is for printers, and `media="all"` is for all devices. Without a `media` attribute, the browser assumes that the style sheet can be used in all media.

There are some print-specific CSS properties that enable the designer to specify what size of paper is to be used for printing, such as letter, legal, or A4, and where to place page breaks, but these properties are poorly supported. Also, text size more commonly uses points as the unit of measurement. Points are more appropriate for printers than computers, televisions, or cell phones.

Create a Print Style Sheet

In this exercise, you create a print style sheet. You use the design-time feature during the design of the print style sheet to hide the styles in bridge.css. You create the print style sheet, and modify the `<link>` tag to specify that the print style sheet is intended for the printer and bridge.css is intended for the screen.

1   In the open file, index.html, create a new style sheet using the selector **body**, and choose **New Style Sheet File** from the Design in options. Type **print.css** in the File name field and click Save.

2   In the Type category, choose **Times New Roman, Times, serif**. Set the color to **#000** and click OK.

3   Right/Control-click in the CSS Style panel and choose Design-time. Click the **+** button to add bridge.css to Hide at Design Time and click OK/Choose.

4   Create a new style for the **h1** selector in the print.css file. In the Border category, create a solid, thin, black border around all sides. Click OK.

5   Create a new style for the form, **p#navbar** selector in the print.css file. In the Block category, set Display to none and click OK.

6   Create a new style for the **a** selector in the print.css file. In the Type category, choose none from the Decoration group of radio buttons, and set the Text color to **#000**.

     The navigation bar has no value on paper, so it was hidden. On a similar note, links in the document also have no value on paper, which is why the underlines were removed and the text color was changed to the same as normal paragraph text.

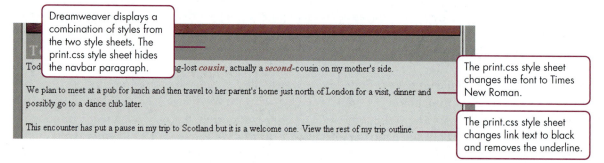

Dreamweaver displays a combination of styles from the two style sheets. The print.css style sheet hides the navbar paragraph.

The print.css style sheet changes the font to Times New Roman.

The print.css style sheet changes link text to black and removes the underline.

FIGURE 2.50

7   Right/Control-click in the CSS Styles panel and choose Design-time. Click the **–** button to enable the display of bridge.css.

8   Open the Code window and locate the line beginning with `<link href="print.css"` (approximately line 8). Move the insertion point to the left of **>** and press the Spacebar. Type **m**, choose media, and press Enter/Return. Type **p**, choose print, and press Enter/Return.

9 Locate the line beginning with `<link href="bridge.css"`. Using the same methods as in Step 8, set the `media` attribute to `screen`. Close the Code window when finished.

```
5  <title>My Travels around Europe and Asia</title>
6  <meta http-equiv="Content-Type" content="text/html; charset=iso-8859-1">
7  <link href="bridge.css" rel="stylesheet" type="text/css" media="screen">
8  <link href="print.css" rel="stylesheet" type="text/css" media="print">
9  </head>
```

When media has been set, the browser knows when to use the style sheet: screen for onscreen display and print when printing the page.

FIGURE 2.51

10 Preview the page in your browser, and either print the page or choose File>Print Preview in your browser.

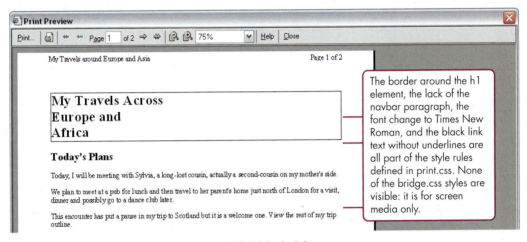

The border around the h1 element, the lack of the navbar paragraph, the font change to Times New Roman, and the black link text without underlines are all part of the style rules defined in print.css. None of the bridge.css styles are visible: it is for screen media only.

FIGURE 2.52

11 Close your browser and return to Dreamweaver, leaving index.html open for the next exercise.

LESSON 9   Using Alternate Style Sheets

An alternate style sheet is a feature of CSS that cannot be duplicated in HTML without completely redesigning the Web site. An alternate style sheet is essentially a second (or third or more) style sheet that has been created for the Web page or Web site. In developing the alternate style sheet, you may completely rethink your design and layout of the Web page or you may just apply very limited changes, such as colors. The differences between primary and alternate style sheets are not in the creation or methodology used, but in how they are attached to the Web pages. Another difference between primary and alternate style sheets is that when you have at least one alternate, you are able to provide your visitors with the option of switching between style sheets. Finally, if you want to use alternate style sheets, all of your style sheets, including the primary, should be external style sheets. It is possible but more difficult to switch between primary and alternate style sheets if the primary is an embedded style sheet.

To Extend Your Knowledge

POINTS VS. PIXELS VS. EMS VS. ...

There are many units of measurements available to CSS: some have good browser support and others do not. The units of measurements can be classified as absolute units and relative units.

Absolute units of measurement are fixed and unchanged. The most understood absolute unit is the point: there are 72 points per inch so a 12-point font is one-sixth of an inch in height. Another absolute unit is the pixel: you have used this often to set the dimensions of images, thickness of borders, and dimensions of some elements, such as the height of the h1 element. Pixels are absolute because the only way you can change the number of pixels on your computer monitor is to change the resolution. CSS also supports inches and centimeters, but those are more appropriate for setting dimensions on the printed page than on-screen.

Relative units of measurement create dimensions or sizes that change, depending on the situation. Percentage is measured relative to the dimensions of the container or default font size. For example, if the table width is set to 50%, the outer table is 50% of the width of the browser window, a nested table is 50% of the width of the containing cell, and so on. All browsers have a default setting for font size (commonly set to point sizes between 12 and 14 points). This is the base font size for paragraph or normal text. Setting the h1 size to 200% displays the text at 24 to 28 points, depending on the browser. Em is another relative unit of measurement. For all intents and purposes, you can think of ems as percentages divided by 100: 1em = 100% and 0.8em = 80%.

Percentages make good sense to people, but unfortunately, some browsers do not interpret percentages well for text size: 0.8em text size should be the same as 80%, but in IE, it is not. Furthermore, font sizes less than 70% on IE5.2 for the Macintosh are very difficult to read, whereas 70% on IE6 for Windows is readable, albeit small.

For reasons of accessibility, the W3C recommends that you use a relative font size. This recommendation targets people who have poor vision and would like to enlarge the font on their computer screen to make it easier to read. Font sizes specified in absolute units cannot be resized, whereas relative units can be resized. Although the menu option varies from browser to browser, under the View menu is a font- or text-size option enabling you to change the size. If other elements use em as the unit of measurement, such as a table with of 30em, its width also change when you change the text size from the menu. Go to webstandards.org and resize the text size. Go to cnn.com and try the same process. CNN.com uses (at the time of writing) points for font size that cannot be resized in a browser. The Opera browser is the exception, in which the zoom feature resizes everything, including images, no matter what units were used.

You have learned how to create an external style sheet. You have used design-time to create a new style sheet, the print style sheet. Using design-time allowed you to see the changes to the style of the page as you created them without interference from the screen style sheet. A print style sheet is not considered an alternate style sheet because it is intended for a different medium. An alternate style sheet is one that has been designed for the screen and displays the same Web page with a different look. There are two changes that you need to make to the `<link>` tag to set an additional style sheet as an alternate style sheet: you must modify the `rel` attribute from `rel="stylesheet"` to `rel="alternate stylesheet"`, and you must apply a name to the alternate style sheet using the `title` attribute, so that the user can choose the alternate style sheet.

There are two methods for allowing visitors to switch between alternate style sheets. The easiest method is available to the Mozilla and Opera browsers. In these browsers, you choose View>Use Style or View>Style and choose the style sheet — the browser automatically unloads the current style sheet, loads the selected style sheet, and redisplays the page using the current style sheet. Unfortunately, Internet Explorer does not support alternate style sheets within the application. The second method is called "style-sheet switching." It depends on either a JavaScript or server-side script with a link on a Web page to choose the style sheet. These methods are supported by all browsers.

CSSZenGarden.com is a Web site designed specifically to highlight CSS-based redesigns of a single page. In order to achieve this, every contributor creates the equivalent of an alternate style sheet, submits it to the site and, using a server-side application, visitors to the site can choose style sheets from the links provided. Besides the promotion of CSS, there are a number of applications where alternate style sheets are beneficial. Some Web designers use them to provide more accessible versions of their Web pages with higher-contrast color schemes, and/or larger fonts. Other Web designers use it to show off their design talents by demonstrating different design options for their Web sites. On a similar note, Web designers could use it to demonstrate to their clients some of the different design options they have come up with for their Web sites.

Attach an Alternate Style Sheet

In this exercise, you are given an alternate style sheet that you must attach to the Web page, configure properly, and test in your browser.

1. **In the open file, index.html, Right/Control-click in the CSS Styles panel and choose Attach Style Sheet. Add the style sheet using the Link method, and browse to choose sphinx.css. Click OK/Choose, then OK again.**

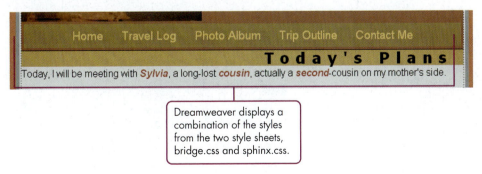

Dreamweaver displays a combination of the styles from the two style sheets, bridge.css and sphinx.css.

FIGURE 2.53

2. **Switch to the Code view and scroll up to approximately line 7 where you find the `<link>` tag to the bridge.css style sheet.**

3   Click to the left of the > at the end of the tag and press the Spacebar. Type **t**, choose `title` from the Code Hint, and press Enter/Return. Type `London Bridge`.

4   Find the `<link>` tag for the sphinx.css file. Insert `alternate` before stylesheet in the rel attribute to produce `rel="alternate stylesheet"`.

5   Click to the left of the > at the end of the tag, and press the Spacebar. Type **m**, press Enter/Return to choose `media`, type **s**, and press Enter/Return to choose `screen`. Insert a `title` attribute, as in Step 3, and title the style sheet `The Sphinx`.

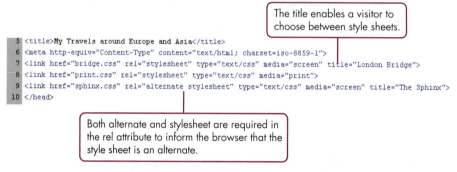

The title enables a visitor to choose between style sheets.

Both alternate and stylesheet are required in the rel attribute to inform the browser that the style sheet is an alternate.

FIGURE 2.54

6   Switch back to the Design view and preview the page in your browser.

7   Switch style sheets using the appropriate method for the browser: in Opera, choose View>Style; in Mozilla, choose View>Use Style; in Firefox, click the icon in the Status bar and choose The Sphinx.

If alternate style sheets are available, Firefox provides a pop-up menu list of the style sheets. The name you applied using the title attribute is used to identify the style sheets.

FIGURE 2.55

8   Close your browser, return to Dreamweaver, and close index.html.

To Extend Your Knowledge

BROWSER SUPPORT FOR CSS

There are many CSS properties and values for the properties. Even the best browsers, which currently are the Mozilla-based browsers (Mozilla, Firefox, and Camino), suffer from bugs, weaknesses, misinterpretations, or lack of support for some CSS properties or values. Current browsers support most of the CSS1 properties, with the exception of some units of measurement, such as the ex. However, CSS2 is not fully supported, and it would be nice to know which browsers support what properties. There are two sources of this type of information: browser-support charts and Dreamweaver's results panel.

Westciv.com has an excellent series of CSS browser-support charts at westciv.com/style_master/academy/browser_support/; you can also purchase a printed copy of these charts (with more information) from that Web site. At blooberry.com/indexdot/css/, you can find a wealth of CSS information, and for each property, browser support is indicated. Other CSS browser-support charts are available if you search for css support chart using your favorite search engine.

Dreamweaver also provides support information through the Browser Check function. You click the Browser Check button to the right of the Document Title field at the top of the Document window, and choose Show All Errors. In the Results panel that opens up below the Property inspector, any code that is poorly supported or unsupported is flagged with red (serious problem for the identified browsers), yellow (warning, may not appear as intended), or white (informational, unsupported code but has no visible effect) markers. To check your CSS file for browser-support issues, open the CSS file in Dreamweaver, run the browser check, and review the messages in the Results panel.

S U M M A R Y

In this project, you learned how CSS works and how to make it work for you. You learned what an element selector is and how to group element selectors so that the same style declaration can apply to multiple elements. You learned the difference between class and id selectors, how they should be used, and how to apply them to your Web pages. You learned about inheritance of CSS properties, about relationships between elements, and how to use these principles to reduce dependency on classes and to create sophisticated style rules. You learned about pseudo-classes and how they can be applied to links. You learned how the **<span>** tag is used to create custom styles. You created an embedded style sheet, discovered how to export it to an external style sheet, and learned how an external style sheet you can attach to every page in a Web site to create a consistent look and feel. You learned how the design-time feature of Dreamweaver is beneficial for the development of other style sheets without interference from the primary style sheet. You created a print style sheet and learned how it can be used to create a style for printing and to hide elements that have no usefulness on paper. You learned how to attach alternate style sheets so that your visitors or clients can be presented with different styles of the same page.

KEY TERMS

absolute units	generic class/id	relative units
block	id	selector
cache	inline	style declaration
class	inline style	style-declaration block
DOM	page weight	style rule
element selector	PDA	values
embedded style sheet	properties	version 4 browsers
external style sheet	regular class/id	

CHECKING CONCEPTS AND TERMS

SCREEN ID

Identify the indicated areas from the list below:

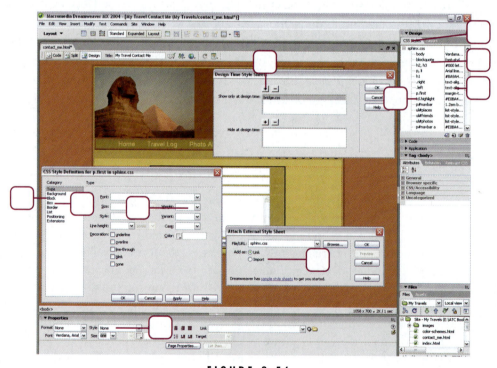

FIGURE 2.56

a. Enable or disable bold

b. @import

c. Style declaration

d. Show more style sheets at design time

e. Category containing width, height, margins, and padding

f. Element selector

g. CSS Styles panel

h. List of available styles

i. Regular class selector

j. Category containing text alignment

MULTIPLE CHOICE

Circle the letter of the correct answer for each of the following:

1. Identify the correct application of the selector `.alert`.

   a. `<p class="alert">`, `<a class="alert">`

   b. `<blockquote id="alert">`, `<h1 class="alert">`

   c. `<h2 id="alert">`, `<h2 id="alert">`

   d. All of the above

2. `a {color: red;}` is an example of _____.

   a. an element selector

   b. a style rule

   c. a style declaration block

   d. a regular class

3. The correct format of a child selector is _____.

   a. a:child

   b. p+p

   c. h1, h2

   d. ul>li

4. A style sheet between the `<head>` and `</head>` tags is called _____.

   a. applied

   b. enclosed

   c. embedded

   d. exported

5. An external style sheet is attached to a Web page using _____.

   a. `<link href="hicontrast.css" rel="alternate stylesheet" type="text/css" media="screen" title="High Contrast">`

   b. `<link href="styles.css" rel="stylesheet" type="text/css">`

   c. `<link href="print.css" rel="stylesheet" type="text/css" media="print">`

   d. All of the above

6. The Design Time Style Sheets dialog box allows you to _____.

   a. create element selectors

   b. hide and display style sheets

   c. create and delete style sheets

   d. attach or detach style sheets

7. To change the appearance of a link when the mouse pointer rolls over it, you use _____.

   a. `p.navbar:active {color: red;}`

   b. `a:visited {background-color: blue;}`

   c. `a.body:hover {text-decoration: none;}`

   d. `p#navbar a {padding: 0px; padding-left: 15px; padding-right; 15px;}`

8. Which is an example of a group of id selectors?

   a. `p#navbar {color: red;}`, `p#footer {color: blue;}`

   b. `.style1, .style2 {font-weight: bold;}`

   c. `p#navbar, .style1 {text-align: center;}`

   d. `#navbar, #footer {text-decoration: underline;}`

9. Which color code produces the color black?

   a. `#00000`

   b. `#black`

   c. `#000`

   d. All of the above

10. In a Web page in which you have `<h2>Job Experience</h2><p>I made hamburgers at <a href="http://www.bk.com">Burger King</a>.</p>`, which selector would change the color of Burger King to blue?

    a. `h2+p>a`

    b. `p a, blockquote a`

    c. `body a`

    d. All of the above

DISCUSSION QUESTIONS

1. You have experienced the power, flexibility, and versatility of CSS, and, as a designer, you can make great use of these features. What reasons might non-CSS designers have for not learning and applying CSS in their Web-site designs? What means can you think of to encourage designers to learn more about and use CSS?

2. The **media** attribute of the **<style>** tag has several options; **screen**, **print**, and **all** are the most commonly used. You have been asked to create a **handheld** media (cell/mobile phones and PDAs) style sheet for the My Travels Web site (the one used for much of this project). Assume that the devices can display color and images (as most current ones can) and assume that these devices support all current CSS selectors and properties. What changes would you make to the style sheet and/or Web page(s) to allow users to comfortably browse this Web site using these small screen devices?

SKILL DRILLS

Skill Drills reinforce project skills. Each skill reinforced is the same, or nearly the same, as a skill presented in the lessons. Detailed instructions are provided in a step-by-step format. Work through these exercises in order.

1. Lay the Foundation Styles

In the following exercise, you're going to build the basic styles for the Philosophy Department's Web site. You create the body styles and the basic layout styles. Although the instructions state to click OK at the end of creating a style rule, you can click Apply after each new property has been assigned to see the changes taking place gradually.

1. Create a new site definition called **Philosophy** from the Project_02>Philosophy folder.

2. One by one, open and examine the three Web pages in the folder.

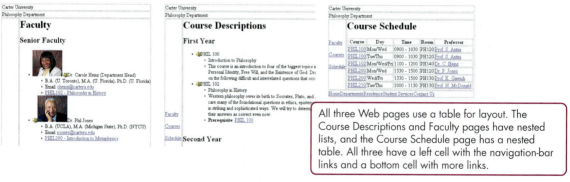

> All three Web pages use a table for layout. The Course Descriptions and Faculty pages have nested lists, and the Course Schedule page has a nested table. All three have a left cell with the navigation-bar links and a bottom cell with more links.

FIGURE 2.57

3. Open faculty.html. Create a new style for the **body** selector, set Define in to New Style Sheet File, and click OK. Type **styles.css** in the File name field and click Save.

4. In the Type category, set the Font to Verdana, Arial, Helvetica, sans-serif. In the Background category, set the Background Image to images>body-bg.png, Attachment to fixed, Horizontal Position to center, and Vertical Position to top. Click OK.

5. Create a new CSS style for the **table#body** selector. In the Background category, set the Background Color to **#000000**, the Background Image to images>table-bg.jpg, Repeat to no-repeat, Horizontal Position to left, and Vertical Position to top. In the Box category, set Width to **750** pixels, uncheck Same for All for Margins, and set both Left and Right margins to auto. Click OK.

6. Click in the table in the Document window. Right/Control-click the **<table>** tag in the Tag selector and set the ID to body.

7. Create a new CSS style for the selector **td#header**. In the Type category, set the Font to Georgia, Times New Roman, Times, serif; the Size to **4** ems; the Weight to bold; and the Color to **#1C438C**. In the Box category, set the Height to **178** px. Click OK.

8. Click inside the top cell containing the text Carter University. Right/Control-click the **<td>** tag in the Tag selector and set the ID to header.

9. Create a new CSS style for the selector **td#dept**. In the Type category, set the Weight to bold, the Line Height to **30** pixels, and the Color to **#FFFFFF**. In the Block category, set Text Align to right. In the Box category, uncheck Same for All for Padding, and set the Right padding to **15** pixels. In the Border category, uncheck Same for All for all border properties, and create a bottom border that is solid in style, medium in thickness, with a color of **#5C7FA7**. Click OK.

10. Click inside the second cell containing the text Philosophy Department. Right/Control-click the **<td>** tag in the Tag selector and set the ID to dept.

FIGURE 2.58

11. Keep faculty.html open for the next exercise.

2. Create the Navigation-Bar Styles

In this Skill Drill, you create the styles for the left navigation bar. You create a navbar id for the **<td>** tag. You then create styles based on descendent selectors using the **td#navbar** as the ancestor, so that these styles are not confused with any other styles. By using the id selector, you do not need to create or assign multiple classes to the content within the navbar cell.

1. Create a new CSS style for the **td** selector. In the Block category, set Vertical Align to top and click OK.

    By default, table-data cells are aligned left (horizontally) middle (vertically); this change forces the content of all table-data cells to the top.

2. Create a new CSS style for the **td#navbar** selector. In the Block category, set Text Align to center. In the Box category, set the width to **120** pixels. In the Border category, uncheck Same for All, and create a Right border with a solid style, a medium thickness, and a color of **#5C7FA7**. Click OK.

3. Click inside the left cell containing the three text links. Right/Control-click **<td>** tag in the Tag selector and set the ID to navbar.

    It is possible to select the **<td>** tag of the left cell and add the code, **id="navbar"**, using the Tag editor before creating the style for the id. However, creating the style first adds the id name to the ID list. It's easier to choose an id from the list to apply than to use the Tag editor. At times, however, you may have to add the id using the Tag editor before creating the style or for the purposes of JavaScript.

4. Create a new CSS style for the **td#navbar p** selector. In the Box category, set all paddings and margins to **0** pixels. Click OK.

5. Create a new CSS style for the **td#navbar a** selector. In the Type category, set Color to **#FFFFFF**, Decoration to none, and Weight to bold. In the Block category, set Display to block. In the Box category, set the width to **120** pixels, and set all Paddings and Margins to **0** pixels. In the Border category, create a bottom border that is solid, **1** pixel thick, with a color of **#5C7FA7**. Click OK.

FIGURE 2.59

6. Keep faculty.html open for the next exercise.

3. Create the Content-Area Styles

The content cell contains the greatest variety of HTML tags, such as headings, paragraphs, links, lists, and nested tables. For this reason, it takes more effort to create the styles for the content area. Additionally, some HTML elements may not exist in the current page (such as a nested table), so you may have to add to the style sheet after examining other pages.

1. Create a new CSS style for the **td#content** selector. In the Type category, set Color to **#DDDDDD**. Click OK.

    The content cell, with the exception of the top portion, has a black background, which is the table background color. The text color could have been set to white, but white can be too bright against a black background. **#DDDDDD** is a light gray that provides decent contrast without appearing too bright.

2. Click inside the main content cell. Right/Control-click **<td>** tag in the Tag selector and set the ID to content.

3. Create a new CSS style for the **td#content h1, td#content h2** selector. In the Type category, set Weight to normal. In the Box category, set all margins to **5** pixels and all paddings to **0** pixels. Click OK.

    Headings, by default, are bold. They are also larger in size (headings 1 to 3 are larger than normal paragraph text, which is equivalent in size to heading 4). Therefore, these headings stand out on the basis of their size. Remember, styles using CSS do not affect the HTML structures of the document. Removing bold from the appearance of these headings does not change their heading level, just their appearance, and removing bold is only one of multitudes of different style changes that you could apply to these elements.

4. Create a new CSS style for the selector **td#content ul**. In the Type category, set Weight to bold, and set Line Height to **1.3** ems. In the List category, set Type to none. Click OK.

    Both the outer and nested list take on the same style. The next style rule uses a selector that targets the nested list.

5. Create a new CSS style for the selector **td#content ul ul**. In the Type category, set Weight to normal. In the Box category, set the bottom margin (only) to **20** pixels. In the List category, set the Type to square. Click OK.

    This rule reverses the bold and bullet settings applied in the previous rule. The bottom-margin setting creates a space below each nested list.

6. Create a new CSS style for the **td#content img** selector. In the Box category, set Float to right, all paddings to **0** pixels, and the right margin to **5** pixels. In the Border category, set all borders to solid style, **2**-pixel thickness, and a color of **#666666**. Click OK.

    This style rule is very generic. On other pages, there may be images that you might not want to float to the right. Therefore, you may have to modify the selector for this page to **td#content ul img** or, if that is not specific enough, you may have to create a class, such as **img.faculty**. For the purposes of this Skill Drill, this selector is sufficiently specific.

7. Create a new CSS style for the **td#content a** selector. In the Type category, set Color to **#97B5EB**. Click OK.

FIGURE 2.60

8. Leave faculty.html open for the next exercise.

4. Create the Footer Styles

The footer is just another navigation bar, but, compared with the left navigation bar, its layout is different (horizontal) and allows for a different styling.

1. Create a new CSS style for the **td#footer** selector. In the Type category, set Line Height to **2** ems. In the Background category, set Background Color to **#2E3B6B**. In the Block category, set Text Align to center. In the Border category, create a top border with a solid style, medium thickness, and a color of **#5C7FA7**. Click OK.

2. Click inside the bottom cell. Right/Control-click **<td>** tag in the Tag selector and set the ID to footer.

3. Create a new CSS Style for the **td#footer a** selector. In the Type category, set Color to **#DDDDDD**, Weight to bold, and Decoration to none. In the Box category, set all margins to **0** pixels, and set the paddings as: Top to **0** pixel, Right to **15** pixels, Bottom to **0** pixel, and Left to **15** pixels. Click OK.

4. Create a new CSS Style for the **td#footer a+a** selector. In the Border category, create a left (only) border with a solid style, **3**-pixel thickness, and a color of **#FFFFFF**.

   Internet Explorer does not support the adjacent selector, a+a, in Step 4, although Dreamweaver and the Mozilla, Opera, and Safari browsers support it. To create this style for IE, you must create a class or an id to style the first link in the footer differently from the other links.

5. Right/Control-click the **td#footer a+a** selector in the CSS Styles panel and choose Go to Code. Delete **a+a** and replace it with **a.notfirst** to create **td#footer a.notfirst** as the selector. Close styles.css and save the changes.

6. Click the second link (Departments) in the Design window, Right/Control-click the selected **<a>** tag in the Tag selector, and apply the class notfirst. One by one, select the remaining links to the right and apply the notfirst class to them.

FIGURE 2.61

7. Keep faculty.html open for the next exercise.

5. Create the Pseudo-Class Styles

Unlike all of the styles created so far, the pseudo-class styles cannot be tested in Dreamweaver. Therefore, after creating these styles, you preview and test them in your browser.

1. Create a new CSS style for the **td#content a:hover** selector. In the Type category, set Decoration to none and click OK.

2. Create a new CSS style for the **td#content a:active** selector. In the Type category, set Decoration to none, Color to **#FFFFFF**, and click OK.

3. Create a new CSS style for the **td#content a:visited** selector. In the Type category, set Color to **#DDDDDD**, and click OK.

4. Create a new CSS style for the **td#navbar a:hover** selector. In the Type category, set the color to **#5C7FA7**. In the Border category, create a bottom (only) border with a solid style, **1**-pixel thickness, and a color of **#FFFFFF**. Click OK.

   It is common practice not to create a **:visited** pseudo-class for navigation-bar links. (An **:active** pseudo-class style could be created but won't be.)

5. Create a new CSS style for the **td#footer a:hover** selector. In the Type category, set Color to **#46537D**. In the Background category, set Background Color to **#BBBBBB**. Click OK.

6. Preview the page in your browser. Roll your mouse pointer over the links in the content, navbar, and footer cells. Click any of the links in the content cell and watch the link color flash white (the **:active** pseudo-class). Click the back button in your browser and note the color of the visited link.

7. Close your browser, return to Dreamweaver, and close faculty.html.

6. Apply the Style Sheet to the Other Web Pages

When you linked to the other pages, you noticed that they were not styled. The next step is to attach the style sheet you created to the other Web pages in this site. Most of the style rules depend on ids, such as **table#body** and **td#navbar**. These ids do not yet exist in these pages. Even when the style sheet is attached, the id hooks won't be present and most of the styles will not appear. If there are classes, they, too, must be applied to the elements that require them. The only class is the **notfirst** class that must be applied to all but the first link in the footer cell.

1. Open courses.html.

2. Right/Control-click in the CSS Styles panel and choose Attach Style Sheet. Using the Add as Link option, choose styles.css.

3. Click in the table. Right/Control-click the **<table>** tag in the Tag selector and set its ID to body.

4. Click in the top cell. Right/Control-click the **<td>** tag in the Tag selector and set its ID to header.

5. Click in the second cell. Right/Control-click the **<td>** tag in the Tag selector and set its ID to dept.

6. Click in the left cell. Right/Control-click the **<td>** tag in the Tag selector and set its ID to navbar.

7. Click in the main cell. Right/Control-click the **<td>** tag in the Tag selector and set its ID to content.

8. Click in the bottom cell. Right/Control-click the **<td>** tag in the Tag selector and set its ID to footer.

9. One by one, click the links in the footer cell (excluding Home), Right/Control-click the **\<a\>** tag in the Tag selector, and set the class to notfirst.

10. Close courses.html, saving your changes.

11. Open schedule.html. Repeat Steps 2 to 9.

12. Save the changes to schedule.html and leave it open for the next exercise.

7. Create New Styles

The document structures in the content cells of the Faculty and Course Descriptions pages are very similar. However, there is a nested table in the Course Schedules page for which no style has been developed. In this exercise, you create a style for the nested table.

1. Create a new CSS style for the **td#content table** selector. In the Background category, set the Background color to **#21355A**. In the Box category, set all margins to **20** pixels. In the Border category, create a border around all sides that is solid, thin, and has a color of **#CCCCCC**. Click OK.

2. Create a new CSS style for the **td#content th, td#content td** selector. In the Block category, set Text Align to center. In the Box category, set all paddings to **5** pixels. Click OK.

FIGURE 2.62

3. Close schedule.html, saving your changes.

CHALLENGE

Challenge exercises expand on, or are somewhat related to, skills presented in the lessons. Each exercise provides a brief narrative introduction, followed by instructions in a numbered-step format that are not as detailed as those in the Skill Drill section. Work through the exercises in the order presented.

1. Create a Print Style Sheet

In this Challenge exercise, you create a print style sheet for the Philosophy Department Web site.

1. Open schedule.html from the Philosophy site.

2. From the CSS Style panel, open the Design Time dialog box and set styles.css to be hidden.

3. Create a new CSS style using **body** as the selector. Set Define in to New Style Sheet File, and name it **print.css**. Set the Font to Arial, Helvetica, sans-serif; the text color to **#000000**; and all margins and paddings to **0** pixels.

4. Create a new CSS style for the **a** selector. Set the text color to **#000000** and Decoration to none.

5. Create a new CSS style for the **table#body** selector. Set the box width to **100**%. Create a bottom border that uses the solid style, is **5** points in thickness, and has a color of **#000000**.

6. Create a new CSS style for the **td#header** selector. Set the font size to **18** points, the weight to bold, and the font to Times New Roman, Times, serif. Create a bottom border that uses the double style, is **3** points in thickness, and has a color **#000000**.

   The solid, dotted, and dashed border styles can be as thick or thin as you wish, but the other styles require at least a medium, 3-pixel, or 3-point thickness. Experiment with different thicknesses — you can use the relative measurements (thin, medium, or thick) or pixels for on-screen presentation and points for printing.

7. Create a new CSS style for the **td#dept** selector. Set the font size to **13** points and the text alignment to right.

8. Create a new CSS style for the **td#footer p, td#navbar p** selector. Set Display to none.

9. Create a new CSS style for the **td#content table** selector. Set the width to **100**%, the bottom margin to **20** points, and a border around all sides that is solid in style, **1** point in thickness, with a color of **#000000**.

10. Right/Control-click the **td#content table** selector in the CSS Styles panel and choose Go to Code. Add the following new style declaration to the **td#content table** style rule: **border-collapse: collapse;**. Close print.css, saving your changes.

    When adjacent cells have a border around each cell, the cell-border thicknesses are doubled. The **border-collapse: collapse** declaration removes the duplicate border when cells share a border. Dreamweaver does not display collapsed borders, but all current browsers support this CSS property.

11. Create a new CSS style for the **td#content td, td#content th** selector. Set the text alignment to left, all paddings to **5** points, and borders around all sides that are solid in style, **1** point in thickness, with a color of **#000000**.

12. Unhide styles.css using the Design Time dialog box. Switch to the Code view and add **media="screen"** to the styles.css **<link>** tag and **media="print"** to the print.css **<link>** tag. Return to the Design view and close schedule.html, saving your changes.

2. Add Additional Styles to the Print Style Sheet

In this Challenge exercise, you attach the print style sheet to the other two pages and determine whether or not additional style rules need to be created to accommodate document structures that are not found in the Course Schedules page.

1. Open faculty.html.

2. Attach print.css to faculty.html and set the media attributes for the two style sheets as you did in Step 12 of the previous exercise.

3. Using the Design Time Style Sheets dialog box, hide styles.css.

4. Examine the appearance of the Web page, and note the differences in document structures that exist in this page — notably the images, lists, and nested lists.

5. Using any of the style properties learned in this project, create new style rules to accommodate the new document structures in this page. Do not create any new classes or ids — use the elements, ids, and classes that currently exist (the only class is the notfirst class in the footer) and their relationships to apply the styles.

6. When finished, redisplay styles.css using the Design Time Style Sheets dialog box, and then close faculty.html, saving your changes.

7. Open schedule.html and apply the same procedures as outlined in Steps 2 and 3. Examine schedule.html and determine whether or not additional style rules are needed. If so, create them, but keep in mind that the structure of schedule.html is very similar to that of faculty.html, and changes you make to the style sheet may affect the Faculty page.

8. When finished with schedule.html, preview the page in your browser, and either print or print preview the page. Link to the other pages, also, and print or print preview those pages, as well.

FIGURE 2.63

9. Close your browser, return to Dreamweaver, and close schedule.html.

3. Create an Alternate Style Sheet

In this Challenge exercise, you will be given some freedom to create your own alternate style sheet.

1. Open index.html from the My Travels site and open color-schemes.html from the My Travels site.

2. In the color-schemes.html page are images and color schemes to match the images. Choose an image to replace the image of the London Bridge. Click in the cells containing the background colors and make note of the hexadecimal color codes. You can close color-schemes.html or keep it open to refer to as you are working.

3. If you are not happy with the colors for your chosen image, you may create your own color scheme using the same technique employed for these images. Set your chosen image as the background image for the h1 element, replacing the image of the London Bridge. Click the color button and, using the eyedropper, pick a color from the image. Note the hexadecimal color code for the color. Open your browser and go to either color.twysted.net or colorschemer.com/online.html. Type the hexadecimal color code into the hexadecimal color field, and click the Use It or Set Hex button (depending on which site you have chosen to use). Make note of the colors in the scheme (whether or not they are provided, you can also use white, black, and grays) and return to Dreamweaver.

4. Using the Files panel, make a copy of the bridge.css file and name it with your personal name (no spaces in the filename — use a hyphen or underscore to create a fake space). The filename will be beneficial in the next Challenge exercise.

5. Attach your new style sheet to index.html.

6. Using the Design Time Style Sheets dialog box, hide all other style sheets.

7. Apply as many or as few of the colors from the color scheme as you want to the text and background colors by modifying the existing selectors. You can also change alignment, and add or delete borders.

8. When you have finished modifying the styles, open the Code window and apply the screen media attribute and the title attribute to the new style sheet `<link>` tag, and modify the rel attribute to alternate stylesheet. Return to the Design view and unhide the style sheets from the Design Time Style Sheet dialog box.

9. If you have access to the Opera, Mozilla (or Firefox or Camino) or Safari browser, preview the page in that browser and switch to your new style sheet.

10. Return to Dreamweaver, leaving index.html open for the next exercise.

4. Use a JavaScript Style-Sheet Switcher

In this Challenge exercise, you set up a JavaScript style-sheet switcher. If you have used the Mozilla, Opera, or Safari browser, you have seen how you may switch between style sheets. However, as soon as you switch to another page, the style sheet reverts to the primary style sheet. Style-sheet switchers remember which style sheet you chose and remember the style-sheet selection for all pages in your site.

There are two steps to setting up a style-sheet switcher. Assuming you already have an alternate style sheet, the first step is to attach the alternate style sheet to all of the pages in your site. The second step is to create a mechanism with which you can choose a style sheet: in this exercise, you use a menu list. The third step is to attach the external JavaScript file to all of the pages in your Web site. Once configured, you choose a style sheet from the list and browse your Web site.

If you are working in a classroom setting, get together with some of your classmates and share the style sheets you created in the previous Challenge exercise. You can then switch between even more style sheets than those you created.

1. Open index.html. In the navbar paragraph, click to the right of Contact Me, and type **Styles** (you won't be able to see the black text against the black background). Double-click Styles and link the selected text to switcher.html.

? If you have problems

If the text Styles appears as soon as you typed it, it is because you added this text to the Contact Me link text. Do not delete it, but select Styles, remove the contact_me.html link from the Link field in the Property inspector, and press Enter/Return. With the Styles text still selected, link it to switcher.html.

---

2. If you are working in a classroom setting, share your style sheet with some classmates by copying the files to a floppy disk or a common folder on the network, or emailing them. Save the ones you have received in the My Travels site. Attach the shared style sheets as alternate style sheets (**rel="alter-nate stylesheet"**) and create a title for each.

3. Open the Code window. Select and copy all of the **<link>** lines to the clipboard.

4. Open switcher.html, open the Code window, if necessary, and paste the copied lines above the closing **</head>** tag. Also, write down on some paper the title attributes for all of the attached alternate style sheets (you can omit print.css).

   The JavaScript code has been added to this file on line 6: do not disturb it.

5. In switcher.html, switch to the Design mode, click the menu list at the bottom, and then click the List Values. Click The Sphinx in the Value column, click the + to add new list items, and add the new title attributes noted in Step 4 in both the Item Label and Value fields. Press Tab after each entry to add more. Click OK when finished.

6. Preview the page in your browser and test the link switcher. Return to Dreamweaver when finished.

   The style switcher works in this page but it will not work in the other pages because the JavaScript code needed to remember the chosen style sheet is not attached to the other pages.

7. Open the Code window. Select from line 6 to the last **<link>** tag, and copy it into the clipboard.

8. Close switcher.html. In the open index.html, select and delete the **<link>** tags in the Code window, and paste the copied lines from switcher.html. Close, saving your changes.

9. One by one, open the remaining pages in this site, delete the **<link>** tag lines from the **<head>** section, and paste the copied lines. When finished, close saving your changes.

10. Open index.html and preview it in your browser. Switch to a different style and then follow one of the links to a new page.

    There are two types of functions in the JavaScript program: one is used to switch style sheets when chosen from the list; the other function enables the other pages to remember the chosen style sheet.

11. Close your browser, return to Dreamweaver, and close index.html.

P O R T F O L I O   B U I L D E R

Convert a Web Page to CSS

Many Web sites do not make much use of CSS other than for basic text styling and for links, with the :hover property. Search for the Web site of a business and view the HTML code. When you find one for which the code contains **<font>** tags and a tables-based layout, save the HTML code as a file on your computer.

1. Examine the code for **vlink**, **link**, **alink**, and **bgcolor** attributes in the **<body>** tag and record the colors. Delete these attributes from the **<body>** tag.

2. Create an embedded style sheet and reinstate these colors using CSS.

3. Examine the **<font>** tags and record the font names, font sizes, and font colors as well as what tag (**<p>**, **<h2>**, **<blockquote>**, or **<b>**) the **<font>** tag is modifying.

4. Record the location of the **<font>** tag, such as **<p>** tags in the left table cell have green text whereas **<p>** tags in the right table cell have blue text.

5. Delete all **<font>** tags and **bgcolor** attributes of **<body>**, **<table>**, **<tr>**, and **<td>** tags. (When deleting the **<font>** tags, don't forget to delete the closing **</font>** tags, as well.)

6. Assign ids to different table cells.

7. Create CSS selectors and rules to replace the **<font>** tags.

8. Look for **bgcolor** attributes in the **<table>**, **<tr>**, and **<td>** tags, and record the colors.

9. Delete the **bgcolor** attributes from the **<table>**, **<tr>**, and **<td>** tags, and reinstate these colors using CSS.

10. Compare the file size of the CSS page with that of the non-CSS page.

Using CSS for Layout

OBJECTIVES

In this project, you learn how to

- Set up the <div> tag for CSS layouts

- Apply padding, borders, margins, width, and height

- Apply list properties and change the display type

- Float content

- Create fixed, liquid, and elastic layouts

- Use the scroll option of CSS

- Use layers for layout and export to a table

- Work with a tracing image

WHY WOULD I DO THIS?

If tables are for data and frames are deprecated in XHTML 1.1, how do you create page layouts? Certainly, tables and frames are fine for the time being, but, if you want to make your design future-proof, you should use CSS for layout. Why CSS, you might ask. As you have read many times in this book and in *Essentials for Design: Dreamweaver MX 2004 Level I*, CSS is for style or appearance and layout is one such appearance. If you gave the same HTML page to different people to design, they would produce different layouts. As long as they did not touch the structure of the HTML page (with the obvious exception of attaching classes and ids to elements), the structure would remain the same, but the appearance or style would differ. This is why CSS for layout makes sense.

CSS for layout is also known as "CSS-P" or "positional CSS." With CSS-P, you can specify the position of elements or blocks on a page. Be aware, however, that CSS for layout is quite difficult to achieve; it reveals bugs in browsers, and is either not supported or improperly supported by older browsers. Designers who use CSS for layout must ask themselves some questions about their site and their audience before they begin using CSS for layout. If a significant percentage (significant is evaluated by the designer) of their audience might be using older browsers, the designer may not want to alienate these individuals. In such cases, the designers can take an intermediate position, using a simple table structure for layout and CSS for text styling. The appearance of the site might then be somewhat different from the fully CSS version, but it could be an acceptable compromise.

You have already encountered some of the CSS properties used in layout in previous projects. These properties include, **vertical-align**, **line-height**, **display**, **width**, **height**, **padding**, **margin**, and **float**. Other CSS properties that play a role in CSS layout include **position**, **overflow**, **top**, **right**, **bottom**, **left**, and **z-index**. In this project, you also learn about the **<div>** tag and how to use it as a container for groups of elements.

There are a number of advantages, for both the designer and the owner of the Web site, to using CSS for layout. The advantages are identical to those we discussed at the beginning of the previous project: CSS offers power, variety, versatility, reduced page weight, and easier redesign. Some of the design features, however, go beyond what you have learned so far: you can move different containers around, such as from side to side or up and down on a page. In addition, because the layout is stored in a style-sheet file, you can use a style-sheet switcher to change not only the colors and fonts, but also the layout of the elements on the page.

You are probably familiar with the CSSZenGarden.com site, which we have mentioned previously as an excellent example of what can be done with CSS. As you recall, the HTML page always remains the same. Although prospective "redesigners" of the CSSZenGarden.com page have access to the HTML page to examine it and learn how the content is structured, they cannot change the HTML code. In the following figure, the original design (top left) appears with a variety of other designs, including a panoramic-style layout. Many designers in the past have argued that CSS can only be used to create boring designs: CSSZenGarden.com is an archive of designs that demonstrate how wrong that statement is. Use the site as an inspiration of what can be achieved using CSS.

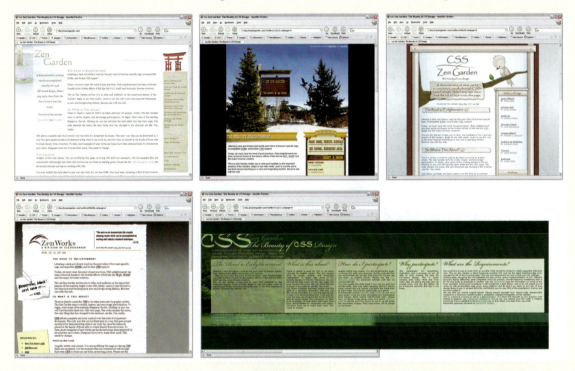

FIGURE 3.1

In addition to CSS for layout, in this project you learn about Dreamweaver layers. Dreamweaver layers are essentially **<div>** elements that use CSS-P to position and size the element. You may insert text, images, or any other Web-page content within layers. Although Dreamweaver calls these elements layers; they are nothing more than **<div>** elements with CSS-P. However, in Dreamweaver, layers have a greater role than just CSS layout. You can use layers to lay out elements on a page, and then convert those layers to a table-based layout. Like the Layout mode used in the Tables project, this is a very free-form method of creating a layout. You can leave the layers as they are and keep the layout as a CSS layout, or you can convert the layout to tables.

You also learn to use a tracing image. A tracing image is a full-sized image or screenshot of the Web page you are creating. (The term tracing image suggests how one might use tracing paper to create a design by placing a picture behind it.) If you create a Web page using Photoshop or any other graphic-design software, you can save this image of the layout and place it behind the current Document window. Using the background image, you can then take the individual elements of the page, insert them into layers, and place them on top of the tracing image. Using Dreamweaver's layers feature, you can drag the layers into position and then export the page to a table-based layout.

V I S U A L   S U M M A R Y

When you create CSS layouts, you often use the **`<div>`** tag to separate content into divisions or sections. Commonly, you select some content within a page and wrap it with a **`<div>`** tag by clicking the Insert Div Tag button on the Layout Insert bar. At times, however, you may not have any content for the **`<div>`** tag; if you don't, you could first insert the tag and then add content.

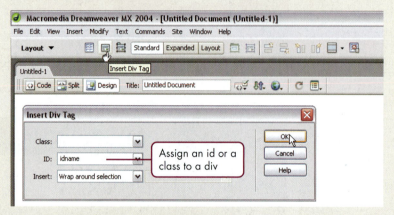

FIGURE 3.2

Another function of Dreamweaver you learn is the creation of layers. In this project, you use layers to create a container in which you may add content. Clicking the Draw Layer button on the Layout Insert bar allows you to draw a layer. Layers have sizing handles with which you may increase or decrease their size. Layers also have a layer handle above the top-left corner: using the layer handle, you may drag the layer into position. You may also modify the properties of a selected layer using the Property inspector.

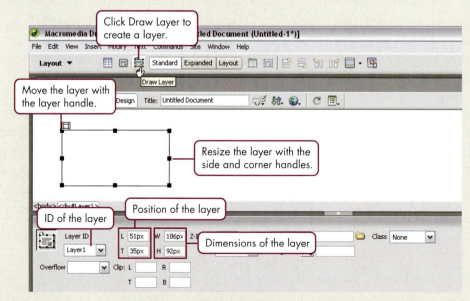

FIGURE 3.3

LESSON 1   Using the <div> Tag for CSS Layouts

In the last project, you learned a little about the **<span>** and **<div>** tags. Neither has any purpose relating to content structure — they provide no meaning for the content in the tags. The purpose of these tags is to deliver CSS styles. When you create a custom style in Dreamweaver, for example, the style is delivered using the **<span>** tag.

As you recall, the difference between these tags is that the **<span>** tag is an inline tag whereas the **<div>** tag is a block tag. An inline tag is a tag that appears in a block tag, such as the **<b>** bold and **<a>** anchor (link) tags in a **<p>** tag. A block tag fills the width of the container and separates its content from other blocks above and below it, like paragraphs and headings. If you were to type your first and last name and place them separately in **<span>** tags, such as **<span>**Firstname**</span>** **<span>**Lastname**</span>**, the two words would appear beside each other on the same line. However, if you were to replace the **<span>** tags with **<div>** tags, your first and last names would appear on separate lines.

When you create a CSS layout, you must collect the major sections of the Web page into different containers using the **<div>** tag. For example, you may need to put the header, navigation bar, body content, and footer into separate **<div>** blocks. There are many circumstances that influence the number of **<div>**s you need. For example, if your footer contains just one block, such as a paragraph, you don't need to surround it with a **<div>**. One way to look at the requirement for **<div>**s is to think about the layout in terms of table cells. This is especially easy if you are converting the layout from a tables-based layout to a CSS-based layout. Just like tables, if you have two blocks in a single row, you need to surround each block with **<div>**s (like table cells), and then surround a collection of **<div>**s with another **<div>** (as table rows encapsulate table cells).

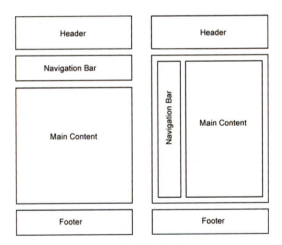

FIGURE 3.4

Separate Content into Divisions

In this exercise, you surround different sections of content with **`<div>`** tags. You then save the file with a different file name. In doing so, you set up the beginning of two parallel layouts that you construct in the next few exercises, using the same HTML structure. Remember, if a section of content contains just one block, it is not always necessary to surround it with an additional **`<div>`** tag.

1 Define the Project_03>GMMS folder as a site called GMMS. Do not click Done — leave the Site Definition dialog box open for the next step.

2 Remove all other sites from the list (except the GMMS site you defined in Step 1). Click Done when finished.

3 Open index.html and examine the content.

At the top is a header graphic followed by a list of links that later become the navigation bar, a heading-1 title, a group of graphics, the rest of the body content with some headings and decorative images, and a footer with the copyright and a contact-us link.

4 Press Control/Command-A to select all of the content.

5 Switch the Insert bar to Layout Insert bar and click the Insert Div Tag button.

6 Type body in the ID field, ensure Insert is set to Wrap Around Selection, and click OK. Click anywhere in the Document window to deselect.

FIGURE 3.5

7 Click the GMMS header graphic, and, using the same procedures as in Step 6, surround it with a div that has an id of header.

8 With the image still selected, in the Tag selector Right/Control-click the `<p>` tag and choose Remove Tag.

Both the **`<div>`** and **`<p>`** tags are block tags. It is not necessary to use both in this case, although in other situations it may be necessary.

FIGURE 3.6

9   Click in the unordered list of links, Right/Control-click the `<ul>` tag in the Tag selector, choose Edit Tag, type (with the aid of Code Hints) `id="navbar"`, and press Enter/Return.

FIGURE 3.7

10   Click to the left of Introduction. Scroll down to the bottom of the page and Shift-click to the right of August 2003. Wrap the selection with a `<div>` tag with the id of `content`.

11   Click in the last paragraph with the copyright, and then click the `<p>` tag in the Tag selector. Using the same procedures as in Step 6, wrap the selection in a `<div>` with the id of `footer` and then remove the `<p>` tag.

12   Save the changes to index.html, and keep it open for the next exercise.

LESSON 2   Understanding the CSS Box Model

The **CSS box model** describes how the width, height, content, padding, border, and margin work with each other. Each has an effect on the dimensions of a particular element, but their domains within the dimensions are different.

Using the example of an image which is 200 × 200 pixels, the content is 200 pixels in width by 200 pixels in height. The next layer outside of the content is padding. If you add 10 pixels in padding, the total dimensions taken by the `<img>` tag is 220 × 220 pixels (10+200+10). A background image or background color appears within the padding, but not outside of it. The border surrounds the padding: adding a 5-pixel border to this image, increasing the total dimensions to 230 × 230 pixels (5+10+200+10+5). Finally, the margin surrounds the border, and if a 20-pixel margin is added, the total dimensions would be increased to 270 × 270 pixels (20+5+10+200+10+5+20). Any background applied to the `<img>` tag does not appear in the margin: the margin is transparent and would show the background of the element behind it, such as the paragraph, table cell, or body.

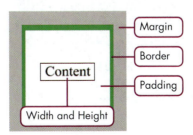

FIGURE 3.8

You can specify all padding, borders, and margins for all sides of an element, or just for specific sides. Their dimensions may be specified in pixels, points (for print style sheets), or ems. Other units of measurement are allowed, such as inches or percentages, but either they don't make sense (inches for on-screen display) or they have inconsistent browser support (percentages). Width and height can also use the same units of measurement, but although percentage may be used for width with reasonable support, measuring the height as a percentage has inconsistent support.

Margin may also be specified as auto, which means that whatever space exists between the element and its container is filled with margin space. This option can be used to center an element within its container, such as a table. If you apply center to the table, the contents of the table are centered, not the table itself. If you apply center to the body with the intent of centering the table, the table will be centered, but so will every element in the table — every paragraph, every heading, and every cell. Using auto margins does not cascade the centering to every element within; it just applies to the current element. However, in order for auto margins to apply, the element must have a fixed dimension. For example, if you have a table in the body of a Web page, you must specify a table width, such as 400 pixels. When you apply auto margins to the left and right of the table, the table is centered in the body.

Create and Attach the Common Style Sheet

In this exercise, you create a common style sheet that will contain the common styles of both layouts.

1   **Make sure index.html is open (from the previous lesson).**

2   **Right/Control-click the CSS Styles panel, and create a new style for the body selector. Set Design In to New Style Sheet File and, in the file name field, type styles.css.**

3   **Set the Font to Arial, Helvetica, sans-serif; the text Color to #436336; the Background Color to #405E33; and click OK.**

4   **Create a new CSS style for the div#body selector (Advanced) in the styles.css file. Set the background color to white and click OK.**

FIGURE 3.9

5   **Leave index.html open for the next exercise.**

Set the Widths of the Body Divs

In this exercise, you set the width and position of the body **<div>**s.

1   **With index.html open, click the GMMS logo graphic.**

Note that its width is 730 pixels.

2   **Right/Control-click the CSS Styles panel and edit the div#body style. In the Box category, set the Width to 730 pixels and click OK.**

3   **Click the Document Window Site button in the bottom-right corner of the Document window and make note of the 800 × 600 maximized dimensions.**

FIGURE 3.10

The difference between the width of the GMMS header graphic and the browser window is 30 pixels, allowing us to work with as much as 15 pixels on either side of the body div.

4   **Edit the body style rule. In the Box category, set all padding to 0 pixels and all margins to 10 pixels. Click OK.**

5   **Edit the div#body style rule. In the Border category, create a solid, 5-pixel black border around all sides. In the Box category, uncheck Same for All for Margins, and set both Right and Left margins to auto. Click OK.**

FIGURE 3.11

6   **Preview the page in your browser. Increase and decrease the width of the browser window.**

As long as the browser window is 760 pixels or more in width, the body div remains centered in the browser window.

7   **Return to Dreamweaver, but leave index.html open for the next exercise.**

To Extend Your Knowledge

WEB ACCESSIBILITY TOOLBAR

The Web Accessibility toolbar for Internet Explorer (nils.org.au/ais/web/resources/toolbar/) primarily focuses on helping Web-site developers test and validate their pages for accessibility and other W3C standards. It has the added benefit, however, of a browser-window resize function in which developers can preview their pages in a browser window set to 640 × 480, 800 × 600, 1024 × 768, or any custom size. Be aware that some of the functions of the toolbar are displayed in a pop-up window: if you have the Google toolbar or any other pop-up blocker installed, some functions of the accessibility toolbar may be blocked. To use any of these pop-up features with the Google toolbar installed, press the Control key when selecting that pop-up function — this allows the pop-up window to open and the function to work as designed. A similar extension has been developed for the Mozilla browsers called the "Web Developer extension." Both toolbars are quite similar in function (although developed by different people) and should be one of the required tools of Web developers.

Experiment with Padding and Margin

In this exercise, you see the differences between padding and margin with respect to the relative position of the border and the background color.

1   **In index.html, create a new CSS style for the h1, h2 selector. In the Background category, set the Background Color to #BED6B4. In the Border category, create a Top border (only) that is solid, 1 pixel thick, with a color of #405E33. Click Apply (not OK).**

FIGURE 3.12

2   In the Box category, uncheck Same for All for margins, and set both the Top and Left margins to **50** pixels. Click Apply.

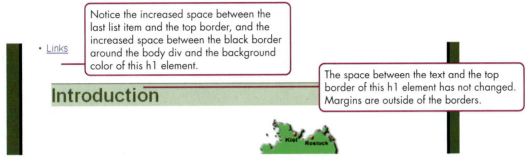

Notice the increased space between the last list item and the top border, and the increased space between the black border around the body div and the background color of this h1 element.

• Links

The space between the text and the top border of this h1 element has not changed. Margins are outside of the borders.

Introduction

FIGURE 3.13

3   In the Box category, reset the Margin settings, uncheck Same for All for Padding, and set Top Padding to **5** pixels and left padding to **10** pixels. Click OK.

Introduction

Padding left and top increase the distance to the top border and to the left edge. The background fills in the padding area.

FIGURE 3.14

4   Scroll down to the bottom of the page and click in the footer div. Create a new CSS style for the `div#footer` selector. In the Background category, set the Background Color to **#BED6B4**. In the Border category, create a Top border (only) that is solid, **1** pixel thick, with a color of **#405E33**. In the Box category, set both Top and Bottom Padding to **20** pixels. Click OK.

August 2003

© GMMS 2000 - 2004
Contact Us

FIGURE 3.15

5   Create a new CSS style for the **p** selector. Set both Left and Right Padding to **10** pixels. Click OK.

6   Keep Dreamweaver and index.html open for the next exercise.

To Extend Your Knowledge

CSS HACKS

Although the box model seems fairly simple to understand, unfortunately, Internet Explorer 5.x for Windows does not render the box model correctly. IE5.x takes the width measurement and then measures the margin, border, and padding inside the dimensions. According to IE5.x, the total width (and height) in the example given in the lesson lead-in would be 200 pixels with a 20-pixel margin, a 5-pixel border, a 10-pixel padding, allowing the content only 130 pixels space: 130 = 200-(2×20 pixels margin)-(2×5 pixels border)-(2×10 pixels margin). If you were designing only for IE5.x, you could easily fix this by changing the width to 270, but any other recent browser, including IE6 for Windows or IE5.2 for Macintosh, interpret the box model correctly, creating a discrepancy between the size of the element in IE5.x and the other browsers.

Commonly, designers deal with this by employing one of the many **CSS hacks**, CSS tricks to fool different browsers into displaying various CSS properties correctly. All current browsers display many CSS properties and values correctly and consistently, such as background colors and fonts. However, some CSS properties are misinterpreted and others are not supported at all. Some misinterpretations may be corrected using hacks. Some CSS misinterpretations cannot be corrected so hacks are created to hide the misinterpreted CSS from the offending browser. Some CSS properties are not displayed at all by some browsers, so the designer must either accept the deficiency or use JavaScript to create the effect. IE7 is JavaScript by Dean Edwards (dean.edwards.name/IE7) created to fix some deficiencies in the Internet Explorer (5+) browsers.

To hack or not to hack is the decision of the designer. To consider the use of CSS hacks requires that the designer know and understand CSS, which browsers have CSS deficiencies, what these deficiencies are, and finally, how to apply these hacks. Some hacks fix one browser but cause problems in another. Unfortunately, there is no single book or Web site that documents all of the browser issues and the hacks that you can use to fix them.

LESSON 3   Using List Properties

CSS list properties apply only to ordered (numbered) and unordered (bullet) lists, not to definition lists. You may change the bullets by selecting from **square**, **circle** (open), or **disc** (closed circle). You may change the numbering style to **decimal** (1, 2, 3, …), **upper-roman** (I, II, III, …), **lower-roman** (i, ii, iii, …), **upper-alpha** (A, B, C, …), **lower-alpha** (a, b, c, …), or **none**, which displays nothing. This CSS property is called **list-style-type**. You can style an unordered list to use a numbering style and visa versa, although that would be considered a misuse of CSS.

Lists may also use graphic bullets instead of the text-character bullets through the **list-style-image** property. However, you cannot use other characters, such as the French quotation marks »: if you want to use this or any other character, use a graphics application to make a screen capture of the character and create a graphic from it. Recognize that you cannot assign alternate text to graphic bullets. Adding a NEW graphic bullet to a list item to indicate a new product may provide information to sighted users but without alternative text, this information is unavailable to people who use screen readers. You may use decorative graphics, such as a photo of a mosquito against a list item that discusses West Nile virus, as long as the photo is not critical to the understanding of the text content.

Generally, you assign the same bullet, counter, or graphic to all list items in the list. You do this by assigning the list property to the `<ul>` or `<ol>` tag. Nested lists inherit the same property, so if you want the nested list to use a different style, use a descendent selector, such as **ul ul**, to style the nested list differently. However, you may also assign list styles to individual list items through classes or ids.

Restyle the Navigation-Bar List

In this exercise, you restyle the navigation-bar list. You don't change the underlying HTML structure — it is still an unordered list of links — but through styles, you can reshape the appearance of the list.

1 In the open file, index.html, create a new CSS style for the `ul#navbar` selector. In the Background category, set the Background Color to **#BED6B4** and click Apply.

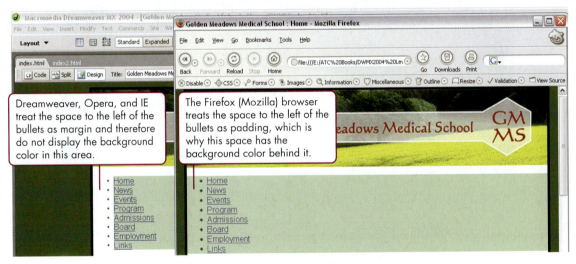

FIGURE 3.16

2 In the Box category, set the width to 150 pixels and click Apply. Also, in the Box category, set all padding and all margins to 0 pixels and click Apply.

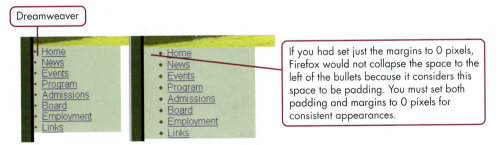

FIGURE 3.17

3   In the Border category, uncheck Same for All, and create a top border that is solid, **3** pixels thick, with a color of **#405E33**. Create a bottom border that is solid, **2** pixels thick, with a color of **#405E33**. Click Apply.

In a later exercise, you will create a bottom border for all of the links that will be 1 pixel thick. The bottom border of the last link (1 pixel) will add to the bottom border of this list, creating a 3-pixel bottom border.

FIGURE 3.18

4   In the List category, set Type to none and click OK.

FIGURE 3.19

5   Keep both index.html and Dreamweaver open for the next exercise.

To Extend Your Knowledge

NAVIGATION BARS ARE JUST LISTS

For the most part, navigation bars are just lists of links, whether or not they have been formatted as such. Using the methods shown here, you see that it is very possible to completely redesign the look of an unordered list of links into a more familiar navigation-bar appearance. In fact, by creating a style in which the `li` element uses `display: inline`, the individual list items don't fall below one another but in a line across the Web page, enabling you to create a horizontal navigation bar from an unordered list. Add background images, such as folder tabs, and you have a completely unique navigation bar just by styling an unordered list.

LESSON 4   Changing the Display Type

We discussed the terms inline and block previously — inline means that an element is enclosed in a block, and block means that it fills the full width of the container and separates its contents from surrounding block elements. In the previous exercise, despite the fact that the unordered list was narrowed to 150 pixels and the text of the heading-1 element can fit to its right, because both lists and headings are blocks, they still separate their contents from each other vertically.

The CSS display property allows you to change an inline element to a block element and a block element to an inline element. There are more display-property values than these — **list-items**, **table-cells**, **table-rows**, and many others. Unfortunately, most browsers do not support them or don't support them well. (It's a pity, as there are be many useful applications of **table-cell**.)

Demonstrate Inline Display

In this exercise, you see an example of transforming a block element so it displays as an inline element. In this exercise, you change h2 and the following paragraph both into inline elements. It is not enough to change just the h2 element, because the following paragraph remains a block element and will force the h2 element away from the paragraph block. There are other ways of creating a similar effect, but this one is sufficient to demonstrate the change in display.

1   **In the open index.html file, create a new CSS style using the selector h2, h2+p.**

2   **In the Background category, set the Background Color to white (#FFFFFF). In the Box category, set the Left Padding to 0 pixels and the Right Padding to 10 pixels. In the Border category, set the Top border to none. In the Block category, set Display to inline and click OK.**

3   **Scroll down to the Research heading and paragraph.**

The paragraphs above and below are unaffected because the **h2+p** selector applies only to the paragraph immediately following the h2 element. Therefore the paragraphs above and below keep their block formatting and separate themselves from the inline paragraph (**h2+p**) between them. IE cannot display this style rule because IE does not understand the adjacent selector (+), but if the paragraph used a class or id selector, it would display the effect properly, as shown in the following graphic.

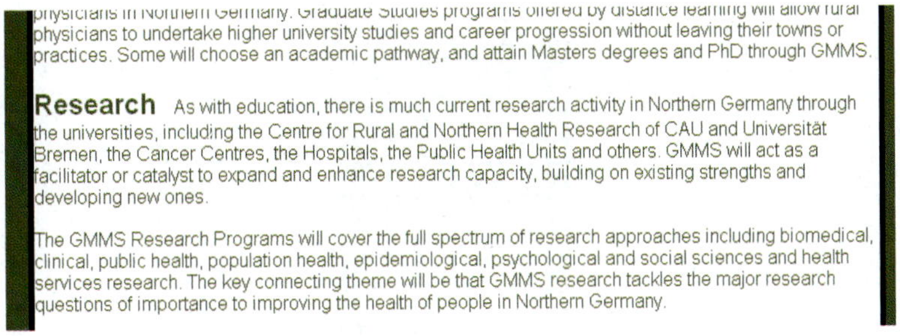

FIGURE 3.20

4   **Right/Control-click the h2, h2+p rule in the CSS Styles panel and delete it.**

5   **Keep Dreamweaver and index.html open for the next exercise.**

Change the Display of the Anchor Element

In this exercise, you change the display of anchor text from inline to block. Normally, anchor text is inline, commonly in the block of a paragraph. By changing it to block, it then fills the width of the container: the container in this case is the list-item tag. This increases the clickable area of the link to the full width of the list-item tag. List-item tags are block tags and normally fill the width of the unordered (or ordered) list tags. Now the anchor tag will fill the width of the list-item tag.

1   In the open index.html file, create a new CSS style based on the `ul#navbar a` selector.

2   In the Type category, set Decoration to none. In the Border category, create a bottom (only) border that is solid, 1 pixel thick, with a color of #405E33. Click Apply.

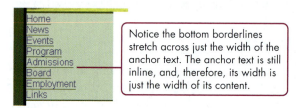

Notice the bottom borderlines stretch across just the width of the anchor text. The anchor text is still inline, and, therefore, its width is just the width of its content.

FIGURE 3.21

3   In the Block category, set Display to block and click Apply.

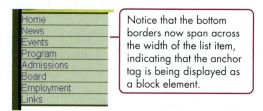

Notice that the bottom borders now span across the width of the list item, indicating that the anchor tag is being displayed as a block element.

FIGURE 3.22

4   In the Type category, set the Color to #405E33, and set Weight to bold. In the Block category, set Text Align to center. In the Box category, set the Height to 20 pixels, and set both Left and Right Padding to 2 pixels. In the Border category, create a Right (only) border that is solid, 3 pixels in thickness, with a color of #405E33. Click OK.

FIGURE 3.23

5   Keep index.html open for the next exercise.

Swap Padding and Border Space

In this exercise, you learn a technique for highlighting a link when the mouse pointer is over it using the **:hover** pseudo-class. The technique thickens the right and left borders. If you were to try this technique without fully understanding how it works, by adding a border to the left and right, you would increase the total width of the anchor block, shifting the contents to the right (to make room for the new border on the left). To create this effect properly, you steal some width from the padding and add it to the border. For example, 2-pixel padding + 150-pixel content width + 2-pixel padding (154 pixels) is the same as 2-pixel border + 150-pixel content width + 2-pixel border (154 pixels). By swapping padding space for border space, the total width remains the same but the thicknesses of the padding and border change. This technique could also be applied using margin space — just always add up the total padding+border+margin space and ensure that the total remains the same.

1   In the open index.html page, create a new CSS style for the `ul#navbar a:hover` selector.

2   In the Background category, set the Background Color to **#E7EFE2**. In the Box category, set both Left and Right Padding to **0** pixels. In the Border category, create a Right border that is solid, **5** pixels thick, with a color of **#405E33**, and a Left border that is solid, **2** pixels thick, with a color of **#405E33**. Click OK.

The original right border was 3 pixels in thickness. Adding the 2 pixels borrowed from the padding creates a 5-pixel thick right border. There was no left border, so the 2 pixels of padding were borrowed to create a 2-pixel left border.

3   Preview the page in your browser and note the thickening of the border as the mouse pointer hovers over the links.

FIGURE 3.24

4   Keep index.html open for the next exercise.

LESSON 5 Floating Content

When you choose right or left alignment for images, text wraps around it on the opposite side. Left and right alignment of images can be replaced with the **float** property of CSS, but float is not limited to just images. As with virtually all CSS, almost any element may be floated. Unlike images that are inline elements, block elements may also be floated. Divs and paragraphs may be floated without converting their display to inline.

Float the Navigation Bar

In this exercise, you float the navigation bar that causes the heading and paragraph text below to wrap around it.

1 In the open index.html file, edit the ul#navbar style. In the Box category, set Float to left and click OK.

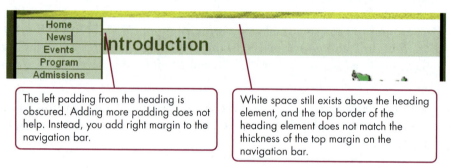

FIGURE 3.25

The left padding from the heading is obscured. Adding more padding does not help. Instead, you add right margin to the navigation bar.

White space still exists above the heading element, and the top border of the heading element does not match the thickness of the top margin on the navigation bar.

2 Create a new CSS style for the h1 selector. In the Box category, set the Top Margin to 0 pixels. In the Border category, create a Top border that is solid, 3 pixels in thickness, with a color of #405E33. Click OK.

3 Edit the ul#navbar style rule. In the Box category, uncheck Same for All for margins. Leave the Top, Bottom, and Left margins set at 0 pixels, but change Right to 10 pixels, and click OK.

FIGURE 3.26

4 Click the left graphic of the group of four (Universitat Bremen) and then Shift-click the map graphic. Wrap the selection with a <div> tag with the id of images.

5 Right/Control-click the <p> tag in the Tag selector and remove it.

6   Create a new CSS style for the `div#images` selector. In the Box category, set the Width to **184** pixels and Float to right. Click OK.

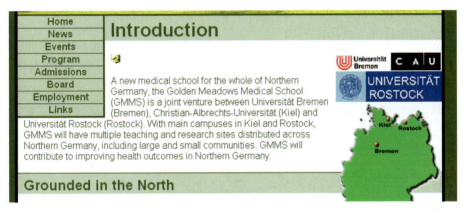

FIGURE 3.27

7   Create two new CSS styles for the selectors `img.left` and `img.right`. Set `img.left` with the Float property set to left and `img.right` with the Float property set to right.

8   Right/Control-click the photos, and choose either CSS Styles>left or CSS Styles>right to apply the left class to the first (surgery photo) and last (Dr. Sandra Werner) photos, and the right class to the middle montage photo.

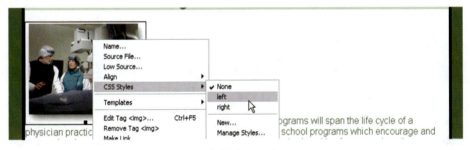

FIGURE 3.28

9   Save the changes to index.html, leaving it open for the next exercise.

Add Final Touches to the Web Page

In this exercise, you add the last couple of styles to finish the design of the Web page.

1   In the open index.html file, scroll to the bottom of the page and click in the signature block of text.

2   Create a new CSS style for the `p.signature` selector. In the Type category, set Style to italic. In the Block category, set Text Align to right. Click OK.

3   With the insertion point in the signature block, Right/Control-click the <p> tag in the Tag selector and set the class to signature.

| 4 | Right/Control-click the div#footer selector in the CSS Style panel and choose Edit. In the Block category, set Text Align to center and click OK. |

Dr. Sandra Werner, Founding Dean
Golden Meadows Medical School
August 2003

© GMMS 2000 - 2004
Contact Us

FIGURE 3.29

| 5 | Save the changes to index.html but leave it open for the next exercise. |

To Extend Your Knowledge

FLOATING LAYOUTS

The layout method used so far simply positions a couple of elements, and, in the case of the navigation bar, floats other elements. The float option is commonly used for creating CSS layouts and is very easy to apply. Furthermore, this technique can be extended to create 2- and 3-column layouts that are commonplace on many commercial Web sites. You float the left column to the left and the right column to the right, and the content appears between them.

LESSON 6   Working with Alternate Layout Methods

There are three basic methods for creating CSS layouts: fixed, fluid (also called "liquid"), and elastic. With each method, there are pros and cons. A fixed layout is suitable for a rigid design, but can cause some problems with usability and accessibility if the design is too rigid. Fluid and elastic layouts are, as their names suggest, more flexible, but can create challenges if you take a rigid design and format it using one of these methods. People who support accessibility tend to employ either of the flexible methods of layout.

A *fixed layout* is one in which the components of the page are given specific widths, such as the navigation bar is 150 pixels wide and the main content is 550 pixels wide. As users increase or decrease the width of their browsers, the width of the layout does not change. The advantage of this method of layout is that the design can be easier to create and the design and layout remain consistent at any browser width. The disadvantage is that if the fixed width is too wide for some smaller computer screens, the user is forced to scroll back and forth to read the content.

Liquid layouts are those in which the widths of the components of the page are relative to the width of the browser window — as the browser window increases or decreases, the layout increases or decreases with it. Liquid layouts use percentage as the unit of measurement of the widths of the components of the page. The advantage of this type of layout is that it supports all browser widths, from displays as large as 1600 × 1200 to cell phones. The disadvantage of this type of layout is that in a medium-width browser, such as 1000 pixels wide, one paragraph might be 3-4 lines long, but in a wider browser window, it might only be 1-2 lines long, creating a strange appearance. Another disadvantage is that studies have shown that reading wide paragraphs is harder than reading narrower paragraphs, so a person with a large, high-resolution monitor may not read as well as someone with a smaller one. This assumes, of course, that the person with the large monitor has set the width of the browser window to the full width of the monitor.

An *elastic layout* is one in which the width of the layout depends on the size of the fonts. This method requires that the widths be specified in em units. This layout method has the advantage of changing width in response to the user's text-size settings. All current browsers allow users to change their-text size settings — in IE, choose View>Text Size; in Mozilla, choose View>Increase (Decrease) Text Size. As the size of the text changes, so does the width of the layout, which means that the number of lines each paragraph takes does not change as the layout width increases or decreases. This layout method is one of the most accessible methods of layout in that it mimics a magnifying glass, enabling users with poor vision to enlarge both the text size and the layout size. However, care must be taken when using this layout method to prevent enlarged text size from increasing the layout width so that users are forced to scroll back and forth to read the content. The disadvantage of this method is that certain designs may not flow well when the layout is resized. When selecting this method, designers must be aware of the resizing issue, and test and account for it in their design.

A *hybrid layout* is one that combines two or even all three methods. For example, the navigation bar may be elastic in width, the content area may be liquid, the right column containing advertising may be fixed, and the total width may be liquid. This is a very common method of using CSS for layout and can often be used to meet two goals at the same time — fixed components maintain the design and flexible components support usability and accessibility.

There are two changes users can make that can affect the layout and design of the page. They may resize their browser width. If either the fixed or elastic method was employed, a narrow browser width may cut off part of the page. You must design and test these layouts using a narrower browser width, such as 760 pixels. (Remember, you learned earlier that the width of a maximized browser window at an 800 × 600 screen resolution is 760 pixels.) Another change users may make is altering their browser's text size. A fixed layout width may encounter problems with this because if the navigation bar is a fixed width and the text size is increased, the link text in the navigation bar wraps to a second line, possibly creating design problems. A designer may prevent this from happening by setting text sizes using a fixed unit of measurement, such as points, but this prevents users from resizing the text if they need larger text sizes for reading properly. An elastic layout may encounter problems if the user enlarges the text too much and the layout flows outside of the browser window. However, you can combine the CSS property, `max-width` (unfortunately, not supported by IE), with an elastic layout to limit the expansion of the layout.

As with any aspect of CSS, users have ultimate control. Most browsers support a user style sheet with which the users may override any or all of the CSS styles you create. Most, if not all, sighted users do not use user style sheets, but users with color blindness or poor vision may choose to override some or all CSS styles with their own. As a result, you, the designer, must recognize that your Web page designs using CSS may not be visible to everyone exactly as you designed them. But as long as the HTML document is sound, the primary information of the Web page will be available to everyone, whatever the design. Therefore, the more you employ CSS for layouts (and fewer tables), the easier it is for users to apply their own style sheets for their own needs.

Modify Layout to Elastic Method

In this exercise, you modify the layout and change the body div from a fixed-width layout to an elastic-width layout, in which changes in text size change the width of the layout.

1   **In the open file, index.html, edit the div#body style rule. In the Box category, change the Width from 730 pixels to 45.6 ems and click OK.**

Browsers, by default, equate 1 em = 16 pixels = 12 points. By dividing 730 pixels by 16 pixels/em, the result is 45.625 ems. The rounding error of 0.025 ems is equal to 0.4 pixels; too small to worry about.

2   **Preview the page in your browser.**

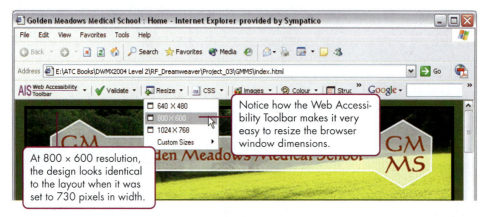

FIGURE 3.30

3   **Increase the width of the browser window.**

❓ If you have problems

Depending on the resolution of your computer monitor, you may not be able to increase the browser-window size. Use these figures as an indication of what happens when the width of the browser window is increased.

FIGURE 3.31

4 Increase the text size by choosing View>Text Size>Larger in IE or View>Increase Text Size in Mozilla.

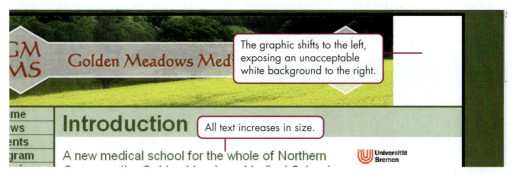

The graphic shifts to the left, exposing an unacceptable white background to the right.

All text increases in size.

FIGURE 3.32

5 Return to Dreamweaver.

6 Create a new CSS style for the `div#header` selector. In the Background category, set the Background Color to black. In the Block category, set Text Align to center. Click OK.

7 Preview the page in your browser.

Although this greatly improves the appearance of the header image, other design options are available, such as a background graphic.

FIGURE 3.33

8 Decrease the text size by two steps (choose Smaller in IE or choose Decrease twice in Mozilla).

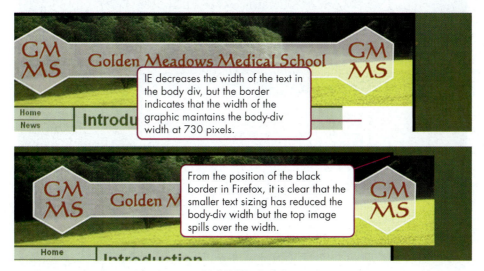

IE decreases the width of the text in the body div, but the border indicates that the width of the graphic maintains the body-div width at 730 pixels.

From the position of the black border in Firefox, it is clear that the smaller text sizing has reduced the body-div width but the top image spills over the width.

FIGURE 3.34

9 Return to Dreamweaver.

10 Edit the div#body style. In the Positioning category, set Overflow to hidden and click OK.

11 Preview the page in your browser.

Setting overflow to hidden hides content, in this case an image, if the width of the content is too wide for the container. Text normally wraps, even if overflow is set to hidden, but if the width of the paragraph has been set wider than its container, overflowing text is hidden.

FIGURE 3.35

12 Return to Dreamweaver but leave index.html open for the next exercise.

Create a Liquid Layout

In this exercise, you modify the body-div layout to a liquid layout that is based on a percentage of the browser-window width. In fact, because the navigation bar remains the same width, set to 150 pixels, this layout is a hybrid layout.

1 In the open file, index.html, edit the div#body style. In the Box category, change the Width to **97.4** % and click OK.

Dividing 730 pixels (content width) by 760 pixels (average width of a 800-pixel-wide browser window) equals 97.4%.

2 Preview the page in your browser.

FIGURE 3.36

3   Reset the text size to normal by increasing its size by one step.

Despite the change in text size, the width of the layout did not change, indicating that text size does not affect fluid layouts.

FIGURE 3.37

4   Increase and decrease the width of the browser window.

In these two screen shots at different widths, the width of the body div obviously expands and contracts with the width of the browser window. The overflow: hidden property also hides some of the image if the browser width is too narrow.

FIGURE 3.38

5   Return to Dreamweaver but leave index.html open for the next exercise.

To Extend Your Knowledge

PULL QUOTES

Pull quotes are excerpts taken from the body of the content and highlighted to emphasize a point. Pull quotes are commonly formatted with larger text, placed in a box, and positioned to the left or the right of the column of text. In a previous exercise, you took a group of figures, surrounded them with a `<div>` tag, and floated the block to the right. You could use the same technique to float a block of text. With text, however, you may want to add more styling, such as font size and color, and perhaps a border and a background color or image. Given that, at times, you may want to create more then one pull quote in a page, you should create a class rather than an id as the CSS selector.

LESSON 7   Scrolling Content

The CSS overflow property has three useful options: hidden, auto, and scroll. You saw the effect of the hidden option on a header graphic — if it is too wide for the body div, the excess or overflow is hidden. The auto and scroll options of the overflow property hide the excess, as well, but the browser provides one or two scroll bars, which enable the user to access the overflow content. The scroll option is like the **scrolling="yes"** option for frames: both scroll bars are always visible, whether needed or not. The auto option displays one or both scroll bars only when needed. This feature is often used on Web sites that demonstrate programming, HTML, or any other code. Rather than occupying large amounts of Web-page space, especially if there are instances of displaying code multiple times, setting the height of the code block along with the overflow auto option, for example, **div.code {height: 5em; overflow: auto;}**, makes the code available without requiring as much space.

Display the Navigation Bar with a Scroll Bar

In this exercise, you modify the navigation bar to create a scrolling navigation bar. When you use the hidden, auto, or scroll overflow options, you must specify the size of the container so that the browser knows when content is too large for the container. You must also take into account the height and width of the scroll bars, which amount to approximately 20 pixels.

1   **In the open file, index.html, edit the ul#navbar style. In the Positioning category, set the Height to 60 pixels, the Width to 170 pixels, Overflow to auto, and click OK.**

2   **Preview the page in your browser and scroll through the navigation bar.**

FIGURE 3.39

3   **Return to Dreamweaver and close index.html.**

To Extend Your Knowledge

FRAMES WITHOUT FRAMES

You may use the overflow: auto (or scroll) property to create a framelike appearance of a complete Web page. As indicated previously, you must specify the dimensions of the div container so that the browser knows when the content exceeds its dimensions. However, setting the height of the container to 100% of the browser window has its drawbacks: padding, borders, and margins increase the height of the element to greater than 100%, so all of these must be set to 0 (0, zero, in any units is zero). Furthermore, IE misinterprets 100% height as 100% of the height of the content, not 100% of the browser window. However, if you specify a browser-window height, such as 420 pixels, for a maximized 800 × 600 screen resolution, it will be too tall for a 640 × 480 monitor and tiny on a 1600 × 1200 monitor. Even for an 800 × 600 monitor, if the user has installed the Google, Accessibility, or any other additional toolbar, the available height is even less. Overflow scroll works best when you can specify the exact dimensions of the container.

LESSON 8   Creating Layouts Using Dreamweaver Layers

Dreamweaver's layers feature has multiple uses — to create a CSS layout, convert a CSS layout to a tables-based layout, and use with **DHTML** (Dynamic HTML, JavaScript that creates dynamic effects). In fact, despite the feature's name, layers are just absolutely positioned **<div>** tags. CSS has seven properties that deal with positioning: **position** (with which you identify the method of positioning); **left**, **right**, **top**, **bottom** (used to identify the position of the div); and **width** and **height**. You don't have to use all of these properties. For instance, you can use just **left** and **top**, if you want to indicate the top-left corner of the **<div>**, along with the type of positioning you want to use.

There are three options for the **position** property: **absolute**, **relative**, and **fixed**. Absolute and relative appear in the options for position in the Positioning category of the CSS Styles dialog box, but fixed does not. Dreamweaver and IE do not support fixed positioning, although Dean Edward's IE7 script does provide a JavaScript solution that enables IE to support fixed positioning. While this lesson focuses on Dreamweaver layers, which generally use absolute positioning, you may also use positioning options on images, paragraphs, headings, or any other HTML element. Commonly, positioning is used for layout and CSS layout uses the **<div>** tag.

Absolute positioning specifies the position of the element relative to the Web page. With an absolute position of **top: 0; left: 0;**, the element appears at the top-left corner of the Web page. If you scroll the Web page, the absolutely positioned element scrolls up and down with the movement of the Web page.

Relative positioning takes into account the current position of the element and enables you to shift the location of the element. For example, **p {position: relative; left: 10px;}** shifts the left edge of paragraphs 10 pixels to the right (whereas left: -10px shifts the paragraph to the left). Be aware, however, that the width of the element is not changed and shifting the element may push it outside of its container.

Fixed positioning is similar to absolute positioning, but instead of being relative to the Web page, fixed positioning is relative to the browser window. Therefore, **div#navbar {position: fixed; top: 10px; left: 10px;}** positions the navbar div 10 pixels down and 10 pixels to the left of the top-left corner of the browser window. Furthermore, when the Web page scrolls, this div does not change in position unless the browser itself is moved across the screen. Commonly, this is used to create a floating navigation bar that doesn't change position when the Web page scrolls, ensuring that it is always visible.

Absolutely positioned content can make it very easy to design a Web page: in Dreamweaver, you can drag the layer around the page and position it as you see fit. However, some components of a Web page do not work well with absolutely positioned elements. It is very difficult, for instance, to position a footer below absolutely positioned content because the length of the content div may be longer or shorter, depending on the content of the page.

The clear property has three values: **left**, **right**, and **both**. The purpose of the clear property is to force content to appear below floated content. In an earlier exercise, the heading-2 text, Grounded in the North, started above the bottom of the group of images. If the clear property were applied, there would be a lot of white space until the height of the image group was cleared, and then the heading-2 text would appear. If the content that must be cleared appears on the left, then you can use **clear: left**; otherwise, you would use **clear:**

right. The third option is **clear: both**, which forces the element below both left- and right-floated content. The clear option is not applied to the floated content but to the content that should appear below it. The clear property won't be needed until a later exercise.

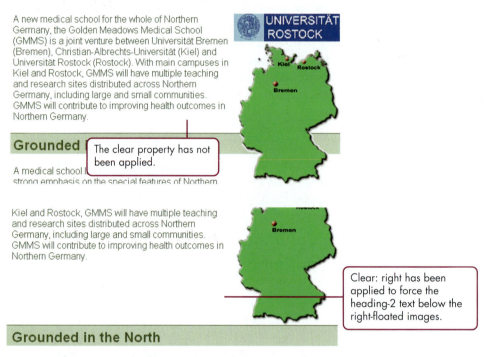

FIGURE 3.40

Create a Layer

In this exercise, you create a layout based on absolutely positioned layers.

1 Create a new Web page and save it (but do not close it) with the filename layers.html.

2 Switch the Insert bar to the Layout Insert bar, and click the Draw Layer button. In the Document window, drag to create a rectangle.

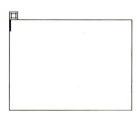

FIGURE 3.41

3   Move the mouse pointer over one of the boundary lines and, when the boundary turns red, click.

The layer handle allows you to drag the layer to another position.

Handles may be used to resize the layer.

FIGURE 3.42

4   With the layer selected, note the Property inspector.

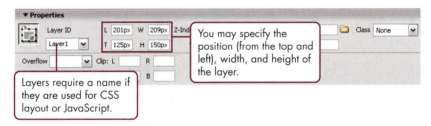

You may specify the position (from the top and left), width, and height of the layer.

Layers require a name if they are used for CSS layout or JavaScript.

FIGURE 3.43

5   Save the changes to index.html, and leave it open for the next exercise.

Populate Layers with Content

In this exercise, you copy content from index.html and paste it into the layers. You position the layers to create a similar layout to the one developed in earlier lessons.

1   In the Property inspector, delete Layer1 from the Layer ID field and type body. Set the Left field to 190px, the Top field to 165px, and the Width field to 580px.

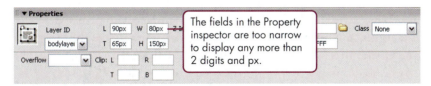

The fields in the Property inspector are too narrow to display any more than 2 digits and px.

FIGURE 3.44

2   Open index.html. Click to the left of Introduction, scroll down, Shift-click to the right of the Contact Us link, and copy the content to the clipboard.

3   Switch back to layers.html (but do not close index.html), and paste the content into the body layer.

4   In the CSS Styles panel, attach styles.css.

FIGURE 3.45

5   Edit the div#body style, remove all border style properties, and click OK.

6   Click the Draw Layer button and draw another layer. Click the layer handle; and, using the Property inspector, name the layer **nb**; and set Left to **40px**, Top to **165px**, and Width to **150px**.

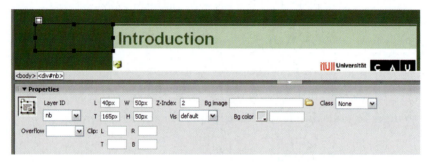

FIGURE 3.46

7   Switch to index.html and click in the navigation-bar unordered list. Click <ul#navbar> in the Tag selector and copy the contents to the clipboard.

8   Return to layers.html and paste the content into the newest layer.

9   Edit the ul#navbar style. In the Box category, set Width to **150** pixels, delete the Height setting, and set all margins to **0** pixels. In the Positioning category, delete the Height and Overflow settings, and ensure that Width is set to 150 pixels. Click OK.

10   Create a new layer above the other two, name it **hdr**, and set Left to **40px**, Top to **15px**, Width to **730px**, and Height to **150px**.

11 Insert the gmms.png image from the images folder into the newest layer.

FIGURE 3.47

12 Save the changes to layers.html, leaving it open.

Examine the Source Code

In this exercise, you examine the source code of the layers.

1 Click the GMMS header graphic and click the Code button to open the Code window.

Notice that despite the position of the header graphic at the top of the Document window, the code for the header appears last in the Code window.

```
61  <div id="hrd" style="position:absolute; left:40px; top:15px; width:730px; height:40px; z-index:3"><img src="images/gmms.png" width="730" height=
62  </body>
63  </html>
64
```

FIGURE 3.48

2 Examine the **<div>** tag that surrounds the **<img>** tag for the header graphic.

The **<div>** tag has a style attribute in which the position type, location, and dimensions of the layer are specified. This is an example of inline styles. If you were using layers to design a CSS layout, to ensure that every page used the same positioning information, you would remove the style information and re-create it in the external style-sheet file so that it would apply to every page.

3 Scroll up the Code window about 10 lines and notice the unordered list containing the navigation-bar code and the nb div surrounding it. Scroll up to the top of the document and locate the h1 element containing the word Introduction.

The source order of the content is the same order in which was created, but not necessarily in the same order as it appears on screen.

4 Switch back to the Design view.

5 Save the changes to layers.html

To Extend Your Knowledge

SOURCE ORDER VS. DISPLAY SPEED

Some designers change the source order of Web-page content to improve the speed at which Web content appears in the browser window. The concept is that if the body arrives before the header or navigation content, the user can start reading the body content while the other components of the page download. While this appears to be beneficial, source order can only be rearranged if the components of the Web page use absolute positioning. In the earlier exercises of this project, if the source order had been changed, then the layout also would have changed — the layout depended on the order of the source code. Given that absolutely positioned content can be more difficult to manage than floating content, source order may be more trouble to manage than it is worth. Furthermore, with the reduction in code that CSS layouts provide (compared with table layouts), the speed of download is dramatically increased and, therefore, pages load much faster anyway. Any improvement provided by source ordering may be much less significant than the improved download speed achieved by using CSS for layout rather than tables.

LESSON 9   Exporting Layers to a Table

Layout tables are one method of free-form creation of a table layout; layers is another method. Once you have created a layout using layers, you may then have Dreamweaver convert the layers-based layout to a tables-based layout simply with the click of a mouse button.

There are a couple of items to be aware of for this process. When positioning the layers, there may be spaces between components. You have the option of allowing Dreamweaver to create empty table cells where these spaces exist and inserting transparent images to keep these spaces apart. When table cells are empty, they collapse upon themselves. Many designers and their design software fill those empty cells with transparent GIFs whose widths are set to the size of the space.

Dreamweaver cannot convert a layers-based layout if layers overlap each other. Table cells are separate from each other and do not overlap. If layers overlap, Dreamweaver informs you that it cannot create tables from the layers because of these overlapping layers. The Layers panel has an option that prevent layers from overlapping, a beneficial option if your intent was to create a tables-based layout from the layers.

Explore Overlapping Layers

In this exercise, you learn how to use the Layers panel to work with layers.

1   **In the open file, layers.html, choose Window>Layers.**

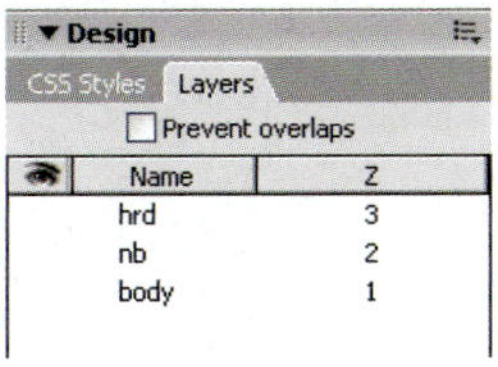

FIGURE 3.49

2   **Click in the text Introduction, click the layer handle, and drag the layer up and to the left so that the body layer partly covers the GMMS header graphic and the navigation bar.**

? If you have problems

If you cannot move the body layer over the other layers, check the Layers panel and ensure there is no check against the Prevent Overlaps checkbox. If there is a check, uncheck it and repeat Step 2.

FIGURE 3.50

3   **Press Control/Command-Z to undo the change.**

4   **In the Layers panel, check the Prevent Overlaps option.**

5   **Try to drag the body layer over the other two layers again.**

In this instance, you cannot overlap layers because of the prevent-overlapping option.

6   **Save the changes to layers.html.**

7   **Choose File>Save as and save the page as table.html.**

Although you may undo the conversion from layers to tables during your Dreamweaver session, you cannot undo it later. Converting a different file enables you to go back to the preconversion layers format at any time.

Convert from Layers to Tables

In this exercise, you convert the layers-based layout to a tables-based layout. Enabling the Prevent Overlaps option and checking it before the conversion ensures that the conversion proceeds successfully.

1   **In the open file, table.html, choose Modify>Convert>Layers to Table.**

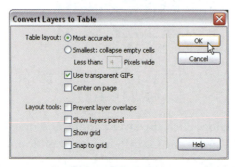

FIGURE 3.51

2   **Use the default settings, as shown in the preceding figure, and click OK.**

Note the table and cell borders, and the empty cells used to maintain the positions of the Web-page section.

FIGURE 3.52

3   **Switch to the Code view and scroll to the bottom of the code.**

```
73    <tr>
74      <td width="30" height="1" valign="top"><img src="transparent.gif" alt="" width="30" height="1"></td>
75      <td width="150" height="1" valign="top"><img src="transparent.gif" alt="" width="150" height="1"></td>
76      <td width="580" height="1" valign="top"><img src="transparent.gif" alt="" width="580" height="1"></td>
77    </tr>
78  </table>
79  </body>
80  </html>
```

The image, transparent.gif, is used three times with different widths. The widths prevent the cells from collapsing and maintain the cells' widths.

FIGURE 3.53

4   Return to the Design view and examine the Files panel.

The file, transparent.gif, was created by Dreamweaver and automatically saved in the site folder.

FIGURE 3.54

5   Close table.html, saving your changes.

To Extend Your Knowledge

PAGE WEIGHT OF TABLES-BASED LAYOUTS

You have read many times before that tables-based layouts cost more in terms of page weight than CSS-based layouts. In the previous exercise, not much weight was added to the code by converting it to a table layout because the number of layers was small and the complexity of the layout was quite simple. Other layouts could very well create much more table code and be of much greater consequence to some users on a slow Internet connection. Whether the table code is relatively small, as in this exercise, or much greater, tables still have the drawback of not displaying until all of the code is received. This delays the display of the page and creates the illusion of a slower connection speed than may be the case.

To Extend Your Knowledge

THE Z-INDEX

The z-index is a property of CSS that has a role when you design layouts, especially if you create layers using Dreamweaver. The z-index is a number that identifies the layering order of overlapping layers. Although the layout you created did not use overlapping layers, at times, overlapping layers may be appropriate for your design. Of course, you would have to ensure that the Prevent Overlaps option is not enabled. When layers overlap, the layer with the higher z-index is above layers with lesser numbers. The numbers do not need to be consecutive — you may use numbers in intervals of 10 or 100, if you wish. If you create a layout that does not use overlapping layers, you don't need the z-index, but Dreamweaver creates it anyway. If the layers do not overlap, the order specified by the z-index then has no effect.

LESSON 10   Using a Tracing Image

Tracing images are very beneficial to designers who use Photoshop or any other graphic-design software for creating a design or layout for their Web site. The designer may prefer to use these applications to create the final graphic layout or may simply create a base mockup of the site. In Dreamweaver, you can place a JPEG, GIF, or PNG of the mockup behind the page you are creating, then take the components of your design, place them in layers, and move them over the tracing image. It is much like working with tracing paper, creating the final layout over a mockup.

The tracing-image function in Dreamweaver has the added feature of adjusting the transparency. If the tracing image is set to full opacity, you cannot see how much of the mockup you have completed.

Just like design-time style sheets, the tracing-image function is just a Dreamweaver design feature that has no effect on the Web page. It does not matter if the tracing-image setting has or has not been deleted after use.

Rearrange Layers According to the Tracing Image

In this exercise, you apply a tracing image behind the layers page. You then rearrange the layers so that they match the tracing image behind it.

1   Open layers.html.

2   In the Property inspector, click the Page Properties button.

3   Choose the Tracing Image category, and browse to choose images>tracing-image.jpg. Drag the slider to set the opacity to 50% and click OK.

4   Uncheck the Prevent Overlaps option in the Layers panel. In the Document window, click in a layer and then, using the layer's handles, drag the layers to the right of the Document window so the tracing image can be seen.

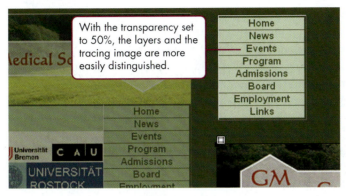

FIGURE 3.55

5   Enable the Prevent Overlaps option in the Layers panel.

6   Using the tracing image as a guide, arrange the layers in position.

7   Close layers.html, saving your changes.

To Extend Your Knowledge

AVOID USING INLINE STYLES

When you create layers in Dreamweaver, it stores the CSS properties inline, in the `<div>` tag. If you are using layers to design your layout and want to use the layers as the final form of the CSS-based layout, you must move the style declarations from the `<div>` tags to the style sheet. Without the style declaration in the style sheet, only the page or pages with the style declaration, i.e., layout information, in the `<div>` tags use the layout you created as you arranged and configured the layers.

There are two methods of moving the style declaration to the style sheet. The first method is to record (or print) the style declaration, create the selector using the id of the `<div>` tag, and then, following the recorded information, re-create the style settings in the CSS Styles dialog box. You can then delete the `style` attribute from the `<div>` tags. An alternative method is to open the Code window and copy the style declaration from the `style` attribute of the `<div>` tag. You then open the style-sheet file, manually create the selector, and paste the style declaration between curly braces {}.

When creating layers, Dreamweaver can use more style properties than are needed. For example, when you draw a layer, it is assigns all of `top`, `left`, `width`, and `height`. The GMMS header graphic does not need the `width` attribute because the `<div>` tag expands to enclose it, so you can safely delete it. The navbar and content divs, however, do need a width, but they don't need the `height` attribute, so you can delete it from the style declaration for these divs. In the GMMS layout, none of the divs overlap (especially if you enable the Prevent Overlaps option), and, therefore, you can safely delete the `z-index` property from all three div style rules.

SUMMARY

In this project you learned that the `<div>` tag is the primary means of separating sections or divisions in the document for layout. You learned about the CSS box model and how width, height, padding, borders, and margins interact with each other. You learned about the different list properties and how to use them to modify a list. You learned how to change the display type of an element. You floated images and floated content in a `<div>` tag. You learned to distinguish fixed, liquid, and elastic CSS layouts, and how to apply them. You used the overflow property to hide or scroll content that did not fit in the dimensions of the container. You created layouts using Dreamweaver layers and exported the layers-based layout to a table-based layout. You also learned about tracing images and how to use them as a guide to assembling a layout.

CAREERS IN DESIGN

DESIGNING WITH CODE

Automation always has its limits. Despite the advances in metal fabrication, for example, the most awe-inspiring custom motorcycle and car designs are crafted by people who not only know how to use sophisticated fabricating equipment or choose the right prefabricated products from the right catalogs, but also can shape a piece of sheet metal with a mallet in ways that can't otherwise be achieved. A graphic or Web designer should also never be limited by the built-in options of a piece of software if other methods are available.

Hand-coding advanced CSS is not unlike hand-fabrication of sheet metal: sometimes the options in Dreamweaver, Photoshop, and other programs are not sophisticated enough to take advantage of all of the options available through CSS. Many great Web designers, including Andy Clarke (malarkey.co.uk), Eric Meyer (meyerweb.com), Doug Bowman (stopdesign.com), Christopher Schmitt (cssbook.com), Dave Shea (mezzoblue.com and csszengarden.com), and Dan Cederholm (simplebits.com), may have great knowledge and experience with Photoshop and other advanced graphic-design applications, but they don't let the limitations of those programs, with regard to CSS, hold back their designs. These designers are also experienced at hand-coding HTML and CSS, and some of them work as well with PHP, ASP, MySQL, and other programming languages and databases. HTML and CSS-coding languages are always ahead of Web-design software. Do not be afraid of code, but, instead, learn how to use it to advance your designs.

KEY TERMS

absolute positioning	DHTML	inline tag
block tag	elastic layout	liquid layout
CSS box model	fixed layout	relative positioning
CSS hacks	fixed positioning	
CSS-P	hybrid layout	

CHECKING CONCEPTS AND TERMS

SCREEN ID

Identify the indicated areas from the list below:

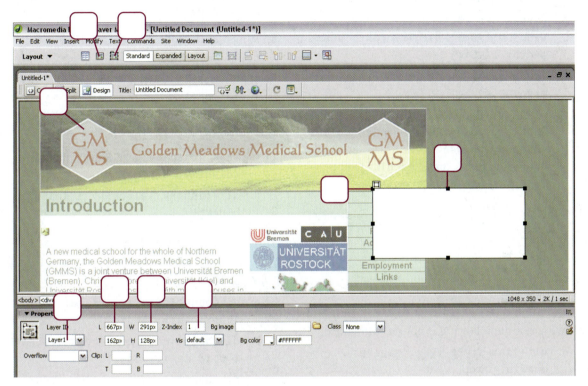

FIGURE 3.56

a. Dimensions of layer

b. Handle to move layer

c. Draw a layer

d. Name of layer

e. Handle to resize layer

f. Position of layer

g. Stack order of layer

h. Tracing image

i. Insert a div tag

MULTIPLE CHOICE

Circle the letter of the correct answer for each of the following:

1. The float property may be applied to
_____.

   a. images

   b. paragraphs

   c. divs

   d. All of the above

2. Elastic layouts expand and contract when
_____.

   a. the designer changes the default font size

   b. the user changes the text size

   c. the user widens the browser window

   d. All of the above

3. Assuming that unspecified properties have dimensions of 0 (zero) pixels, which of the following produces a total width of 240 pixels?

   a. `p {height: 180px; padding: 25px; border: 5px;}`

   b. `div#navbar {border-top: 10px; padding: 10px; margin-right: 40px; width: 240px;}`

   c. `.pull-quote {width: 200px; margin: 40px;}`

   d. `ul li a {display: block; width: 200px; padding: 5px; border-color: #3399CC; border-style: dashed; border-width: 3px; margin-left: 16px; margin-right: 8px;}`

4. When is a tracing image visible on a Web page?

   a. Always

   b. Only when opacity is set to 100%

   c. Never

   d. You must use display: tracing-image

5. Which of the following is not recommended?

   a. `ul {list-style-type: square; margin: 0px;}`

   b. `ol {list-style-type: upper-alpha; border: red;}`

   c. `ul li {list-style-image: url (red-bullet.gif);}`

   d. `ul {list-style-type: decimal;}`

6. Which of the following is correct, given the following style rule? `div#navbar {position: fixed; top: 50px; left: 20px;}`

   a. `div#navbar` moves only with the browser window

   b. `div#navbar` moves when the page is scrolled

   c. `div#navbar` moves with the mouse pointer

   d. None of the above

7. Dreamweaver's layers are _____.

   a. a free-form layout method

   b. convertible to tables

   c. fixed-position divs

   d. All of the above

8. Which of the following change both default display properties?

   a. `a {display: inline;} p {display: inline;}`

   b. `strong (display: block;) h2 {display: inline;}`

   c. `span {display: inline;} div {display: block;}`

   d. `ul {display: block;} li {display: block;}`

9. To maintain `div#body` at a position of 100 pixels from the top and 50 pixels from the left of the Web page, use _____.

   a. `div#body {display: fixed; top: 100px; left: 50px;}`

   b. `div#body {position: relative; top: 100px; left: 50px;}`

   c. `div#body {location: 100px 50px fixed;}`

   d. `div#body {position: absolute; top: 100px; left: 50px;}`

10. A fluid layout uses the _____ units of measurement.

    a. em or ex

    b. in or cm

    c. %

    d. points

DISCUSSION QUESTIONS

1. Just because you can create layouts with CSS doesn't mean that you should. Given the statement "HTML is for structure, CSS is for presentation," does layout belong in the domain of CSS or HTML? Explain your point of view.

2. The scroll value of the CSS overflow property creates a framelike appearance. Describe four situations in which the overflow: scroll property may be useful in the design of a Web site.

SKILL DRILL

Skill Drills reinforce project skills. Each skill reinforced is the same, or nearly the same, as a skill presented in the lessons. Detailed instructions are provided in a step-by-step format. Work through these exercises in order.

1. Create a Pull Quote

In this Skill Drill exercise, you create a pull quote by wrapping text with a `<div>` tag, styling the text, and then floating the div. You format the enclosed text as a paragraph so you can apply two background images — a curved top to the top of the div and a curved bottom to the bottom of the paragraph, which creates the appearance of rounded corners. You may click Apply after each property change to see the individual changes to the layout and style of the pull quote.

1. Open index.html from the GMMS site.

2. Scroll down to the Education and Training heading, and click to the left of GMMS in the first paragraph below the heading.

3. From the Layout Insert bar, click the Insert Div Tag button, type **pull-quote** in the Class field, and click OK.

4. Delete the selected text, and type **Community participation will be essential to the success of the Golden Meadows Medical School.**.

5. Using the Property inspector, set the Format to Paragraph.

6. Create a new CSS style for the **div.pull-quote** selector. In the Type category, set Font to Georgia, Times New Roman, Times, serif; Style to italic; Size to **1.3** ems; Weight to bold; and Color to **#FFFFFF**; and then click Apply. In the Block category, set Text Align to right and click Apply.

7. In the Background category, set Background Image to images>pq-top.gif, Repeat to no-repeat, Horizontal to center, and Vertical to top. Click Apply.

8. In the Box category, set Width to **220** pixels, and Float to right. Uncheck Same for All for Padding and set Top to **15** pixels. Uncheck Same for All for margins, and set the Left, Right, and Bottom margins to **5** pixels. Click OK.

9. Create a new CSS style for the **div.pull-quote p** selector. In the Background category, set the Background Color to **#BED6B4**, Background Image to images>pq-bottom.gif, Repeat to no-repeat, Horizontal to center, Vertical to bottom. Click Apply.

10. In the Box category, uncheck Same for All for Padding, and set Top to **0** pixels, and Left, Right, and Bottom to **15** pixels. Set all margins to **0** pixels. Click OK.

11. Preview the page in your browser.

FIGURE 3.57

12. Return to Dreamweaver but keep the file open for the next exercise.

2. Create a Two-Column Layout

In Skill Drill 2, you transform the GMMS layout into a more-traditional two-column layout, in which the navigation bar appears to fill the left side of the layout. In fact, the navigation bar won't extend down the left side. You change the background behind it to the same color as the background of the navigation bar. You use the clear property to push the footer below the main content. You may click the Apply button after each property change to watch the changes take place gradually.

1. In the open file, index.html, from the GMMS site, edit the ul#navbar style and set all margins to 0 pixels. Remove the Bottom border settings.

2. Edit the ul#navbar a style and remove the Right border settings.

3. Edit the ul#navbar a:hover style and change the Width of the Right border to **2** pixels.

    The purpose of Steps 2 to 4 is to remove the bottom and right borders from the navigation bar and the links. You will reapply the right border to the navigation bar as a left border on the new div#content block.

4. Edit the div#body selector. Set the Width to **730** pixels and the Background Color to **#BED6B4**.

5. Create a new CSS style for the **div#content** selector. Set the Background Color to **#FFFFFF**. In the Box category, set the Width to **577** pixels and Float to right. In the Border category, create a Left (only) border that is solid, **3** pixels wide, with a color of **#405E33**.

    The footer floats up below the navigation bar on the left.

6. Click anywhere in the footer text. Edit the div#footer selector — set its Width to **730** pixels and click Apply. In the Box category, set Clear to right and click Apply. In the Border category, change the thickness of the Top border to **3** pixels and click OK.

7. Preview the page in your browser.

FIGURE 3.58

3. Create Scrolling Content

In this Skill Drill, you cause the content div to display a scroll bar, thereby creating a framelike appearance.

1. Edit the div#content style. In the Positioning category, set the Height to **200** pixels and Overflow to auto. Click OK.

    We chose the height of 200 pixels to accommodate 800 × 600 browsers in which the browser window height is 420 pixels. After taking into account the body top margin (10 pixels), the height of the GMMS graphic (150 pixels), and the footer (estimated as 60 pixels), the remainder is 200 pixels. If you prefer to design for a screen resolution of 1024 × 768, the div#content height may be set at 380 pixels.

2. Preview the page in your browser and scroll up and down the content.

FIGURE 3.59

3. Return to Dreamweaver and close index.html.

4. Center Content Absolutely

In this Skill Drill, you learn a technique for centering content absolutely, both vertically and horizontally. The vertical-align CSS property has weak support from many browsers with the exception of within table cells. However, if a div is assigned the display property of table cell, **vertical-align** works; because IE does not support **display: table-cell**, **vertical-align** won't work. The technique used in this Skill Drill does work in current browsers. The technique is to absolutely position the top-left corner of the div at 50% from the top and 50% from the left, which positions the top-left corner in the very center of the page no matter what the height or width. Then set both left and top margins to a negative value that is half the width and height of the div. By using negative values, the div is then pulled to the left by half of its width and towards the top by half of its height, resulting in the center of the div being at the center of the browser window.

1. Create a new HTML page and save it as **splash.html**.

2. Attach styles.css to the page.

3. Insert images>gmms.jpg, assign it the alt text of **Golden Meadows Medical School**, and link it to index.html.

4. Click the image, choose the **<a>** tag in the Tag selector, and click the Insert Div Tag button from the Layout Insert bar. Assign it an id of **splash** and click OK.

5. Create a new CSS style for the div#splash selector and define it in This Document Only.

6. In the Box category, set the Width to 730 pixels and the Height to 150 pixels, and click Apply.

7. In the Positioning category, set Type to absolute, Top to 50%, and Left to 50%. Click Apply.

8. In the Box category, uncheck Same for All for margins. Set the Top Margin to –75 pixels (half the height), set the Left Margin to –385 pixels (half the width), and click OK.

9. Create a new CSS style for the body selector and define it in This Document Only. Set all padding and margins to 0 pixels and click OK.

10. Preview the page in your browser and resize the browser's width and height.

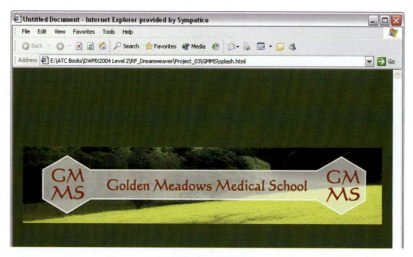

FIGURE 3.60

11. Return to Dreamweaver and close splash.html.

CHALLENGE

Challenge exercises expand on, or are somewhat related to, skills presented in the lessons. Each exercise provides a brief narrative introduction, followed by instructions in a numbered-step format that are not as detailed as those in the Skill Drill exercises. Work through the exercises in order.

1. Prepare to Convert a Tables-Based Layout to a CSS-Based Layout

In this Challenge exercise, you convert a Web page that uses a limited number of tables to a CSS-based layout. Although Dreamweaver surrounds its tables and table cells with dotted lines, at times, it is difficult to see the lines. In this exercise, you surround the table and the table cells with contrasting borders so that the structure of the table is visible.

1. Define a new site called **PH-P3** from the Project_03>PH-P3 folder and open table-layout.html.

2. In the CSS Style panel, create a new style for the **table** selector in styles.css. In the Borders category, create a solid, thin, red border on all sides and click OK. Create a new style for the **td** selector in styles.css. In the Borders category, create a solid, thin, yellow border on all sides and click OK.

   This table-based layout is quite simple but some tables-based layouts that you may have to work on may be much more complex. Highlighting tables and cells using contrasting border colors is an effective means of determining the number and location of tables and table cells.

3. One by one, Right/Control-click the table and td style rules you have just created and delete them.

4. Select all of the contents within the top cell (header), click the Insert Div Tag button from the Layout Insert bar, assign it an id of **header**, and click OK.

5. In response to the message regarding the multiple uses of the id header, click OK.

   The duplicate application of the id header is only temporary.

6. Select all of the contents within the department cell, click the Insert Div Tag button from the Layout Insert bar, assign it an id of **dept**, and click OK. Click OK to acknowledge the multiple uses of the id.

7. Select all of the contents within the navigation-bar cell, click the Insert Div Tag button from the Layout Insert bar, assign it an id of **navbar**, and click OK. Click OK to acknowledge the multiple uses of the id.

8. Select all of the contents within the main-content cell, click the Insert Div Tag button from the Layout Insert bar, assign it an id of **content**, and click OK. Click OK again.

9. Select all of the contents within the footer cell, click the Insert Div Tag button from the Layout Insert bar, assign it an id of **footer**, and click OK. Click OK again.

10. Choose File>Save as and save the file as css-layout.html, leaving it open for the next exercise.

2. Remove Table Tags

In this exercise, you remove the table tags from the Web page and reset the CSS selectors to refer to div elements instead of table and td elements. In the previous exercise, you surrounded the individual sections of content with **<div>** tags. In this exercise, you delete all of the table tags (**<table>**, **<tr>**, and **<td>**) that are mixed in with the **<div>** tags. Ensure that you don't delete any of the opening **<div>** tags or closing **</div>** tags.

1. In the open file, css-layout.html, scroll to the top of the page and switch to the Code view.

2. Locate the code **<table id="body">** and the code **<div id="header">** a couple of lines below. Delete all of the table code between the **<body>** tag and the **<div id="header">** tag.

3. At the end of the **<div id="header">** line is the closing **</div>** tag. Select and delete all table code between the **</div>** and **<div id="dept">**.

4. Locate the **</div>** that closes the dept div, and select all table code between the **</div>** and **<div id="navbar">**.

5. Locate the **</div>** tag that closes the navbar div, and select all table code between the **</div>** and **<div id="content">**.

6. Scroll down, locate the **</div>** that closes the content div, and select all table code between the **</div>** and **<div id="footer">**.

7. Locate the **</div>** that closes the footer div, and select all table code between the **</div>** and the closing **</body>** tag.

8. Switch to the Design view, and press Control/Command-A to select all text in the Web page. Wrap the selected text in a div with the id of **body**.

9. Save the changes but keep css-layout.html open for the next exercise.

3. Adjust CSS Style Rules for CSS Layout

In this exercise, you change the selectors by removing the references to table and td in the selectors and replace them with divs. You also adjust some of the style rules so that they work well with divs.

1. In the open file, css-layout.html, Right/Control-click style.css in the CSS Styles panel and choose Go to Code.

2. Keeping all of the style declarations intact, replace all references to table or td in the selectors with div. For example, change table#body to **div**#body, td#header to **div**#header, and continue. When finished, close styles.css, saving your changes.

3. To recreate the two-column appearance of the navbar and content divs, change the style declarations as follows. Edit the div#navbar style rule, remove the right border, and set Float to left. Edit the div#content style; create a left border that is solid, **4** pixels in width, with a color of **#5C7FA7**; set the width to **626** pixels; and float div#content to the right.

4. To correct the footer, edit the div#footer style rule, set the width to **750** pixels, and set clear to right.

5. Delete the td style rule as it is no longer necessary.

6. Close css-layout.html.

4. Create a CSS-Based Photo Album

In this exercise, you display a series of photographs as if they were in 35mm slide mounts. This is a very basic (yet elegant) display of photo thumbnails that simply uses **<img>** tag styling. Each thumbnail has the same proportions: one dimension is 120 pixels and the other dimension is 80 pixels. Some photos were taken in landscape (wide) format and others were taken in portrait (tall) format. This exercise relies on the thumbnails being the same dimensions. Using a landscape or portrait class, the thumbnails of the photos display properly in their slide mounts.

There may be other information you want to associate with the photo thumbnails, such as a description of the photos, but that would require additional layers of tags, such as a **<div>** tag around each slide. In Eric Meyer's recent book, *More Eric Meyer on CSS*, he demonstrates a more sophisticated method. While it does allow the designer to add more information about each photo thumbnail, the method involves more tags and more effort.

1. Create a new site called **MT-P3** using the Project_03>MT-P3 folder.

2. Open photo_album.html.

3. Create a new CSS Style for div#slides in a new style-sheet file called **photos.css**. In the Block category, set Text Align to center.

4. Create a new style for the **img** selector. In the Background category, set the Background Image to photos>slide-bg.gif. In the Box category, set all margins to **1** pixel. Click OK.

5. Create a new style for the **img.landscape** selector. In the Box category, uncheck Same for All for Padding; set Top, Right, Bottom, and Left padding to **35** pixels, **15** pixels, **35** pixels, and **15** pixels, respectively.

   The slide-bg.gif background image is 150 × 150 pixels in dimension, and the landscape thumbnails are 120 pixels wide by 80 pixels high. Divide the differences in dimensions by half, and assign the values to the different sides as padding. Remember: padding allows the background of the current element to show through; margin allows the background of the element behind to show through.

6. Create a new style for the **img.portrait** selector. In the Box category, uncheck Same for All for Padding; set Top, Right, Bottom, and Left padding to **15**, pixels, **35** pixels, **15** pixels, and **35** pixels respectively.

7. One by one, Right/Control-click the images and assign the landscape (wide) or portrait (tall) class to the images.

8. Preview the page in your browser. Strangely, Dreamweaver does not display this exercise properly; you must preview it in a browser.

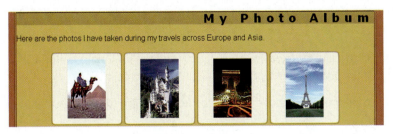

FIGURE 3.61

9. Return to Dreamweaver, close photo_album.html, and close Dreamweaver.

PORTFOLIO BUILDER

Plan a CSS Layout

Many Web sites provide templates for Web-site designs, such as 4templates.com. However, most such designs use tables for layout rather than CSS and **<div>** tags. You have been hired by a local café to create their Web site. They selected a design from 4templates.com — item number VA0019OR. Your task is to plan the Web site using this design but employing CSS for layout.

1. Go to 4templates.com and click the Search Templates link in the right column.

2. In the Match Item # field, type **VA0019OR**, click Submit, and then click the thumbnail image of the design.

3. Print the two layouts.

4. Identify which images should be in the foreground with **<img>** tags and alt attributes and which images should be background images.

5. Divide the page into large sections, such as header, footer, and main content. If necessary, create sections within the major sections.

6. Assign ids to **<div>** tags that occur only once and classes to **<div>** tags that occur multiple times.

7. Sketch a plan of how you would lay out the Web page using CSS.

PROJECT 4

JavaScript Behaviors

OBJECTIVES

In this project, you learn how to

- Code JavaScript in a tag

- Create a JavaScript function

- Use the Behaviors panel

- Create alerts and status-bar messages

- Create a jump menu

- Use image rollovers

- Configure a sophisticated navigation bar

- Set up a form-validation script

WHY WOULD I DO THIS?

JavaScript is useful in Web-site design for creating dynamic effects that would otherwise not be possible, such as randomly changing decorative graphics, image rollovers in navigation bars, and drop-down menus. Some JavaScript behaviors enhance design, such as image rollovers, and some behaviors enhance usability, such as form validation.

HTML is static and, with the exception of the **:hover**, **:active**, and **:focus** properties, CSS is also static. JavaScript, however, can create dynamic effects that respond to user actions. Commonly, JavaScript dynamic effects are known as "behaviors" because they respond to events or actions. One event might be loading the page into the browser — think of pop-up windows that appear with advertising when you go to a Web site. Another event could be the movement of the mouse pointer over a particular region of the Web page. Image rollovers or pop-up menus commonly use mouse events to trigger these functions. Clicking a submit button in a form can also trigger a behavior — if you have not completed all of the required fields in a form, a message may appear to alert you.

JavaScript is a client-side scripted programming language. *Client-side* refers to the fact that it is run in the browser, not on the Web server. However, this has not always been the case. The Netscape Web server, Compass, can run JavaScript as a server-side language and Microsoft's ASP (Active Server Pages) language can use JavaScript. Although the popularity of Compass has since declined, JavaScript continues to be popular as a client-side language. JavaScript is also known as "ECMAScript." ECMA (European Computer Manufacturers Association) is a European standards body, not unlike the ISO, International Standards Organization, and has been involved in the standardization of JavaScript. The current version, JavaScript1.5, is equivalent to ECMAScript-262, Edition 3.

JavaScript is a *scripted programming language*, meaning that it is not *compiled* (converted to a compact form of machine-only readable code) but uses the programming code as raw text. When the browser receives the code, it reads and runs the code. All programming languages have a human-readable format, which is what the programmers use to write the programs. However, many programming languages, such as C++, are compiled before they are run, a process that converts the human-readable code into machine language that runs much more quickly but which people cannot read.

There are other client-side scripting languages: JScript is Microsoft's version of JavaScript and VBScript (Visual Basic Script) is another Microsoft client-side scripting language, both of which run only in Microsoft Internet Explorer (IE). JavaScript also is available, in a modified format, in PDF (Portable Document Format) documents, and is commonly used to perform PDF form validation. ActionScript is a client-side scripting language embedded in Flash animations and is similar to JavaScript.

Despite JavaScript's benefits, you should realize that not all users can use the JavaScript functions for a number of reasons. For example, Lynx (a text-only browser) does not run any version of JavaScript, IE3 does not run recent versions of JavaScript, most browsers allow the users to disable JavaScript, and some users don't use a mouse (many JavaScript triggers depend on mouse actions). Therefore, when you design a Web site in which you would like to use JavaScript, be aware of your target audience. If you use JavaScript to create nonessential decorative behaviors, such as image rollovers or rotating decorative images, then the absence of JavaScript in a visitor's browser won't be critical. Form validation, however, is more critical to many sites. Because users have the option of disabling JavaScript in their browsers, Web-site designers should never depend on JavaScript validation as it may not always run. You should instead use server-side validation, which cannot be disabled or avoided. You can also use JavaScript to create content dynamically, but if JavaScript is unavailable to some users, they won't receive the same content as those with fully functional JavaScript. Not all browsers support CSS, but if applied properly, the content does not depend on CSS. You should consider this when you apply JavaScript — your Web site should not depend on it.

V I S U A L   S U M M A R Y

Dreamweaver provides several JavaScript behaviors that you can configure through dialog boxes. The behaviors are listed in the pop-up menu of the Behaviors panel. By default, the Behaviors panel is not open, but you can open it by choosing Window>Behaviors.

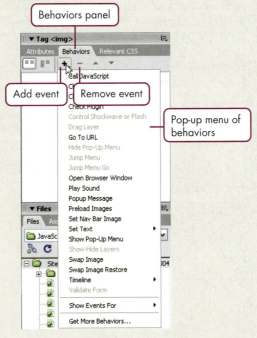

FIGURE 4.1

You can insert behaviors from the pop-up menu of the Behaviors panel. You can also change the event of an existing behavior or, using the Remove Event button, delete an event.

FIGURE 4.2

Macromedia has created the behaviors listed in the pop-up menu for Dreamweaver, and you can configure the behaviors through their own dialog boxes. Each behavior has its own options. Some behaviors have very few options, such as the Status-bar text, which requires only a single line of text whereas other behaviors are more complex, such as the Navigation Bar behavior. Although there are many more JavaScript programs available from other Web sites such as Hotscripts.com, you must configure them by opening the file in Code view and edit the code: Dreamweaver's behaviors are much easier to configure, especially for those who are not comfortable working with code.

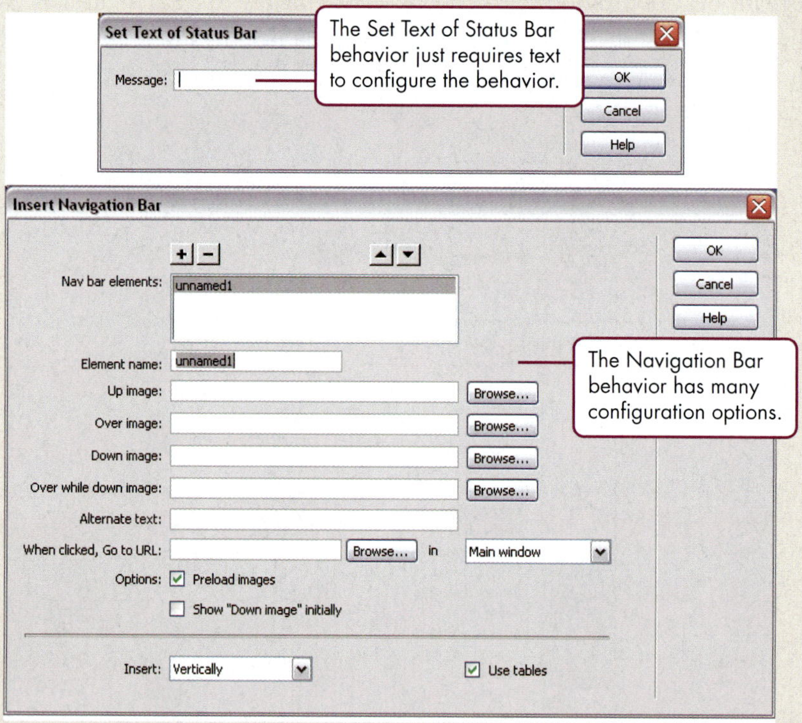

FIGURE 4.3

You can also hand-code JavaScript in the Code window. Dreamweaver applies syntax coloring to JavaScript to help identify improperly written code, but doesn't provide code hints for JavaScript.

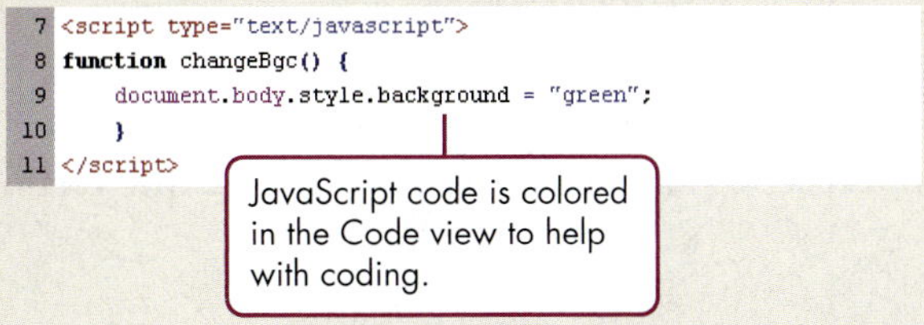

```
7  <script type="text/javascript">
8  function changeBgc() {
9      document.body.style.background = "green";
10     }
11 </script>
```

> JavaScript code is colored in the Code view to help with coding.

FIGURE 4.4

LESSON 1   Working with Basic Events and Methods

JavaScript uses events to trigger the operation of a behavior. ***Events*** are actions that JavaScript monitors and, when the event occurs, the behavior runs. Not all events trigger all JavaScript behaviors — a behavior must be directly associated with an event to trigger its operation. Events all begin with on, such as **onclick**, **onmouseover**, **onload**, **onsubmit**, and **onfocus**. Like CSS, JavaScript can be written inline within an HTML tag. In this format, the event is an attribute of the tag followed by an attribute value, the JavaScript command, such as **onclick="this.style.color = 'blue';"**. As you can see, the attribute value must be quoted; in this example, double quotes surround the attribute value. At times, you may also need to quote information in the attribute value, such as blue in this example. The quotes may be double quotes or single quotes: **onclick="this.style.color = 'blue';"** is the same as **onclick='this style.color = "blue";'** but **onclick="this.style.color = "blue';** and **onclick="this.style.color = "blue";"** would both fail because the quotes don't nest properly.

You must select the appropriate event for the action you want to use to trigger an event. For example, **onload** and **onunload** in the **<body>** tag initiate a behavior when the page loads or ***unloads*** (when the user leaves the page), **onclick** is commonly associated with a link or **<a>** tag, **onsubmit** is associated with a submit button to trigger a validation script, and **onchange** is commonly associated with a select list like the JavaScript style switcher in Project 2. Some events are similar and provide options for keyboard users: you can use **onkeydown** with **onclick** to give keyboard and mouse users the same functionality.

An ***event handler*** is the JavaScript code that runs when the event is triggered. In the preceding example, **this.style.color = 'blue';** is the event-handler code. Each JavaScript instruction ends with a semicolon, but if the function has just one line of code, it is not necessary (although it is good form) to add a semicolon at the end. However, like CSS, which has a similar ***syntax*** (grammar of code), adding a semicolon to the end of every line is good form and prepares the code in case you need to add another line of code. Most JavaScript is written with each instruction on its own line and each line ending with a semicolon. You can write a complete JavaScript program on one line as long as you add semicolons to the end of each statement, but this format would be very difficult for the programmer to read and ***debug*** (locate and fix errors).

Change Background Color with JavaScript

In this exercise, you write some basic JavaScript code that changes the background color of the page. You work with different events and combine events in one HTML tag.

1   Define the Project_04>JavaScript folder as a site called **JavaScript** using the methods outlined in previous projects. Do not click Done — leave the Site Definition dialog box open for the next step.

2   Click the first site in the list from a previous project and click the Remove button. When asked to confirm the removal, click Yes. Repeat until you have removed all sites from the list (except the JavaScript site you defined in Step 1). Click Done when finished.

3   Open background.html, click to the right of the Red link, and switch to the Split view.

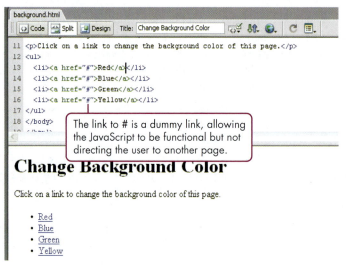

FIGURE 4.5

4   Click between the "#" and > of the Red link, press the Spacebar, type **onc** (the Code Hint chooses onClick), and press Enter/Return.

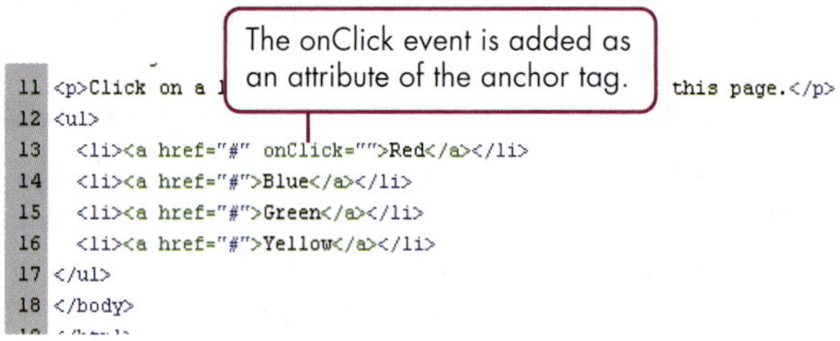

FIGURE 4.6

5   Between the two double quotation marks, type `body.style.background = 'red';`.

Red must be surrounded by single quotation marks because double quotation marks surround the entire event handler.

```
11  <p>Click on a link to change the background color of this page.</p>
12  <ul>
13    <li><a href="#" onClick="body.style.background = 'red';">Red</a></li>
14    <li><a href="#">Blue</a></li>
15    <li><a href="#">Green</a></li>
16    <li><a href="#">Yellow</a></li>
17  </ul>
18  </body>
```

The semicolon is not necessary at this time but, like CSS, is good form to use every time.

FIGURE 4.7

6   Preview this page in your browser and click the Red link.

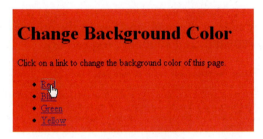

FIGURE 4.8

7   Return to Dreamweaver, but keep background.html open for the next exercise.

Change Background to Other Colors

In this exercise, you add the JavaScript code to the other links to provide additional background-color options.

1   In background.html, select `onClick="body.background.style.color = 'red';"` and copy/paste it to the same position in the three remaining links. Ensure that there is a space in front of onClick.

2   In the pasted code, change the colors from red to match the color indicated by the link text.

```
11  <p>Click on a link to change the background color of this page.</p>
12  <ul>
13    <li><a href="#" onClick="body.style.background = 'red';">Red</a></li>
14    <li><a href="#" onClick="body.style.background = 'blue';">Blue</a></li>
15    <li><a href="#" onClick="body.style.background = 'green';">Green</a></li>
16    <li><a href="#" onClick="body.style.background = 'yellow';">Yellow</a></li>
17  </ul>
18  </body>
```

FIGURE 4.9

3   Preview the page and test the links.

4   Return to Dreamweaver, but leave background.html open for the next exercise.

Add a Behavior to an Event Handler

In this exercise, you add another behavior to the event handler to perform two changes from just one event. You learn about the **this** keyword, which always refers to the owner of the function being executed.

1   In background.html, after the semicolon of the red event handler, press the Spacebar and type `this.style.color = '#FFFFFF';`.

```
11  <p>Click on a link to change the background color of this page.</p>
12  <ul>
13    <li><a href="#" onClick="body.style.background = 'red'; this.style.color = '#FFFFFF';">Red</a></li>
14    <li><a href="#" onClick="body.style.background = 'blue';">Blue</a></li>
15    <li><a href="#" onClick="body.style.background = 'green';">Green</a></li>
16    <li><a href="#" onClick="body.style.background = 'yellow';">Yellow</a></li>
17  </ul>
18  </body>
```

FIGURE 4.10

2   Copy and paste the new code to the same position in the other event handlers, and change #FFFFFF to #FFFF00, #808080, and #0000FF, respectively.

```
11  <p>Click on a link to change the background color of this page.</p>
12  <ul>
13    <li><a href="#" onClick="body.style.background = 'red'; this.style.color = '#FFFFFF';">Red</a></li>
14    <li><a href="#" onClick="body.style.background = 'blue'; this.style.color = '#FFFF00';">Blue</a></li>
15    <li><a href="#" onClick="body.style.background = 'green'; this.style.color = '#808080';">Green</a></li>
16    <li><a href="#" onClick="body.style.background = 'yellow'; this.style.color = '#0000FF';">Yellow</a></li>
17  </ul>
18  </body>
```

FIGURE 4.11

3   Preview the page in your browser, click the links, and note the changes in the text colors.

? If you have problems

If at any time, the effect does not seem to work as it should, compare your code against the code displayed in the figures. Determine which line and which part of the code do not work — background color or text color. Examine that section of the code for differences from your code.

4   Return to Dreamweaver, but leave background.html open for the next exercise.

Use onMouseOver as the Event

In this exercise, you change the event from **onClick** to **onMouseOver**. The **onMouseOver** event is triggered when the mouse pointer moves over the element in this event.

1   In background.html, change all instances of onClick to onMouseOver.

```
11  <p>Click on a link to change the background color of this page.</p>
12  <ul>
13    <li><a href="#" onMouseOver="body.style.background = 'red'; this.style.color = '#FFFFFF';">Red</a></li>
14    <li><a href="#" onMouseOver="body.style.background = 'blue'; this.style.color = '#FFFF00';">Blue</a></li>
15    <li><a href="#" onMouseOver="body.style.background = 'green'; this.style.color = '#808080';">Green</a></li>
16    <li><a href="#" onMouseOver="body.style.background = 'yellow'; this.style.color = '#0000FF';">Yellow</a></li>
17  </ul>
18  </body>
```

FIGURE 4.12

2   Preview the page in your browser, move your mouse pointer over the links, and notice that there is no need to click a link to change the background color and text color.

3   Return to Dreamweaver, but leave background.html open for the next exercise.

Restore Original Colors with onMouseOut

In this exercise, you restore the original background and text colors when the mouse pointer moves off a link. Currently, the link colors do not revert to their original colors when another event is triggered. There is no event that is the opposite of **onClick** although **onDblClick** could be used. **onMouseOver** and **onMouseOut** are naturally opposing events.

1   In background.html, click between " and > in the Red link, press the Spacebar and type
onMouseOut="body.style.background = '#FFFFFF'; this.style.color = '#000000';".

2   Copy/paste this code (without modification) to the same position in the three other links.

```
';" onMouseOut="body.style.background = '#FFFFFF'; this.style.color = '#000000';">Red</a></li>
0';" onMouseOut="body.style.background = '#FFFFFF'; this.style.color = '#000000';">Blue</a></li>
80';" onMouseOut="body.style.background = '#FFFFFF'; this.style.color = '#000000';">Green</a></li>
0FF';" onMouseOut="body.style.background = '#FFFFFF'; this.style.color = '#000000';">Yellow</a></li>
```

FIGURE 4.13

3   Preview this page in your browser and notice that when you move your mouse pointer off any of the links, the colors revert to the original black text against a white background.

4   Return to Dreamweaver, but leave background.html open for the next exercise.

To Extend Your Knowledge

CHARACTER CASE OF JAVASCRIPT

Some JavaScript code is not case sensitive and other code is case sensitive. Events are not case sensitive: **onclick** and **onClick** are interchangeable. Most other functions are not case sensitive, but if you plan to create your own behaviors, have a reference manual available and check the case of the code before you add it to your behavior. For example, you can use JavaScript to change the CSS properties of an element just as you changed the background and text colors in the previous exercise. You can also change the **font-weight** or **font-family** CSS properties using **style.fontWeight** and **style.fontFamily**. These JavaScript properties are case sensitive and do not work with any other spelling.

LESSON 2   Using JavaScript Functions

JavaScript *functions* are little programs that may have 1 or 1,000 lines of JavaScript statements, each of which is defined once in a program and can be *executed* (run) many times. In the previous lesson, you created JavaScript code that grew in size as you added more features to it. Instead of adding to the code in the anchor tags, in this lesson you export the code to a function and execute the function.

Functions have a specific syntax: the keyword **function** precedes the name of the function which is followed by parentheses **()**, such as **function addNumbers()**. The actual code is enclosed by curly braces **{}**, such as **{ total=firstNum+secondNum; }**. Commonly, the layout of the code is to have the function name and opening curly brace on the first line, each line of code indented, and then the closing curly brace on a line after the last line of code but not indented.

```
function addNumbers(firstNum, secondNum) {

        total=firstNum+secondNum;

        document.write("<p>The total is " & total & ".</p>");

    }
```

Many functions perform their actions based on *parameters* (information) passed to them. In the preceding example, the two numbers to be added are passed to the function and collected by firstNum and secondNum, the parameters of this function. The words firstNum, secondNum, and total in this example are *variables*, placeholders or containers for information. If we wanted to add 2 and 5, we could create a function in which the code is **total=2+5**; but that would limit the versatility of the function so adding 3 and 7 would require creating another function. The next question is where the values for firstNum and secondNum come from. The values are placed in the code which calls the addNumbers function, such as **onClick="addNumbers(2, 5);"**.

The last line in the function is a *method*, a predefined functionality in JavaScript. The **document.write()** method writes the total to the page using the **<p>** paragraph tag to format the answer. Two types of information are provided in this example: the *literal text* (raw text) surrounded by double quotation marks (you could use single quotation marks, instead) and the variable called total. Variables should not be enclosed in quotation marks or, in this example, the word total rather than the value of total would be written to the page. Literals and variables are *concatenated* (joined) with ampersands (**&**).

Functions are created between **<script>** tags located in the head section of an HTML document. The only required attribute of the **<script>** tag is the **type** attribute that should be set to **type= "text/javascript"**. Some older browsers do not understand the **type** attribute and prefer the **language** attribute, as in **language="JavaScript"**. Sometimes the version of JavaScript is specified, such as **language="JavaScript1.2"**. If you are developing for an older browser, you must use the **type** attribute for current compatibility and should use the **language** attribute for compatibility with older browsers.

This is a very basic and brief introduction to JavaScript. Much more is available through JavaScript than we can cover in this book. If you would like to learn more, consult *Essentials for Design: JavaScript*. The rest of this project focuses on applying the JavaScript behaviors prewritten for you in Dreamweaver.

Create a JavaScript Function

In this exercise, you create a JavaScript function in the **<style>** block.

1   **In background.html, click at the end of the </title> tag and press Enter/Return.**

2   **Type <sc and press Enter/Return to accept script. Press the Spacebar and type t, press Enter/Return to accept type, type t, press Enter/Return to accept text/javascript, and type >.**

3   **Press Enter/Return twice to split the opening and closing <script> tags, leaving a blank line between them.**

```
 6 <title>Change Background Color</title>
 7 <script type="text/javascript">
 8
 9 </script>
10 </head>
```

FIGURE 4.14

4   **In the empty line between the opening and closing <script> tags, type function changeProperties(bgc) { and press Enter/Return. Type document.body.style.background = bgc; and press Enter/Return. Type }.**

Note the syntax highlighting — function is bold and document.body is magenta. If you misspell function, it does not display as bold so you should examine the code.

```
 7 <script type="text/javascript">
 8 function changeProperties(bgc) {
 9     document.body.style.background = bgc;
10 }
11 </script>
```

JavaScript programmers commonly move the curly brace to the same position as the f of the function it closes.

FIGURE 4.15

5   **Save your changes, but leave background.html open for the next exercise.**

Add the Function to the Event Handler

In this exercise, you call the changeProperties function from the event handler. The bgc parameter collects the background-color information from the event handler.

| 1 | In background.html, scroll down to the Red link and delete the event handler code for the onMouseOver event, leaving onMouseOver="". Leave the onMouseOut event alone for now. |

| 2 | Between the two quotation marks, type `changeProperties('red');`. Copy and paste this code to the three other onMouseOver event handlers, replacing red with the appropriate color. |

```
15  <h1>Change Background Color</h1>
16  <p>Click on a link to change the background color of this page.</p>
17  <ul>
18    <li><a href="#" onMouseOver="changeProperties('red');" onMouseOut="body.style.bac
19    <li><a href="#" onMouseOver="changeProperties('blue');" onMouseOut="body.style.b
20    <li><a href="#" onMouseOver="changeProperties('green');" onMouseOut="body.style.l
21    <li><a href="#" onMouseOver="changeProperties('yellow');" onMouseOut="body.style.
22  </ul>
23  </body>
```

FIGURE 4.16

| 3 | Preview the page in your browser, roll your mouse pointer over the links, and notice that the changeProperties function has replaced the inline code. |

| 4 | Return to Dreamweaver and scroll up to the changeProperties function in the Code window at approximately line 8. |

| 5 | Type `, txtc` after `bgc` changing it from `(bgc)` to `(bgc, txtc)`. |

| 6 | Click to the right of `(bgc, txtc)  {;` and press Enter/Return. Type `document.body.style.color = txtc;`. |

| 7 | Scroll down to the links and add `, 'yellow'` to the changeProperties parameter for the red link, `, 'silver'`, `, 'white'`, and `, 'blue'` to the remaining links. |

```
6  <title>Change Background Color</title>
7  <script type="text/javascript">
8  function changeProperties(bgc, txtc) {
9      document.body.style.color = txtc;
10     document.body.style.background = bgc;
11 }
12 </script>
13 </head>
14 <body>
15 <h1>Change Background Color</h1>
16 <p>Click on a link to change the background color of this page.</p>
17 <ul>
18   <li><a href="#" onMouseOver="changeProperties('red', 'yellow');" onMouseOut="body.style.background = '#FFFFFF'; this.st
19   <li><a href="#" onMouseOver="changeProperties('blue', 'silver');" onMouseOut="body.style.background = '#FFFFFF'; this.s
20   <li><a href="#" onMouseOver="changeProperties('green', 'white');" onMouseOut="body.style.background = '#FFFFFF'; this.s
21   <li><a href="#" onMouseOver="changeProperties('yellow', 'blue');" onMouseOut="body.style.background = '#FFFFFF'; this.s
22 </ul>
23 </body>
```

FIGURE 4.17

8   Preview the page in your browser and move your mouse pointer over the links.

This keyword is more difficult to use with functions because the code is not in the tag so the association of this with a specific tag is not clear. It is possible to re-create the previous behavior in a function, but the coding is much more complex.

FIGURE 4.18

9   Return to Dreamweaver, but leave background.html open for the next exercise.

Restore the Color Properties with Another Function

In this exercise, you replace the **onMouseOut** code with a function to restore the color properties of both the text and background. The function created in this exercise uses the same color properties every time, therefore it has no parameters. Nevertheless, **( )** must always follow the function name in both the **<script>** block and in the event handler.

1   In background.html, scroll up to the closing curly brace (}) of the changeProperties function in the Code window, click to the right of this closing curly brace, and press Enter/Return.

2   Create a new function by typing `function restoreProperties() {`, press Enter/Return, press Tab, type `document.body.style.background = "white";`, press Enter/Return, type `document.body.style.color = "black";`, press Enter/Return, press Backspace, and type `}`.

3   Scroll down to the links and replace all of the onMouseOut event handlers with `onMouseOut="restoreProperties();"`.

```
12  function restoreProperties() {
13      document.body.style.background = "white";
14      document.body.style.color = "black";
15  }
16  </script>
17  </head>
18  <body>
19  <h1>Change Background Color</h1>
20  <p>Click on a link to change the background color of this page.</p>
21  <ul>
22    <li><a href="#" onMouseOver="changeProperties('red', 'yellow');" onMouseOut="restoreProperties();">Red</a></li>
23    <li><a href="#" onMouseOver="changeProperties('blue', 'silver');" onMouseOut="restoreProperties();">Blue</a></li>
24    <li><a href="#" onMouseOver="changeProperties('green', 'white');" onMouseOut="restoreProperties();">Green</a></li>
25    <li><a href="#" onMouseOver="changeProperties('yellow', 'blue');" onMouseOut="restoreProperties();">Yellow</a></li>
26  </ul>
```

FIGURE 4.19

4   Preview the page in your browser, move the mouse pointer over the links and back off again, and notice that the functions are changing and restoring the color properties of the page.

5   Return to Dreamweaver, switch to the Design view, and close background.html.

To Extend Your Knowledge

EXTERNAL JAVASCRIPT FILES

Functions, as you have learned, are better than inline JavaScript code, but even in a `<script>` block, they apply only to the current page. Many JavaScript behaviors, such as drop-down menus, may be beneficial to all pages in the site. Therefore, you don't want to have to recode the behavior in every page or even copy/paste the `<script>` block to every page. If one aspect of the code changes, then you must change every page with the code. Just like CSS, JavaScript can be stored in an external JavaScript file and attached to every page on the site. The attachment method is a bit different but the principle is the same. In the `<script>` tag, you use the `src` attribute followed by the name of the JavaScript filename (which should end with .js), such as `<script type="text/javascript" src="background.js">`. In CSS, if a selector does not exist in a page, the selectors styles cannot apply; similarly, if an event handler is not added to a new page, the JavaScript behaviors do not run. When you create a new page that should use the behaviors stored in the external JavaScript file, the JavaScript file must be attached and the appropriate tags must have event handlers to invoke the functions.

LESSON 3 Creating JavaScript Alerts

On their own, JavaScript alerts are not very useful. However, when combined with other functions, they can be very beneficial. For example, in a form-validation script that detects that the email address has not been completed, a JavaScript alert can pop up to alert the user of this omission. Alerts can be confused with pop-up windows: alerts simply display a text message whereas pop-up windows open a new Web page. Many recent browsers have pop-up blockers: they are designed to block pop-up windows and have no effect on pop-up alerts.

Learning to create JavaScript alerts is a good introduction to the Behaviors panel in Dreamweaver. Although the alert is created to pop up, by default, when the page loads, you can change the event that triggers the alert and can make the change in the Behaviors panel. You must also ensure that the tag to which you want to attach the behavior is the tag that is currently selected. You learn that the Behaviors panel displays some behavior options when one tag is selected and other behavior options when another tag is selected. This is important when you perform form validation: you must ensure that it is the email field being checked for an email address, not the comments field.

Explore the Behaviors Panel

In this exercise, you explore the Behaviors panel and learn what Dreamweaver behaviors may be attached to which elements on a page.

1 Define a new site called **MT-P4** from the **Project_04>MT-P4 folder.**

2 Open **contact_me.html.**

3   **Choose Window>Behaviors to open the Behaviors panel.**

If you want a larger view of the Behaviors panel, close the Design panel group.

4   **Note that the Tag panel-group heading displays the <body> tag.**

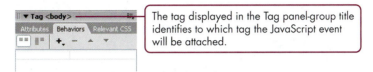

The tag displayed in the Tag panel-group title identifies to which tag the JavaScript event will be attached.

FIGURE 4.20

5   **Click the plus symbol below Behaviors.**

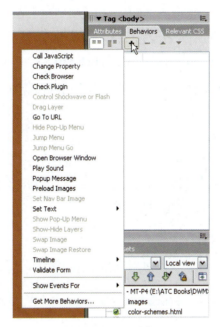

FIGURE 4.21

6   **Do not choose any of the options, but click in the heading-1 text, My Travels Across Europe and Africa. Reopen the Behaviors pop-up menu.**

Most of the options are not available because few Dreamweaver behaviors can be attached to the **<h1>** tag.

7   **Click in any of the navigation-bar links below the heading and reopen the Behaviors pop-up menu.**

The Show Pop-up Menu is a behavior that you can attach to a link but not to the **<body>** or **<h1>** tags.

8   **Keep contact_me.html open for the next exercise.**

Create an onLoad Alert Message

In this exercise, you create an alert message that appears when the page loads.

1   In contact_me.html, check the Tag panel-group heading and ensure that the **<body>** tag is identified.

?   ## If you have problems

If the Tag panel-group heading does not identify the **<body>** tag, either click to the left or right of the main table or click the **<body>** tag in the Tag selector.

2   Open the Behaviors pop-up menu and choose Popup Message.

3   Type **I appreciate your comments.** and click OK.

FIGURE 4.22

4   Examine the Behaviors panel.

The onLoad event means that when the page loads in the browser, this behavior executes.

This behavior is attached to the **<body>** tag, which is best for onLoad and onUnload events.

FIGURE 4.23

5   Click onLoad in the Behaviors panel, and then click the arrow to open the list of other events.

If you want to change the event that triggers the current behavior, you can select it from this list.

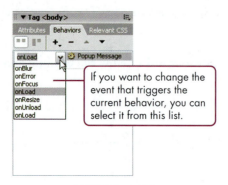

FIGURE 4.24

6 Preview the page in your browser. Click the OK button after the alert pops up.

FIGURE 4.25

7 Return to Dreamweaver.

8 In the Behaviors panel, change the event from onLoad to onUnload and preview the page in your browser.

9 Click the Home link in the navigation bar.

This time, the pop-up message does not appear when the page loads but when you click on the link to go to another page and the current page unloads.

10 Return to Dreamweaver, but leave contact_me.html open for the next lesson.

To Extend Your Knowledge

JAVASCRIPT STATISTICS

According to Peter-Paul Koch ("Separating Behavior and Presentation," digital-web.com/articles/separating_behavior_and_presentation/), approximately 98% of users use a recent browser, but between 10 and 15% of users do not run JavaScript. This means that many users have intentionally disabled JavaScript in their browsers. As with all statistics, more information would be useful, but to obtain more detailed information requires paying TheCounter.com or StatMarket.com for their collected data. Nevertheless, the information is both startling and revealing, and increases the importance of understanding your site's audience before implementing JavaScript.

LESSON 4   Displaying Messages on the Status Bar

You can use the Status bar to display additional information about a page or a link. To display a Status-bar message for a page, you use the **onLoad** event to trigger the display of the message when the page loads and **onUnload** to clear the Status-bar message when the visitor moves to another page. Similarly, when creating a Status-bar message for a link, you use **onMouseOver** to display the message and **onMouseOut** to clear the message. JavaScript can be used to create scrolling text in the Status bar, which can be very annoying after awhile.

Create Status-Bar Messages

In this exercise, you create a Status-bar message for each link in the navigation bar.

1   In contact_me.html, click the Home link in the navigation bar.

2   Open the Behaviors pop-up menu and choose Set Text>Set Text of Status Bar. Type `Return to the home page of My Travels site` and click OK.

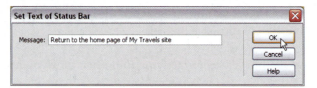

FIGURE 4.26

3   Preview the page in your browser, move your mouse pointer over the Home link, and observe the Status bar.

FIGURE 4.27

? If you have problems

If you are previewing this page in IE, you see the Status-bar message. However, in Mozilla browsers, the message does not appear because the JavaScript code that Dreamweaver creates for the Status-bar messages is incomplete. IE is lenient enough to understand what is intended by the code, but other browsers can be stricter in their requirements for the code and do not display it.

4   Move the mouse pointer off the link and notice that the Status-bar text remains.

5   Return to Dreamweaver, but leave contact_me.html open for the next exercise.

Clear the Status-Bar Message

In this exercise, you create an empty Status-bar message. You use the **onMouseOut** event to display the empty Status-bar message. This clears the Status bar of any text when the mouse pointer is away from the link.

1   In contact_me.html, open the Code window.

2   Scroll to line 15, locate **status=msgStr;**, and type window. in front of status. If you are previewing in the Firefox or Mozilla browser, preview the page again to check that the new code displays the Status-bar text.

window. is missing from in front of status in the code produced by Dreamweaver.

```
14 function MM_displayStatusMsg(msgStr) { //v1.0
15     window.status=msgStr;
16     document.MM_returnValue = true;
17 }
```

FIGURE 4.28

3   Close the Code window.

4   Click in the Home link again, open the Behaviors pop-up menu, and choose Set Text>Set Text of Status Bar.

5   Click OK without typing any text.

6   In the Behaviors panel, click the second onMouseOver event and change it to onMouseOut.

After changing the event, the behaviors reorder alphabetically.

FIGURE 4.29

7   Right/Control-click the onMouseOut behavior and choose Edit Behavior. Ensure that the onMouseOut behavior is associated with the empty Status-bar message. Click OK when finished.

FIGURE 4.30

| 8 | Preview the page in your browser, move your mouse pointer over the Home link, and then move it away from the link. |

Note that the Status-bar message now disappears when the mouse pointer moves off the link.

| 9 | Return to Dreamweaver and close contact_me.html |

To Extend Your Knowledge

STATUS-BAR MESSAGES ARE NOT ACCESSIBLE

It would appear that Status-bar messages is a useful means of providing additional information about linked pages before the visitor clicks the link. However, although the additional information about the linked pages is beneficial, Status-bar messages are not the place to put the information if you are concerned about accessibility. Many screen-reader programs do not update the content they read to the user when content changes dynamically, like Status-bar text. The **title** attribute of the anchor tag is designed for this use. This is not to say that you shouldn't use Status-bar text; you should simply be aware that Status-bar text isn't accessible to users of screen-reader software, can't be resized for users who have poor vision, and won't appear if JavaScript is disabled.

LESSON 5 | Creating Jump Menus

Jump menus are very commonly used because of their elegance. Essentially, *jump menus* are select lists of Web-page links that use JavaScript to open the page automatically when the visitor chooses a destination from the list. One benefit of jump menus is that they are compact despite the number of items you may have in the list. It would not be appropriate to use a jump menu as the navigation system for a Web site because, by default, it depends on JavaScript, which means that some visitors may not be able to use it. Also, it depends on the **onChange** event handler. The **onChange** event occurs when a mouse user clicks one of the options from the list. The **onChange** event also occurs when a keyboard user moves from one option to another. This means that keyboard users trigger the **onChange** event just by scrolling through the options without even choosing one: they are never able to go to any link except the first one.

Jump menus are just simple select lists with two differences: the **<select>** tag contains an **onChange** event that watches for the selection of an option, and the values of the options are URLs. When the visitor chooses an option from the list, the **onChange** event is triggered and JavaScript immediately jumps the user to the destination.

Create a Jump Menu

In this exercise, you create a jump menu to different Web sites from the Travel Log page. The URLs do not need to be external links — they can be links to pages within the site using either absolute or relative paths, or they can be links to anchors on the current or other pages within the site. The only URL to which you cannot create a jump with jump menus is a mailto link.

1   Open travel_log.html and click in the empty paragraph below the paragraph These are links to Web sites of places I have visited.

2   From the Forms Insert bar, insert a form and name it `links`.

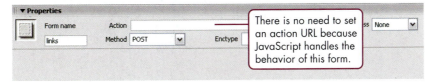

FIGURE 4.31

3   Click in the form outline and then click the Jump Menu button on the Forms Insert bar.

FIGURE 4.32

4   In the Text field, type `Select a destination`; in the When Selected, Go to URL field, type `#`; and in the Menu Name field, type `jumpmenu`.

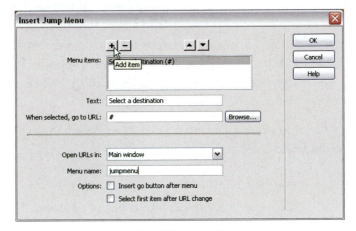

FIGURE 4.33

5   Click the Add Item button (+) near the top of the Insert Jump Menu dialog box, type `Egypt` in the Text field, and type `http://www.lonelyplanet.com/destinations/africa/egypt/` in the URL field.

6   Complete three more entries as follows:

Add Item button	Text	URL
Click	Greece	http://www.lonelyplanet.com/destinations/europe/greece/
Click	Spain	http://www.lonelyplanet.com/destinations/europe/spain/
Click	France	http://www.lonelyplanet.com/destinations/europe/france/

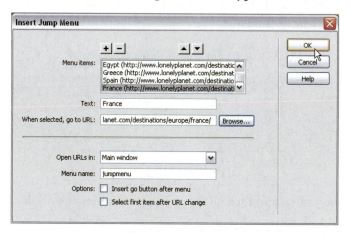

FIGURE 4.34

To Extend Your Knowledge

THE GO-BUTTON OPTION FOR JUMP MENUS

Dreamweaver's Jump Menu function offers the option to insert a **go button** (a submit button with the value set to go) after the menu. This option supports JavaScript-disabled browsers. If JavaScript is enabled in a browser, the go button is unnecessary because the jump menu operates using JavaScript. However, more than just the go button is required to enable JavaScript-disabled browsers to visit the same links. The action URL must be complete and must point to a server-side script that redirects the user to the page chosen from the jump-menu list.

If your Web server uses ASP, you would point the action URL to jumpmenu.asp and set the Method to Get. The jumpmenu.asp file would contain:

```
<%

var destination = Request.QueryString("jumpmenu")

Response.redirect(destination)

%>
```

A similar solution is available for all server-side languages and enables all JavaScript-disabled browsers to go to the links provided by the select list.

7   Click OK.

8   Preview the page in your browser and choose an option from the list.

9   Return to Dreamweaver and close travel_log.html.

LESSON 6   Creating Image Rollovers

JavaScript is very popular for creating image rollovers. The *image rollover* is a JavaScript behavior that replaces one image with another when the mouse pointer rolls over the original image. This effect is very similar to that created by the CSS **:hover** pseudo-class, but CSS has limitations. For example, CSS cannot use fonts that are not available on a visitor's computer, nor can it create a glow around text or other graphical decorative effects. You can only assign the image rollover behavior to links: the **onMouseOver** and **onMouseOut** events do not trigger actions for all tags, although you can successfully assign some other tags, such as **<input>** tags in forms, to the **onMouseOver** and **onMouseOut** events.

Examine Web sites that use JavaScript image rollovers and you will see that many use quite simple effects that could be recreated with CSS properties. Keep in mind, however, that you must create an image for both states of the image rollover — **onMouseOver** and **onMouseOut**. If you need to add more rollovers, such as additional links in a navigation bar, you must open the template files for both rollover states in your image-editing application (you did remember to save the templates, didn't you?) and create the new graphics. Correcting a spelling mistake in a graphic also takes more effort than editing the HTML page.

Although this discussion may seem quite critical of image rollovers, consider it instead a caution. Picture the effects you want to create in the two states of the rollover and determine whether you can create the effect using CSS or only with a graphic. If the only means to create effects depend on graphics, then go ahead and create the graphics and set up the rollovers.

For the most part, image rollovers are not inaccessible because they are purely decorative. However, in Dreamweaver you can create image rollovers that roll over two images (or more) at the same time. If the second image provides additional content that is not available if JavaScript is disabled, then you must evaluate your audience and determine whether or not it is significant that some of your (or your employer's/client's) visitors do not receive the additional content.

Assign Image IDs

In this exercise, you create image rollovers of text images with a glow around the text, a graphical treatment not available through CSS. The first step in this process is to assign an id to each image so that the JavaScript knows which image to act on.

1   Open f1cars.html from the JavaScript site.

2   Click the Ferrari text graphic near the bottom of the page, and, in the Property inspector, type `ferrari` in the name field.

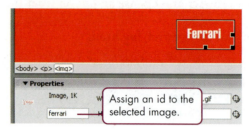

FIGURE 4.35

3   One by one, assign ids that are the same as the text they represent to the remaining images (excluding the F1 Cars logo graphic and the large photo montage).

4   Save the changes, but leave f1cars.html open for the next exercise.

Configure Image Rollovers

In Dreamweaver, image rollovers use the Swap Image behavior. A similar behavior — Swap Image Restore — swaps the new image back to the original image when the mouse pointer moves off the link area. The Swap Image Restore behavior has other uses than simple image rollovers, but this behavior is directly tied to the Swap Image behavior: you don't need to assign the two behaviors separately. Choosing the Restore Images onMouseOut option in the Swap Image dialog box enables the Swap Image Restore behavior.

1   In f1cars.html, click the Ferrari graphic link and choose Swap Image from the Behaviors pop-up menu.

2   Ensure that the ferrari image is selected in the Images field of the Swap Image dialog box.

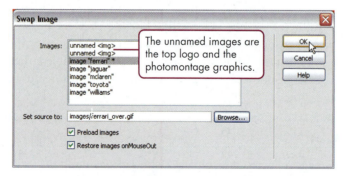

FIGURE 4.36

3   Click the Browse button of the Set Source to option, and choose images>ferrari_over.gif.

4   Ensure Preload Images and Restore Images onMouseOut are enabled and click OK.

You must configure the individual images separately.

5   Examine the Behaviors panel and note the two behaviors listed for the Ferrari graphic link.

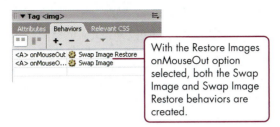

With the Restore Images onMouseOut option selected, both the Swap Image and Swap Image Restore behaviors are created.

FIGURE 4.37

6   Click the Jaguar graphic link and choose Swap Image from the Behaviors pop-up menu. Using the same procedures as in Steps 3 and 4, choose jaguar_over.gif and click OK.

7   Repeat Step 6 for the three remaining graphic links, choosing mclaren_over.gif, toyota_over.gif, and williams_over.gif as the sources for the swapped images. Click OK after each is set.

8   Preview the page in your browser and move your mouse pointer over each of the graphic links.

FIGURE 4.38

9   Return to Dreamweaver and close f1cars.html.

To Extend Your Knowledge

PRELOADING IMAGES

The Preload Images option is very useful because it causes JavaScript to load the **onMouseOut** images when the page loads: the **onMouseOut** images are only part of the page because of JavaScript, not because they are part of the HTML. If the Preload Images option is unchecked, then the display of the **onMouseOut** image is delayed while your browser downloads the image from the Web site. However, if you have many image rollovers, preloading all of the images can significantly delay the page loading into the browser while all of the images preload. A visitor with a slow dialup connection to the Internet may not appreciate the wait.

The **defer** attribute of the **<script>** tag can speed up the display of a Web page that uses JavaScript. You can use the **defer** attribute as follows: **<script   type="text/javascript" language="JavaScript" src="script.JavaScript" defer></script>**. The **defer** attribute delays the execution of the identified scripts but it does not defer the download of the external script. The advantage of this attribute is that the Web page can display without hindrance from any running scripts. However, the **defer** attribute, despite being part of W3C's HTML4 standard, is only supported by IE version 4 and later, although this does mean that most users will benefit from it.

LESSON 7   Creating a JavaScript Navigation Bar

Dreamweaver offers a sophisticated navigation-bar feature that allows you to configure your navigation bar with multiple links and to give each link up to four states. The four states are up, over, down, and over while down. The up and over states are the same as the **onMouseOut** and **onMouseOver** states, respectively. The down and over while down states are basically **onMouseOut** and **onMouseOver**, respectively, as well, but differ in that the down states are used when the links correspond to the current page. This is helpful because it indicates to visitors what page they are on.

As much as Dreamweaver tries to simplify the process of creating a navigation bar, the process is still quite involved. For this reason, although you only have 3 Web pages in this lesson, as each link has 4 states, you work with 12 graphic images.

Examine the Graphics for the Four States

In this exercise, you examine the 12 graphics that are used in this lesson. You see the differences between the 4 states for each navigation link.

1   Open states.html from the JavaScript site.

2   Examine the similarities and differences between the 12 graphics.

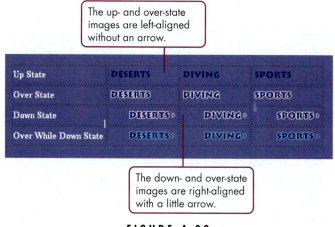

FIGURE 4.39

3   Close states.html.

Set Up the Deserts Navigation Images

In this exercise, you set up the navigation-bar images for the desert_fotos.html page. Remember to add alternative text when using graphical links so that users who cannot see graphics can still use your pages.

1   Open desert_fotos.html and click in the left empty table cell.

2   Switch the Insert Bar to the Common Insert bar and choose Navigation Bar from the Images drop-down menu.

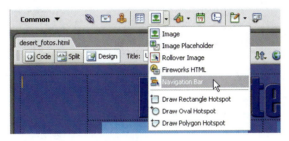

FIGURE 4.40

3   Type **deserts** in the Element Name field.

4   For the Up, Over, Down, and Over While Down images, browse to choose nb_desert_up.gif, nb_desert_over.gif, nb_desert_down.gif, and nb_desert_down_over.gif, respectively, from the images folder.

5   Type **Deserts** in the Alternate Text field.

6   In the When Clicked, Go to URL field, browse to select (or type) **desert_fotos.html**.

7   Set Insert to Vertically and ensure Use Tables is checked.

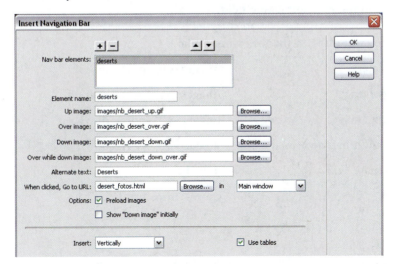

FIGURE 4.41

8   Do not click OK or close the Insert Navigation Bar dialog box as you need it for the next exercise.

Prepare the Image States for the Other Pages

In the previous exercise, you set up the states of the images for the Desert Photos pages. In this miniature Web site, however, every page links to every other page and you must configure the links and graphics for all other pages through this dialog box.

1   In the Insert Navigation Bar dialog box, click the plus symbol (Add Item button) above the Nav Bar Elements field.

FIGURE 4.42

2   Type **diving** in the Element Name field.

3   Set the images according to the following table:

Up Image	images>nb_diving_up.gif
Over Image	images>nb_diving_over.gif
Down Image	images>nb_diving_down.gif
Over While Down Image	images>nb_diving_down_over.gif
Alternate Text	Diving
URL	diving_fotos.html

4   Click the Add Item button

5   Type **sports** in the Element Name field.

6   Set the images according to the following table:

Up Image	images>nb_sports_up.gif
Over Image	images>nb_sports_over.gif
Down Image	images>nb_sports_down.gif
Over While Down Image	images>nb_sports_down_over.gif
Alternate Text	Sports
URL	sports_fotos.html

7   Click OK.

8   Save the changes, but leave desert_fotos.html open for the next exercise.

Copy the Navigation Bar to the Other Pages

You have created the navigation bar for the desert_fotos.html page. Your next step is to copy the table of navigation-bar links to the other pages.

1   In desert_fotos.html, click one of the navigation-bar graphics.

2   In the Tag selector, select the nested <table> tag to select the nested navigation-bar table.

FIGURE 4.43

3   Copy the selected table to the clipboard.

4   Open diving_fotos.html (without closing desert_fotos.html), click in the left empty table cell, and paste the copied table.

5   Save your changes to diving_fotos.html, but leave it open for the next exercise.

6   Open sports_fotos.html (without closing the other two pages), click in the left empty table cell, and paste the copied table.

7   Save your changes to sports_fotos.html, but leave it open, as well, for the next exercise.

Configure the Down States of the Navigation Bars

In this final exercise, you configure the down states of the navigation bars in each of the three pages. (You must do this page by page, so there was no point in trying to configure it earlier.)

1   In sports_fotos.html, click the Sports navigation-bar graphic.

2   Right/Control-click any of the behaviors in the Behaviors panel and choose Edit Behavior.

FIGURE 4.44

3 In the Set Nav Bar Image dialog box, ensure that the Element Name is sports, check the Show "Down Image" Initially checkbox, and click OK.

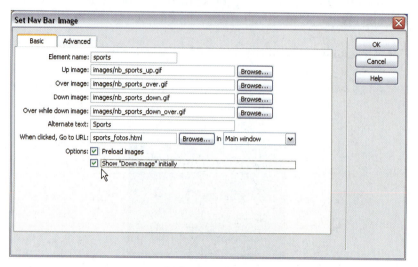

FIGURE 4.45

? **If you have problems**

If the Element Name is not sports, cancel the dialog box, click the sports graphic, and edit this behavior again.

---

4 Close sports_fotos.html, saving your changes.

5 In diving_fotos.html, click the Diving navigation-bar graphic, edit the Set Nav Bar behavior in the Behaviors panel, enable the Show "Down Image" Initially option, and click OK.

6 Close diving_fotos.html, saving your changes.

7 In desert_fotos.html, click the Deserts navigation-bar graphic, edit the Set Nav Bar behavior in the Behaviors panel, enable the Show "Down Image" Initially option, and click OK.

8 Preview the page in your browser, hover over the links, and click the links.

Note that the down states indicate the current page. Observe, as well, the different onMouseOver and onMouseOut states for both the down and not-down states.

FIGURE 4.46

9 Return to Dreamweaver and close desert_fotos.html.

To Extend Your Knowledge

SCREEN-READER SOFTWARE AND JAVASCRIPT

Most people who use screen-reading software use either JAWS or GW Window-Eyes. These programs work as a layer over the Windows operating system and Windows software, such as IE. Most screen-reader users have not disabled JavaScript in IE and, therefore, JavaScript is operational. However, unless the JavaScript developer has written the JavaScript to accommodate keyboard use, many JavaScript functions can cause problems for these users. This is why accessibility and JavaScript are often at odds — JavaScript is often enabled for screen-reader users who:

- cannot take advantage of it, for example, in mouse events

- use the keyboard instead of the mouse; many JavaScript functions do not use keyboard events to trigger behaviors or the keyboard events trigger the events incorrectly

- do not receive information about changing content, such as an action in one area of the screen triggers content to appear in another part of the screen, such as the Status bar

One possibility is to provide a JavaScript link stating "Disable JavaScript features" so a user with a JavaScript-enabled browser can view the pages without the JavaScript features. The developer of the pages must then code the JavaScript features to look for the cookie that indicates that JavaScript features are not to run. The developer must also ensure that the essential features of the page continue to be available and usable without JavaScript. However, such a feature is not part of the Dreamweaver collection of behaviors and requires an experienced JavaScript developer to create.

LESSON 8 Validating Forms

JavaScript form validation is very beneficial for a number of reasons. It provides immediate feedback to the visitor and saves extra demand on the server. This results in savings in server demand — also a savings in ***bandwidth*** (the number of bytes downloaded from the Web server) — and time because the validation is performed right on the visitor's computer. Another benefit to such client-side validation is that the validation script can be written to ***set the focus*** (move the insertion point) to the field in error.

There are two methods of alerting a visitor that the data in a form is not valid. The quicker method to configure initiates the validation script when the user clicks the submit button. The **onSubmit** event triggers the validation script: it intercepts the submission of the form data to the form-processing application. Within the form-processing script, it determines whether the validation is OK (true) or not OK (false). When the form-validation script has completed, a line in the JavaScript script sends either a **return true** or **return false** back to the browser. If **return true** is sent back, the browser then submits the data to the action URL. However, if **return false** is sent back from the form-validation script, the browser does not send the data.

The other method of form validation is to have the validation occur at every field. This is no more difficult than the other method; it is just more involved as there are more steps to the process because each field requires configuring with validation criteria. Generally, this type of field-by-field validation uses the **onBlur** event, triggered when the visitor moves the focus away from the field by tabbing to the next field or clicking in another field.

Not all fields require validation: for instance, you can allow visitors not to insert their names or email addresses if they don't want you to respond to their comments. However, you may prefer to require that both the subject and comment be completed.

Forms can also be validated on the basis of content. For example, email addresses must be formatted correctly, and phone-number fields must contain only numbers. Dreamweaver's form-validation script is fairly basic, but nevertheless beneficial. Performing full and complete validation of complex forms, however, with all the bells and whistles requires custom programming. Although there may be some common formats, such as the email-address format, only you know what you need for your specific requirements, and therefore, only you can specify how the validation is to proceed.

Remove an Unneeded Behavior

In this exercise, you learn to remove an unneeded behavior from the Behaviors panel.

1 Open contact_me.html from the MT-P4 site.

2 In the Behaviors panel, click the Set Text of Status Bar event, and then click the Remove Event button (– symbol).

FIGURE 4.47

3 Keep contact_me.html open for the next exercise.

Validate the Fields of a Form

In this exercise, you configure validation for all fields to occur at the same time. When you configure form validation in this manner, you use the **onSubmit** event to trigger the validation script when the user clicks the submit button.

1 In contact_me.html, click anywhere in the form in the Document window but not on any labels or fields.

2 Click the <form#contactme> tag in the Tag selector.

3 In the Behaviors panel, choose Validate Form from the Behaviors pop-up menu.

4 With name selected in the Named Fields list, set the Value to Required, set Accept to Anything, but do not click OK.

5   Click email in the Named Fields list, set the Value to Required, and set Accept to Email Address.

6   Click subject in the Named Fields list, set the Value to Required, and set Accept to Anything.

7   Click comments in the Named Fields list, set the Value to Required, and set Accept to Anything.

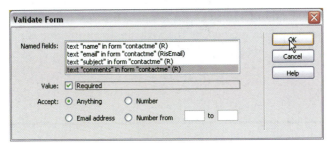

FIGURE 4.48

8   Click OK and preview the page in your browser.

9   Click the Send Me Your Comments button and note the alert message that appears, identifying what fields need valid data.

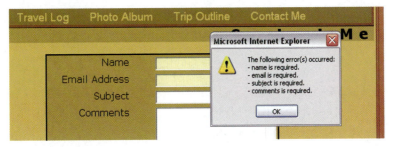

FIGURE 4.49

10   Click OK, return to Dreamweaver, and close contact_me.html.

To Extend Your Knowledge

NEVER DEPEND ON CLIENT-SIDE FORM VALIDATION

JavaScript form validation is very beneficial as it returns the error much more quickly to the visitor, saves bandwidth by reducing the number of round trips to the server, can be configured to alert the user of a problem as soon as the user moves from a field, and can be configured to set the focus of the insertion point on the field in error. Despite all of these benefits, remember that JavaScript may be unavailable or disabled. Never depend on JavaScript validation alone because the form's contents may not be valid without JavaScript. Always back up client-side validation with server-side validation.

SUMMARY

In this project, you learned about inline JavaScript, events, event handlers, and functions. You created some inline JavaScript and learned how embedding the code within a function is more efficient. You used Dreamweaver's Behaviors panel to create pop-up alerts and Status-bar messages. You created a jump menu to provide a list of links, which, when selected, would take the visitor to the selected URL. You created image rollovers and a sophisticated navigation bar with four different states. You learned to configure a form-validation script that can validate field by field or all of the form at once. You also learned that, when you consider using JavaScript, you must evaluate the target audience of the Web site to ensure that the JavaScript will not be a barrier for your visitors.

KEY TERMS

alert	image rollover	onSubmit
bandwidth	JavaScript	onUnload
behavior	JScript	parameter
client-side	literal	pop-up window
concatenate	method	<script>
ECMAScript	onClick	scripted programming language
event	onBlur	server-side
event handler	onChange	syntax debug
execute	onLoad	variable
focus	onMouseOver	VBScript
function	onMouseOut	

CHECKING CONCEPTS AND TERMS

SCREEN ID

Identify the indicated areas from the list below:

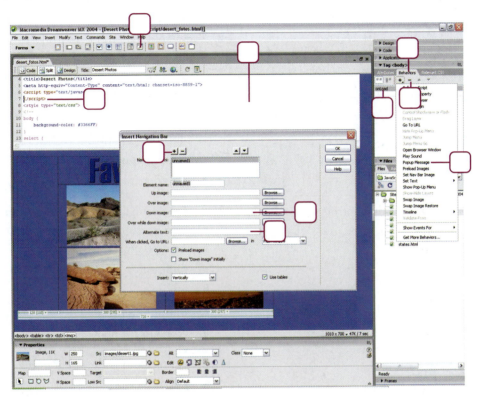

FIGURE 4.50

a. Behaviors panel

b. Source field for down state

c. Code window

d. Create a pop-up message

e. Add Item button

f. <script> tag

g. Remove Behavior button

h. Create a jump menu

i. Alternate text for navigation-bar item

j. onLoad event

MULTIPLE CHOICE

Circle the letter of the correct answer for each of the following:

1. In `<a href="filename.html" onClick="function();">`, onClick is _____.

   a. an event

   b. an attribute

   c. a trigger

   d. All of the above

2. JavaScript code can be written between which tags?

   a. `<% Language="JavaScript" %>`

   b. `<script></script>`

   c. `<javascript></javascript>`

   d. `<a></a>`

3. One advantage of exporting JavaScript code to an external file is _____.

  a. it runs faster

  b. it is available to multiple pages

  c. it is protected from being viewed by even the most experienced visitor

  d. None of the above

4. JavaScript is _____.

  a. a client-side programming language

  b. also known as ECMAScript

  c. not always accessible

  d. All of the above

5. Client-side form validation _____.

  a. responds more quickly to errors

  b. can save bandwidth

  c. can be disabled

  d. All of the above

6. To improve the speed of image rollovers, you would _____.

  a. always use the down state

  b. enable the preload option

  c. keep the filenames short

  d. All of the above

7. Which of the following is true?

  a. Status-bar text can be colored and enlarged.

  b. JavaScript is enabled in all browsers.

  c. Pop-up windows may contain Web pages.

  d. None of the above.

8. You would like to provide links to the five most popular pages on your Web site, a collection that changes each month. Which JavaScript behavior is most suitable for this task?

  a. pop-up window

  b. navigation bar

  c. jump menu

  d. unordered list

9. To invoke a behavior in a page when a visitor's browser opens the page, you would use the following event:

  a. `onOpen`

  b. `onLoad`

  c. `onMouseOver`

  d. None of the above

10. Which block of code would not fail?

  a. `onClick{popupPhoto();}`

  b. `onClick="document.body.`
      `style.color="red";"`

  c. `onClick='validate();'`

  d. None of the above

DISCUSSION QUESTIONS

  1. You have created a form to collect information about your magazine subscribers. It has the following fields: Title (Mr., Mrs., Dr., etc.), First Name, Last Name, Street Address 1, Street Address 2, City/Town, State, Zip, Phone, Fax, Toll-Free Phone, Email Address, Age, Family Income, and Number of Family Members. What fields would you make required fields? Without worrying about how to code the JavaScript, give English instructions that describe the validation that should be performed on each required field, such as Number of Family Members: numbers only, maximum 2 digits, greater than 0.

  2. Pop-up windows can be very annoying when overused. However, used with discretion, they can be a beneficial method of presenting information. List at least four situations when the use of pop-up windows could be beneficial to the usability of a Web site.

SKILL DRILL

Skill Drills reinforce project skills. Each skill reinforced is the same, or nearly the same, as a skill presented in the lessons. Detailed instructions are provided in a step-by-step format. Work through these exercises in order.

1. Create a Double Rollover

In this Skill Drill, you set two images to swap when the mouse pointer moves over one. You could extend this technique to swap many images at the same time. However, that would mean that more and more images must preload, which would delay the loading of the Web page.

1. Open f1cars.html from the JavaScript site.

2. Click the photomontage image and, in the Property inspector, assign it the name **large**.

3. Click the Ferrari graphic link in the Document window.

4. Right/Control-click Swap Image in the Behaviors panel (not Swap Image Restore) and choose Edit Behavior.

5. Choose image "large" from the Images list, click the Browse button, choose images>ferrari_car.jpg, click Select/Choose, then click OK.

6. Click the Jaguar graphic link, edit the Swap Image behavior, choose the "large" image, assign the source to images>jaguar_car.jpg, click Select/Choose, then click OK.

7. Repeat Step 6 for the Mclaren, Toyota, and Williams graphic links, setting the "large" image swap image to mclaren_car.jpg, toyota_car.jpg, and williams_car.jpg, respectively.

8. Preview the page in your browser and notice that both the graphic text link and the large image swap images.

FIGURE 4.51

9. Return to Dreamweaver and close f1cars.html.

LEVEL 2   200   Project 4   JavaScript Behaviors

2. Validate One Field at a Time

In this Skill Drill exercise, you associate the validate-form script with specific fields. The advantage of this method is that when the visitor enters either invalid data or no data in a required field, the script immediately alerts the visitor that a problem exists. This may be most beneficial in long forms where the submit button may be distant from the first fields.

1. Open contact_me.html from the MT-P4 site.

2. Click anywhere in the contact form, Right/Control-click the Validate Form behavior in the Behaviors panel, and choose Delete Behavior.

3. Click the Subject field in the Document window.

4. Choose the Validate Form behavior from the pop-up menu of the Behaviors panel.

5. Choose the subject field from the Named Fields list, enable the Required option, set Accept to Anything, and click OK.

6. Click the Comments field in the Document window.

7. Choose the Validate Form behavior from the pop-up menu of the Behaviors panel.

8. Choose the comments field from the Named Fields list, enable the Required option, set Accept to Anything, and click OK.

9. Preview the page in your browser, click in the Subject field, and, without typing anything, tab to the Comments field and note the alert.

10. Click OK to acknowledge the alert and then tab to the submit button.

11. Click OK to acknowledge the alert.

12. Return to Dreamweaver and close contact_me.html.

3. Open Images in Pop-Up Windows

In this exercise, you set links to open in new pop-up windows.

1. Open planets.html from the JavaScript site.

2. Click in the hotspot for Mercury (the first planet from the Sun).

3. Choose Open Browser Window from the Behaviors pop-up menu.

4. Use the Browse button beside the URL to Display field to choose images>mercury.jpg. Set both the Window Width and Window Height to **300**, type **image** in the Window Name field, and click OK.

5. In the Behaviors panel, click the event onMouseOver, and choose onClick from the list of events.

6. Configure the Venus, Earth, Mars, Jupiter, Saturn, Uranus, Neptune, and Pluto hotspots using the same methods as you did in Steps 2 to 5 to open the images of the planets in new windows.

7. Preview the page in your browser and, one at a time, click the hotspots to display the enlarged images in pop-up windows.

? If you have problems

Some browsers are configured, through their own features or add-on software, to prevent pop-up windows. If you have this feature installed or configured, you may need to either disable or override it (the Google toolbar allows you to open a blocked pop-up window by pressing the Control button when clicking the pop-up window link). However, most pop-up blockers do not prevent requested windows, in other words, windows that open in response to onClick events.

---

8. Return to Dreamweaver and close planets.html.

4. Create an onMouseOver Photo Album

In this Skill Drill, you use the onMouseOver event over a photograph thumbnail to make a larger photograph appear. You also disable the onMouseOut event so that the last photo remains. This allows the user to move the mouse pointer away and still see the larger photograph.

1. Before you begin, define a new site called **TO-P4** from the Project_04> TO-P4 folder.

2. Open staff.html.

3. Click the center photograph and, in the Property inspector, assign the name **largePhoto**.

4. Click the top-left photograph and note the filename in the Property inspector.

   You need to know the filename to be able to swap in the larger image with the same filename.

5. With the top-left photograph selected, choose Swap Image from the Behaviors panel pop-up menu.

6. From the Images list in the Swap Image dialog box, choose image "largePhoto". Click the Browse button and set the source to photos>alan.jpg. Uncheck Restore Images onMouseOut and click OK.

7. Repeat Step 6 for the remaining photos in the outer cells of the table.

   The thumbnail photographs and the larger photographs both have the same filename for the same person but are stored in different folders.

8. Preview the page in your browser and move your mouse pointer over the thumbnail photos.

9. Return to Dreamweaver and close staff.html.

CHALLENGE

Challenge exercises expand on, or are somewhat related to, skills presented in the lessons. Each exercise provides a brief introduction, followed by instructions in a numbered-step format that are not as detailed as those in the Skill Drill exercises. Work through the exercises in order.

1. Open an Additional Frame Using JavaScript

A link can open only one Web page at a time, whether the page is in a framed or nonframed layout. You can create the illusion of opening multiple pages from one link by linking to a frameset page, however it is not the link but the frameset that is opening multiple pages.

You can use JavaScript to open a second (or more) Web page from a single link. In fact, the Web pages may be in completely separate frames. A benefit to this particular snippet of JavaScript code is that the JavaScript only opens one frame; the other frame is opened by a standard link and target. This means that if someone were to view this page with a browser that does not run JavaScript, he or she would still be able to open one page in the frameset.

In this exercise, you hand-code the JavaScript code, but the code is quite short and simple. You could easily extend it to open a third, fourth, or more frames if you wanted, but that is beyond the scope of this exercise.

1. Before you begin, define a new site called **Calendar** from the Project_04>Calendar folder.

2. Open calendar.html from the Calendar site, preview the frameset in your browser, and test the links in the top-left calendar.

   The links open the details of the day in the frame below the calendar, but the frame to the right of the calendar frame remains empty — it contains an empty HTML page. You will create JavaScript that changes the Web page in the right frame to a Web page that contains the number of the selected calendar day in addition to the day's details below.

3. Return to Dreamweaver, click in the top-left frame containing the calendar table, and open the code window.

4. Find line 6, which contains the **\<title\>** tag, click to the right of the closing tag (**\</title\>**), and press Enter/Return.

5. Type **\<sc** and press Enter/Return to accept the script, type **t** and press Enter/Return to accept type, type **t** and press Enter/Return to accept text/javascript, type **\>** to close the tag, and then press Enter/Return twice.

6. Move the insertion point up one line, type **function alsoOpen(pageurl) {**, and press Enter/Return. Type **top.dayframe.location = "days/" + pageurl;** and press Enter/Return. Type **}**.

7. Scroll down to line 40, the line that contains the link to feb1.html.

8. Click between **target="detailsframe"** and **\>**, press the Spacebar, and type **onClick="alsoOpen('day1.html');"**.

9. Copy and paste this block into the same position in the link code to feb2.html through feb7.html, changing day1.html to the appropriate day number for the current link.

10. Switch to the Design view, save the changes, preview the page, and test the links in your browser.

    This time you should see the both the day's details and the day number change.

? If you have problems

If the day-number Web page does not appear in the dayFrame as it should, return to february.html in Dreamweaver and carefully check the code.

---

11. Return to Dreamweaver and close calendar.html.

2. Fill Fields with JavaScript

JavaScript can provide many practical uses, such as helping visitors complete a Web form. For example, in a situation where both the shipping and billing addresses are the same, wouldn't it be easier to simply click an option to indicate that both addresses are the same and have JavaScript populate the second series of address fields with the data from the first series? It is not difficult to create this script, although it is not one in Dreamweaver's list of behaviors: you must hand-code it.

There are two stages to this procedure. The first stage is selecting the type form control with which you invoke the JavaScript. Two form controls come to mind quickly: a checkbox where checked means yes and unchecked means no, or two radio buttons corresponding to yes and no. Although it is slightly easier to insert one checkbox than two radio buttons, the JavaScript is more complicated because, with one checkbox, the JavaScript must determine the state, checked or unchecked, to determine which action to take, whereas separating the yes and no into two radio buttons simplifies the JavaScript. The second stage of this procedure is to configure the `onClick` event for the yes and no buttons to invoke two different functions — the yes button to populate the shipping-address fields with the billing-address data and the no button to clear the shipping-address fields of any data that may exist in them.

1. Open order_form.html from the TO-P4 site.

2. Click the Same as Shipping Address button and switch to the Code view.

3. To the left of the > character at the end of the selected radio-button code, press the Spacebar, and then type `onClick="sabay();"`.

    sabay is an abbreviation for Same As Billing Address Yes, the function that populates the shipping fields with the billing-fields data when the user clicks this radio button.

4. Five lines below is the radio-button code for the no radio-button option. Click to the left of the **>** character at the end of the radio-button code, press the Spacebar, and then type `onClick="saban();"`.

    saban is an abbreviation for Same As Billing Address No, the function that clears the shipping-fields data when the user clicks this radio button.

5. Scroll up to line 7 and (with the assistance of code hints) type `<script type="text/javascript" src="script.js"></script>`.

   The `sabay()` and `saban()` functions will be created in an external JavaScript file with the filename script.js.

6. Choose File>New. From Category, choose Basic Page; from Basic Page, choose JavaScript; and click Create. Click at the end of the first line and press Enter/Return.

7. Type `function sabay() {` and press Enter/Return.

8. Type `document.order.shipping_street.value = document.order.billing_street.value;` and press Enter/Return.

9. Repeat Step 8 five more times, replacing street (on both sides of the equal sign) with `city`, `state`, `zip`, `phone`, and `fax`. After the last line, press Enter/Return, type `}`, and press Enter/Return.

10. Create a function named `saban()` and repeat Steps 7 to 9, except on the right side of the equal sign, type `""` before the semicolon, such as `document.order.shipping_street.value = "";`. When finished, close script.js, saving your changes.

```
 1  // JavaScript Document
 2  function sabay() {
 3      document.order.shipping_street.value = document.order.billing_street.value;
 4      document.order.shipping_city.value = document.order.billing_city.value;
 5      document.order.shipping_state.value = document.order.billing_state.value;
 6      document.order.shipping_zip.value = document.order.billing_zip.value;
 7      document.order.shipping_phone.value = document.order.billing_phone.value;
 8      document.order.shipping_fax.value = document.order.billing_fax.value;
 9  }
10
11  function saban() {
12      document.order.shipping_street.value = "";
13      document.order.shipping_city.value = "";
14      document.order.shipping_state.value = "";
15      document.order.shipping_zip.value = "";
16      document.order.shipping_phone.value = "";
17      document.order.shipping_fax.value = "";
18  }
```

FIGURE 4.52

11. Preview order_form.html in your browser, enter some information in the billing-address fields, and click the radio buttons.

12. Return to Dreamweaver and close order_form.html.

3. Create, Copy, and Configure a Navigation Bar

In this Challenge exercise, you create and install a navigation bar for Tropiflora Online. The images all follow the same pattern: once you have set one up, the rest fall into the same pattern. After you create the base navigation bar, you copy it to the other pages. Finally, you configure the down state for each page.

1. Open index.html from the TO-P4 site and click in the empty leafy cell on the left.

2. Choose Insert>Image Objects>Navigation Bar from the menu.

3. Type **home** in the Element Name field. Using the Browse button, set images>nb_home.gif as the Up Image, set images>nb_home_over.gif as the Over Image, images>nb_home_down.gif as the Down Image, and images>nb_home_down_over.gif as the Over While Down Image. Set Alternate Text to **Home**. Set the link URL to index.html. Ensure that Show "Down Image" Initially is not checked. Set Insert to Vertically and ensure Use Tables is checked. Click the Add Item (+) button.

4. Using the same procedures as in Step 3, set the **about**, **products**, **staff**, **location**, and **contact** elements. Click OK when finished all of them.

5. Click in the new navigation bar, click the **<table>** tag in the Tag selector to select the nested navigation-bar table, and copy it to the clipboard.

6. Close about.html, and, one by one, open the rest of the pages and paste the copied navigation-bar table into the left, empty, leafy cell. Close each page after pasting.

7. Open index.html. Click the Home graphic in the navigation-bar table, double-click the Set Nav Bar Image behavior in the Behaviors panel, enable the Set "Down Image" Initially option, and click OK. Close index.html.

8. One-by-one, open about.html, contact.html, location.html, and staff.html, and set their respective graphics in the navigation bar to the down state.

9. One-by-one, open products.html, bromeliads.html, tillandsias.html, succulents.html, and order_form.html, and, in all cases, set the Products graphic as the down image. Close the file when finished.

    All of these pages are part of the products group so the Products navigation-bar graphic should be the down image for them all.

10. Open index.html and preview the page in your browser, moving the mouse pointer over the links and clicking the links to verify the over, down, and over while down states.

11. Return to Dreamweaver and close index.html.

P O R T F O L I O   B U I L D E R

Create Custom Buttons and Image Rollovers

JavaScript image rollovers are very similar to the **:hover** CSS property and it makes sense to consider the **:hover** property for basic rollover effects. For example, if two image graphics use a commonly available font with different flat colors behind the text, then using JavaScript to swap the images is overkill. This effect is more easily achieved using the **:hover** CSS property. However, you cannot use CSS to create graphics effects, such as glows or animations. These are situations where graphics are required and, by extension, JavaScript rollovers. This book focuses on using Dreamweaver, so in this assignment you use an online button-creation application at buttongenerator.com. If you also have and are familiar with graphics software that allows you to create such images, go ahead and use the software instead to create the images for the effects you design.

1. Go to buttongenerator.com. Browse through the five pages of button styles and select a button style. (You can change the color, font, and text, so don't think that you're limited to the displayed buttons.)

2. Change the Mode to Advance Form. Select the Initial State and Mouse Over State button styles. Set the Button colors (the color of the button, not the text).

3. Create four text labels — **Home**, **Products**, **Services**, **Contact Us** — and select a font from the list. (The frame of font images previews the fonts.)

4. When finished configuring the options, experiment to see what some of them do. Click the Click Here to Generate Your Button button at the bottom of the form.

5. When the buttons appear, Right/Control-click on each of the buttons and save them to your Project_04 folder. (Depending on your browser, you may have to save them first and then move them.)

6. Create a Web page called buttons.html with a 4-row, 1-column layout table and insert one of each pair of buttons into the cells and link the buttons to buttons.html. Using the Behaviors panel, use the onMouseOver event to swap the buttons with their alternates. Preview the page in your browser.

7. If you feel up to the challenge, return to buttongenerator.com. Create two more button states using the same basic style and text but change some other aspect of the appearance so that you have four variations of the same button. Save these new buttons to the same folder and use all four states to create the four states of a navigation bar.

PROJECT 5

Animation and DHTML

OBJECTIVES

In this project, you learn how to

- Distinguish components of the Timelines panel

- Add images, layers, and behaviors to animations

- Time the operation of behaviors

- Set animations to play automatically

- Make animations repeat

- Create movement of layers

- Create a DHTML navigation menu

WHY WOULD I DO THIS?

Everyone loves animation, especially on the Web, and more and more sites offer animation to encourage visitors to return. Nothing works as well as movement to grab the eye when jumping from site to site. While it doesn't offer the same horsepower as its sister program, Flash, Dreamweaver's animation capabilities can add motion to an otherwise static page.

Creating animation using Dreamweaver is a combination of some of the topics that we covered in earlier projects: HTML, CSS, images, layers, and JavaScript behaviors. The combination of these items creates **DHTML** (Dynamic HTML). The term DHTML was coined to distinguish basic JavaScript behaviors, such as pop-up windows, from advanced behaviors, such as animations. W3Schools.com goes so far as to state that DHTML is more of a marketing term than an actual technology. Although DHTML isn't a W3C technology, it depends on many of them.

Although there are essential similarities between simple JavaScript and the more complex DHTML, an example may clarify the difference. Simple JavaScript can be used to dynamically create HTML, such as `document.write("<p>This is a paragraph.</p>");`. This code writes a paragraph to the Web page. An example of DHTML extending this concept might be code that dynamically creates a layer with embedded content so the layer follows your mouse pointer around the page and changes colors every 10 seconds. Fold-out lists, drop-down menus, and randomly falling snowflakes are some examples of DHTML.

In many cases, DHTML involves timing. For example, it is very easy to display a hidden layer named menu using `onMouseOver = "document.menu.style.display = 'block'";`. This is the type of effect that you would use to display a menu when the visitor's mouse pointer moves over the top heading of the menu. However, as soon as you move your mouse pointer off the link that displays the menu, for example, to choose an item from the menu, the menu either disappears or is obscured by another that appears on top of it. This is solved using a timer that holds the current menu visible for a few seconds, allowing you enough time to make your choice before it disappears.

Creating these type of complex behaviors is beyond the skills of most Web designers, but Dreamweaver has the features necessary to create many DHTML effects and behaviors. Using the Timelines panel, you can create a number of these complex effects without writing one character of code. With some ingenuity, you can create many interesting DHTML effects, including games.

There are several drawbacks to DHTML, the first being browser versions. DHTML commonly uses the **DOM** (Document Object Model) to manipulate objects in the Web page. The DOM is a tree-like description of an HTML element in the current document. You can see a very similar visualization of the DOM in the Tag selector, such as `<body><p><a#home>`, which means a link with the id of home within a paragraph within the body of the Web page. Although the syntax of the DOM differs from that of the Tag selector, the basis is similar. The problem with browser versions is that Netscape Navigator 4.x (NN4), IE, and the more-standards-compliant browsers (Mozilla and Opera7+) each use different methods of accessing the DOM, and older browsers do not support DOM-based JavaScript at all. You must make your DHTML code, therefore, support all current browsers, or indicate that your site does not support certain browsers (which was more common in the past but is currently frowned upon), or just accept that some or all DHTML may not be available to all of your visitors.

Another drawback to DHTML is that it is rarely accessible. Many DHTML effects support only mouse events, and although some may be configured to support keyboards, to do so often requires significant JavaScript experience and skills. However, if the DHTML is decorative or provides functionality that only adds to HTML that currently exists, then although those who need accessibility may not be able to use the DHTML, they may be able to use the base HTML of the document. For example, if a DHTML menu is used to enhance an existing HTML menu, then if the DHTML menu can't be used without a mouse, the base HTML menu is a reasonable fallback.

A similar caveat regarding DHTML applies either when browsers don't support JavaScript or when visitors have disabled JavaScript in their browsers. If the designer depends on the DHTML being functional, these visitors would not be able to use the DHTML and would miss a key functionality of your Web site. You must take care, when you consider using DHTML scripts, to determine whether or not your target audience will be able to use the DHTML and decide how to deal with visitors who cannot.

V I S U A L   S U M M A R Y

Many animations created with DHTML require timing, whether the timing is at the beginning or during the animation. Creating timing with JavaScript code is very complex, but Dreamweaver offers the Timelines panel to assist with this. It is a visual tool enabling you to configure the timing of different events without having to type a single character of JavaScript. A *keyframe* is a frame at which a change in the animation occurs as well as the start and finish of the animation.

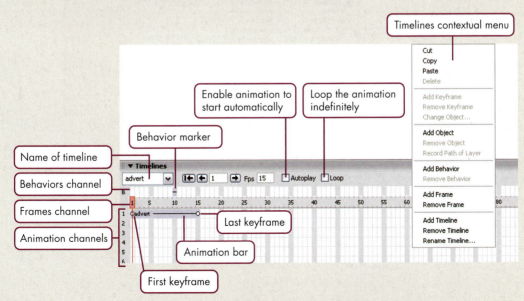

FIGURE 5.1

In order to create animations, the JavaScript must be able to uniquely identify the object being animated. To do this, in the Property inspector you add a name to either the image or the layer, depending on which you are animating. Although Dreamweaver automatically creates unique ids for both, it assigns names like image1, image2, image3, etc. or layer1, layer2, layer3, etc., neither of which may convey much to you. You should assign more meaningful names to the images or layers.

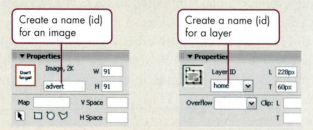

FIGURE 5.2

Although you can create many animations using the Timelines panel, you can also create a DHTML menu that does not use the Timelines panel. The menus can be quite complex with subnavigation menus, and can be configured in many different ways. The Show Pop-Up Menu dialog box consists of four tabs that enable you to create and configure your DHTML menu, as needed.

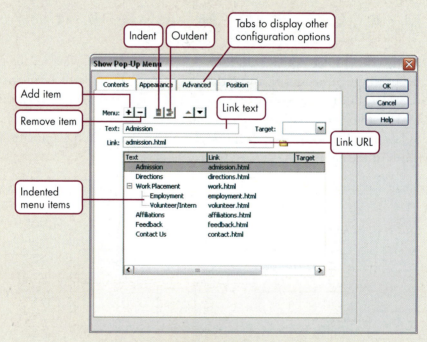

FIGURE 5.3

LESSON 1   Exploring the Timelines Panel

This lesson explores objects and the Timelines panel. Dreamweaver's DHTML can only act upon two types of objects: images and layers. Although Dreamweaver can perform some animation with images, images cannot be moved with DHTML, only layers can be moved. However, images can be swapped. In *Project 3: Using CSS for Layout*, you learned that layers play a role in JavaScript as well as in CSS. Dreamweaver layers are `<div>` tags absolutely positioned with CSS style properties. You learned that JavaScript can modify CSS in the `body.style.color='red'` exercise. Other aspects of CSS can also be modified, including position. For this reason, layers, which have CSS positional properties, can be moved whereas images (unless contained in a layer) cannot be moved.

In order for any DHTML to work on an object, that object must have an individual id. It is not necessary to assign ids to all objects, however, just those to which DHTML will be applied. As discussed earlier, ids play a role in JavaScript as well as in CSS, and DHTML is especially dependent on ids. Other objects may have ids for CSS and that is fine. Having unique ids is especially important for DHTML because you don't want two objects running the same DHTML — in fact, the DHTML may not work for either if there are two or more instances of the same id.

The other tool you learn to use is the Timelines panel. Many DHTML effects depend on timing, if only to create a delay. Dreamweaver's Timelines panel allows you to manipulate the timing of effects, such as delaying the initiation of, prolonging, and repeating a behavior. By default, the Timelines panel is not visible; you can open it by choosing Window>Timelines. The Timelines panel consists of numerous animation channels, allowing you to animate multiple objects at the same time with their own patterns of animations. You can also create multiple timelines so that you can create independent animations.

In the previous project, you learned to trigger image swapping with the **onMouseOver** event. In this project, you create a timed behavior in which image swapping occurs at timed intervals, hence you need the Timelines panel. Like images and layers, you can add behaviors to the Timelines panel, but only if an object already exists on this panel.

? If you have problems

This project depends on the Timelines panel. During the development of Dreamweaver MX 2004, Macromedia did not include the Timelines panel in version 7.0, but later reinstated the panel in version 7.0.1. To determine which version you have, either examine the splash screen when you launch Dreamweaver or choose Help>About and click the About window. If the version states 7.0, you must download the upgrade patch (free) from Macromedia to complete this project.

Add an Image Object to the Timelines Panel

In this exercise, you add an image to the Timelines panel. There are two methods of adding an object to the Timelines panel: you can drag an image to the panel or you can select an image in the Document window, Right/Control-click in the Timelines panel, and choose Add Image from the contextual menu.

1   **Define the Project_05>TO-P5 folder as a site called TO-P5 . Do not click Done, but remove all previously defined sites from the Manage Sites dialog box and then click Done.**

2   **Open index.html.**

3   **Drag images>anim1.gif from the Files panel to below the Contact link in the left navigation bar.**

4   **Type advert in the Name field of the Property inspector.**

FIGURE 5.4

5   **Choose Window>Timelines to open the Timelines panel below the Property inspector.**

6   **Type advert in the Timelines name field.**

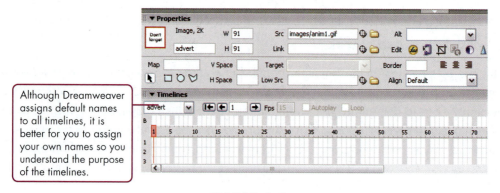

FIGURE 5.5

7 Drag the anim1.gif image from the Document window to animation channel 1 of the Timelines panel at frame1.

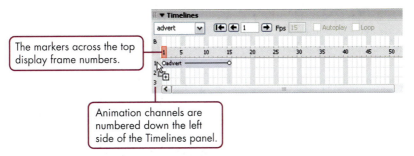

The markers across the top display frame numbers.

Animation channels are numbered down the left side of the Timelines panel.

FIGURE 5.6

8 Read the alert and then click OK to acknowledge it.

FIGURE 5.7

9 Save the changes, but keep index.html open for the next lesson.

To Extend Your Knowledge

DHTML IS VERY COMPLEX

DHTML can be used to create some very interesting and useful effects. However, the JavaScript code used to create DHTML behaviors and effects can be quite complex. Be aware that although there are many free DHTML scripts that you can download from DHTMLCentral.com, Javascripts.com, or HotScripts.com, in order to configure them, you have to modify the code to fit them to your needs. Some scripts, such as ones creating the effect of falling snowflakes, may be immediately useable, but others may require a significant investment in time. You wouldn't need to modify the code, just the options, and many authors of these types of scripts present the options at the top of the script code with instructions on what you can change and which options are available.

LESSON 2 Adding Behaviors to the Timelines Panel

The purpose of the Timelines panel is to time the action of behaviors. There are many ways to use timing with a behavior. Timing can delay the start of a behavior, can trigger different behaviors at different times, and can extend or shorten the duration of a behavior.

Two channels in the Timelines panel have a role in the timing of behaviors: the Behaviors channel and the Frames channel. The Frames channel selects the frame in which a particular behavior is to be triggered. Timeline events are unlike the JavaScript events you have encountered before: Timeline events all start with onFrameX where X represents the frame number, such as onFrame15. These are not standard JavaScript events, but events created by and for the JavaScript code to enable the behaviors to occur at the appropriate times.

To add a behavior to the Behaviors channel, you click in the Behaviors channel at the frame at which you want the event to occur. You then click the Add Event button in the Behaviors panel, choose a behavior, and configure it. When you add a behavior to the Timelines panel, a marker appears in the Behaviors channel at the selected frame. When you click the marker, you can view the details of the behavior in the Behaviors panel and, if necessary, modify the behavior. You can even drag the behavior marker to another frame to trigger the behavior at another time.

Add the Swap-Image Behavior to the Timelines Panel

In this exercise, you add behaviors to the Timelines panel to trigger the swapping action at different times. There are four images. You add the Swap Image behavior to four different frames and, at each time, select a different image.

1 In the open file, index.html, drag the ending keyframe of the advert animation bar in the Timelines panel to the mark at frame 60.

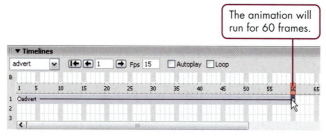

The animation will run for 60 frames.

FIGURE 5.8

2 Click at the 15-frame mark in the Behaviors channel.

FIGURE 5.9

3 From the pop-up menu of the Behaviors panel, choose Swap image.

FIGURE 5.10

4 Choose image "advert" from the Images list, click the Browse button to choose images>anim2.gif, ensure that Preload Images is checked, and click OK.

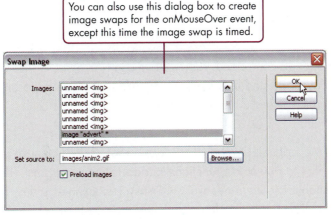

You can also use this dialog box to create image swaps for the onMouseOver event, except this time the image swap is timed.

FIGURE 5.11

5 Examine the Behaviors panel.

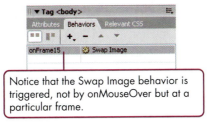

Notice that the Swap Image behavior is triggered, not by onMouseOver but at a particular frame.

FIGURE 5.12

6 Click in the Behaviors channel of the Timelines panel at frame 30. Using the same procedures as in Steps 3 and 4, add a Swap Image behavior and set the source of the advert image to images>anim3.gif.

7 Using the same procedures as in Step 6, add a Swap Image behavior at frame 45, setting the source of the image to anim4.gif. Add a final Swap Image behavior at frame 60, setting the source of the image to anim1.gif.

FIGURE 5.13

8 Preview the page in your browser and observe that the image did nothing.

9 Return to Dreamweaver, but leave index.html open for the next lesson.

To Extend Your Knowledge

OTHER SOURCES OF DHTML SCRIPTS

There are many sources of DHTML scripts available on the Web. Some examples are DHTMLCentral.com, HotScripts.com, and DynamicDrive.com. All of these sites offer tutorials as well as free scripts for you to download and use. Recognize that these scripts generally require you to hand-code any changes you need to make the scripts work for you, such as colors, speed of animation, or organization of menu items.

Another source of DHTML scripts is Dreamweaver extensions. Extensions are part of all Macromedia products and enable users to download functions to add to the programs. There are more than just DHTML extensions available for Dreamweaver, such as prepackaged styles, form-validation scripts, and accessibility-testing functions. To download more extensions, choose Commands>Manage Extensions, click the Macromedia button, and browse the extensions available to download and install. Some extensions are free and others are available for a fee; Macromedia created some and outside developers created others. The advantage these extensions have over free downloadable scripts is that they operate visually: you can configure the extensions using dialog boxes without needing to deal with the code.

LESSON 3   Setting Animations to Play Automatically

Although the behaviors are set up, no event is yet set to initiate the timeline of behaviors. You learned in the previous project that many JavaScript events invoke behaviors. In this case, the most appropriate event is the **onLoad** event that invokes the animation as soon as the page loads into the visitor's browser; by default, the **onLoad** event is assigned to the **<body>** tag, as in **<body onLoad="MM_timelinePlay('advert');"**. (All Dreamweaver behavior functions begin with MM, indicating Macromedia created them.) At other times, you may want to trigger a behavior with an **onMouseOver** event assigned to an **<a>** tag. You could do that also with this behavior by cutting the **onLoad** event from the **<body>** tag, creating an **onMouseOver** event for the same function, and assigning it to an anchor tag.

Although the **onLoad** event triggers the **MM_timelinePlay()** function to begin immediately, you could easily delay the start of the animation by sliding the animation bar to the right so that it doesn't start at frame 1 but, perhaps, at frame 30. You would also have to slide the behaviors in the same direction by the same amount. By doing so, you would create a delay in the start of the animation but not in the invoking of the **MM_timelinePlay()** function. The countdown would begin immediately but the animation would start 30 frames later.

Enable the Autoplay Option

In this exercise, you set the Autoplay option, creating an onLoad event that triggers the running of the timeline and the behaviors within it.

1   **In the open file, index.html, enable the Autoplay option.**

FIGURE 5.14

2   **Click OK to close the dialog box.**

FIGURE 5.15

3   From the Frames channel, click any frame that does not have a behavior marker.

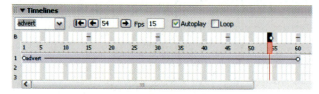

FIGURE 5.16

4   Click in the Document window, click the `<body>` tag in the Tag selector, and note the Behaviors panel.

These two behaviors start as soon as the Web page loads. The Play Timeline behavior is important for triggering initiation of timeline behaviors.

FIGURE 5.17

5   Preview the page in your browser and watch the animation of swapping images.

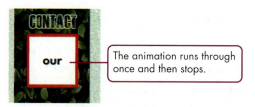

The animation runs through once and then stops.

FIGURE 5.18

6   Return to Dreamweaver, but leave index.html open for the next lesson.

LESSON 4   Looping Behaviors

It is fine for the behavior to begin when the page loads but, in this case, we want the behavior to loop through the series of images multiple times. This requires enabling the loop option. When you enable this option, Dreamweaver creates an onFrame trigger and assigns it the Go to Timeline Frame behavior.

The Go to Timeline Frame behavior has two options that enable you to modify the looping behavior. You can specify the number of times that you want your animation to loop. By default, the Loop field is empty, which means that the loop is to continue infinitely, but you can specify any number of loops. The other option is to specify which frame the loop is to return to. If you shift the animation bar and the behavior markers in the Behaviors channel to the right by 30 frames, you delay the start of the animation. When the animation loops, you may not want to loop the delay but have the loop return to frame 30. There is a third option in the Go to Timeline Frame dialog box — you can choose which timeline to apply the looping modifications — but with just one timeline, you won't need that for this lesson.

Enable the Loop Option

In this exercise, you enable the looping behavior so that the animation repeats. You also learn to modify the behavior and specify the number of times the animation should loop.

1 In the open file, index.html, check the Loop option in the Timelines panel, and then click OK to acknowledge the alert message.

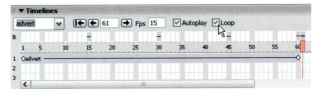

FIGURE 5.19

2 Preview the page in your browser and notice that the animation continues to loop.

3 Return to Dreamweaver.

4 Click frame 61 in the Behaviors channel.

FIGURE 5.20

5 Right/Control-click the Go to Timeline Frame behavior in the Behaviors panel and choose Edit Behavior.

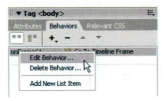

FIGURE 5.21

6 Set the Loop field to 3 and click OK.

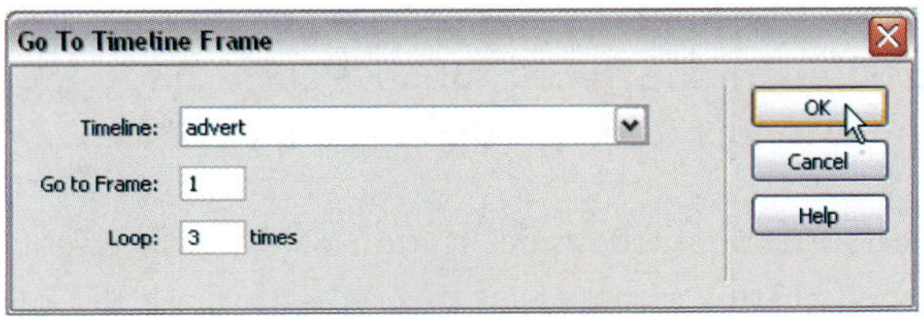

FIGURE 5.22

7 Preview the page in your browser and count the number of times that the animation loops.

8 Return to Dreamweaver, but leave index.html open for the next exercise.

Finalize the Animation

The animation works fine except that it ends displaying the Don't Forget image, which doesn't make a lot of sense. It would be better for it to end with the Specials image. In this exercise, you shift the position of the behaviors in the Behaviors channel so that the last loop ends with the Specials graphic. You also link the graphic to the specials.html page.

1 In the open file, index.html, drag the behavior marker at frame 60 (not frame 61) to frame 1.

This has the effect of swapping in the Don't Forget image at the beginning of the animation. On the first loop, this behavior is unnecessary; when the last loop ends, however, the Specials image is not swapped out but remains in place.

2 Shift the behavior markers for the three remaining behaviors one frame to the right — to 16, 31, and 46, respectively — but leave the last behavior marker at frame 61.

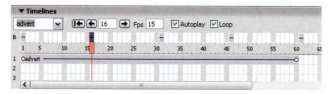

FIGURE 5.23

3 Link the image in the Document window to specials.html.

4 Preview the page in your browser, and notice that the animation ends with the Specials image.

5 Return to Dreamweaver and close index.html.

LESSON 5 Creating Movement with DHTML

You can also use DHTML to create movement, however, you can only apply movement to layers. In the previous project, you learned that JavaScript can modify CSS in the **body.style.color="red"** exercise. You can also modify other aspects of CSS, including position. For this reason, layers, which have CSS positional properties, can be moved whereas images (unless contained in a layer) cannot be moved. For example, just as **style.color** can be modified using JavaScript to change the CSS color property (text color), **style.posTop** can be used by JavaScript to change the top position of a layer.

In many ways, creating animation through the modification of CSS via JavaScript is easier than assigning a behavior to the Timelines panel. In this series of lessons, you animate the movement of a layer using the Timelines panel and JavaScript, which change a CSS property.

To Extend Your Knowledge

BROWSER DETECTION WITH JAVASCRIPT

In the mid- to late-1990s, the browser wars were in effect: browser manufacturers Netscape and Microsoft were trying to attract developers to develop for their browsers and thus attract users to use their browsers. Both Netscape Communications and Microsoft, therefore, added proprietary HTML tags that enhanced Web pages as well as their own JavaScript functions. As a result of different approaches to JavaScript, developers who wanted or, for business reasons, needed to support both browsers had to learn which JavaScript functions were common to both and where they differed. Furthermore, because the code affected, developers had to have JavaScript detect which browser the visitor was using and, based on the result, one block or another of JavaScript code would run.

The drawback to this was the massive duplication of code needed to provide the same function in multiple browsers. With the return to Web standards, most current browsers are more similar to each other than before, but IE still has some differences. The way that JavaScript detected which browser was in use was by a script asking the browser which browser and version it was, such as Netscape 4 or IE 5. However, as soon as a new browser arrived on the market, all of the browser-detection scripts were out of date. The more current method of browser detection is not based on asking which browser and version number but by determining capabilities. For example, `if (document.getElementById ||` `document.all || document.layers)` is the currently recommended method of asking the browser if it can handle DHTML. The code `document.getElementById` detects if the browser is DOM-compliant, `document.all` detects if the browser is IE (IE is not fully DOM-compliant), and `document.lay-` `ers` detects if the browser is Netscape4. Other methods of detection are possible, but browser-version detection is no longer recommended: object detection is preferred.

Create and Prepare the Layers

The first stage in creating an animation using Dreamweaver's Timelines panel is to create and prepare the layers. There are two stages to this process: first, create the layers and, second, assign unique ids to the layers. By default, Dreamweaver creates layer ids for you but, as with many other Dreamweaver functions, you may prefer to assign your own names to the ids that make more sense to you than layer1 and layer2. In this exercise, you draw the layers, resize them, insert a graphic into each, and assign a unique id to each layer.

1. **Open about.html from the TO-P5 site.**

2. **Click the Draw Layer button (Layout Insert bar) and create a layer in the left navbar cell.**

3. **Type nbhome in the Layer ID field of the Property inspector. Also, set both the top and left positions of the nbhome layer to 20 px, the width to 119 px, and the height to 34 px.**

4   From the images folder, insert the nb_home.gif image into the nbhome layer.

The mouse pointer was placed over the outline of the div to highlight it because the dark outline of the layer is difficult to discern against the dark leafy background.

FIGURE 5.24

5   Repeat Steps 2 to 4 as follows:

Layer ID	Left	Width	Top	Height	Image
nbabout	20px	119px	54px	34px	nb_about.gif
nbproducts	20px	119px	88px	34px	nb_products.gif
nblocation	20px	119px	122px	34px	nb_location.gif
nbstaff	20px	119px	156px	34px	nb_staff.gif
nbcontact	20px	119px	190px	34px	nb_contact.gif

FIGURE 5.25

6   Save your changes to about.html, leaving it open for the next exercise.

To Extend Your Knowledge

SOPHISTICATED DHTML MENUS FOR A FEE

Although OpenCube.com and HierMenusCentral.com are not the only developers of sophisticated DHTML menu systems for a fee, they are certainly very prominent. Their products are not inexpensive, but for the fees you pay, you receive support from the company, free upgrades, and confidence that the menus work in many browsers. The Visual QuickMenu Pro suite from OpenCube.com also provides a visual editor with which you can create, edit, and configure the menus just as you do in Dreamweaver.

LESSON 6 | Adding Layers to the Timelines Panel

The second stage of preparation for a DHTML animation is to add the layers as objects to the Timelines panel. You must add layers one at a time, and ensure that you are adding the layers, not the images that exist within the layers, or you won't be able to make the images move.

Add the Layers to Animation Channels

In this exercise, you drag the handles of the layers to the animation channels of the Timelines panel.

1 In the open file, about.html, assign menu as the name of the timeline.

2 In the Document window, click the Home graphic in the left navbar cell, and then click the layer handle.

3 Drag the layer handle to the first animation channel of the Timelines panel and position the animation bar at frame 1.

4 Repeat Steps 2 and 3 to add the remaining layers to animation channels in the Timelines panel.

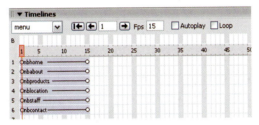

FIGURE 5.26

? If you have problems

If the Timelines panel is not high enough, you can drag the control handle at the top of the Property inspector up, which expands the height of the Timelines panel.

5 Save your changes to about.html, leaving it open for the next exercise.

LESSON 7 Animating the Layers

Animating the movement of the layers is very simple. Each animation bar in the animation channels has a first and last keyframe. Depending on the complexity of the animation, other keyframes may exist or may be added. A *keyframe* is a frame that serves as a reference point in an animation. There may be multiple keyframes in an animation, but there must be a minimum of two: the first and last frames. In a straight-line animation where a ball moves in a straight line at the same speed from one location to another, only two keyframes are required. However, if the ball is thrown in an arc and the ball slows down as it increases in height and speeds up on the way down, multiple keyframes are required to mark significant changes in direction and speed. *Tweening* is the process of creating the individual frames between the keyframes. The term comes from *in-betweeners* who are assistant animators hired to draw the frames between the keyframes.

To animate the movement of these layers, you click a keyframe and set a property of the layer in the Property inspector. In this lesson, you create an animation that moves the layers into place when the page loads. This means that at the first keyframe, the layers must be moved out of position; at the last keyframe, the layers must be in their current positions; and the DHTML creates the tweening. Currently, the first and last keyframes have the same positions. However, to modify the starting position of the layer, you click the first keyframe and modify the property in the Property inspector. You leave the last keyframe alone so that when the animation finishes running, the current position of the layers, which also is the property of the last keyframe, is where the layers end up at the end of the animation.

Prepare the Initial State of the First Frame

In this exercise, you modify the top position of the layers at the first keyframe. The layers move above the browser window. All of the layers are 34 pixels in height. To move the layers immediately above the browser window, you set the top position of the layers to –34 pixels. By leaving the last keyframe as it is, as the animation progresses, the layers move from the initial –34 pixels to the current position.

1   **In the open file, about.html, click the first keyframe of the nbhome animation bar in the Timelines panel.**

2   **In the Property inspector, set Top to -34 px.**

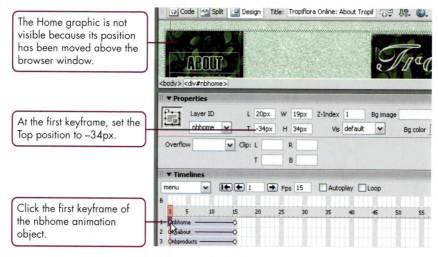

The Home graphic is not visible because its position has been moved above the browser window.

At the first keyframe, set the Top position to –34px.

Click the first keyframe of the nbhome animation object.

FIGURE 5.27

3 | Repeat Steps 1 and 2, setting the top position of each object in the Timelines panel to -34 px at the first keyframe.

4 | Save your changes to about.html, leaving it open for the next exercise.

Test and Preview the Animation

Of course, you can preview the animation in your browser, but you can also preview the animation in Dreamweaver. If you click at different frame positions along the timeline, the objects display their states — in this lesson, the positions as they would be at that particular stage in the timeline. This is a very beneficial method of checking the states of the layers as the animation progresses. To see the animation in real-time, you must preview the animation in your browser.

1 | In the open file, about.html, click frame 1 in the Frames channel of the Timelines panel.

2 | Click frames 2, 3, 4, and so on to frame 15.

Notice that the layers gradually move into place.

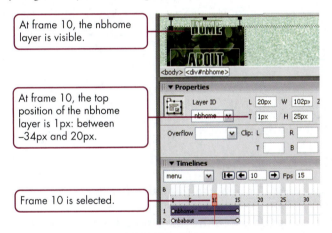

At frame 10, the nbhome layer is visible.

At frame 10, the top position of the nbhome layer is 1px: between –34px and 20px.

Frame 10 is selected.

FIGURE 5.28

3 | Check the Autoplay option in the Timelines panel, and then click OK to acknowledge the warning.

4 | Preview the page in your browser and observe the movement of the layers.

5 | Return to Dreamweaver, but leave about.html open for the next exercise.

Modify the Timings of the Animations

In this exercise, you modify the animations in two ways. The first modification changes the duration of the animation — all animations start at the same time but end at different times. The second modification is to change the duration of the animations so that they start at different times but end at the same time.

1   In the open file, about.html, drag the last keyframe of the nbhome animation bar to frame 65.

2   Repeat Step 1 as follows:

Animation bar	Position of Last Keyframe
nbabout	55
nbproducts	45
nblocation	35
nbstaff	25

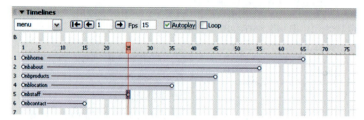

FIGURE 5.29

3   Preview the page in your browser.

4   Return to Dreamweaver.

5   Drag the first keyframe of the nbhome animation bar to frame 50.

6   Drag the nbabout animation bar so that the last keyframe is at frame 65. Drag the first keyframe of the nbabout animation bar to frame 40.

7   Repeat Steps 5 and 6 as follows:

Animation bar	First Keyframe	Last Keyframe
nbproducts	30	65
nblocation	20	65
nbstaff	10	65
nbcontact	0	65

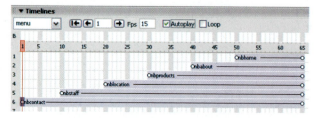

FIGURE 5.30

8   **Preview the page in your browser.**

9   **Return to Dreamweaver.**

10   **Choose Window>Timelines to close the Timelines panel.**

11   **Close about.html.**

To Extend Your Knowledge

OTHER JAVASCRIPT RESOURCES

Dreamweaver comes with two resources that may be helpful for a JavaScript developer: the O'Reilly HTML reference and the O'Reilly JavaScript reference. The usefulness of the JavaScript reference is obvious, but the HTML reference may not be as clear. At the end of each reference for an HTML tag is a reference as to how the tag can be targeted by the DOM, such as `document.formname` or `document.anchors`.

LESSON 8   Creating a DHTML Navigation Bar

DHTML navigation bars are very popular applications of DHTML because they provide a compact method of providing a navigation system that offers links to virtually every page on a Web site. Generally, you move your mouse pointer over the links and a pop-up list of additional links appears, some of which may further offer pop-up lists of additional links and so on. These behaviors are generally based on complex JavaScript code and, for that reason, there is an industry surrounding the development and sale of these types of scripts. OpenCube.com and HierMenusCentral.com are two such companies that create DHTML menus for sale. Fortunately, Dreamweaver has a function that allows you to create and configure DHTML menus through dialog boxes.

There are some drawbacks to this type of menu system. The menu does not work if a visitor's browser does not support JavaScript or the particular version of JavaScript for which the DHTML menu was created. This causes a serious problem if there is no navigation bar, even a basic one, which does not depend on JavaScript. Secondly, even when JavaScript is available, if the subnavigation menus fold out to the right (as they commonly do) and disappear off the right side of the screen, they may be inaccessible unless the browser window is widened, assuming, of course that it is not already maximized.

This use of JavaScript is not simply decorative but functional. It is important that there be a fallback position if JavaScript is not available. Furthermore, the menus should be tested at different browser resolutions, primarily lower resolutions such as 800 × 600 or even 640 × 480, to ensure that any ***fold-out menus*** (menu items that pop out to one side or the other) on the right side of the browser window remain accessible in the browser window.

It might appear that DHTML menus have a bad reputation. In fact, most DHTML menus are inaccessible without a mouse, and many are completely dependent on JavaScript, so many usability experts recommend against their use. DHTML menus may be compared with frames as a technology or feature that has had some popularity but second thoughts recommend against its use. They may be used with care if you have properly assessed the target audience of the Web site.

Dreamweaver provides DHTML menus through the Show Pop-Up Menu behavior. You create your menu using a fairly complex dialog box that allows you to add menu items; change their order; configure their colors, borders, width, and height; as well as set the position of the menu.

Add the Pop-Up Menu Items

In this exercise, you create a pop-up menu.

1   Define a new site from the JCW-P5 folder and call it `JCW-P5`.

2   Open index.html and click in Education in the horizontal navigation bar below the logo graphic.

3   From the Behaviors panel drop-down menu (choose Window>Behaviors if the Behaviors panel is not open), choose Show Pop-Up Menu.

4   In the Text field, replace New Item with `Wildlife Safari`. Either type or use the Browse for File button (folder icon) to set Link to `wildlife_safari.html` and press Tab.

You must press Tab after typing the link so that the link is properly registered in the list of menu items below.

FIGURE 5.31

5   Do not click OK but click the Add Item button (+).

FIGURE 5.32

6 Repeat Steps 4 – 5 as follows:

Text	Link	Add Item button
Birthday Adventure	birthday_adventure.html	Click
Night Safari	night_safari.html	Click
Safari Zoo Camp	zoo_camp.html	Click
Wildlife Adventure Camp	adventure_camp.html	Don't click

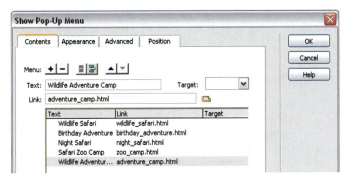

FIGURE 5.33

7 Keep the dialog box open for the next exercise.

Configure the Appearance of the Menu

In this exercise, you create the appearance of the menu so that it matches the appearance of the nonJavaScript menu to which it is attached.

1 In the Show Pop-Up Menu dialog box, click the Appearance tab at the top.

2 Ensure that the menu is set to Vertical Menu. Choose Arial, Helvetica, sans-serif from the Font list. Set the Size to 16, and click the B (bold) button.

FIGURE 5.34

3   In the Up State column, click the Text color button and move the eyedropper pointer to the sand-brown area of the page.

Using the eyedropper, choose the background color of the main-content region.

FIGURE 5.35

4   Using the same technique as in Step 3, set the Cell color to the dark-green background of the top navigation bar.

5   Use the same techniques to set the Over State Text and Cell colors, but reverse them.

FIGURE 5.36

6   Keep the Show Pop-Up Menu dialog box open for the next exercise.

Configure the Advanced Properties

The Advanced tab of the Show Pop-Up Menu dialog box allows you to configure the table-cell properties of the menu. These properties include the height and width of the table cells and their border properties. In this lesson, you configure the DHTML menu to match the appearance of the static menu.

1   In the Show Pop-Up Menu dialog box, click the Advanced tab.

2   Leave Cell Width alone. For Cell Height, change Automatic to Pixels and set the height to **30**. Set Cell Padding, Cell Spacing, and Text Indent to **0**, and Menu Delay to **1000** ms.

FIGURE 5.37

3   Ensure Pop-Up Borders is checked and set Border Width to 1. Click the Border Color button and, using the eyedropper, carefully select the light-green border surrounding the static menu items. Set Shadow and Highlight to the same colors.

FIGURE 5.38

4   Keep the Show Pop-Up Menu dialog box open for the next exercise.

Set the Position of the Menu

In this final stage, you set the position of the menu so that it opens below the static menu. Dreamweaver provides you with four predefined positions or you can configure the position of the menu using the x and y positions.

1   In the Show Pop-Up Menu dialog box, click the Position tab.

2   Set X to 0 and Y to 32. Ensure that Hide Menu on onMouseOut Event is checked and click OK.

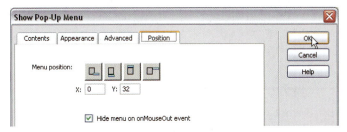

FIGURE 5.39

3   Preview the page in your browser and move your mouse pointer over the Education link.

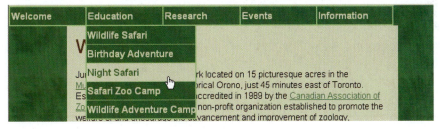

FIGURE 5.40

4   Close your browser and return to Dreamweaver.

5   Close index.html.

To Extend Your Knowledge

USE <NOSCRIPT> FOR NONJAVASCRIPT BROWSERS

The <noscript> tag is similar to the <noframes> tag in that the content is only visible if scripting is not available in the browser. When JavaScript is available, the <noscript> content remains invisible, but if JavaScript is unavailable, <noscript> content is visible. Therefore, you enclose menus that are not dependent on JavaScript with <noscript> tags so that if the DHTML-navigation menu items are not available because JavaScript is unavailable, these <noscript> menu items are visible and usable.

To reduce some of the dependency on JavaScript, you could add a DHTML menu to a nonJavaScript navigation bar and configure just those categories that contain additional pages with a DHTML menu. Although this method is better, in that not all links depend on the DHTML menu, many links would still depend on JavaScript. To accommodate nonJavaScript users, you can create static subnavigation menus and enclose them between <noscript> tags. This hides these additional menus when JavaScript is available and reveals them when JavaScript is unavailable, satisfying most JavaScript requirements. However, if the menu uses JavaScript functions not available in older JavaScript-enabled browsers, neither the DHTML menu nor the nonJavaScript menus are visible. Always be sure to carefully consider your target audience to determine whether or not a DHTML menu is suitable.

SUMMARY

In this project, you learned to work with the Timelines panel. You learned to add images to the animation channels of the Timelines panel. You learned that images must have an id. You also discovered that image animation is limited to image swapping. You explored how to increase and decrease the length of an animation by increasing and decreasing the length of the animation bar in the animation channel of the Timelines panel. You learned how to add a behavior to the Timelines panel, and how to change the timing of the behavior by moving the behavior marker in the Behaviors channel. You added layers to the animation channel and used the Timelines panel to create animation by changing the CSS properties of the layers. You also learned to modify the animation by changing the duration, starting frames, and ending frames of the animation bars.

KEY TERMS

animation	DHTML	keyframe
animation bar	DOM	layer
animation channel	fold-out	loop
autoplay	frames	object
behavior	Frames channel	onLoad
Behaviors channel	id	timeline

CHECKING CONCEPTS AND TERMS

SCREEN ID

Identify the indicated areas from the list below:

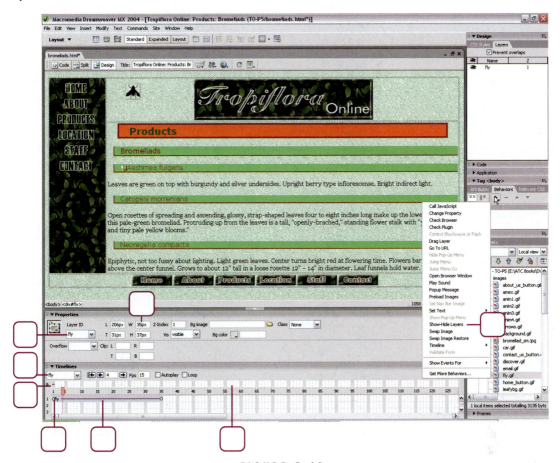

FIGURE 5.41

a. Layer properties

b. Keyframe

c. Layer id

d. Behaviors channel

e. Behaviors pop-up menu

f. Behavior marker

g. Timeline name

h. Animation bar

MULTIPLE CHOICE

Circle the letter of the correct answer for each of the following:

1. DHTML _____.
   a. is a W3C technology
   b. are database-generated Web pages
   c. is a combination of HTML, JavaScript, and CSS
   d. All of the above

2. Parts of the Timelines panel include _____.
   a. animation channels, Loop checkbox
   b. Behaviors panel, Frames panel
   c. Behavior markers, image placeholder
   d. keyframes, Autostart checkbox

3. You can add _____ to the Timelines panel.
   a. behaviors
   b. images
   c. layers
   d. All of the above

4. What type of event triggers timed behaviors in the Timelines panel?
   a. onLoad
   b. onFrame
   c. onClick
   d. onMouseOver

5. Which item creates the onLoad event for the <body> tag?
   a. The Loop checkbox
   b. A behavior marker at frame 1
   c. The Autoplay checkbox
   d. None of the above

6. Which of the following correctly describes tweening?
   a. Add a behavior to the Behaviors channel
   b. Actions that occur between keyframes
   c. The people hired by animators to draw frames between keyframes
   d. The process of delaying the start of or extending the duration of an animation

7. Which of the following is not a consideration when evaluating the use of DHTML?
   a. HTML/XHTML version
   b. Accessibility
   c. Usability
   d. Browser version

8. Which of the following would not prevent an animation bar in the Timelines panel from being moved using DHTML?
   a. The animation bar represents an image
   b. The object has no id
   c. The object has no class
   d. None of the above

9. DHTML menus should be tested _____.
   a. in multiple browsers
   b. by potential users
   c. at different screen resolutions
   d. All of the above

10. What type of effect might be impossible to create with DHTML?
   a. Fireworks
   b. A clock with moving hands
   c. A fade-in/fade-out slideshow
   d. None of the above

DISCUSSION QUESTIONS

1. You have been asked to consult on a Web-development project with regard to DHTML and animations. It is important to the client that they not lose any potential customers but it is also important that they use JavaScript and DHTML menus. Prepare a list of pros and cons for the use of these technologies that you could present to your client and identify how, without worrying about the details of the code, the cons may be avoided or circumvented.

2. CSS has properties with specific options. The trick to creative design is learning how to combine the properties. The same may be said about DHTML and Dreamweaver's behaviors — alone, they may seem simple and uninteresting, but combined, they can produce very interesting results. Examine the list of behaviors available from the Behaviors panel and describe some ways they could be combined with each other and the Timelines panel to create interesting results.

SKILL DRILL

Skill Drills reinforce project skills. Each skill reinforced is the same, or nearly the same, as a skill presented in the lessons. Detailed instructions are provided in a step-by-step format. Work through these exercises in order.

1. Create Additional DHTML Menus

In this Skill Drill, you add more DHTML menus to other menu categories that have items below them. Once you have created one DHTML menu, many of the appearance settings are carried forward from the previous menu, reducing the number of steps required to create a new menu of the same appearance.

1. Open index.html from the JCW-P5 site.

2. Click Events in the static navigation bar.

3. Choose Show Pop-Up Menu from the Behaviors pop-up menu.

4. Replace New Item in the Text field with **Halloween Safari** and choose halloween.html as the link.

5. Add a new item, type **Special Occasions** in the Text field, and choose special_occasions.html as the link. Add a new item, type **Pasha Day**, and choose pasha.html as the link.

6. In the Advanced tab, set the Cell Height to **30** pixels. Set Cell Padding, Cell Spacing, and Text Indent to **0**. Set Border Width to **1**.

7. In the Position tab, set X to **0** and Y to **32**, and click OK.

8. Preview the page in your browser and test the new menus. (Dreamweaver remembers color settings from the last time that the Show Pop-Up Menu was used. If you notice the colors may not be correct, use the instructions from Lesson 8 and set the Text and Cell colors and the Border properties.)

FIGURE 5.42

9. Return to Dreamweaver and close index.html.

2. Use the Show-Hide Layers Behavior to Create Pop-Up Menus

The Show Pop-Up Menu behavior (previous exercises) is a fully dynamic method — the menus do not exist in HTML, but JavaScript dynamically creates the content and displays the content when the mouse pointer moves over the trigger link. The Show-Hide Layers method is similar to the animated graphic layers of Lessons 5, 6, and 7, in which you used JavaScript to modify the CSS top-position property of the layers. The layers existed in HTML but were animated with DHTML. The Show-Hide Layers behavior is similar in that the layers also exist in HTML and are animated with JavaScript, but using the CSS visibility property rather than position.

The principle behind this behavior is that the timeline changes the visibility of the layer. The layer starts out hidden; the onMouseOver event triggers the timeline, displaying the layer for the duration of the timeline; and then, when the timeline has run to completion, the layer is hidden again. To create this animation, you must set the initial visibility of the layer to hidden. You add the layer to the Timelines panel, add the Show-Hide Layers behavior to frame 1 to show the layer, and add the Show-Hide Layers behavior to the last frame to hide the layer again. You then add the Play Timeline behavior to a link to trigger the operation of the timeline. You also add the Go to Timeline Frame behavior to the same onMouseOver event so that the animation restarts from frame 1 when triggered again.

1. Open products.html from the TO-P5 site.

2. Choose Window>Layers to open the Layers panel and Window>Timelines to open the Timelines panel.

3. Click in the left column of the Layers panel on the same row as menu to display a closed eye.

   The closed eye indicates that the initial visibility state of the layer is hidden.

4. In the Document window, drag the layer handle of the menu layer to the first animation channel of the Timelines panel, and then drag the last keyframe to frame 45.

5. Type **menu** in the Timelines name field.

6. Click in the Behaviors channel at frame 1. Choose Show-Hide Layers from the pop-up menu of the Behaviors panel. With the menu layer selected, click Show, and then click OK.

7. Click in the Behaviors channel at frame 45. Choose Show-Hide Layers from the pop-up menu of the Behaviors panel. With the menu layer selected, click Hide, and then click OK.

8. In the Timelines panel, click the menu animation bar to deselect the most recently created behavior in the Behaviors channel. Click the Products menu graphic in the left navigation-bar cell. From the Behaviors panel pop-up menu, choose Timeline>Play Timeline. Click OK.

   There is only one current timeline so you don't need to choose one; otherwise, you would need to choose the timeline to play.

9. With the Product graphic still selected, choose Timeline>Go to Timeline Frame from the Behaviors panel pop-up menu. Ensure that the menu timeline is selected, Go to Frame is set to **1**, and the Loop field is empty. Click OK.

10. Set both behaviors in the Behaviors panel to trigger with the onMouseOver event.

11. Preview the page in your browser.

FIGURE 5.43

12. Return to Dreamweaver and close products.html.

3. Create the Appearance of Random Image Swaps

In this exercise, you create the appearance of random image swaps. In fact, the image swaps are regular in timing, but the five images each have different timelines, enabling you to set their timings individually.

1. Create a new site called **Seabreeze** from the Project_05>Seabreeze folder and open index.html.

2. Click the left photographic image near the top, and name the image **one** in the Property inspector. Name the remaining four photographic images in the wave **two**, **three**, **four**, and **five**.

3. Drag image one to the Timelines panel, and stretch the animation bar from frame 1 to frame 50. Name the timeline **swapOne**.

4. At frame 25, click in the Behaviors channel. Choose Swap Image from the Behaviors panel pop-up menu. Choose image one, and set the swap source to swap_images>one_swap.jpg.

5. At frame 50, click in the Behaviors channel. Choose Swap Image from the Behaviors panel pop-up menu. Choose image one and set the swap source to swap_images>one.jpg.

6. Enable both the Autoplay and Loop options.

7. Right/Control-click and choose Add Timeline.

8. Repeat Steps 3 to 7, as follows:

Timeline Name	Number of Frames	First Image Swap	Second Image Swap
swapTwo	60	frame 30, two_swap.jpg	frame 60, two.jpg
swapThree	70	frame 35, three_swap.jpg	frame 70, three.jpg
swapFour	80	frame 40, four_swap.jpg	frame 80, four.jpg
swapFive	90	frame 45, five_swap.jpg	frame 90, five.jpg

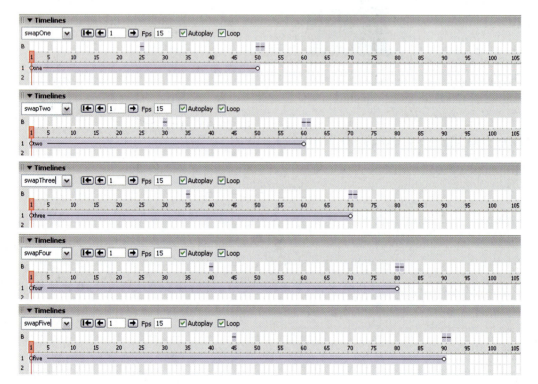

FIGURE 5.44

9. Preview the page in your browser.

10. Return to Dreamweaver and randomly reposition the position of the first swap-behavior marker. You can also resize the length of the animation bars, but remember to reposition the second swap-behavior marker to the end of the animation bar, and the loop-behavior marker to the frame following the end of the animation bar. Preview the revised animation.

11. When finished, close index.html.

4. Prepare <noscript> Content for JavaScript-Disabled Browsers

In this exercise, you surround a static menu with **<noscript>** tags so that any visitors who browse with JavaScript-disabled browsers can use your site, even if you have DHTML menus. Browsers with JavaScript enabled will not display the contents of the **<noscript>** tag, whereas browsers with JavaScript disabled will see the **<noscript>** content. (This method does accommodate JavaScript-disabled browsers. If a visitor is using an older JavaScript-enabled browser, however, the browser may not be able to interpret current JavaScript functions and, at the same time, because it has JavaScript enabled, it won't display the **<noscript>** content.)

Each browser has its own means of disabling JavaScript. However, if you are using IE, you can download an accessibility toolbar from nils.org.au/ais/web/resources/toolbar/index.html with which you can easily disable JavaScript. Firefox and Mozilla users can download the Developer toolbar from chrispederick.com/work/firefox/webdeveloper/ that also makes it easy to disable JavaScript. Opera users may simply choose Tools>Quick Preferences and uncheck Enable JavaScript. Some browsers simply require you to refresh the page to enable any changes. Other browsers require you to shut them down and relaunch them to enable any changes.

1. Open halloween.html from the JCW-P5 site.

2. Click in the left navigation-bar table, and then click the **<table#sidenav>** tag in the Tag selector.

3. Choose Insert>Tag.

4. In the Tag Chooser dialog box, choose HTML>Scripting>noscript, click Insert, click OK, and click Close.

5. Close the Code window and preview the page in your browser.

    If you have a JavaScript-enabled browser, you won't see the side navigation bar, but you can view the source code of the page from your browser and see that the table does exist between **<noscript>** tags.

6. Return to Dreamweaver and close halloween.html.

CHALLENGE

Challenge exercises expand on, or are somewhat related to, skills presented in the lessons. Each exercise provides a brief introduction, followed by instructions in a numbered-step format that are not as detailed as those in the Skill Drill exercises. Work through the exercises in order.

1. Create Fold-Out Menu Items

In this exercise, you extend the DHTML menu to include menu items within menu items. When you enter the items into the menu, you initially start adding them as if they were part of the main menu. You then select them and demote them to items within a menu item.

1. Open index.html from the JCW-P5 site.

2. Click in the Information link, and choose Show Pop-Up Menu from the Behaviors panel pop-up menu.

3. Add the following menu items:

Text	Link	Click Add Item
Admission	admission.html	Yes
Directions	directions.html	Yes
Work Placement	employment.html	Yes
Employment	employment.html	Yes
Volunteer/Intern	volunteer.html	Yes
Affiliations	affiliations.html	Yes
Feedback	feedback.html	Yes
Contact Us	contact.html	No

4. Click the Employment item and click the Indent Item button.

5. Click the Volunteer/Intern item, click the Indent Item button, then click the Outdent Item button.

The Indent Item button indents the selected item to a level below the preceding item. In this case, it is indented too far and must be outdented.

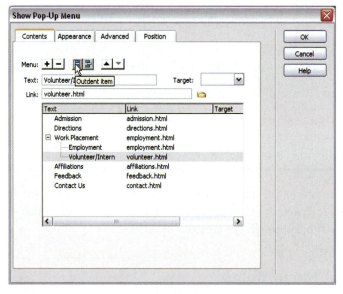

FIGURE 5.45

6. In the Advanced tab, set the Cell Height to **30** pixels. Set Cell Padding, Cell Spacing, and Text Indent to **0**. Set Border Width to **1**.

7. In the Position tab, set X to **0** and Y to **32**, and click OK.

8. Preview the page in your browser and test the new menus.

    If the colors appear different, return to Lesson 8 for instructions on how to create the same colors as used in the rest of the pop-up menu.

FIGURE 5.46

9. Return to Dreamweaver and close index.html.

2. Animation from Recorded Movement

The animations of movement you have created so far involve changing numbers, such as position. Dreamweaver's Timelines panel can also record the movement of a layer and play it back. In this exercise, you record the movement of an image of a fly (in a layer) and then play it back. You also set the animation to loop three times and return to a different frame.

1. Open bromeliads.html from the TO-P5 site.

2. From the Layout Insert bar, click the Draw Layer button and draw a layer. Select the layer, name it **fly**, and set the width to **35px** and the height to **37px**. From the images folder, insert the image fly.gif into the layer.

3. Click the layer handle and drag the layer to the left border of the Document window near the Products link.

4. Right/Control-click in an animations channel of the Timelines panel and choose Record Path of Layer.

5. Drag the fly layer around in the simulated movement of a fly and make it disappear off the top of the Document window. When finished, drag the fly animation bar in the Timelines panel to the right so that the first keyframe is at frame 30.

6. To make the fly seem to appear off the left edge of the Document window at the beginning of the animation, click the first keyframe of the fly animation bar and, in the Property inspector, set the left position to **–35px**.

7. To make the fly seem to disappear off the top edge of the Document window at the end of the animation, click the last keyframe of the fly animation bar and, in the Property inspector, set the top position to **–37px**.

8. Enable the Autoplay and Loop options.

9. In the Timelines panel, click the behavior marker for the loop behavior. In the Behaviors panel, Right/Control-click the Go to Timeline Frame behavior and choose Edit Behavior. Set Loop to **3** times, set Go To Frame to **30**, and click OK.

10. Preview the page in your browser.

    The initial delay is because the animation-bar timeline does not begin until frame 30, but as soon as the animation ends, the fly appears immediately at the left because the loop was set to return to frame 30, not frame 1.

11. Return to Dreamweaver and close bromeliads.html.

3. Show and Hide Tabbed Content

In this exercise, you use the Show-Hide Layers behavior to create the appearance of links that display content when clicked. When there are sections in a Web page, you can create links to them. When the visitor clicks on a link to a section, the browser window scrolls to take the visitor to the destination of the link. You can use the Show-Hide Layers behavior to enhance this process. Instead of taking the visitor to the section, you use the Show-Hide Layers behavior to show the selected layer and hide all other layers.

You can modify this use of the Show-Hide Layers behavior so that JavaScript-disabled browsers can navigate the page without the behavior. However, there is always the possibility that some JavaScript-enabled browsers are too old to understand some of the JavaScript functions and, as always, these visitors may have some difficulty with this script.

1. Define a new site called **PHIL-P5** from the Project_05>PHIL-P5 folder. Open phil100.html from this site and preview it in your browser.

   This Web page is long, but there are tablike links at the top that take the visitor to the different sections in the page.

2. Return to Dreamweaver and open the CSS Styles panel.

   Notice the two style sheets. Styles.css is the primary one with a style rule that hides the different sections of this page. Static.css is the secondary style sheet with a style rule to reverse the hiding so that the sections can be seen. (The purpose of this becomes evident later in the exercise.)

3. Edit the td#content div style rule in static.css. In the Positioning category, delete static from the Type property and click OK.

   Without the style rule in static.css setting the position to static, the position: absolute rule in styles.css is able to display, which has the effect of stacking all layers over one another.

4. In the Timelines panel (choose Window>Timelines to open it, if it is closed), click at frame 1 in the Behaviors channel.

5. In the Behaviors panel (choose Window>Behaviors to open it, if it is closed), add the Show-Hide Layers behavior. Set the guidelines layer to show and hide the four other layers. Click OK when finished.

6. Name the timeline **menu** and enable Autoplay in the Timelines panel.

7. Click in the Requirements link. In the Behaviors panel, add the Show-Hide Layers behavior. Set the requirements layer to show and all others to hide. Click OK.

8. Repeat Step 7 as follows:

Click Link	*Show Layer*	*Hide Layers*
Grading	grading	all others
Texts	texts	all others
Assignments	assignments	all others
Lectures	lectures	all others

9. Preview the page in your browser and click the links.

    Notice that the links do not move the page down (very much) but, instead, the Web page displays the new layer in place of the previous one. However, if JavaScript is disabled in a browser, the visitor sees the mess of overlapping layers that appears in Dreamweaver. The next steps correct this.

10. Return to Dreamweaver. and edit the td#content div style rule in the static.css style sheet. In the Positioning category, set Type to Static and click OK.

    The appearance is much better in Dreamweaver but will conflict with the behavior. The next step hides the static.css style sheet when JavaScript is enabled.

11. Switch to the Code view and scroll to approximately line 79 — the **<link>** tag for static.css. Choose the **<link>** tag, Right/Control-click the selection, and choose Insert Tag. Choose HTML>Scripting>noscript and click Insert, OK, and Close.

12. Switch to the Design view and preview the page in your browser.

    You see the same effect and appearance as before except that, if you are able to disable JavaScript from your browser, unlike after Step 10, the layers of content now do not lie atop each other but fall below each other in a line, just as Dreamweaver displayed this page.

13. Return to Dreamweaver and close phil100.html.

P O R T F O L I O   B U I L D E R

Create Combinations of JavaScript Behaviors

You learned that you can create an image rollover on its own using the Swap Image behavior. You learned how you can change the event that triggers a behavior, such as from onMouseOver to onClick. You learned in this project how you can add a behavior to the timeline, such as animating the Swap Image behavior. By combining the timelines, events, and behaviors, you can create some interesting DHTML effects.

1. Open the Behaviors panel and examine the list of behaviors available.

2. Think of some interesting combinations of events, behaviors, and the timeline, such as triggering the fly animation to occur when the mouse pointer rolls over a particular link rather than when the page loads.

3. Experiment with different combinations to learn what may be possible to create with Dreamweaver's DHTML functions.

4. Create five different animations that may be used in an educational site for younger children.

Snippets, Library Items, and Templates

OBJECTIVES

In this project, you learn how to

- Insert a snippet into a Web page

- Create and save a new snippet

- Create a library item

- Insert a library item into a Web page

- Revise a library item

- Create a template

- Create a child page from a template

- Revise a template

- Create a repeating region

WHY WOULD I DO THIS?

A consistent look and feel is one goal of good design in a Web site and to achieve this, you must find ways to maintain this consistency. One way is to build a template, which many designers have done with or without Dreamweaver. A template would include all of the common components, such as the logo, navigation bar, and footer, but would leave the body area empty, ready to fill with new content as it arrives. A design change requires a large effort to bring all of the pages in line with the new design or layout. Dreamweaver, however, provides very powerful and sophisticated tools for accomplishing this with great ease.

Certainly, one of the tools that can help to build a consistent look to the site is CSS. In *Project 2: Working with Cascading Style Sheets* and *Project 3: Using CSS for Layout*, you learned how to create a style and layout using CSS, and that, with the assistance of a JavaScript style-sheet switcher, you can change the layout and look of a site. However, CSS only affects style, not structure: if you need to add another link to the navigation bar, a jump menu, or a search form to every page, CSS cannot help you. All of these changes are structural changes that require a different approach.

You learned in the previous book how to create a basic Web-site template without any content and save it as a template page. You then opened the template in Dreamweaver, saved it with a different name, and added the content specific for that page and continued the process. This is one method of templating and, until something new is needed, this process would work. It is when you need new common content on every page that this process fails because you must add the new content, such as an additional link, to every page. Dreamweaver has two tools that ease this process: library items and templates.

The Dreamweaver templating function allows you to create a **master template page** for a group of pages on your site. Once you have created the master template, you can lock areas you don't want modified and unlock content areas. If you discover that you have forgotten a link or any other structural change, you merely edit the master template page, make whatever changes necessary, and save the changes. When you change the master template, Dreamweaver automatically transfers the changes to the other pages that were built from the template — the **child pages**, pages built from the master, take on the change(s) applied to it. Of course, depending on the nature of the change, you may need to tweak your CSS, as well.

The other Dreamweaver technology that assists with the development of a consistent look and feel for a site is called "library items." In many respects, they are similar to Dreamweaver templates in that all pages that use a library item take on the same changes if the master library item changes. The difference between library items and templates is that templates are whole pages whereas library items are just parts of pages. For example, a department store may have the same header, footer, and primary navigation for all pages, but the clothes-department navigation bar may be different from the furniture-department navigation bar. Therefore, you would build a template for the header, footer, and primary navigation, and would use library items for the departmental navigation bars.

In this project, you also learn to use snippets. **Snippets** are parcels of code that may be just a single word, a paragraph, or larger. Although snippets and library items may be the same size, there are significant differences between them that affect their use. Library items, like templates, are linked to their masters, so if a change is made to the master, the change cascades to all uses of the library item. Not so with snippets: if you make a change to the stored snippet, only it changes, not any instances of its use. Secondly, templates and library items are specific to site definitions, which is perfectly reasonable: it would not make sense to use or even have access to the Tropiflora templates and library items from the Jungle Cat World site. However, snippets are global and may be used in any site — if you create a useful snippet when working on one site, you can open the snippets folder from another site and use that same snippet.

In this project, you learn how to create, modify, and use snippets, library items, and templates. You learn how to use them to create a consistent look and feel to your site. You learn that library items and templates could be considered the structural equivalents of CSS, and discover how using both of these technologies can greatly simplify your design and development of a Web site.

V I S U A L   S U M M A R Y

Snippets are stored in the Snippets panel that is part of the Code panel group. To open the Snippets panel, you choose Window>Snippets or click the Code panel group and then the Snippets tab. Snippets are organized into folders: when you create your own snippets, you may add them to currently existing folders or you may create your own folders. Be careful when considering the deletion of a folder: to restore a Snippet folder that was part of the Dreamweaver installation, you must reinstall Dreamweaver.

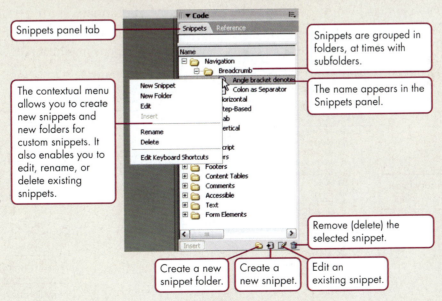

Snippets panel tab

The contextual menu allows you to create new snippets and new folders for custom snippets. It also enables you to edit, rename, or delete existing snippets.

Snippets are grouped in folders, at times with subfolders.

The name appears in the Snippets panel.

Remove (delete) the selected snippet.

Create a new snippet folder.

Create a new snippet.

Edit an existing snippet.

FIGURE 6.1

When you create or edit a snippet, you must assign it a name, choose the type of snippet, and insert the code; the description is optional. Wrap-selection snippets have two components, the before block and the after block, and both blocks display separately in the Snippet dialog box. Insert-block snippets have just one part, shown in the Insert Code field of the Snippet dialog box.

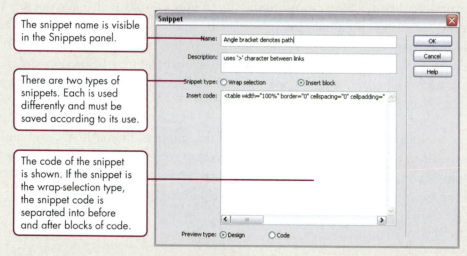

The snippet name is visible in the Snippets panel.

There are two types of snippets. Each is used differently and must be saved according to its use.

The code of the snippet is shown. If the snippet is the wrap-selection type, the snippet code is separated into before and after blocks of code.

FIGURE 6.2

You find library items in the Library folder of the Site folder or in the Library section of the Assets panel. The Library folder does not exist in a site until you create the first library item. Library items have the filename extension .lbi. If you select a library item in the Assets panel, a preview of the library item appears at the top of the panel.

You can use any of the buttons at the bottom of the Library Assets panel to insert the selected library item into the Web page, to create a new library item, or to edit or delete the selected library item. You can also insert the library item into the page by dragging the appropriate .lbi file from the Library folder in the Files panel into the Web page. However, if you double-click a library item, either from the Library folder of the Files panel or the Library Assets panel, it opens in edit mode.

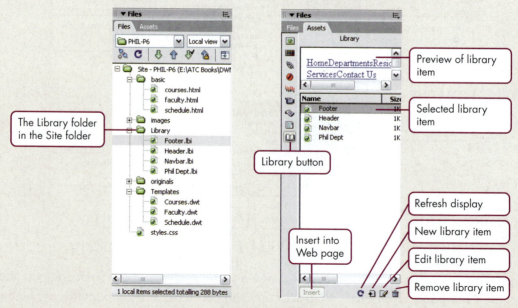

The Library folder in the Site folder

Preview of library item

Selected library item

Library button

Insert into Web page

Refresh display

New library item

Edit library item

Remove library item

FIGURE 6.3

When preparing a new template file, you use the Templates drop-down menu from the Common Insert bar to specify editable and repeating regions. In this project, you create the template by working with an existing page — one with the features you need in a Web page for the site — and preparing it as a template.

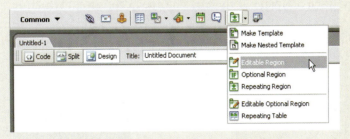

FIGURE 6.4

When you create and save a template, Dreamweaver creates a Templates folder below the Site folder and the template is stored there. Dreamweaver templates have the .dwt (Dreamweaver templates) extension. Templates are also listed in the Templates Assets panel from which you may apply the template, create a new one, and edit or delete an existing one. You can create multiple templates, each for a different purpose.

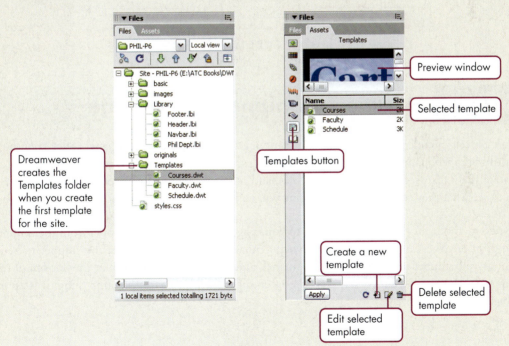

FIGURE 6.5

When you build a child page from a template, you choose File>New and click the Templates tab. You then choose the site from which the template is stored and choose the specific template, if necessary. You can see the template in the Preview window. The child page of the template allows you to edit or create content in the editable regions but not in the noneditable regions, preventing you or other users of the template from damaging the template; it thereby enforces a consistent structure from page to page.

FIGURE 6.6

LESSON 1   Inserting a Snippet into a Page

Snippets are parcels of code that are stored in the Snippets folder in the Snippets panel. They are grouped into folders in the Snippets panel, and each snippet has a description to enable you to identify what it contains. Some contain plain text, some contain small tables, and others even contain JavaScript. Experimentation will allow you to see what they contain and may inspire you with some ideas of how you might be able to use them.

There are two methods for inserting snippets into your page. You can drag the snippet from the Snippets Asset panel into position. You can also click in the Document window where you want the snippet to be inserted, click to choose the snippet in the Snippet Assets panel, and click the Insert button at the bottom of the panel. As with many features of Dreamweaver, there are often different ways to do the same thing; it is up to you to decide which method you prefer.

Insert a Snippet

In this exercise, you add a snippet to the order form. When you ask for credit-card information in an order form, you must collect both the month and year of the expiration date. A select list of month numbers already exists in the Snippets panel. You can quickly insert and use this snippet in a Web page.

1 | Define the Project_06>TO-P6 folder as a site called **TO-P6**. Do not click Done, but remove all previously defined sites from the Manage Sites dialog box, and then click Done.

2 | Open order_form.html, scroll down, and click in the empty cell to the right of Expiration Date.

3 | Type **Month:** and press Spacebar.

4 | Open the Snippets panel by selecting Window>Snippets.

5 | In the Snippets panel, double-click the Form Elements folder, and then double-click the Dropdown Menus folder to open it.

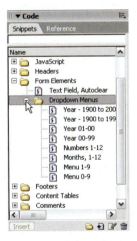

FIGURE 6.7

6 | Drag the Months, 1-12 snippet to the right of Month: in the table cell.

FIGURE 6.8

7 | Click the new List control. From the Property inspector, change its name to **cc_exp_month** and press Enter/Return.

FIGURE 6.9

8 | Save your changes to order_form.html, but leave it open for the next exercise.

To Extend Your Knowledge

CONTENTS OF SNIPPETS

You can create and insert snippets to use in the **<head>** or **<body>** section of the Web page. In most cases, you will probably create snippets to use in the Document window or the **<body>** section of the Web page. However, there are HTML tags that Dreamweaver does not offer through its menus or that are missing some of the attributes, such as the **rel** attribute of the **<style>** tag, and, therefore, snippets may be the way you want to store and reuse them.

Snippets may contain virtually any tag content or text content, with some limitations. There are no limitations on what you can insert into a snippet — you could even, for instance, insert all of the code of an HTML document in a snippet, but you wouldn't be able to use the snippet because a Web page cannot have two **<body>**, **<html>**, **<head>** or **DTD** (Document Type Definition) tags. Therefore, avoid the **DTD**, **<body>**, **<head>**, and **<html>** tags in your snippets. Also do not use snippets to create parts of tags or components, such as **<tr><td>**, which are the opening tags of a table row and a table cell, because it is quite possible that you won't always remember to complete the unfinished tags.

Remember, also, that Dreamweaver does not check the validity of snippets, so if you try to create a **<bold>** tag, Dreamweaver does not check your snippet for valid tags, whereas Dreamweaver does check the Web page if you try to create such a tag on your page. It is best to create the content in Dreamweaver so that it creates good and valid code, and then you can create a snippet from that code.

LESSON 2   Creating a New Snippet

Dreamweaver does not contain all of the snippets that you might find useful. You may create snippets of your own that might be useful in other projects. You may also discover pieces of code on other Web sites that could be useful to you, such as a list of countries of the world or the states of the US. In both cases, these parcels of code are quite long so saving them as reusable snippets could save you a lot of typing time in the future.

There are two types of snippets: wrap selection and insert block. The insert-block snippets are blocks of code that appear where you insert them. There is only one component to the snippet. The wrap-selection type of snippet consists of two pieces of code: one that appears before and one that appears after. When you create a new snippet, you must first determine which type of snippet it will be and enable the appropriate options in the Snippet dialog box.

Create a New Snippet

In this exercise, you create a new insert-block snippet and save it for later use. The code does not yet exist so you must create it first. This snippet will be the years from 2004 to 2010, created for use as the credit-card expiration year. You save the snippet in a new folder that you create in the Snippets panel.

1   **In the open file, order_form.html, click to the right of the cc_exp_month List control.**

2   **Type Year: and from the Forms Insert bar, insert a new List. Name it years. Populate the list values with 2004, 2005, 2006, 2007, 2008, 2009, and 2010.**

FIGURE 6.10

3   **In the Snippets panel, close any open folders.**

4   **Right/Control-click below the last folder in the Snippets panel and choose New Folder.**

FIGURE 6.11

5   **Type your name (such as Bob) and press Enter/Return.**

6 Click the new list of years in the Document window. Right/Control-click the new folder in the Snippets panel and choose New Snippet.

FIGURE 6.12

7 In the Name field, type `Years, 2004 to 2010`. In the Description field, type `A select list of years from 2004 to 2010`. Set Snippet Type to Insert Block. Set Preview Type to Design and click OK.

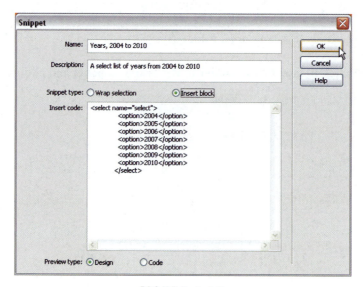

FIGURE 6.13

8 Click the year list in the Document window and, in the Property inspector, name the list `cc_exp_year`.

FIGURE 6.14

9 Save the changes to order_form.html, but leave it open for the next exercise.

To Extend Your Knowledge

WRAP-SELECTION SNIPPET TYPE

The wrap-selection snippet allows you to surround selected content with two parts of a snippet: the insert-before and insert-after parts. This is very handy if you use an HTML tag that Dreamweaver does not present except in the Tag Chooser dialog box. You may find that opening the Tag chooser to insert a tag is cumbersome; the wrap-selection snippet may be more to your liking. For example, if you find that you use the <q> quote tag often, you may create a quote-tag snippet, where the insert-before code is <q> and the insert-after code is </q>. To use the quote-tag snippet, simply select the quote text, insert the quote-tag snippet, and the quote will be surrounded by the <q> and </q> tags.

LESSON 3   Creating Library Items

Most people are familiar with the concept of a template; we explore the Dreamweaver template function later in this project. A template is a complete Web page without the information that changes from page to page. A library item is a small component, such as a menu bar or header, not a complete Web page. Although smaller and more focused, a library item is still a powerful tool and time saver. The power of a library item is not simply the consistency from page to page that uses it, but also that if you make a change to the library item, any page using it reflects the change. Need to add a new link to the navigation bar? Just create a navigation bar library item and, when you add a new link to it, all pages that use that library item reflect that change, whether there are 4 or 4,000 pages on your site.

The first step in working with a library item is to create it. The library item must first exist as a component of your pages (at least one page) and then you may add it to the library-items folder or assets. When you create your first library item, Dreamweaver creates a Library folder in the Site folder; any library items you create will be stored there. Library items are also listed as assets of the site and, as such, are found in the Library collection of the Assets panel.

Create a Library Item

In this exercise, you create a library item from the Tropiflora logo image. As you do so, Dreamweaver creates the Library folder for you. You see that when you examine a library item in the Property inspector, it displays the library-item properties, not the properties of the content in the library item.

1   **In the open file, order_form.html, click the Tropiflora Online graphic at the top of the page.**

2   **Open the Assets panel either by clicking the Assets tab at the top of the Files panel or by selecting Window>Assets.**

3 Click the Library icon at the bottom of the list of icons on the left side of the Assets panel.

FIGURE 6.15

4 Drag the Tropiflora Online graphic into the Library Assets panel. Type `Tropiflora Logo` and press Enter/Return.

FIGURE 6.16

5 Click the Files tab to view the Files panel and click the Refresh button (or press F5).

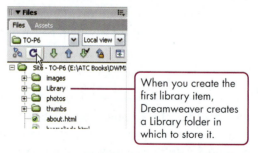

When you create the first library item, Dreamweaver creates a Library folder in which to store it.

FIGURE 6.17

6 Click the graphic at the top of the Document window and observe the Property inspector.

The properties of this image are now properties of a library item. To view the image properties, you must open or edit the library item.

FIGURE 6.18

7 Close order_form.html, saving your changes.

To Extend Your Knowledge

CONTENTS OF LIBRARY ITEMS

Snippets may contain code for either the **\<head>** or **\<body>** section of an HTML document, but a library item may only contain **\<body>** section content, with one exception. This means that the content must be viewable in the Document window in the Design view. The exception to this rule applies when JavaScript is involved.

Many JavaScript scripts have two components: the event handler as an attribute of a tag in the **\<body>** section of the HTML document and the function called by the event handler that is in the **\<head>** part of the HTML document. For example, an image rollover has the **onMouseOver** and **onMouseOut** events and event handlers in the **\<a>** tag, but the Swap Image behavior function is written in the **\<head>** section of the HTML document. If you create a navigation bar with image rollovers in it and save it as a library item, you might assume that because the Swap Image JavaScript is in the **\<head>** section and the navigation bar is in the **\<body>** section, the Swap Image JavaScript would not be carried by the library item. If you create the behavior using Dreamweaver's own behaviors and the Behavior panel, however, Dreamweaver does transfer the JavaScript with the library item. Examine the JavaScript function for the Swap Image behavior in the **\<head>** section of the HTML document and you will see that the function begins with **MM_**. All Dreamweaver behavior functions begin with **MM_**. This has special significance to Dreamweaver library items because Dreamweaver recognizes that the event handler in the navigation bar is calling a JavaScript function that begins with **MM_** and Dreamweaver automatically adds that JavaScript function into the **\<head>** section of any page in which you insert the library item.

However, if you create a custom JavaScript script that has a function in the **\<head>** section of the HTML document, Dreamweaver does not know to copy the function to pages that use the custom function; you must copy it yourself. On the other hand, if you create a template with the custom script, because the template is a complete Web page, the custom code in the **\<head>** section will be transferred to pages built from the template.

LESSON 4   Inserting Library Items into Other Pages

You can only apply the power of library items if the library item exists on other pages. Although the Tropiflora Online graphic appears on all other pages of this site, it does not exist as a library item on these other pages, just as a graphic. To set this graphic as a library item on the other pages, you must replace the graphic with the library item of the same graphic.

You might not generally replace common elements with library items while working on an existing site. Instead, you would be likely to use library items as you design the site for the first time using templates. When you build a new page from the template, it has the library items already in it because they were in the template. At times, however, you may be asked to rebuild a Web site and you might use library items in the rebuilding. Therefore, you would identify the common elements on the pages, store them as library items, and then replace the common elements with the library items created from them. In doing so, you have prepared the common elements so that should any further changes be required later, you could update all of the common elements with the alterations.

There are two methods for inserting a library item into a page. You can click at the position where the library item is to go and drag the library item from the Library Assets panel. Your other option is to click at the position where the library item is to go, click the library item in the Library Assets panel, and click the Insert button at the bottom of the panel. You cannot add a library item from the Library folder of the Files panel nor by double-clicking the library item: double-clicking just opens the library item in edit mode.

Add the Library Item to the Other Pages

In this exercise, you add the Tropiflora Logo library item to the other pages in the site. You switch between the Files and Assets panels to open the page, and then insert the library item. There are no real shortcuts although you may open the page using File>Open.

1 Open about.html and click the Tropiflora Online graphic at the top of the page.

2 Switch to the Assets panel and click the Tropiflora Logo library item. (If necessary, first click the Library icon at the bottom left of the Assets panel.)

3 Click the Insert button at the bottom of the Assets panel.

FIGURE 6.19

? If you have problems

If the Tropiflora Logo library item did not replace the Tropiflora Online graphic but, instead, appeared beside it, the graphic was not selected when you clicked the Insert button. You may either delete the Tropiflora Online graphic or you may press Control/Command-Z to undo, click the Tropiflora Online graphic, and reinsert the library item.

| **4** | Close about.html, saving your changes. |

| **5** | Repeat Steps 1 to 4 with the remaining HTML pages in the site. |

To open the pages you can switch to the Files panel, open the file, and then switch to the Assets panel to insert the library item. You may also choose File>Open to open the page, keeping the Assets panel open all of the time.

To Extend Your Knowledge

LIBRARY ITEMS ON THE WEB SITE

Most of the content that you create in the Site folder will be uploaded to the Web server and, generally, is publicly viewable. However, library items and template files have no role in a Web site outside of its design and development. Dreamweaver will upload the Library and Template folders if you upload the whole site to the Web server unless you are selective or you cloak these folders. Cloaking is a feature of Dreamweaver with which you may mark folders and file types: Dreamweaver does not upload cloaked files and folders. You learn to cloak folders and file types in *Project 7: Managing Your Live Web Site.*

LESSON 5   Revising a Library Item

Simply replacing the Tropiflora Online graphic with a library item that contains the same graphic is not the value of the library-items feature. The value is that if you change an aspect of the library item, all pages that use the library item receive the updated content, as well. In this lesson, you edit the Tropiflora Logo library item and, as you do so, you see how every page containing the library item is updated with the changes.

You have two choices for editing a library item: you can open the Library folder of the Files panel and double-click the library item, or you can double-click the library item in the Assets panel. In edit mode, the library item appears alone in a new Document window. You may make changes to it as you see fit. As soon as you close the Document window, you are prompted to save the library item. If you choose to save, you are then prompted to update all pages that use the library item.

Edit a Library Item

In this exercise, you change two aspects of the Tropiflora Logo library item: you add alt text to the image and you change the image. You make both changes at the same time. After you close the Document window containing the library item, you save the changes and update the pages that contain the library item.

| **1** | Open the Assets panel and double-click the Tropiflora Logo library item. |

You don't need to have a document open to edit a library item.

| **2** | Double-click the image in the Document window and replace it with images>tropiflora_online2.jpg. |

3   Type Tropiflora Online in the Alt field and press Enter/Return.

FIGURE 6.20

4   Close, saving the library item.

5   Click Update to update the pages that contain the library item.

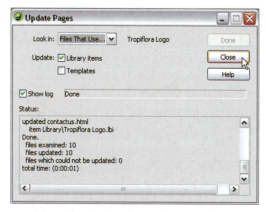

FIGURE 6.21

6   After the update is complete, you see a report on the update process. Click Close after reviewing the report.

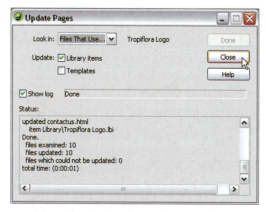

FIGURE 6.22

To Extend Your Knowledge

SSI IS SIMILAR TO LIBRARY ITEMS

In **SSI** (server-side includes) — a technology very similar in function to library items — common parcels of code are inserted into Web pages. The technology differs, however, in that the insertion occurs when the visitor requests the page, not during the design of the Web page. In most cases, SSI requires access to a Web-programming language, such as PHP or ASP, but if your Web server is running Apache Web-server software, you can use SSI without a Web-programming language.

The drawback to library items is that if you have many pages that use the same library items, whenever you change a library item, Dreamweaver must inject the changes to the library item into all of the pages. With many pages, this process can take a long time. SSI simply uses a command that states "insert file abc.inc here," but that command is not processed until a visitor requests the page. As long as the SSI command remains the same, the code in the include file can change as much as you like during the development of the site.

The primary difference between library items and SSI is that when you use library items, the complete code of the library item exists within the Web pages that use the library item, but the SSI command is just a line of code that states the filename of the include to insert. This difference has another effect on file uploading: because the code of library items are in the pages that use them, it does not matter if the Library folder is uploaded to the Web server because the pages on the Web site do not rely on the presence of the files in the Library folder. However, SSI is a command to the Web server to insert the include file into the page before delivering it to the visitor. You must, therefore, remember to upload the include files to the Web server; otherwise, the SSI command tries to include a nonexistent file.

Dreamweaver supports SSI in the Design view: you can create the code for SSI and Dreamweaver displays the contents of the included file in the Design view. However, you cannot see the effect of SSI if you preview a local page in your browser unless your computer is running either Apache Web-server software or a Web-programming language. (You learn to use SSI in the final project of this book.)

LESSON 6   Creating Templates

There are two methods for creating a template: start from scratch and prepare a Web page as a template or take an existing page and save it as a template. The method you choose may simply be based on your preferences; there are no compelling reasons to choose one method over another. However, be certain that the template is in good shape when you start to use it. Although you may make changes to the template later, you shouldn't make too many changes, because the more child pages you create from the template, the longer the update process takes. When you have laid out the common elements of a template, you save the file as a template by choosing File>Save as Template, where you can also add a description of the template in case you create several for the same site.

Templates are commonly thought of as Web pages with the common elements of the Web pages for the site. However, Dreamweaver templates are more sophisticated than that — the common elements are protected from change unless you edit the template file. This is beneficial because if you are working on a page based on a template, you cannot make changes to the common elements on that page, thus rendering parts of that page different from other pages. Instead, if you discover a mistake with the template while working on a child page, you edit the template, fix the mistake, and update all of the pages that use the template with the fix.

After you have laid out the common elements of the template, you must identify what areas of the template are editable. By default, none of the parts of the template are editable, which means that when you create a child page from the template, you can't add any content. If you forget to specify an editable region (or regions) when you save the template, you will be warned that the template has no editable regions; you can then go back and assign editable regions. Only in child pages are some regions noneditable. In the template all regions may be edited, but to make the template useful for creating child pages, you must set at least one editable region.

Templates, like library items, are stored in their own Templates folder. Templates also are collected in the Assets panel in their own group, which is accessible by clicking the Templates icon, the second from the bottom. Templates may contain library items, a feature that can greatly simplify the development of a Web site. This saves the work of re-creating the components of the library item in each template if a library item is quite complex and used throughout the site, or if you have multiple templates for the Web site, all containing the same library item. Of course, if you change the library item, both templates and child pages update with the change.

Create a Template from an Existing Page

In this exercise, you create a template from an existing page. In a situation where you need to add more pages to a site and want to use the Dreamweaver template technology, it makes sense to take an existing page and develop it into a template. You must remember to set the editable area or you won't be able to use it to create child pages.

1 Open about.html from the TO-P6 site.

2 Choose File>Save as Template.

3 Type **Basic** in the Save as field and click Save.

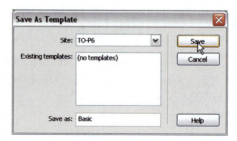

FIGURE 6.23

4   **Click Yes to update the links in the template.**

The links in the about.html page are relative to the location of about.html, the root folder of the site. However, templates are stored in a Templates folder, so the links must be adjusted to compensate for the location of the recently created template.

FIGURE 6.24

5   **Examine the filename tab.**

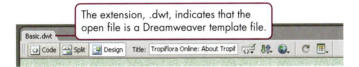

The extension, .dwt, indicates that the open file is a Dreamweaver template file.

FIGURE 6.25

6   **Choose File>Close. Do not check the Don't Warn Me Again checkbox, but instead click Cancel.**

Unless another user before you has checked the Don't Warn Me Again checkbox, this warning appears, indicating that there are no editable regions in the template.

FIGURE 6.26

? If you have problems

If someone before you has checked the Don't Warn Me Again checkbox, you won't see the warnings in Steps 4 or 6 and the template file closes. You must reopen Template.dwt from the Templates folder. You may have to refresh the Files panel by clicking the Refresh button at the top of the Files panel. If you have had to reopen Template.dwt, continue with Step 7.

7   Click OK to acknowledge the information.

FIGURE 6.27

8   Click in the main content cell of the page, click the `<td>` tag in the Tag selector, and press Delete.

9   With the `<td>` tag in the Tag selector still selected, switch to the Common Insert bar, and choose Editable Region from the Template drop-down menu.

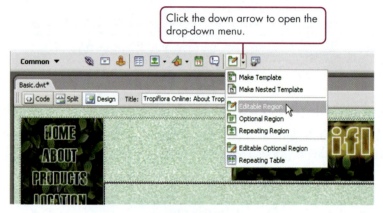

FIGURE 6.28

10   Name the editable region `Content Region` and click OK.

FIGURE 6.29

11   Examine the Document window and notice the blue label identifying the editable region.

FIGURE 6.30

12   In the document Title field at the top of the Document window, remove About Tropiflora and replace it with `Template`.

FIGURE 6.31

13   Close Basic.dwt, saving your changes.

To Extend Your Knowledge

TEMPLATES AND LIBRARY ITEMS

Templates may contain library items as well as regular HTML components. There may be times when you need to create different templates for a Web site, such as a template for a product-category page as well as a template for a product-detail page. Both may use the same footer content (links to the contact, copyright, privacy, and other pages) and primary navigation (links to primary product-category pages). There is no need to go to the trouble of re-creating these components of the templates each time you create a new template and risk creating them differently. If you create a library item for each of these components, you just need to insert them into the two templates and any other templates that you create later. Then, if you need to make a change to any of these library items, the update process not only updates the child pages created from the templates but also updates the templates themselves.

LESSON 7   Creating a Child Page from the Template

Once you have created a template, you can use it to build other pages, child pages. To create a child page from a template, you choose File>New to create a new page. Click the Templates tab at the top of the New dialog box, choose the site from which the template is to be drawn, choose the template page from the list, and click Create (or double-click the template page name).

When creating a child page, you learn that there are only two sections of a page that are editable: the editable regions, of which there may be more than one, and the document Title. Only these sections can be edited in a child page. Even in the Code view, you cannot edit any section outside of the editable regions.

To enable this functionality, Dreamweaver creates special tags based on the standard HTML comment tags: <!-- and -->, for which special Dreamweaver-specific attributes are added. For example, the code inserted into the page to indicate the editable region named Content Region is **<!-- TemplateBeginEditable name="Content Region" -->**Content Region**<!-- TemplateEndEditable -->**. In any other HTML editor, these tags could be edited and deleted, but in a child page of a template while using Dreamweaver, these tags cannot be edited. Dreamweaver respects the purpose of these tags — to identify editable and noneditable regions. It is not HTML but Dreamweaver that prevents the designer from editing noneditable regions.

Create a Child Page from the Template

In this exercise, you create a new page from the Basic template. When creating a new page from a template, you change the mode of the New dialog box to New from Template by clicking the Templates tab. In that mode, the dialog box displays all sites current in Dreamweaver on the left, and, after you click a site, any templates that have been created for the selected site display in the middle.

1 Choose File>New and click the Templates tab.

2 Click the TO-P6 site, choose the basic template, and click Create.

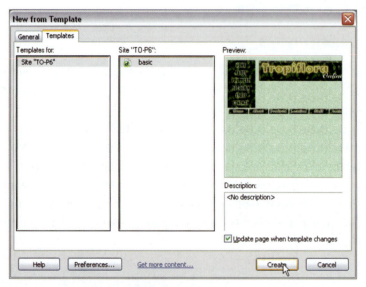

FIGURE 6.32

To Extend Your Knowledge

MACROMEDIA CONTRIBUTE

Not only Dreamweaver but also another of Macromedia's products, Contribute, respects the template-specific coding. Contribute, in version 3 at the time of this writing, is an application specifically developed for contributors to a Web site. Not all people adding content to a Web site are Web designers or Web developers. Some contributors simply add content to new pages. Furthermore, the cost of the Contribute application is significantly less than the cost of Dreamweaver, making it quite affordable for an organization to purchase a few copies of Dreamweaver and many more copies of Contribute for the content writers. Contribute can use templates, but, unlike Dreamweaver, Contribute can neither create nor edit templates, thus reassuring the Dreamweaver designer that the templates will not be damaged by Contribute users.

3   **Move your mouse pointer around the template, including over the Content Region.**

The editable region is named and surrounded by an aqua border.

Outside of the editable regions, the mouse pointer changes to indicate uneditable regions.

A yellow border surrounds the template. A label at the top right identifies the name of the template.

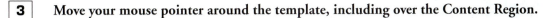

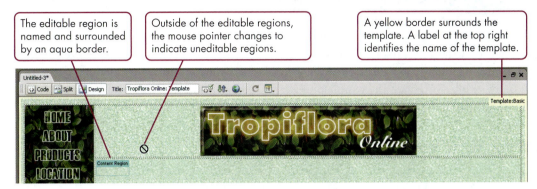

FIGURE 6.33

4   **Without closing the Untitled page, open basic_events.html. Select all of the text in the page, copy it to the clipboard, and close the page.**

5   **Click in the Content Region of the Untitled page and paste the copied content.**

6   **Delete Template from the document Title field and replace it with Upcoming Events.**

FIGURE 6.34

7   **Close, saving the new child page as events.html.**

To Extend Your Knowledge

DRAWBACKS TO TEMPLATE TECHNOLOGY

As you have learned, both library items and template technologies are very beneficial for the development of a Web site, and its consistent look and feel. As mentioned earlier, CSS can help with this, too. However, whenever you need to make a change to either a template or a library item, the update process runs and updates all pages affected by the changes. If there are only 10 pages in a site, at most, only 10 pages need to be uploaded to the Web server. However, if there are 10,000 pages on a site, this is more problematic. Although all 10,000 pages can be uploaded, the upload can take a very long time and the update process may also take a very long time. Many Dreamweaver professionals recommend limiting the use of Dreamweaver template technologies to sites with 50 or fewer pages. Larger sites should consider the use of SSI or other technologies.

LESSON 8   Revising a Template

You have created a new page from the template but no pages are linked to the new page. In this exercise, you assume that all of the pages on the site were created from this same template. Therefore, when you add a link in the template to the new page, all pages built using the template are revised to include the new link. The process is quite simple: you open the template, make the change, save the template, and when Dreamweaver asks if you want to update all pages built from the template, you click Update.

Revise the Template

In this exercise, you open the Basic template and make two changes. In both cases, you create links to the new events.html page. Just like library items, when you save the changes to a template, you are prompted to update all pages that use the template.

1   **From the Templates folder, open Basic.dwt.**

You can also open a template by opening the Assets panel, clicking the Template icon, and double-clicking the name of the template.

2   **In the left navigation-bar table, click the Products graphic link, and choose Modify>Table>Insert Rows or Columns. Set the Insert Rows or Columns dialog box to insert one row Below the Selection and click OK.**

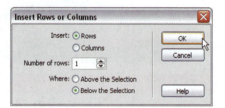

FIGURE 6.35

3   **Into the empty cell, insert the images>nb_events.gif graphic and link it to events.html. Add Events as the alternate text.**

FIGURE 6.36

4 | Click the Products graphic link in the bottom navigation bar and choose Modify>Table>Insert Rows or Columns. Set the Insert Rows or Columns dialog box to insert one column After the Selection and click OK.

FIGURE 6.37

5 | Insert the images>events_button.gif graphic into the empty cell, and link it to events.html. Add Events as the alternate text.

6 | Close Basic.dwt, saving your changes.

7 | When prompted, click Update. When finished, click Close.

8 | Reopen events.html and observe that both navigation-bar graphics appear in the page.

LESSON 9 Creating Repeating Regions in a Template

Repeating regions of a template enable you, the designer, to create a consistent look and feel within small parts of a page. There are times when a type of information may be repeated multiple times in a page. For example, you may create a What's New page where each story has a title, date, author, and *précis*, (a summary of the main points of a story). You may want to design a format or layout for this collection of components and allow the collection to be repeated as many times as necessary. You would, therefore, create a template with repeating regions. In the repeating regions, you can have a mixture of both editable and noneditable regions. For example, the date area might be editable but the word Date, the heading, might not be editable.

Repeating regions are more work to set up but quite simple to use. When you are working on a child page developed from a template with a repeating region, you can add and delete repeating regions and change their order. For example, when a story has been added out of date order, you may move it up or down into the correct order. Also, if a story is old and no longer appropriate on the What's New page, you can remove it by deleting its repeating region.

When you create a template with a repeating region, you should lay out one of the regions with actual content so that you can arrange it properly and determine which content needs repetition and which does not. Then you select the content that is to be editable and set it as editable regions (with names). You select the content that is to be repeated and set it as a repeatable region (also with a name). Finally, you save the template and build a child page from the template.

Create a Template with a Repeating Region

In this exercise, you create a template with a repeating region. You set some of the content area to be editable and specify which region in the template may be repeated. Finally, you save the template.

1   Open about.html from the TO-P6 site, choose File>Save as Template, and name it `Books`. When asked to update links, choose Yes.

2   Click in the main content cell, click the `<td>` tag in the Tag selector, and press Delete.

3   Click in the empty cell, type `From the Bookshelf`, format the block as Heading 2, and press Enter/Return.

4   Create a 2-row, 2-column table that is 50% in width (and leave all other settings blank).

5   With the table still selected, set the alignment to center in the Property inspector.

6   Select the two cells in the top row and check the Header option in the Property inspector.

7   In the top-left cell, type `Title`, and in the top-right cell, type `Price`.

FIGURE 6.38

8   Click in the bottom-left cell, click the last `<td>` tag in the Tag selector, and choose Editable Region from the Templates drop-down menu of the Common Insert bar. Name the Editable Region `Title` and click OK.

9   Click in the bottom-right cell, click the last `<td>` tag in the Tag selector, and choose Editable Region from the Templates drop-down menu of the Common Insert bar. Name the Editable Region `Price` and click OK.

10   With the insertion point in the bottom row, click the last `<tr>` tag in the Tag selector, and choose Repeating Region from the Templates drop-down menu of the Common Insert bar. Name the Repeating Region `Book Details` and click OK.

Dreamweaver adds Repeat: to the name of the repeating region.

FIGURE 6.39

11   Remove About Tropiflora from the document Title field and replace it with `Template`.

12   Close Books.dwt, saving your changes.

Create a Child Page Using the Repeating Region

Creating a child page from a template with repeating regions uses the same procedures as you used in the previous template until you need to repeat the regions. As you notice, there are four icons above the repeating region: a plus symbol (+) to add a copy of the repeating region, a hyphen (-) to remove the current repeating region, an up arrow to move the current repeating region up in order, and a down arrow to move the current repeating region down in order.

1   Choose File>New, choose the Templates tab, and choose books from the TO-P6 site.

FIGURE 6.40

2   Change the document title to `Products: Books`.

3   Choose File>Save and save the child page as `books.html`.

4   Click in the Title editable area and type `Bromeliads: A Cultural Manual`. Click in the Price editable area and type `$39.95`.

5   Click the plus symbol (+) to add a new repeating region.

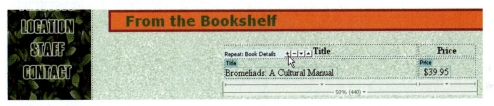

FIGURE 6.41

6   Type `The Tillandsia Handbook` in the Title editable region and `$27.00` in the Price editable region.

7   Add a new repeating region, type `Bananas You Can Grow` as the title, and type `$19.95` as the price.

8   Add a new repeating region, type `Succulents: The Illustrated Dictionary` as the title, and type `$24.95` as the price.

9 Using the up and down areas at the top of the repeating region, sort the books so that, from top to bottom, the books are Bananas You Can Grow, Bromeliads: A Cultural Manual, Succulents: The Illustrated Dictionary, and The Tillandsia Handbook.

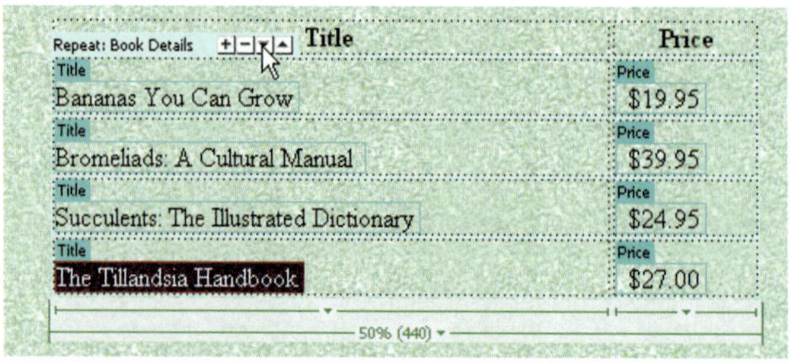

FIGURE 6.42

10 Click in the Bananas You Can Grow repeating region and click the hyphen button (-) to delete the repeating region. (This book is no longer available.)

11 Close books.html, saving your changes.

To Extend Your Knowledge

PROGRAMMING THE TEMPLATE TECHNOLOGY

Dreamweaver's template technology is much more sophisticated than what you have seen, including capabilities such as conditional and optional regions in a template. Dreamweaver's templates have a programming language and the code described to you earlier for a template's editable and noneditable regions is just the tip of the iceberg. Unfortunately, most of these features and functions are based on programming concepts that are outside of the scope of these books. The template programming language is based on JavaScript, but unlike the Behaviors panel, many of the features of this language are not available through dialog boxes and require hand-coding.

For additional information about the programming technology of Dreamweaver templates, review the information available in the Help resources of Dreamweaver or at macromedia.com/devnet/mx/dreamweaver/templates.html.

CAREERS IN DESIGN

WORKING WITH DOCUMENTS DESTINED FOR PRINTING AND THE WEB SITE

Web designers may be assigned different roles and responsibilities in an organization, depending on a variety of factors, including their knowledge, skills, and experience, as well as the size of the department. Among the possible roles and responsibilities they may take on are print-based graphic and publication design.

Communications departments often continuously produce print-based publications from smaller single-page documents such as press releases to larger documents of 100 pages or more. Many such documents are destined for multiple paths — printed to paper, saved as PDFs, and made into Web pages. However, the ways in which readers use these types of documents differ from each other depending on the final formats, and Web designers should be aware of the differences. Although it is possible to export a publication from a graphic-design or desktop-publishing application to Web-page format, the result may not be satisfactory for either the end user or the Web-site designer.

A printed publication is commonly read from beginning to end, but information on Web sites is typically scanned by users searching for specific information, a much more focused approach. A one- or two-page press release may be posted to a Web site with little or no modification, but longer documents require restructuring and reorganization. As a result, a large document must be split into multiple pages so that the users may more easily find the information they are seeking. It may also be necessary to include a link to a search engine or even build a search engine into the Web site. You may download code from Google.com, or one of several other search engines, that creates a form on your site linked to the search engine and provides search-engine functionality to enable searching for content from pages within your site. This functionality goes a long way to helping the users of your site search for the information they are seeking.

In other words, File>Save As is not an appropriate method for transferring content from a print publication to a Web site. Web designers and their managers should be aware that the two different media require different treatments. Effective use of templates and CSS can greatly ease the creation of Web pages from multipage publications and should be considered from the outset when the project is initiated.

SUMMARY

In this project, you learned several means of efficiently updating and planning for updating your Web sites. You learned to insert a snippet into your document. You created a new snippet and a folder in the Snippets panel, and stored the snippet for later use. You learned about library items and how they can help you create a common look and feel to your Web site. You learned how they are beneficial to the development of a Web site and enable you to make changes that are reflected throughout your Web site. You created, inserted, and updated a library item. You also learned about templates and how they, too, help with the development and rebuilding of a Web site. You discovered how to create a template from a combination of a library item and nonlibrary-item code. You created a template from an existing page, but also learned that you could create the template from scratch. You created a child page from the template, modified the template, and saw the child page update with the changes. You created a template with a repeating region. You built a child page from the template with the repeating region, added more repeating regions, and sorted them.

KEY TERMS

child page

editable region

insert after

insert before

insert block

Library folder

library item

master template

repeating region

snippet

template

Templates folder

update

wrap selection

CHECKING CONCEPTS AND TERMS

SCREEN ID

Identify the indicated areas from the list below:

FIGURE 6.43

a. Snippets panel

b. Noneditable region

c. Template name

d. Add repeating region

e. Snippet name

f. Create new page from template

g. Library folder

h. Name of an editable region

i. Assets panel

MULTIPLE CHOICE

Circle the letter of the correct answer for each of the following:

1. Which of the following is true?
   a. Snippets can be opened from either the Snippets panel or the Snippets folder of the current site.
   b. A snippet of an <img> tag contains both the HTML code and the image.
   c. Snippets can contain a JavaScript event handler.
   d. None of the above.

2. By default, all areas in a template are _____.
   a. not editable
   b. unstyled
   c. table cells
   d. All of the above

3. Templates can be created using _____.
   a. library items
   b. snippets
   c. HTML
   d. All of the above

4. To insert a library item into a document, you can _____.
   a. drag it from the Templates folder
   b. select the content in the page and click the New Library Item button
   c. choose the item in the Library Assets panel and click the Insert button
   d. All of the above

5. Which of the following can contain the **<body>** tag?
   a. an editable region
   b. a snippet
   c. a library item
   d. a template

6. To wrap a selected block of text with <span class="sidebar"> before it and </span> after it, you would create _____.
   a. a library item
   b. a snippet
   c. a template
   d. None of the above

7. Which layout method is not supported by templates?
   a. layers
   b. CSS
   c. frames
   d. tables

8. Which feature does not apply to templates?
   a. consistent HTML structure
   b. site-wide updating
   c. less effort for contributors to a Web site
   d. consistent appearance and styles

9. Which component of a Web page is always editable in a template?
   a. **<body>** content
   b. **<title>** content
   c. **<!-- -->** comments
   d. None of the above

10. Which feature is not site-specific?
   a. snippets
   b. templates
   c. library items
   d. All of the above

DISCUSSION QUESTIONS

1. You have been asked to design a Web site for a client. You plan to use Dreamweaver templates to provide consistency to the structure. Your client would like you to show them a few sample pages before giving final approval. Would you or would you not use templates and/or library items in the sample pages? Explain your reasoning.

2. The snippet function can save a significant amount of time in the development of a Web page by reducing some of the tedious development time. Review the procedures and methods you have used in the past to create components of a Web page, list those that could be saved as a snippet for later use, and explain why. If you think of others uses for snippets that you haven't tried yet, add those to your list as well.

SKILL DRILL

Skill Drills reinforce project skills. Each skill reinforced is the same, or nearly the same, as a skill presented in the lessons. Detailed instructions are provided in a step-by-step format. Work through these exercises in order.

1. Create Snippets from Code

It is very easy to add a snippet, such as a list of the states of the US, from a Web page in Dreamweaver: you just open the page in Dreamweaver, click the list in the Design view, and add it to the Snippets panel. It is more difficult to copy code. The purpose of this Skill Drill is not to make it difficult for you to copy some useful code and save it as a snippet. The purpose is to create a more realistic scenario whereby you might find a piece of code on someone else's Web site and want to save it for use on yours. You would, therefore, have to view the source code from your browser, search through the code for the code you want to copy and save as a snippet, and then copy/paste it into the Snippets panel. Recognize that you should not save copyrighted code unless you ask permission of the owner of the Web site. In this Skill Drill, the information is publicly available and not copyrighted.

1. Open survey.txt from the TO-P6 site.

2. Scroll to line 245. Select lines 245 to 297, inclusive, and copy the code into the clipboard.

3. Right/Control-click your named folder in the Snippets panel and choose New Snippet.

4. Name the snippet **States of the US**. In the Description, type **A select list of the states of the US**.

5. Set Snippet Type to Insert Block and set Preview Type to Design.

   If the selected code does not automatically appear in the Insert Code area, paste the selected code into it.

6. Click Close/OK.

7. In the open file, survey.txt, select lines 19 to 237, inclusive, and copy the code to the clipboard.

8. Create a new snippet in your named folder called **Countries** with a description of **A select list of the countries of the world.**

9. Set Snippet type to Insert Block and set Preview Type to Design.

    If the selected code does not automatically appear in the Insert code area, paste the selected code into it.

10. Click Close/OK.

11. Close survey.txt.

2. Insert Snippets into a Web Page

In this Skill Drill, you insert the snippet containing the list of states that you saved in the previous exercise. You use it to replace a text field in which the visitors are expected to type their billing and shipping states. To meet the needs of the form-processing application, you must rename the form field names from the default names stored with the snippet.

1. Open order_form.html from the TO-P6 site.

2. Click the State text field in the Billing Information area of the form and delete it.

3. From your named folder in the Snippets panel, insert the States of the US snippet.

4. Click the new list field and change the name of the form control in the Property inspector to `billing_state`.

5. Repeat Steps 2 to 4 with the state text field in the Shipping Information area of the form. Name the new form control `shipping_state`.

6. Close order_form.html, saving your changes.

3. Create and Add Library Items to the Template

In this Skill Drill, you enhance the Basic.dwt template by making more of the common components — the left and bottom navigation bars — into library items so, if you need to, you can use them in other templates.

1. Open Basic.dwt from the Templates folder of the TO-P6 site.

2. Click any of the graphic links in the left navigation bar.

3. In the Tag selector, click the `<table>` tag to the right of the `<td#navbar>` tag.

4. Open the Assets panel and click the Library icon at the bottom of the column of icons on the left.

5. At the bottom of the Assets panel, click the New Library Item button, read the message, and click OK. Name the new library item `Left Navbar`.

6. In the Document window, click any of the graphic links in the bottom navigation bar.

7. In the Tag selector, click the nested `<table>` tag.

8. At the bottom of the Assets panel, click the New Library Item button, read the message, and click OK. Name the new library item `Bottom Navbar`.

9. Close Basic.dwt, saving your changes.

10. When prompted, click Update and then Close.

4. Build a Site with Revised Templates

In this Skill Drill, you use the revised template to rebuild most of the pages from the TO-P6 site folder, ensuring that the entire site uses the same template and library items. After completing this exercise, you are prepared to make any changes to the site that you or the owner of the site requires — your changes will cascade through all of the pages.

1. Choose File>New, if necessary click the Templates tab, choose the basic template from the TO-P6 site, and click Create.

2. Open about.html from the TO-P6 folder.

3. Drag to select all of the content in the main content cell and copy it to the clipboard. Close about.html.

4. Paste the copied content into the editable region. Set the document Title field to **Tropiflora Online: About Tropiflora**.

5. Close, saving your changes to about.html and overwriting the existing file.

   The links will be broken until you save the file and Dreamweaver updates the links.

6. Repeat Steps 1 to 5 as follows:

Source of Content	Document Title Field	Save as Filename
bromeliads.html	**Tropiflora Online: Products: Bromeliads**	bromeliads.html
contactus.html	**Tropiflora Online: Contact Us**	contactus.html
index.html	**Tropiflora Online: Home**	index.html
location.html	**Tropiflora Online: Location**	location.html
order_form.html	**Tropiflora Online: Products: Order Form**	order_form.html
products.html	**Tropiflora Online: Products**	products.html
staff.html	**Tropiflora Online: Staff**	staff.html
succulents.html	**Tropiflora Online: Products: Succulents**	succulents.html
tillandsias.html	**Tropiflora Online: Products: Tillandsias**	tillandsias.html

5. Create a Template with Repeating Regions

In this Skill Drill exercise, you create a staff directory with a repeating region. Each repeating region consists of a table with a left cell containing an editable image placeholder and cells on the right containing the name, phone number, and email address of each staff member. The heading cells between the two columns are not editable.

1. Open about.html from the TO-P6 site, choose File>Save as Template, and name it **Staff Directory**. When asked to update links, choose Yes.

2. Remove About Tropiflora from the document Title field and replace it with **Staff Directory**.

3. Delete the content in the main content cell. Type **Staff Directory** and format it as Heading 2. Click to the right of the text and press Enter/Return.

4. Create a **4**-row, **3**-column table that is **500** pixels wide. Leave all other fields empty and click OK.

5. With the table selected, set the alignment of the table to center from the Property inspector.

6. Select the three cells of the bottom row and merge them. From the HTML Insert bar, insert a horizontal rule into the merged cell.

7. Merge the three remaining cells in the left column. Set the merged cell's horizontal alignment to center and vertical alignment to middle.

8. From the Common Insert bar, Images drop-down menu, insert an image placeholder named **photo**, with dimensions of **100** by **100**, into the merged cell.

9. In the middle column, type **Name:**, **Phone Number:**, and **Email Address:**. Select the three cells and apply bold.

10. In the right column, type **name**, **phone**, and **email** in the three cells.

11. Click in the right cell containing the word name, click the **<td>** tag in the Tag selector, and, from the Common Insert bar, set it as an editable region named **Name**. Repeat the same procedure for the two other cells on the right, naming the editable regions **Phone** and **Email**, respectively.

12. Click in the left cell with the image placeholder and click the **<td>** tag in the Tag selector. Set this cell to be an editable region named **Photo**.

13. Click the nested **<table>** tag to select the inner table. From the Common Insert bar, set this table to be a repeating region named **Staff Details**.

FIGURE 6.44

14. Close Staff Directory.dwt, saving your changes.

6. Fill a Template with Repeating Regions

In this Skill Drill exercise, you use the Staff Directory template and build a staff directory using repeating regions. The advantages of repeating regions become very clear when you develop a layout using them. You never have to think about the process of creating a nested table; you just click the Add button and a new region appears, identical in structure to the previous one. This is a real time saver.

1. Choose File>New, click the Templates tab if necessary, choose staff directory, and click Create.

2. Save the new file as `staff-directory.html`.

3. Double-click the image placeholder and replace the placeholder with alan.jpg from the thumbs folder. In the Name editable region, type `Alan`. In the Phone editable region, type `351-2267 ext. 122`. In the Email editable region, insert an email link using the Email button on the Common Insert bar and the address `alan@tropiflora.com` in both the Text and E-mail fields of the Email Link dialog box.

FIGURE 6.45

4. Add a new repeating region by clicking the plus symbol (+). Replace the image placeholder with alex.jpg from the thumbs folder. In the Name editable region, type `Alex`. In the Phone editable region, type `351-2267 ext. 134`. In the Email editable region, insert an email link using the Email button on the Common Insert bar and the address `alex@tropiflora.com` in both the Text and E-mail fields of the Email Link dialog box.

5. Repeat Step 4 with the following information:

Photo	*Name*	*Phone*	*Email*
david.jpg	`David`	`351-2267 ext. 133`	`david@tropiflora.com`
debbie.jpg	`Debbie`	`351-2267 ext. 214`	`debbie@tropiflora.com`
dennis-linda.jpg	`Dennis and Linda`	`351-2267 ext. 115`	`cathcarts@tropiflora.com`
gregoria.jpg	`Gregoria`	`351-2267 ext. 212`	`gregoria@tropiflora.com`
jeff.jpg	`Jeff`	`351-2267 ext. 144`	`jeff@tropiflora.com`
pilar.jpg	`Pilar`	`351-2267 ext. 114`	`pilar@tropiflora.com`
ray.jpg	`Ray`	`351-2267 ext. 224`	`ray@tropiflora.com`
veronica.jpg	`Veronica`	`351-2267 ext. 234`	`veronica@tropiflora.com`

6. Close staff-directory.html, saving your changes.

CHALLENGE

Challenge exercises expand on, or are somewhat related to, skills presented in the lessons. Each exercise provides a brief introduction, followed by instructions in a numbered-step format that are not as detailed as those in the Skill Drill exercises. Work through the exercises in order.

1. Create Library Items from a CSS Layout Page

In the preceding exercises, you learned that that you can create library items where the pages use tables for layout. However, the containers of the contents of tables-based layouts are the **<td>** table-data cells and they cannot be separated from the rest of the table structure. When you create a library item from a table cell, you create a library item of the contents of the table cell, not the table cell and its contents. When using CSS-based layouts where the **<div>** tags are the containers, the situation is different in that the **<div>** tag and its contents can be captured in the library item.

In this exercise, you create library items from a CSS-based layout. Because the layout uses **<div>** tags as containers and CSS to position the containers, Dreamweaver warns you each time you create a library item from a **<div>** that the styles will not be saved with the library item. This is fine because the styles are stored in an external style sheet. However, there is a problem that may not be clearly evident. If you create a library item of a **<div>** with the id of header and then edit the library item and change or remove the id, the styles do not apply to that **<div>** and its contents because the id, which is used as a selector, does not exist in the form that CSS needs. Be aware of the need to maintain ids and classes for CSS styling when you modify a library item.

1. Define a new site called **PHIL-P6** from the Project_06>PHIL-P6 folder.

2. Open faculty.html from the basic folder.

3. Open the Assets panel to the Library Items panel.

4. Click in Carter University at the top of the page, click **<div#header>** tag in the Tag selector, and drag the selected block to the Library Items Assets panel. Click OK to acknowledge the message about styles. In the Library Items Assets panel, name the new library item **Header**.

   It may seem odd to store the name of the college in a library item because it is unlikely that the name would change. However, you may need to change the contents of the header div, and to effect the change across the whole Web site, you must store the change in a library item.

5. Click in Philosophy Department, click the **<div#dept>** tag in the Tag selector, and drag the selected block to the Library Items Assets panel. Click OK to acknowledge the message about styles. In the Library Items Assets panel, name the new library item **Phil Dept**.

   Again, to accommodate the possibility that the department div might change in the future, you create a library item. This library item would only be used on pages for the Philosophy Department. The university's Web pages would need other library items for the other departments, as well.

6. Click in the left navigation bar and click the **<div#navbar>** tag in the Tag selector. Click the New Library Item button at the bottom of the Library Items Assets panel. Click OK to acknowledge the message about styles. In the Library Items Assets panel, name the new library item **Phil Navbar**.

   Each department can have its own navigation-bar links so the Philosophy Department navigation bar is saved as its own library item.

7. Scroll down if necessary, click in the footer, and click the **<div#footer>** tag in the Tag selector. Click the New Library Item button at the bottom of the Library Items Assets panel. Click OK to acknowledge the message about styles. In the Library Items Assets panel, name the new library item **Footer**.

   Like the Header library item, the Footer library item would be consistent across all of the university's Web pages and is saved as a library item to allow for the possibility of additional links.

8. Keep faculty.html open for the next exercise.

2. Create a Template with Nested Library Items

In this exercise, you prepare the template for the Faculty page. You use the library items you created and specify editable regions.

1. In the open file, faculty.html, choose Save as Template and save the template as **Faculty**. When prompted to update links, click Yes.

2. Select the text Faculty Group Name. From the Common Insert bar, choose Editable Region from the Templates drop-down menu, name the New Editable Region **Faculty Group Name**, and click OK.

3. Click in Professor Name and click the **<li#prof_name>** tag in the Tag selector. Choose Editable Region from the Templates drop-down menu, name the New Editable Region **Faculty Details**, and click OK.

4. Save the changes to Faculty.dwt but leave it open.

3. Create the Remaining Templates for the Web Site

In this exercise, you create the Courses and Schedule templates, using Faculty as the base.

1. In the open file, Faculty.dwt, choose File>Save as Template. Read and then click OK to acknowledge the warning. Name the new template **Courses**. At the end of the document Title field, change Faculty to **Courses**.

2. Without closing Courses.dwt, open courses.html from the basic folder, select all of the content, copy it to the clipboard, and close courses.html.

3. Click in the content div of Courses.dwt, click the **<div#content>** tag in the Tag selector, and paste the copied content.

4. Select the text Year. From the Common Insert bar, choose Editable Region from the Templates drop-down menu, name the New Editable Region **Year Group Name**, and click OK.

5. Click in the text PHIL XXX and click the **<li#phxxx>** tag in the Tag selector. From the Common Insert bar, choose Editable Region from the Templates drop-down menu, name the New Editable Region **Course Details**, and click OK.

6. Save the changes to Courses.dwt but leave it open.

7. Choose File>Save as Template. Read and then click OK to acknowledge the warning. Name the new template **Schedule**. At the end of the document Title, change Faculty to **Schedule**.

8. Without closing Schedule.dwt, open schedule.html from the basic folder, select all of the content, copy it to the clipboard, and close schedule.html.

9. Click in the content div of Schedule.dwt, click **<div#content>** tag in the Tag selector, and paste the copied content.

10. Select the text Term. From the Common Insert bar, choose Editable Region from the Templates drop-down menu, name the New Editable Region **Term Group Name**, and click OK.

11. Select PHILxxx in the second row and set it as an Editable Region called **Course**. Select Mon/Wed and set it as an Editable Region called **Days**. Select 0900-1030 and set it as an Editable Region called **Time**. Select PH120 and set it as an Editable Region called **Room**. Select Prof and set it as an Editable Region called **Professor**.

12. Close Schedule.dwt, saving your changes.

4. Create Nested Repeating Regions

Each of the pages created so far in the Challenge exercise may be set up with repeating regions — there is more than one professor, more than one course description, and more than one course listed in the schedule.. However, professors are grouped according to whether they are full or assistant professors, courses are grouped according to their year, and schedules are grouped into different terms. This provides the opportunity for you to learn how to create nested repeating regions.

1. Open Schedule.dwt from either the Template Assets panel or the Templates folder in the Files panel.

2. Click in any cell of the second row of the table and then click the **<tr>** tag in the Tag selector.

3. From the Common Insert bar, choose Repeating Region from the Templates drop-down menu and name the repeating region **Course Region**.

4. Click in the text Term, and then click the **<h2>** tag in the Tag selector. Shift-click to the bottom right of the table to select from the **<h2>** tag to the end of the table.

5. From the Common Insert bar, choose Repeating Region from the Templates drop-down menu and name the repeating region **Term Region**.

6. Close Schedule.dwt, saving your changes.

5. Create Nested Repeating Regions in the Template Pages

In this exercise, you create nested repeating regions in the Courses and Faculty pages. To prepare repeating regions, especially nested repeating regions, takes a bit of practice. The Schedule.dwt template page is slightly easier than the Courses and Faculty template pages, but with careful attention to the instructions, you can set up these nested repeating regions.

1. Open Courses.dwt from the Templates folder or the Templates Assets panel.

2. Click in the text PHIL XXX, and then click the **<ul>** tag in the Tag selector.

3. From the Common Insert bar, choose Repeating Region from the Templates drop-down menu and name the repeating region **Course Region**.

4. Click in the text Year, and then click the **<h2>** tag in the Tag selector. Shift-click to the bottom right of Course Syllabus.

5. From the Common Insert bar, choose Repeating Region from the Templates drop-down menu and name the repeating region **Year Region**.

6. Close Courses.dwt, saving your changes.

7. Open Faculty.dwt from the Templates folder or the Templates Assets panel.

8. Click in the text Professor Name, and then click the **<ul>** tag in the Tag selector.

9. From the Common Insert bar, choose Repeating Region from the Templates drop-down menu and name the repeating region **Faculty Region**.

10. Click in the text Faculty Group Name, and then click the **<h2>** tag in the Tag selector. Shift-click to the bottom right of Course Title.

11. From the Common Insert bar, choose Repeating Region from the Templates drop-down menu and name the repeating region **Faculty Group Region**.

12. Close Faculty.dwt, saving changes.

6. Create and Test Child Pages

In this exercise, you create child pages from the templates and test the nested repeating regions. You learn that each repeating region has its own controls to add, remove, and sort the regions. You can add Fall, Winter, and Spring terms to the Schedule page and, within each term, can display multiple courses in the schedule tables. Nested repeating regions could also be created for the Courses and Faculty pages.

1. Create a new page from the schedule template in the PHIL-P6 site.

2. Click the plus symbol to the right of the Repeat: Course Region label.

3. Click the plus symbol to the right of the Repeat: Term Region label. In the second Term Region, click the plus symbol to the right of the Repeat: Course Region label.

4. Close without saving the changes.

5. Create a new page from the courses template in the PHIL-P6 site. Use the plus symbols to add new Course and Year regions. When finished, close without saving the changes.

6. Create a new page from the faculty template in the PHIL-P6 site. Use the plus symbols to add new Faculty Group and Faculty regions. When finished, close without saving the changes.

PORTFOLIO BUILDER

Assess the Need for Templates and Library Items

You have learned that templates and library items are very beneficial to the development, maintenance, and consistent appearance of a Web site. Some Web sites, such as the Canadian federal governments' Web sites, have a "common look and feel (CLF)" policy. Templates and library items could help realize similar policies. In this assignment, you build a Dreamweaver template for a Web site using a free page from freesitetemplates.com.

1.   Go to freesitetemplates.com. On the left, under the Free Templates heading, are categories of templates. Browse through these templates and find one that appeals to you.

2.   Register and confirm the registration when the email arrives.

3.   Download the file and save it in a new folder called **PB**, under the Project_06 folder.

4.   Create a new site for the **PB** folder called **PB6**.

5.   Open the downloaded page and create library items from selected components of the page.

6.   Create a template from the page and set an editable area.

PROJECT **7**

Managing Your Live Web Site

OBJECTIVES

In this project, you learn how to

- Validate HTML

- Check the accessibility of your pages

- Test for broken links and orphaned files

- Improve your site's search-engine rating

- Prevent certain file types from being uploaded

- Register with a free Web-hosting service

- Upload your Web site to the Web server

WHY WOULD I DO THIS?

You have completed your Web site in Dreamweaver. It has compelling content, an appealing design, and tasteful use of JavaScript. However, the only way that others can experience your efforts is to gather around your computer. This project focuses on preparing and *uploading* (transferring files from your computer to the Internet or a Web server) your Web site to a Web server so that others can view your creation from the comfort of their own computers.

In this project, you learn to prepare your site so search engines can find it, to validate the HTML, and to test for accessibility. You check for broken links, orphaned files, and target-browser problems. You create new folders, reorganize pages, and rename some pages to fit with the new folder structure.

You also learn about different hosting packages and services so that you can find a Web-hosting service that meets your needs and budget. You sign up with a free Web-hosting service and insert its settings into the site definition so that you can upload your site to the Web server.

These are skills you must know to be able to prepare and transfer your Web-site designs to your Web server or your client's Web server. In some cases, Web hosting is set up for you so you don't need to search for a service; in other cases, you may be involved in choosing the domain name and hosting service, and in making other initial decisions about the site. Many of the lessons you learn in this project are those that should be part of your last-minute checklist before *publishing* (uploading) the Web site.

V I S U A L   S U M M A R Y

In this project, you learn to prepare a Web site for uploading to a Web server. Before you upload sites to the Web server, you run a series of checks on the site. These checks ensure that the HTML is valid, there are no broken links or orphaned files, and the site is accessible. You use the Results panel to perform all of these checks. After you run the check, if Dreamweaver detects a problem, you can double-click its entry in the Results panel to open the page with the problem and correct it.

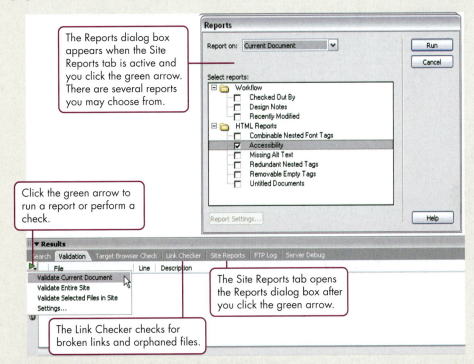

The Reports dialog box appears when the Site Reports tab is active and you click the green arrow. There are several reports you may choose from.

Click the green arrow to run a report or perform a check.

The Site Reports tab opens the Reports dialog box after you click the green arrow.

The Link Checker checks for broken links and orphaned files.

FIGURE 7.1

After checking for errors or problems with the site, you increase the rating of the Web site by, if necessary, improving the content in the document title and creating a description of and keywords for the site.

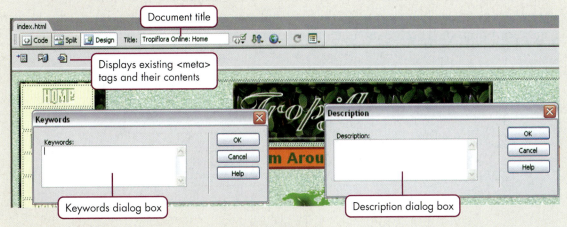

Document title

Displays existing <meta> tags and their contents

Keywords dialog box

Description dialog box

FIGURE 7.2

Once you have performed the checks and added keywords and a description, your Web site is ready to upload to a Web server. You obtain an account with a Web-hosting service — for this book, you create an account with a free Web-hosting service — and receive its FTP information with which you log in to your space on the hosting service and upload files. In order to perform the upload from Dreamweaver, you must register the FTP information in the Site Definition dialog box.

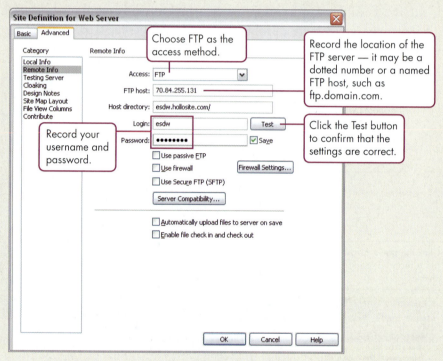

FIGURE 7.3

You FTP the files to the Web server from the Files panel. To upload a site to the Web server, you can either use the Put button at the top of the Files panel or Right/Control-click the site name in the Files panel and choose Put. When you finish, you should disconnect from the Web server, especially if you are on a dial-up connection to the Internet. By default, the view in the Files panel is the Local view, but you can switch it to the Remote view to look at the files on the Web server. You may need to click the Refresh button to refresh the listing of remote files. The Expand/Collapse button expands the display of the Files panel, enabling you to see the local and remote files at the same time, and to copy files (drag and drop) from the Local to the Remote window.

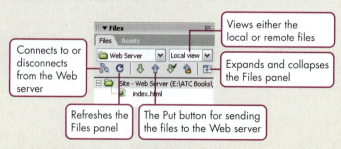

FIGURE 7.4

LESSON 1   Validating HTML

In this lesson, you learn to use the HTML validator that is a built-in function of Dreamweaver. There are several types of errors that a validator can flag. Obvious errors include nonexistent tags, such as the <bold> tag, or mistyped tags, such as <stron> instead of **<strong>**, but if you build your Web site using Dreamweaver and don't play with the code too much, you're unlikely to have these types of errors. Another possible type of error is a missing but required attribute, such as the **alt** attribute of the **<img>** tag. This is an easier type of error to make, especially if you, like many, think that the **alt** attribute is merely an option, not a requirement. If you have not studied the HTML standards, you may not be familiar with the required attributes of tags, so the built-in validator can be a very useful tool. Another error is using a tag that does not exist in the selected version of HTML, such as using the **<style>** tag in HTML 2.0 when it was not part of the HTML 2.0 specification.

The HTML validator is part of the Results panel, which you open by choosing Window>Results. The Results panel has numerous tabs for different types of functions, such as Search, Validation, and Target Browser Check. To run the validation, you choose the Validation tab and click the green arrow — the results of the check appear in the Results window. Double-clicking any of the results selects the erroneous code in the Code window. You can then correct the code in the Code window or switch to the Design view to correct the error in a more familiar environment.

Validate the HTML

In this exercise, you validate the HTML on one page. When you build the pages of a site from the same code base (template), as you have done throughout this book (and *Essentials for Design: Dreamweaver MX 2004 Level I*), an error in one page is likely to occur in the others. In this case, you discover that the error in this page occurs in a library item, so by fixing the library item, you repair all pages that use it.

1. Define the Project_07>TO-P7 folder as a site called **TO-P7**. Do not click Done, but remove all previously defined sites from the Manage Sites dialog box, and then click Done.

2. Open **about.html** and choose **Window>Results.**

3. Click the Validation tab, click the green arrow to the left, and choose Validate Current Document.

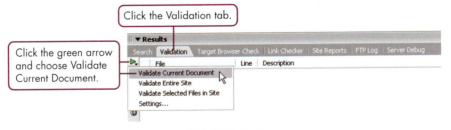

FIGURE 7.5

? **If you have problems**

There is an undocumented feature of Dreamweaver that prevents validation from proceeding. If validation generates no results, work through the following procedures. Click the green arrow and choose Settings. Choose XHTML 1.0 Strict and click OK. Click the green arrow again, choose Validate Entire Site: results appear for the entire site. Click the green arrow again and select Validate Current Document: results appear for just the current document.

4   **Double-click the first result.**

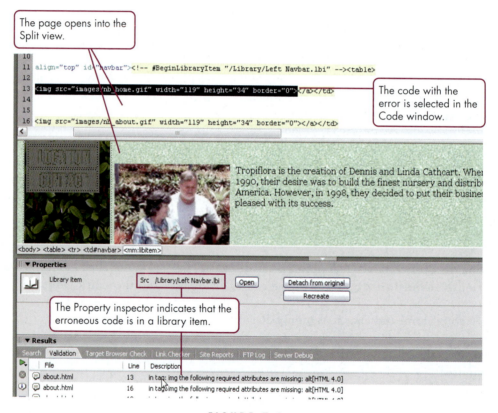

FIGURE 7.6

5 Click the More Info button to the left and read the additional information about the error.

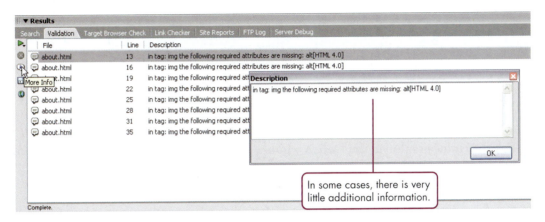

In some cases, there is very little additional information.

FIGURE 7.7

6 Click OK to close the Description window.

7 Double-click the rest of the errors identified by the validation check.

The first seven errors exist in the left navigation-bar library item, the eighth in the Tropiflora-Online-logo library item, and the ninth in the photo of the Cathcarts.

8 Keep about.html open for the next exercise.

Correct the Validation Errors

In this exercise, you correct the validation errors found by checking this page. Seven of the errors exist in one library item and one other in another library item. Both are easy to correct and your fixes cascade to the other pages that use the library items when you update the changes to the library item. The last error exists only on this page.

1 If the ninth error is selected in the Results window, double-click it; if it is not selected, type `Photo of Dennis and Linda Cathcart with Bucky their dog` in the Alt field of the Property inspector.

FIGURE 7.8

2 Double-click the first error in the Results window and click the Open button in the Property inspector.

FIGURE 7.9

3 Click the Home graphic in the Design window and type Home in the Alt field of the Property inspector.

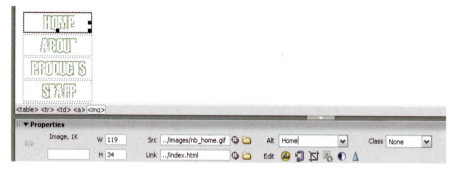

FIGURE 7.10

4 Repeat Step 3 as follows:

Click graphic	Add alt text
About	About Tropiflora
Products	Products
Staff	Staff
Location	Location
Contact	Contact

5 Close Left Navbar.lbi, saving your changes.

6 Click Update and, when finished, click Close.

7 Click the green arrow in the Results panel to run the validation check again.

FIGURE 7.11

8   Double-click the remaining error in the Results window, and open the Tropiflora Logo.lbi library item from the Property inspector.

9   Click the Tropiflora Online graphic and assign it the alt text `Tropiflora Online`.

10   Close the Tropiflora Logo.lbi. library item, saving your changes.

11   Click Update and then click Close.

12   Save the changes to about.html, but leave it open for the next exercise.

To Extend Your Knowledge

ONLINE HTML VALIDATORS

There are two highly recommended online HTML validators: the W3C's validator at validator.w3.org and the Web Design Group's validator at htmlhelp.com/tools/validator. The Web Design Groups validator is good for HTML 4.01 or lower, but has not kept up-to-date with XHTML 1.0 or 1.1. In both validators, you can either validate a page that is already on the Web or upload a page or the code of a page to the validator. If your pages are not yet on a Web server or you are working behind a firewall, you must upload your pages. You can also validate your CSS code at jigsaw.w3.org/css-validator.

LESSON 2   Checking Accessibility

When Sir Tim Berners-Lee created HTML as a means of communication, he intended the World Wide Web to be accessible to everyone. Unfortunately, for a variety of reasons including the evolution of HTML, laziness of Web designers/developers, improper HTML support in Web-design software, and more, many Web sites are not accessible to everyone. Sir Tim Berners-Lee formed the *W3C* (World Wide Web Consortium) to shape the future of HTML and, later, other Web technologies, such as XML and PNG. A committee of the W3C has created *WCAG 1.0*, which is version 1.0 of the Web Content Accessibility Guidelines. The WCAG has divided the guidelines into three levels — Priority 1 (the lowest level), Priority 2, and Priority 3 (also known as "Levels A, AA, and AAA"). The higher the priority or level, the more accessible the Web page. In the US, the *ADA* (Americans with Disabilities Act) has a similar guideline, Section 508. It is similar to WCAG Priority 1, but has a few differences, such as including some items from Priority 2. Other countries have adopted accessibility guidelines for their government Web sites and, in the case of the UK and Australia, for all commercial Web sites as well. Most governments simply adopt the WCAG 1.0 at Priority 1 or 2.

Testing for accessibility is a difficult challenge that most automated checkers cannot completely fulfill. For example, alt text allows people who use screen readers to understand the content of a graphic, such as the navigation-bar graphic buttons in this project's Tropiflora Online Web site. An automated checker can check to see if the alt attribute exists for all images, but it cannot check whether or not Home is the appropriate alt text for the contact.gif graphic. All checkpoints of the WCAG 1.0 require manual evaluation in addition to the automated checks.

UsableNet.com created the accessibility checker which was then added to Dreamweaver. You can purchase an enhanced version of UsableNet.com's LIFT product for additional features. The built-in product does identify both manual and automated checks, allowing you to verify, for example, that the alt text is appropriate for the graphic. The accessibility checker is also part of the Results panel.

Test for Accessibility at Priority 1

In this exercise, you run the accessibility checker against one page. You learn that the accessibility checker identifies manual checkpoints. You also learn more about a checkpoint by using the More Info button to open the Reference panel.

1   **In the open file, about.html, click the Site Reports tab of the Results panel.**

FIGURE 7.12

2   **Click the green arrow to the left.**

3   **Check Accessibility in the HTML Reports folder and click Run.**

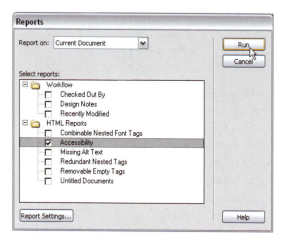

FIGURE 7.13

4   **Scroll through the results and note that all of them are manual checks.**

Each of these items requires that you evaluate the checkpoint and determine whether or not it has been met. All of the automated checks have been passed, so if all of the manual checks pass, then the page meets WCAG Priority 1.

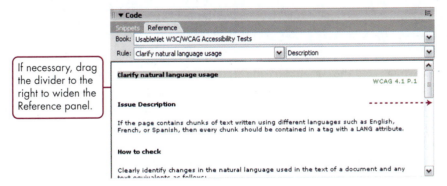

> WCAG 1.1 refers to checkpoint 1.1 and P.1 refers to Priority 1. You may research both at w3.org/TR/WCAG10/full-checklist.html.

FIGURE 7.14

5   **Scroll down to the last item in the list, click it, and then click the More Info button.**

FIGURE 7.15

6   **Read the reference information for this checkpoint.**

In plain English, this checkpoint means that you must identify the language of the HTML page using the **lang** attribute. Also, if parts of the page are in different languages than what is specified in the **<html>** tag, you must add the **lang** attribute to the tag that surrounds the content of a different language or add a **<span>** tag with the **lang** attribute such as **<span lang="fr">Bonjour</span>**.

> If necessary, drag the divider to the right to widen the Reference panel.

FIGURE 7.16

7   **In the Code window, scroll to the top of the HTML document.**

8   **Click to the left of the closing angle bracket > at the end of the `<html>` tag. Press the Spacebar, type `1`, and press Enter/Return to accept the `lang` attribute. Type en between the quotation marks.**

You can find language codes at oasis-open.org/cover/iso639a.html. You can also use country subcodes, such as en-us (American English) or fr-ca (French Canadian).

```
1 <!DOCTYPE HTML PUBLIC "-//W3C//DTD HTML 4.01 Transitional//EN">
2 <html lang="en">
3 <head>
4 <title>Tropiflora Online: About Tropiflora</title>
```

FIGURE 7.17

9   **Choose Window>Reference to close the Reference panel.**

10   **Close about.html, saving your changes.**

The rest of the items met the standard of WCAG Priority 1 but, because the accessibility checker could not determine whether or not the criteria passed or failed the guideline, it displays them all.

To Extend Your Knowledge

KNOWLEDGE IS BETTER THAN CHECKERS

If you must build pages that are accessible, you should be cautious of depending on automated checkers because many checks must be performed manually. Many accessibility checkers seem to suggest that your page meets the standard, but manual checking may reveal that it doesn't meet the standard. You should research accessibility, why it matters, and how the guidelines benefit those who need accessibility. As you become more knowledgeable about accessibility, you significantly reduce your dependence on automated checkers because you incorporate accessibility into your pages as you build them.

LESSON 3   Checking for Broken Links and Orphaned Files

It looks bad for a Web site and the designer if links lead to either the wrong page or no page at all. You should always test your links before you upload your Web page to a public site. In the Results panel is a Link Checker that helps with some of these issues. However, the Link Checker cannot help you with a link to the wrong page, such as a supposed link to the Products page that actually takes you to the Contact Us page. It is possible to do this in Dreamweaver if you use the browse-for-file or point-to-file methods and click the wrong page. You should always verify the link in the Link field as soon as you create it so you catch any mistake like this immediately. You should also test links frequently in your browser.

There are two checks that Dreamweaver's Link Checker can test for: orphaned files and bad links. *Orphaned files* are files that exist in the site definition's folders to which no links have been created. Orphaned files also include graphic files that are not used in any pages of the site: these can be deleted or moved to another folder outside of the site folder. ***Bad links*** are links to pages that don't exist on the current site. Dreamweaver also provides a report on external links but it cannot test them. External links includes email addresses (mailto: links) that Dreamweaver also cannot test. However, you can still review them to see if they should work and test links to external pages by previewing the page in your browser and clicking the links.

Check for Broken Links

In this exercise, you test for broken links. You can test for broken links in a current open page or you can test all pages at once. In order to test for orphaned files, you must first run the site-wide check for broken links.

1   **In the Results panel, click the Link Checker tab.**

2   **Click the green arrow and choose Check Links for Entire Site.**

FIGURE 7.18

3   **In the Report window, double-click products.html.**

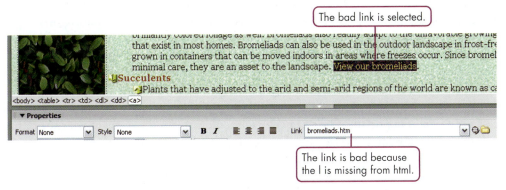

FIGURE 7.19

4   **In the Link field, type the letter 1 (lowercase L) at the end of the filename.**

5   **Run the site-wide link check again.**

6   **From the list, choose Orphaned Files.**

Book.doc is identified as an orphaned file; it is not a required page or document for the Web site.

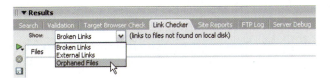

FIGURE 7.20

| 7 | Scroll up to the top of the products page below the Products heading. |

| 8 | Click to the right of Tillandsias, press Enter/Return, and type Books. Select Books and link it to books.html. |

| 9 | Run the site-wide broken link check again and check for orphaned files. |

| 10 | Close products.html, saving your changes. |

LESSON 4 Preparing Your Site for Search Engines

SEO (Search Engine Optimization) is as much an art as it is a science. In the past, you could just stuff words into the `<meta>` tags and your site would appear near the top of a search engine's results page. These days, many of the old *search-engine spamming* (spamdexing — adding keywords to comment tags and alt attributes to falsely increase their use on the Web site) techniques virtually guarantee your site's exclusion from some search engines.

The general rule for promoting your site to search engines is to use reasonable techniques. These include appropriate page titles, keyword and description `<meta>` tags, and headings. The content-to-code ratio is also said to affect search-engine ranking. The more code in a Web page, the more difficult it is for a search engine to get at the content and rank it. By reducing or eliminating the use of tables for layout in your page, you increase the content-to-code ratio and the chances of people finding your Web site through search engines.

As you know, the contents of the `<title>` tag do not appear in the Web page but in the Title bar of the browser, as the name of the page in the Favorites folder, and as the name of the link in a search engine's results page. For the visitor to your site or the search engine, using the `<title>` tag is important for these reasons alone. However, search engines also rank the content of the `<title>` tag quite highly, so crafting quality content in the `<title>` tag is important. The `<title>` tag should contain the name of your site or business plus a brief description of the products, services, or purpose of the site. Limit the `<title>` tag to 10-15 words.

Also pertinent to this discussion is the `<meta>` tag. This is an unusual tag that appears in the `<head>` of an HTML document. It is an empty tag — it does not have a </meta> closing form. The content of the tag appears within attributes of the tag. There are many forms of information that can be contained in the `<meta>` tag, and they are identified by the **name** and **content** attributes. The **name** attribute identifies what type of information is being described, such as keywords, description, or generator (commonly used by Web-design applications to promote themselves in search engines). The **content** attribute contains the actual content, such as the list of keywords, the description, or the name of the Web-design application.

A `<meta>` tag for keywords to promote a computer store could be `<meta name="keywords" content="computer sales retail hardware software monitors cpus hard drives keyboards mice printers">`. You can separate the keywords with commas, but sometimes, when pairs of words are used together, such as hard drive, you may prefer to avoid commas. You should group words in pairs that make sense: important words or phrases next to each other increase *hits* (the number of visitors) because of their proximity to each other in the keywords list. For example, `hard computer drive` would receive fewer hits than `computer hard drive`.

The description **<meta>** tag should describe the purpose of the site or business in a maximum of 25-30 words. The description of your site should include some of the description you have in the **<title>** tag as well as some of the keywords, all of which support each other and together promote your site in search engines.

Improve the Document Title

The most important page on your Web site is the home page, which is commonly used as the gateway to your Web site. For that reason, pay special attention to the **<title>** and **<meta>** tags of this page. In this exercise, you modify the document title to make it more search-engine friendly.

1   **Open index.html from the TO-P7 site.**

2   **In the document Title field, delete Home, replace it with** `Retailer of exotic plants from around the world`, **and press Enter/Return.**

FIGURE 7.21

3   **To insert the description <meta> tag, choose Insert>HTML>Head Tags>Description, and type** `Tropiflora Online is a retailer of tropical and exotic plants from around the world along with growing supplies, books, and expert advice`. **Click OK when finished.**

FIGURE 7.22

4   **To insert the keywords <meta> tag, choose Insert>HTML>Head Tags>Keywords, and type** `exotic tropical plants retail succulents orchids tillandsias bromeliads books growing supplies`. **Click OK when finished.**

FIGURE 7.23

5   **To view the current <meta> tags, choose View>Head Content.**

6 One by one, click the icons below the Document toolbar and examine their contents in the Property inspector.

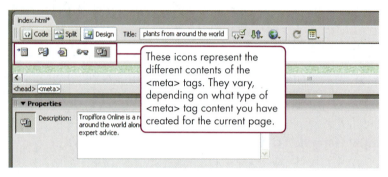

FIGURE 7.24

7 Choose View>Head Content to hide the Head Content icons.

8 Close index.html, saving your changes.

To Extend Your Knowledge

IN-BOUND LINKS HELP RATINGS

When Google.com started in the late 1990s, it used what was then a revolutionary method of ranking pages: the more pages that linked to your site, the more highly your site was ranked. This method was based on the assumption that Web-site designers created links to your site because of its value and its value was displayed by its ranking in search-engine results pages. However, many people now try to promote their sites by joining link exchanges, in which a group of people link to each other's sites to increase the value of their sites. Although this may not be considered spamming, per se, it is a somewhat false method of increasing the ranking of your site. Google.com has since revised its ranking methods, but although in-bound links are not as important as they once were, they still help your ranking on the Google.com search engine. Other search engines, especially older ones, did not use in-bound links as a ranking method but, like Google.com, continually adjust their ranking methodologies and may now include in-bound links.

LESSON 5 Cloaking Resource Files

Cloaking is a Dreamweaver function that allows you to identify files that should not be uploaded to the Web site. For example, you may have Microsoft Word files in the site folder that were sent to you with content for the Web site. You probably would not want these files uploaded to the Web site. Dreamweaver assumes that, for the most part, all files in a site folder are to be uploaded to the Web-hosting service, which is not always the case.

One method of cloaking is to cloak on the basis of file type. This means that no matter what folder a file of that type may be in, it is not uploaded to the Web server. To cloak a file type, you edit the site definition, navigate to the Cloaking category, and add the filename extensions to the list. When files are cloaked, their file icons have a red slash through them.

Cloak the Word .doc Files

In this exercise, you cloak the Microsoft Word .doc files. To do so, you edit the site definition and add the .doc filename extension to the list of cloaked file types. After completing the process, Dreamweaver rebuilds the site cache and any .doc files in the site folder appear with a red slash through the file icon.

1   **In the Files panel, choose Manage Site from the drop-down menu.**

2   **With TO-P7 chosen in the Manage Sites dialog box, click the Edit button.**

3   **Choose the Cloaking category and enable the Cloak Files Ending With option.**

4   **Add .doc (include a space after .fla) to the list.**

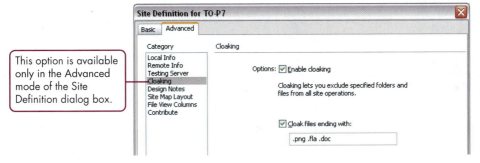

FIGURE 7.25

5   **Click OK and then click Done.**

6   **Observe the Files panel.**

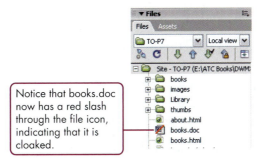

FIGURE 7.26

To Extend Your Knowledge

CLOAKING FOLDERS

When you set cloaking only by file type, you may have problems with PNG files because Fireworks uses PNG files as its working format. If you use Fireworks to create graphics and you save both the original Fireworks graphic and the finished PNG (for use in the Web pages) in the site folder, you may end up uploading both or neither, depending on the cloaking setting, even if the working PNG files and final PNG files are in different folders. For these and other reasons, you may want to create a folder structure in the site folder where you can store the original documents in one folder away from the Web-page files. You then cloak that folder in Dreamweaver and any documents in the folder do not upload. Cloaking by folder is not an option from the Site Definition dialog box, but is available from the contextual menu of the Files panel.

LESSON 6   Registering for a Free Hosting Service

Web-hosting services are so popular these days that it would be impossible to research them all to determine which is best for your needs. Armed with knowledge of what features you need, you can either search on your own or participate in discussion forums to get help, advice, or recommendations. People who are happy with a service are generally also happy to recommend that service, even if they do not receive a commission for their recommendation.

There are many considerations for choosing a hosting service. The first consideration is location of that hosting service. At times, this can be difficult to ascertain because, just as you can work in San Francisco and develop a site for a client in England, a business providing hosting can operate in Italy while its servers are in located in Florida. Generally, if your Web site is for an audience in a particular location, such as North America, you should find a hosting service with servers in North America. There is a definite lag time if the servers are overseas. However, large businesses with interests in multiple continents should purchase a hosting package where the servers are in different continents and mirror each other's content.

Additional basic issues are disk space and bandwidth. Although you can buy services with 1000 MB or more of space for relatively low cost, the average Web site rarely uses that much space. Space is so cheap these days, however, that you can't expect to find a hosting service offering only 10MB of space for 1/100th of the cost of its 1000MB service. Other considerations include email service that allows you to use your domain name as part of your email address, and support for programming languages and databases.

There are different categories of hosting services based on ownership and access to the equipment. ***Shared*** or ***virtual servers*** are the cheapest to rent because you and perhaps 100 other Web sites can exist on the same server. The benefit is that it is cheapest and perfectly suitable for most needs, but if another site on the same server is experiencing a surge in traffic, your site and others on the same server can slow down. ***Dedicated servers*** are rented from the hosting company, but only your site exists on the server. You have the freedom to manage the server yourself, but the hosting service looks after maintenance. ***Co-location servers*** are servers that you own but you rent space within a data center so you can connect it to the Internet. This is the most costly option because you are on your own in terms of maintenance or must be prepared to pay a hefty fee to the data center to do it for you. The final hosting category is ***reseller hosting***, where an individual can rent a large amount of space on a server and then sell off the space in smaller parcels. Generally, resellers just take a commission for being advocates of the hosting service and cannot perform any maintenance or support themselves. It is not uncommon to find some Web-design businesses also selling hosting services; in many cases, they are simply resellers.

One final option for those who have the skills and knowledge is to host their site on their own computer at home, such as dean.edwards.name (apparently, the computer is in his kitchen). This option presents many issues that you must deal with, like those of co-located servers, and you must be prepared to purchase a computer dedicated to hosting. Don't use your working computer, or imperfectly set security could leave your working files open for ***hackers*** (people who, for fun, profit, or maliciousness, attempt to bypass security and gain access to a computer) to access, read, alter, or even delete. They may even hijack your computer for malicious purposes, such as sending out spam. Furthermore, many ***ISPs*** (Internet Service Providers) do not allow servers to be connected to ISP accounts. Check with your ISP if you have the knowledge, skills, and interest to consider this option.

For this book, you register with a free hosting service. Even free services offer a wide variety of options, although, generally, the space and bandwidth are limited as are the features. Most free services make some money back through banner advertising that is forced on your site, whether or not you want it. Most also offer limited services, such as no databases or Web programming languages, although some provide access to some preapproved and prewritten scripts that you can use on your site, such as a hit counter or form mail script. One other consideration for free Web hosting is that some do not support ***FTP*** (File Transfer Protocol) — you must use a Web form to upload your pages to their servers. We have found that 100webspace.com offers a very liberal amount of services, considering that the service is free. In addition to 100MB of space, 100webspace.com also offers free support, no advertising, FTP, ***PHP*** (a Web programming language), and ***MySQL*** (a Web database). The last two features are beneficial for the next project in this book, in which you learn a bit about PHP and MySQL. It is likely that 100webspace.com is attempting to attract users to its free service and then convert them, virtually at the click of a button, to their paid service.

Register with 100webspace.com

In this exercise, you register an account with 100webspace.com. When you receive your email confirmation, you use the account information to log in to your account, browse the control panel, and explore the options. You record the connection information so that you can FTP your pages to your account from Dreamweaver.

1   **Open your browser and navigate to 100webspace.com.**

2   **Under the details of the Free Package, click the Sign Up Now button.**

3   **Complete the registration form. You must provide a valid email address so that you can receive the password and other connection details. Choose Free Hosting and Use a Subdomain. Click the Place the Order button.**

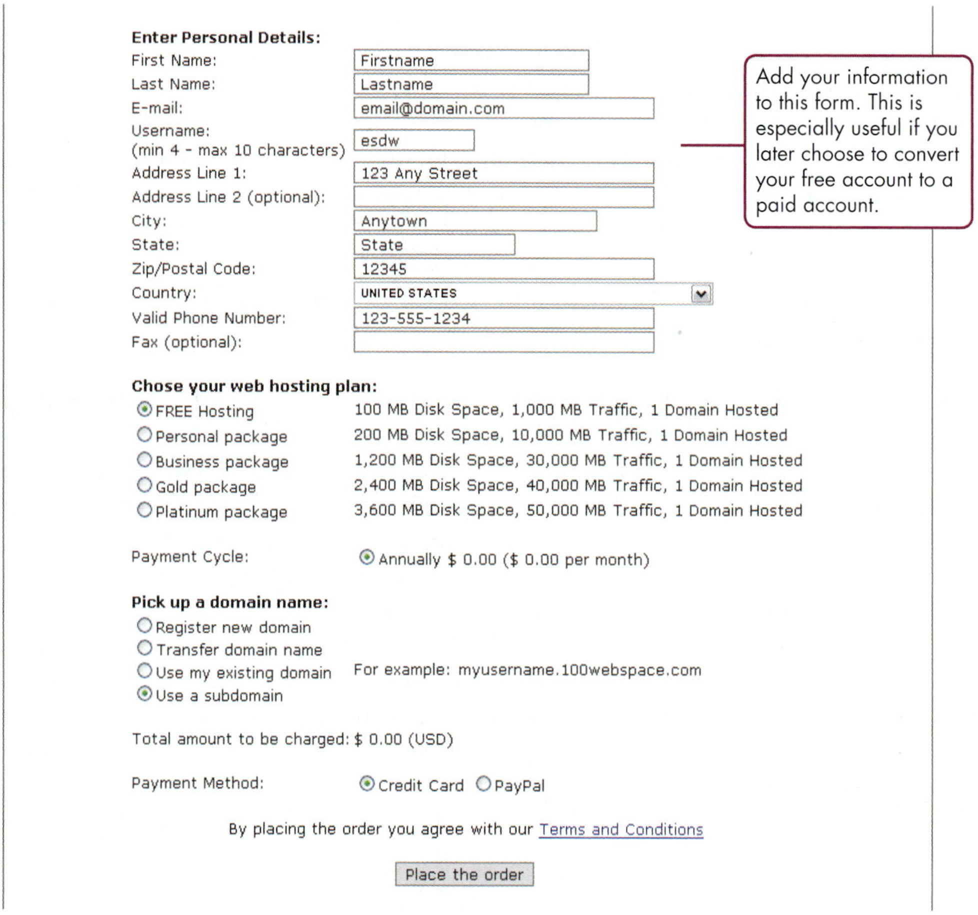

Enter Personal Details:

First Name:	Firstname
Last Name:	Lastname
E-mail:	email@domain.com
Username: (min 4 - max 10 characters)	esdw
Address Line 1:	123 Any Street
Address Line 2 (optional):	
City:	Anytown
State:	State
Zip/Postal Code:	12345
Country:	UNITED STATES
Valid Phone Number:	123-555-1234
Fax (optional):	

Add your information to this form. This is especially useful if you later choose to convert your free account to a paid account.

Chose your web hosting plan:

- ⦿ FREE Hosting — 100 MB Disk Space, 1,000 MB Traffic, 1 Domain Hosted
- ○ Personal package — 200 MB Disk Space, 10,000 MB Traffic, 1 Domain Hosted
- ○ Business package — 1,200 MB Disk Space, 30,000 MB Traffic, 1 Domain Hosted
- ○ Gold package — 2,400 MB Disk Space, 40,000 MB Traffic, 1 Domain Hosted
- ○ Platinum package — 3,600 MB Disk Space, 50,000 MB Traffic, 1 Domain Hosted

Payment Cycle: ⦿ Annually $ 0.00 ($ 0.00 per month)

Pick up a domain name:
- ○ Register new domain
- ○ Transfer domain name
- ○ Use my existing domain   For example: myusername.100webspace.com
- ⦿ Use a subdomain

Total amount to be charged: $ 0.00 (USD)

Payment Method: ⦿ Credit Card   ○ PayPal

By placing the order you agree with our Terms and Conditions

Place the order

FIGURE 7.27

4   **After you successfully register, a login screen appears.**

5 **When you receive the email notification from 100webspace.com, make note of your username and password. (File this email where you can retrieve it later.)**

Depending on the capabilities of your email software, you may not see all of the graphics and colors. The important text information should be easy to find.

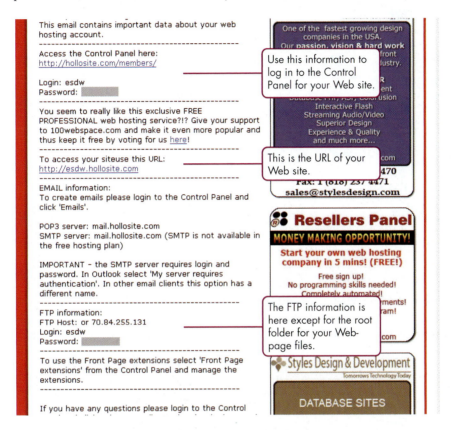

FIGURE 7.28

6 **Type your username and password in the login screen and click Login.**

You may notice that the URL for your login is not 100webspace.com but hollosite.com, freeunixhost.com, or perhaps another domain name. 100webspace.com manages its accounts under these domain names. You must use the information sent to you, not any other information you may see here or from others.

FIGURE 7.29

7 Explore the Control Panel software, which you use to manage your Web site.

FIGURE 7.30

8 From within the Site Manager group, click the File Manager link.

9 Click the www folder link.

Name	Type	Size	Perms	Last modified	Last changed	Last access
⊞Uplevel						
☐ 📁 logs	folder	4096	755	10.10.2004 02:15:46	10.10.2004 02:15:46	10.02.2003 17:26:07
☐ 📁 mail	folder	4096	755	10.10.2004 02:15:46	10.10.2004 02:15:46	09.27.2003 18:37:05
☐ 📁 sys	folder	4096	755	10.10.2004 02:15:46	10.10.2004 02:15:46	09.27.2003 18:38:00
☐ 📁 tmp	folder	4096	755	10.10.2004 02:15:46	10.10.2004 02:15:46	09.27.2003 18:37:05
☐ 📁 www	folder	4096	755	10.10.2004 04:00:46	10.10.2004 04:01:00	10.10.2004 04:01:00

Click the www folder link.

FIGURE 7.31

10 Make note of the name of your site's root folder.

Name	Type	Size	Perms	Last modified	Last changed	Last access
⊞Uplevel						
☐ 📁 esdw.hollosite.com	folder	4096	755	10.10.2004 04:01:41	10.10.2004 04:01:41	10.10.2004 04:01:41

This folder, named differently for each account, is the root folder or host directory for your Web site.

FIGURE 7.32

11 Log out by clicking the logout link at the top right of the control panel.

Record the FTP Information in the Site Settings

In this exercise, you modify the site-definition settings with the settings from your new Web-hosting account. With the settings in place, you can then upload the Web site to your new hosting account.

1   In the Files panel, choose Manage Sites from the drop-down menu.

FIGURE 7.33

2   Choose TO-P7 in the Manage Sites dialog box, and then click Edit.

FIGURE 7.34

To Extend Your Knowledge

OTHER RESOURCES FOR HOSTING INFORMATION

According to Rosemarie Wise, an author with Sitepoint.com, one of the most important business relationships for a Web-site owner should be a Web-hosting company. She has written two long articles for sitepoint.com about Web hosting, which you can find at sitepoint.com/article/complete-guide-hosting-1. The articles are full of valuable information about how to determine your needs and how Web-hosting businesses work. Her own Web site, websiteowner.info, also has a large amount of additional information. Sitepoint.com also has a forum dedicated to hosting at sitepoint.com/subcat/hosting.

3   In the Remote Info category, choose FTP from the Access list, type your FTP host information from the email into the FTP Host field, type your site's root folder name into the Host Directory field, and type your login name and password into their respective fields.

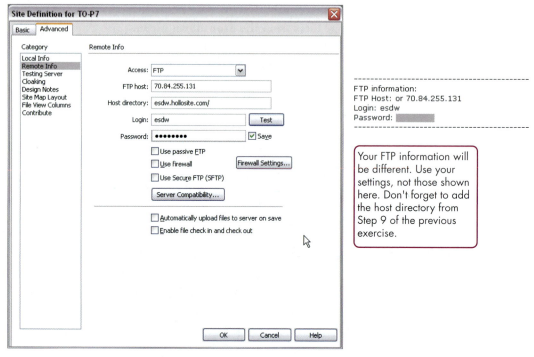

FTP information:
FTP Host: or 70.84.255.131
Login: esdw
Password:

Your FTP information will be different. Use your settings, not those shown here. Don't forget to add the host directory from Step 9 of the previous exercise.

FIGURE 7.35

4   Click the Test button and click OK when the message appears, noting that you have successfully connected to your Web server.

FIGURE 7.36

? If you have problems

If you do not get a successful connection, check your settings.

5   Click OK to close the success message, click OK to close the Site Definition dialog box, and then click Done to close the Manage Sites dialog box.

LESSON 7   **Uploading Your Site to the Web Server**

In this lesson, you upload your site to your hosting account. There are two terms you should be familiar with: put and get. Both are easy to understand: *put* means to upload a file from your computer to the Web server and *get* is the reverse. The terms come from the original FTP methods. In those methods, after you logged in to an FTP server, from a ***command line*** (a window on your system where you typed computer commands), you would type "put" followed by the filename of the file you want to upload or "get" followed by the filename to download the file. (You would use the commands mput and mget to put or get multiple files.) Dreamweaver's FTP functionality is much easier than command line.

To put an entire site, you select the site folder name in the Files panel and choose Put. You upload individual files by selecting a single file or Control/Command-click multiple files and choose Put. You can activate the put command either by clicking the Put button at the top of the Files panel or by Right/Control-clicking a file and choosing Put.

Put Your Site on Your Web Host

In this exercise, you put the entire site on the Web server. Depending on the speed of your connection, it may take a few seconds or a few minutes. For this reason, if you start working on your own as a Web designer, you may want to invest in a high-speed Internet connection to reduce the waiting time.

1   **Click the site name in the Files panel and then click the blue Put button.**

FIGURE 7.37

2   **When asked if you wish to put the entire site, click OK.**

FIGURE 7.38

3   **When you have finished uploading, click the Connect button to disconnect from the Web server.**

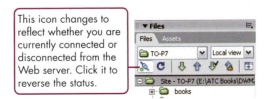

This icon changes to reflect whether you are currently connected or disconnected from the Web server. Click it to reverse the status.

FIGURE 7.39

4   **Open your browser and browse to the URL identified in the email message.**

> The URL is also the same as the host directory for your Web pages. This was done intentionally to keep the process as simple as possible.

FIGURE 7.40

5   **Close your browser.**

SUMMARY

In this project, you learned to validate HTML and fix any errors you found. You checked your site for accessibility and discovered that checking for accessibility involves both automated and manual checks. You learned how to check your site for broken links and orphaned files, and corrected both types of errors. You improved the document title and added keyword and description **<meta>** tags to improve the chances that your site would be found through search engines. You learned how to set file-type cloaking so certain file types do not upload to your Web site. You created an account with a free Web-hosting service, and entered the account information into Dreamweaver so you could FTP. Finally, you uploaded your site to your hosting account and viewed the pages in your browser.

KEY TERMS

ADA	get	reseller hosting
automated checks	hacker	search-engine optimization
bandwidth	hit	Section 508
broken links	hit counter	shared server
cloaking	ISP	spamdexing
co-located server	keywords	upload
command line	manual checks	validate
control panel	MySQL	virtual server
dedicated server	orphaned files	W3C
description	PHP	WCAG
disk space	publish	Web hosting
FTP	put	Web server

CHECKING CONCEPTS AND TERMS

SCREEN ID

Identify the indicated areas from the list below:

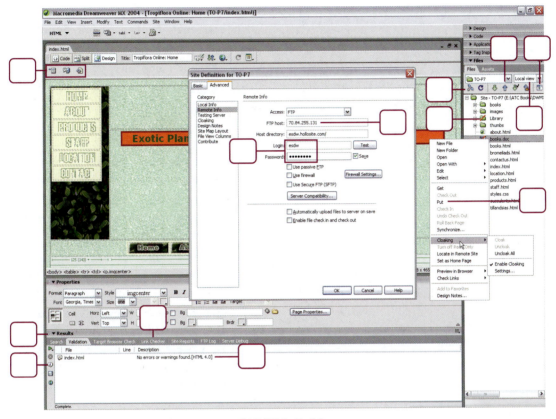

FIGURE 7.41

a. Change view

b. Username and password

c. Contextual menu

d. View <meta> tags

e. Result of a check

f. Link Checker tab

g. Connect/Disconnect

h. FTP URL

i. More Info

j. Collapse/Expand

k. Put

l. Results panel

m. Cloaked folder

MULTIPLE CHOICE

Circle the letter of the correct answer for each of the following:

1. To upload a site to a Web server, click the _____ button.
   a. upload
   b. put
   c. send
   d. ftp

2. In a search engine's results page, the description of a page is _____.
   a. auto generated by the search engine
   b. the <meta> tag description
   c. the first Heading 1
   d. the document title

3. The contents of which tag has the least relevance to search-engine rankings?
   a. headings
   b. paragraphs
   c. document title
   d. `<meta>` keywords

4. The <image> tag is flagged during _____.
   a. CSS validation
   b. HTML validation
   c. Jigsaw validation
   d. a search-engine query

5. Which of the following is correct?
   a. `<p lang="en">"Hi" in French is <span lang="fr">"Salut"</span>.</p>`
   b. `<p lang="en">"Hi" in French is <lang="fr">"Salut"</lang>.</p>`
   c. `<p lang="fr">"Hi" in French is "Salut".</p>`
   d. `<p lang="en">"Hi" in French is <p lang="fr">"Salut"</p>.</p>`

6. In which tag does it not matter if the content is a complete sentence?
   a. `<meta name="keywords" content="content goes here">`
   b. `<meta name="description" content="content goes here">`
   c. `<title>content goes here</title>`
   d. `<p>content goes here</p>`

7. UNIX and Linux operating systems are character case-sensitive. If you have a Web page with a filename of About.html, which link to it would be broken?
   a. `<a href="corporate/About.html"> About the ABC Corporation</a>`
   b. `<a href="about.html#address"> Address of the ABC Corporation</a>`
   c. `<a href="/service/policy/ About.html"> Service policies of the ABC Corporation</a>`
   d. `<a href="About.html?sid=1257& visitor=extrnl&kwrd=staff+Julie"> Our Sales Manager</a>`

8. If you have a decorative image, which <img> tag would be flagged as an issue by an automated accessibility checker?
   a. `<img src="fish.jpg" alt="">`
   b. `<img src="fish.jpg" title="My cat">`
   c. `<img src="fish.jpg" alt="My cat">`
   d. All of the above

9. Cloaking is a Dreamweaver function that _____.
   a. prevents you from creating links to cloaked files
   b. prevents visitors from downloading certain files without a password
   c. deletes certain files from the Web server
   d. prevents certain files from uploading to the Web server

10. A dedicated-server hosting package
_____.

    a. allows you to connect your own server to the Internet

    b. is the least costly hosting option

    c. is limited (dedicated) to HTML pages only

    d. only serves your Web site

DISCUSSION QUESTIONS

1. You have been approached by a small dry-cleaning business to create a Web site to market their products and services. Consider the following aspects — HTML validation, CSS validation, broken links and orphaned files, accessibility checking, keywords, description, document title, cloaking, and Web-site hosting — and discuss which are essential, which are unnecessary, and which have additional options that you would recommend. How would you explain and justify to your client the choices you have made?

2. When you click a broken link, you are directed to a 404 page that displays little more than page not found: 404 is the error number of the HyperText Transfer Protocol (HTTP) for a nonexistent page. Many Web hosting services allow you to create your own 404 pages to replace the default page. Discuss the design and content of a 404 page for the Tropiflora Online Web site.

SKILL DRILL

Skill Drills reinforce project skills. Each skill reinforced is the same, or nearly the same, as a skill presented in the lessons. Detailed instructions are provided in a step-by-step format. Work through these exercises in order.

1. Cloak a Folder

Cloaking by file type is not appropriate for every situation. As noted earlier, the Fireworks working format is PNG, so if your final graphics are PNGs, as well, you may need to cloak your working PNGs while allowing your final PNGs to upload (be uncloaked). Therefore, you cannot simply cloak PNGs by file type, but must move the working PNGs into a working folder and cloak that folder. The Library and Templates folders are not cloaked, by default. Although you can simply cloak the .lbi and .dwt files to prevent the library items and templates from uploading, Dreamweaver still creates empty Library and Templates folders. Cloaking the folders prevents this.

1. In the Files panel, Right/Control-click the Library folder.

2. Choose Cloaking>Settings.

3. Ensure that Enable Cloaking is checked and click OK.

    You must enable cloaking before you can cloak either by file type or by folder.

4. Right/Control-click the Library folder.

5. Choose Cloaking>Cloak.

2. Delete Folders Using the Control Panel

At times, you may need to work with the files and folders directly on the site and not through Dreamweaver, possibly because you are at your client's office instead of your own. Web-hosting businesses have different control-panel software, so the software may have variations, but offer the same essential functions. Some software companies develop control-panel software for Web-hosting companies, so you may find two or more hosting companies with the same control-panel software. In this exercise, you log in to your control panel and delete the Library folder that you cloaked in the previous exercise.

1. Open your browser and go to the URL identified in the email from 100webspace.com in the section Access Your Control Panel Here.

2. Enter your username and password and click Login

3. Click the File Manager link in the Control panel.

4. Click the www folder link in the File manager.

5. Click the folder that represents the site folder for your Web site.

6. Click the checkbox beside the Library folder.

7. Click the Delete button (at the top or bottom of the list of files and folders).

8. In response to the JavaScript alert, asking if you are sure, click OK.

9. Click the Logout link at the top right of the Control panel.

3. Replace a File

Windows and Unix/Linux Web servers are the most popular servers on the Internet. Most Web designers use Windows or Macintosh systems to design Web sites. Windows and Macintosh systems are not case-sensitive for file and folder names whereas Unix/Linux systems are case-sensitive. Therefore, when developing your system, you may create a link to the page index.html but in the anchor tag, you may have typed Index.html. Although you won't encounter any problems when you preview your pages on Windows and Macintosh systems, when you upload and test your links on a Unix/Linux Web server, this link will be broken. This is why we recommend that you always use lowercase filenames and folder names. In this exercise, you discover that a filename in a link begins with an uppercase letter but the filename on the Web server is lowercased and the link is broken. Unfortunately, Dreamweaver's Broken Link checker does not check for letter case or this error would have been discovered earlier.

1. Go to the URL of your Web site and link to the Products page.

2. Under the Top Sellers heading, click the link to Tillandsia Latifola.

3. Click the Back button in your browser and scroll down to the bottom of the page.

    Notice that the bottom image is missing.

4. Click the View Our Tillandsias link.

5. Click the Back button.

6. Launch Dreamweaver and open products.html from the TO-P7 site.

7. Change the Tillandsia Latifola link from Tillandsias.html#tl to **`tillandsias.html#tl`**. Change the View our Tillandsias link from Tillandsias.html to **`tillandsias.html`**. Click the image of the tillandsia and change the src to **`images/tillandsia_sm.jpg`**.

8. Close products.html, saving your changes.

9. Right/Control-click products.html in the Files panel and choose Put from the contextual menu.

    If you are asked if you wish to upload dependent files, click No.

10. When the upload has finished, click the Disconnect button at the top left of the Files panel.

11. Return to your browser, refresh the page, and recheck the links and image.

4. View Both Remote and Local Sites

Most stand-alone FTP software displays two panels of files: commonly the left panel shows your local files and the right panel shows the remote files on your Web server. In order to upload the files to the Web server, you use the two panels to drag files and folders from the local computer folder to the remote computer folder; the upload then proceeds. This option is available to Dreamweaver users, as well, in the expanded view of the Files panel, but the local and remote files are displayed in reverse order to most other FTP software

1. Open books.html and change the publication year of The Book of Bromeliads from 2000 to **2002**.

2. Close books.html, saving your changes.

3. In the Files panel, click Expand/Collapse (the right-most button).

4. To the right of the sites list, click the Connect button.

5. When connected, drag books.html from the right (Local Files) panel to the left (Remote Files) panel.

? If you have problems

You must drag to within the group of files on the left. If you drag below them, Dreamweaver does not allow the upload to happen. Watch the cursor to see that it changes to a copy icon, indicating that the upload is allowed.

---

6. When the upload is complete, disconnect from the site.

7. Click the Expand/Collapse button.

8. In your browser, navigate to books.html (Home>Products>Books) and note the updated publication date of the book.

CHALLENGE

Challenge exercises expand on, or are somewhat related to, skills presented in the lessons. Each exercise provides a brief introduction, followed by instructions in a numbered-step format that are not as detailed as those in the Skill Drill exercises. Work through the exercises in order.

1. Delete All Files and Folders from Your Site

This is the first of a series of exercises in which you display the work you have completed in the projects of this book. The first step is to delete the files and folders that currently exist on your site. You then prepare a home page with links to newly added folders on your site.

1. Open your Web browser and log in to the Control panel of your Web site.

2. Navigate to the www>root folder (replace root with the root folder name of your Web site).

3. In the File manager, click the Check All link below the list of files and folders.

4. Click the Delete button below the Check All link, and then click OK to confirm you want to delete all of the files and folders.

5. Log out from your site.

2. Prepare a New Site in Dreamweaver

In this exercise, you prepare a new site in Dreamweaver using the FTP information from the email message. As an independent Web designer, you may want to demonstrate work in progress on your Web site. You can keep client sites separate by storing each site in a different folder on your site. In this exercise, you prepare the folders for the assorted projects you have worked on recently.

1. In Dreamweaver, create a new site definition called **Web Server** from the Project_07>Web Server folder, but do not close the Site Definition dialog box.

2. Switch to the Remote Info category.

3. Choose FTP from the Access list.

4. Using the information from your email, add the FTP host information into the FTP Host field. Set the Host Directory to the URL of your account. Type your username in the Login field and your password in the Password field.

5. Click the Test button to confirm the settings.

6. Click OK when finished.

7. Click Done to close the Manage Sites dialog box.

3. Create New Folders on Your Web Server

In this exercise, you create a new folder on your Web server through Dreamweaver. By default, the Files panel displays only the local files but by choosing an option, it displays the remote files. The first time you switch to remote files, the Files panel is empty: you must connect to the Web server so that the Files panel can display the remote files. You can then work with the files and folders using the contextual menu, but the menu acts on the remote files, not the local files.

1. In the Files panel, to the right of the list of sites, choose the Remote view.

2. Click the Connect button to connect to the Web server.

3. Right/Command-click below the list of files and choose New Folder.

4. Type **to** and press Enter/Return.

5. Repeat Steps 3 and 4 creating folders called **phil**, **seabreeze**, and **jcw**.

6. Click the Disconnect button to disconnect from the Web server.

4. Assign Remote Folders to Local Sites

In this exercise, you prepare site definitions with both local and remote settings. You use the same server and account information, but you use the new folders as the root folders for the sites or projects on the Web server.

1. Define a new site called **PHIL-P6** from the Project_06>PHIL-P6 folder but do not close the Site Definition dialog box.

2. Switch to the Remote Info category.

3.   Choose FTP from the Access list.

4. Using the information from your email, add the FTP host information into the FTP Host field.

5. Set the Host Directory to the URL of your account and add **/phil** to the end of the URL.

6. Type your username in the Login field and your password in the Password field.

7. Click the Test button to confirm the settings.

8. Click OK when finished.

9. Click Done to close the Manage Sites dialog box.

10. Repeat Steps 1 to 9 as follows:

Local Folder	*Site Name*	*Remote Folder*
Project_05>Seabreeze	**Seabreeze**	URL/seabreeze
Project_05>JCW-P5	**JCW-P5**	URL/jcw

5. Cloak Folders

In this exercise, you cloak the Library and Templates folders of the PHIL-P6 site. It is not sufficient to cloak the .lbi and .dwt files because the Library and Templates folders will be created even if there are no files in them. To prevent the Library and Templates folders from being created and uploaded, you cloak the folders.

1. In the Files panel, choose the site PHIL-P6.

2. In the Files panel, Right/Control-click the Library folder of the PHIL-P6 site.

3. Choose Cloaking and ensure that Enable Cloaking is checked (but do not uncheck it).

4. Right/Control-click the Library folder and choose Cloaking>Cloak.

5. Right/Control-click the Templates folder and choose Cloaking>Cloak.

6. Upload the PHIL-P6 Site

In this exercise, you upload the PHIL-P6 files and uncloaked folders to your Web-server account.

1. Click the Site Name at the top of the Files panel list of files and folders.

2. Click the Put button at the top of the Files panel.

3. After the upload has finished, switch to the Remote view (click the Refresh button, if necessary) and check that the files have uploaded properly to the correct folders.

4. Disconnect from the Web server.

7. Upload the Other Sites to Your Web-Server Account

In this exercise, you upload the remaining three sites that you prepared in Challenge exercise 2. If you feel so inclined, you can edit the index.html page in the Web-server site, adding your name and a style sheet, or replacing the ordered list with a jump menu.

1. Switch to the Seabreeze site.

2. Put the site on the Web server.

3. Using the Remote view, ensure the files have uploaded correctly.

4. Switch to the JCW-P5 site.

5. Put the site on the Web server.

6. Using the Remote view, ensure the files have uploaded correctly.

Create <meta> and <title> Tags for Web Sites

In order to improve their ranking in search engines, Web sites must make good use of the page title, the keywords **<meta>** tag, and the description **<meta>** tag. The home page is especially important because, for many people, it is the first page of the Web site that they encounter.

1.   Open the Yellow Pages book for your community and find three businesses, each with a large advertisement and a Web site.

2.   Read through the advertisements for each.

3.   From the content in the ad, create a document title, a description, and a list of keywords that would be suitable for the home page of the Web site for that business.

4.   Go to the Web site of each business. In each case, view the source code of the home page, and compare their **<meta>** (if any) and **<title>** tags used in the home page of that Web site with the **<meta>** and **<title>** tag contents you created.

PROJECT **8**

Developing with PHP and MySQL

OBJECTIVES

In this project, you learn how to

- Create PHP code
- Use includes
- Work with form data
- Create a database

- Display records from a database
- Insert records into a database
- Select and sort database records

WHY WOULD I DO THIS?

Dynamic pages are pages with at least a portion of dynamic content that the Web server generates when needed. The dynamic portion of the page does not have to be a large portion of the page. It may simply generate a "Good Morning" before 12 p.m. and a "Good Afternoon" after 12 p.m. However dynamic pages can do much more than that, such as displaying a statistic that changes daily, like a list of the most popular products. You may be confused by the similarity of DHTML (Dynamic HTML) and dynamic pages: DHTML is an application of JavaScript that acts at the client-level and can be used to create event-driven animations whereas dynamic pages are created by the Web server. For this reason, creating dynamic pages is the last project in this book.

The proverb "It is difficult to run before you can walk" could apply, a little altered, to the development of dynamic Web pages: it is difficult to create dynamic pages if you don't know HTML. For example, you may wish to display a list of book titles in an ordered list, but if you don't know how to create an HTML ordered list, you won't be able to display the books in this format.

Dynamic pages require a server-side programming language. The most popular server-side languages include PHP (PHP Hypertext Preprocessor), ASP (Microsoft's Active Server Pages), ASP.Net (a more recent version of ASP), ColdFusion (a Macromedia technology), and JSP (Java-Servlet Pages). In this project, we introduce you to PHP because it is easier to learn than some of the others; it is free; it can be installed on Unix/Linux, Macintosh, and Windows computers; and Dreamweaver supports it. PHP also happens to be installed and available in your free Web-hosting account at 100webspace.com (a feature not commonly available to free Web-hosting accounts).

Although PHP can be used quite effectively to create dynamic pages; it and most other server-side languages can also interact with a database. A *database* is a collection of information organized so a computer program can quickly select desired pieces of data. Examples of databases include a telephone directory and a list of clients for a credit-card company. Commonly, ASP and ASP.Net are paired with Microsoft's SQL Server database whereas PHP is commonly set up with MySQL because it, too, is free to download and install. Databases are used to store data, such as product details or news stories. The database is queried (a *query* is a request for information from a database), using a server-side language, for the details of a product or a particular news story. The server-side language then takes the results of the query and adds it to the Web page.

Data in a database is unformatted, that is, it does not contain HTML tags. You use PHP to wrap HTML tags around the database data, such as **<td>** if the data is to be displayed in a table or **<h2>** or **<p>** or other tags, depending on the formatting needed. You, therefore, use PHP to extract the appropriate data from the database, wrap it in HTML tags, and deliver the finished Web page to the visitor who requested the page.

As you can see, you can do much with PHP and the MySQL database. This project can only touch on a few aspects of server-side programming languages and databases. If you'd like to learn more, there are many books about each of these technologies and how to make them work together. Although we focus on PHP and MySQL in this project, you can apply the same principles to other languages and databases.

V I S U A L   S U M M A R Y

Much of this project deals with PHP and SQL code that you type into the Code window of your PHP pages. You may wonder why, with all the visual design tools, Dreamweaver forces you to type code into the Code window for a language (PHP) and a database (MySQL) that it claims to support. Dreamweaver's support is only part of the requirements for a visual development tool — it must also connect with the database, and 100webspace.com, like many other Web-hosting services, does not allow remote access to databases on their server. Secondly, not all programming can be provided through visual tools. As an example, there are many JavaScript functions used in various Web sites that are not provided through the visual interface of Dreamweaver. PHP is no different in this respect. However, Dreamweaver does provide syntax coloring and code hints for PHP functions to help you with the functions.

```
49  <?php
50  $to = "myEmail@address.com";
51  $subject = $_POST['subject'];
52  $comments = $_POST['comments'];
53  $from = "\"" mail(string to, string subject, string message, [string additional_headers], [string additional_parameters])
54  if(mail($to,)) {
55  echo "<h3>Your Message</h3>";
56  echo "<p><strong>From:</strong> " . $from . "</p>";
57  echo "<p><strong>Subject:</strong> " . $subject . "</p>";
58  echo "<p><strong>Comments:</strong> " . $comments . "</p>";
59  echo "<p>We will contact you as soon as we can.</p>";
60  } else {
61  echo "<p>Email failed.</p>";
62  }
63  ?>
```

Dreamweaver provides sophisticated code hints that identify the required and optional components of a function.

FIGURE 8.1

To preview your PHP and MySQL pages in your browser, you must upload them to the server so that it can process the PHP commands and display the results. To simplify this process, you register a testing server in the Site Definition dialog box. In it you specify the type of server configuration, in this case PHP MySQL, and the location of the server. After these settings are in place, when you preview a page in your browser, Dreamweaver uploads the page to the server and your browser displays the page at the server.

Site Definition for TO-P8

Basic | Advanced

Category
Local Info
Remote Info
Testing Server
Cloaking
Design Notes
Site Map Layout
File View Columns
Contribute

Server model: PHP MySQL
Access: FTP
FTP host: 70.84.255.131
Host directory: esdw.hollosite.com
Login: esdw   [Test]
Password: ••••••••   ☑ Save
☐ Use passive FTP
☐ Use Firewall (in Preferences)
☐ Use Secure FTP (SFTP)
[Server Compatibility...]

URL prefix: http://esdw.hollosite.com/
The URL Prefix is the location of the site's root folder on the testing server.

FIGURE 8.2

In this project, you use a number of features of the Control panel at your site. You use the Subdomain Manager to set up a new subdomain. You use the Manage SQL Databases to create a new MySQL database, and you use the PHPMy Admin link (it should actually be PHPMyAdmin) to manage the data in your database.

FIGURE 8.3

You learn that PHPMyAdmin is a PHP application, designed and built to add, delete, and modify the tables in your database as well as the fields and data within the tables of your database. Although PHPMyAdmin is essentially a series of links and Web forms, it is also a database-management application that runs in your Web browser.

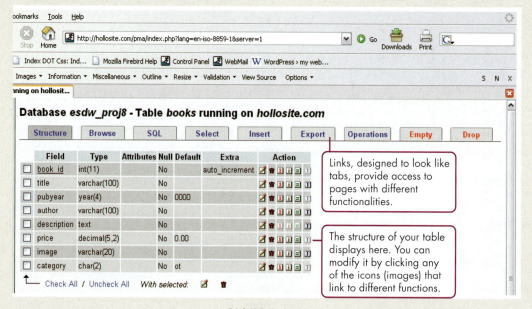

FIGURE 8.4

LESSON 1 Learning to Use PHP

PHP pages generally end with the filename extension .php so the PHP code can be processed. When you want to create a new PHP page, you choose Dynamic Page from the New Document dialog box instead of Basic. From there you choose PHP and click Create. When you save the page, Dreamweaver assumes that you want to give the page the .php extension. The new PHP page has the **<!DOCTYPE>**, **<body>**, and the rest of the basic HTML page tags that appear in a standard HTML page. However, at times your PHP page may contain just PHP code, no HTML at all. In this situation, you would delete all of the HTML code.

Generally, PHP code is intertwined with the HTML code. Based on the instructions in the PHP code, it generates content, such as the "Good Morning" greeting mentioned earlier. When a visitor requests a PHP page, the Web server processes the instructions in the page and delivers the results of the processing to the visitor. The visitor never sees the PHP code, just the HTML and content generated by the PHP code.

PHP code is surrounded by PHP tags: **<?php** at the beginning of the PHP block and **?>** at the end. The Web server processes the code between the PHP tags and replaces the tags and code with the results of the processing. You can have as many PHP blocks in the page as necessary.

Configure Your PHP Subdomain

For you to view the results of the PHP processing, you must use a Web server with PHP installed on it to process the page. For this project, you must upload your pages to your Web-hosting account each time you make a change to the code. In this exercise, you configure the site definition for this project and also configure the Testing Server category of the Site Definition dialog box. The result of this configuration is that when you preview the page in a browser, the page is uploaded to the server and your browser is sent to the page on your hosting account, not to your local page. This means that you can preview the effects of your changes immediately. At times, however, you must refresh your browser to see the effect of the change.

In addition to the new features of Dreamweaver's Site Definition dialog box, you set up a ***subdomain*** (or child domain, a domain that is part of a larger domain name) on your 100webspace.com account. For example, if the domain is www.example.com, then a subdomain replaces the www with another name, such as family.example.com. Technically, the URL of your free account is a subdomain: 100webspace.com's offer for up to five subdomains allows you to create four more subdomains under the same login. Generally, the content of subdomains is stored in folders of your primary account; for example, the pages for family.example.com may be stored in example.com/family.

The advantage of creating and using another subdomain for this project is that you can leave your other pages as they are and work as if you had another free account. After you complete this book, you can delete the project files from your site and also remove the subdomain.

1   Using the information you received in your email from Project 7, open your browser, go to the login page for your account, and log in to the Control panel.

Control Panel login

| Username: | esdw |
| Password: | ******** |

Login

FIGURE 8.5

2   In the Site Manager group, click the Subdomain Manager link.

LATEST NEWS & UPDATES (0)

FIGURE 8.6

3   In the Subdomain field, type your login name and add 2 to the end of it.

4   If you have a choice of domains, choose your original domain.

5   Leaving the rest of the settings as they are, click the Add Subdomain button at the bottom.

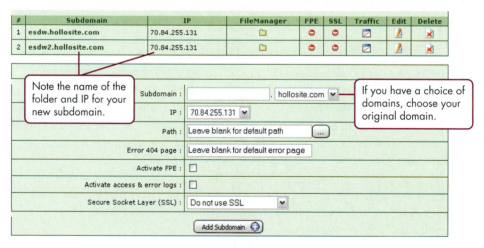

FIGURE 8.7

6   Return to Dreamweaver and create a new site definition from the Project_08>TO-P8 folder called TO-P8.

7   In the Remote Info category, set Access to FTP.

8 Using the information from the email you received from 100webspace.com, set the Host Directory to the URL of your new subdomain folder, insert your Login and Password, and then click the Test button to verify the settings.

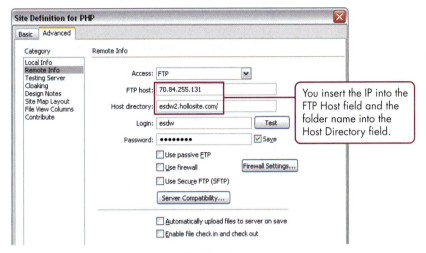

FIGURE 8.8

9 Switch to the Testing Server category. Choose PHP MySQL from the Server Model list. Choose FTP from the Access list. Check the URL Prefix at the bottom of the dialog box and ensure that it contains only http:// followed by the URL of your subdomain.

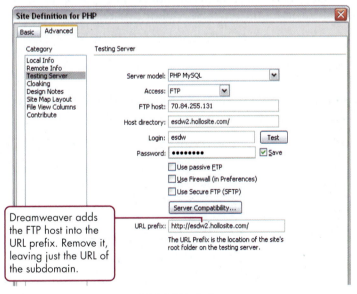

FIGURE 8.9

10 Click OK, and then click Done when finished.

11 In the Files panel, click the Site Name at the top of the list of files, and then click the Put button to upload the pages to the subdomain of your account.

12 When asked if you want to put the entire site, click OK.

To Extend Your Knowledge

DEFAULT PAGE NAMES

You learned that most Web servers are configured to use index.html or index.htm as the default HTML filenames. If you create a link to domain.com/folder, the Web server notes that no filename is specified and delivers the page with the default filename to the visitor. If you are building PHP pages, generally, the default filename is index.php. As with HTML pages, different Web hosts may configure their servers differently: if index.php does not work, contact the support desk of the hosting company for clarification.

Be aware that if you have both index.html and index.php in the same folder, creating a link to that folder may deliver index.html instead of index.php or vice versa. Don't create two index files in the same folder.

Create a PHP Test Page

In this exercise, you embed a PHP function in an HTML page. The **phpinfo()** function provides two benefits. First, if it runs properly, it confirms that PHP is installed and running properly on the server. This is particularly beneficial if you have installed PHP on your personal computer and want confirmation that the install was successful. Second, **phpinfo()** produces a report on the configuration of PHP on the server. There are numerous settings, options, and add-ons available for PHP, and knowing what is available to you enables you to take advantage of them. However, when your hosting account is a shared-server account (paid or free), you must accept the settings configured for the server. A dedicated hosting account allows you to modify the configuration as you require.

1 Choose File>New.

2 In the New Document dialog box, under Category, click Dynamic Page, under Dynamic Page, in the middle pane, click PHP. Click Create.

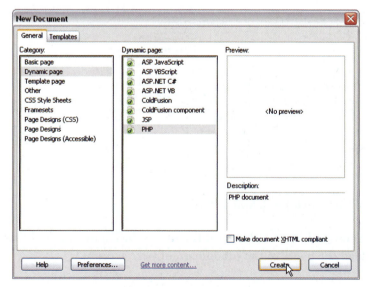

FIGURE 8.10

3   Save the blank page as `phpinfo.php`.

4   Switch to the Code view.

5   In line 9, the blank line below the `<body>` tag, type `<?php phpinfo(); ?>`.

Dreamweaver uses syntax coloring for PHP code as well as HTML and JavaScript.

FIGURE 8.11

6   Save the changes to phpinfo.php.

7   Preview the page in your browser.

Dreamweaver uploads the page to the server, and the Testing Server setup in the Site Definition dialog box prompts Dreamweaver to direct your browser to phpinfo.php at your hosting account.

The fact that the PHP information page displays confirms that you have entered the code correctly, that the page had been uploaded to the server, and that PHP has been installed on the server.

FIGURE 8.12

8   Keep your browser open and return to Dreamweaver.

9   Close phpinfo.php.

To Extend Your Knowledge

BUILDING YOUR OWN WEB SERVER

You can install PHP on your own computer, but if you share a computer or are in a classroom setting, that may not be allowed. You also need to install Web-server software, such as Apache, for PHP to work with your Web pages. Later in this project you learn to use MySQL, a Web-database application. Installing all three applications and getting them to work together is more difficult than installing and configuring most standard business applications. Your account at 100webspace.com has all three applications installed and configured, thereby eliminating any concern about your installing this fairly complex mix of applications. However, Apache, PHP, and MySQL are also all free to download and install. If you feel adventurous, you may want to do so. If you do, the result will be that you have a working Web server running on your computer complete with PHP and MySQL.

Echo Content and HTML

The **echo ""**; function writes into the page the content between the "". This content may be text, such as "**Good Morning**", or HTML code, or both, like "**<p>Good Morning</p>**".

| 1 | Create a new Dynamic PHP page and save it as `echo.php`. |

| 2 | In line 9, the blank line below the <body> tag, type `<?php echo "Good Morning"; ?>`. |

```
 8  <body>
 9  <?php echo "Good Morning"; ?>
10  </body>
11  </html>
```

FIGURE 8.13

| 3 | Save the changes and preview the page in your browser. |

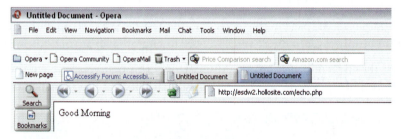

FIGURE 8.14

| 4 | View the source code of the page by Right/Control-clicking in your browser window and selecting View Source (or something similar — the option may differ in other browsers). |

```
 1  <!DOCTYPE HTML PUBLIC "-//W3C//DTD HTML 4.01 Transitional//EN" "http://www.w3.org/TR/html4/loose.dtd">
 2  <html>
 3  <head>
 4  <meta http-equiv="Content-Type" content="text/html; charset=iso-8859-1">
 5  <title>Untitled Document</title>
 6  </head>
 7
 8  <body>
 9  Good Morning</body>
10  </html>
```

> There is no sign of the PHP code other than the results of the processing.

FIGURE 8.15

| 5 | Close the source-code viewer and return to Dreamweaver. |

| 6 | Type <h1> before Good (but to the right of the quotation marks) and </h1> after Morning (but to the left of the quotation marks). |

```
 8  <body>
 9  <?php echo "<h1>Good Morning</h1>"; ?>
10  </body>
11  </html>
```

FIGURE 8.16

7 Save the changes and preview the page in your browser again.

FIGURE 8.17

8 View the source code again.

FIGURE 8.18

9 Close the source-code viewer and return to Dreamweaver.

10 Keep echo.php open for the next exercise.

Concatenate Variables with Strings

To *concatenate* is to join two or more pieces of data to create a string. Concatenation uses the **.** (dot) opera-tor. The code **1+2**, uses the addition operator to produce 3, but **"1"."2"** produces "12" and **"John "   .**
"Doe" produces "John Doe". A *string* is content between quotation marks whereas a *numeral* is a number not enclosed by quotation marks. Programming *variables* are storage containers of string or numeral data. Variables only exist during the processing time of the PHP and are destroyed after processing. To maintain data from page view to page view, you must write it to a file or a database.

Data is assigned to a variable using the assignment operator **=**. (To compare the equality of two strings, numerals, or variables, you use **==**, such as **1 == 1**.) Variables must have a **$** prefix, such as **$firstName**. To assign data to a variable, you use the format **$variableName = data**, such as **$firstName = "Bill"** or **$age = 50**.

1 In the open file, echo.php, delete echo **"<h1>Good Morning</h1>";** and press Enter/Return twice to separate **<?php** and **?>** with a blank line between them.

FIGURE 8.19

2 In the blank line, type **$name = "myname";** (replace myname with your actual name) and press Enter/Return.

Each PHP command must end with the semicolon.

3   Type `$birthYear = 1960;` (replace 1960 with your actual year of birth) and press Enter/Return.

4   Type `$currentYear = 2004;` (replace 2004 with the current year, if different) and press Enter/Return.

5   Type `$age = $currentYear - $birthYear;` and press Enter/Return.

6   Type `echo "<p>My name is " . $name . ".</p>";` and press Enter/Return.

7   Type `echo "<p>I was born in " . $birthYear . ".</p>";` and press Enter/Return.

8   Type `echo "<p>This year, I will be " . $age . " years old.</p>";`.

```
8  <body>
9  <?php
10 $name = "James";
11 $birthYear = 1960;
12 $currentYear = 2004;
13 $age = $currentYear - $birthYear;
14 echo "<p>My name is " . $name . ".</p>";
15 echo "<p>I was born in " . $birthYear . ".</p>";
16 echo "<p>This year, I will be " . $age . " years old.</p>";
17 ?>
18 </body>
19 </html>
```

FIGURE 8.20

9   Save the changes and preview the page. (You may have to press F5 to reload the page in your browser to see the results of the new code.)

My name is James.

I was born in 1960.

This year, I will be 44 years old.

FIGURE 8.21

10   Return to Dreamweaver and close echo.php.

To Extend Your Knowledge

PHP IS LOOSELY TYPED

Some programming languages are very strictly typed, which means that when you create a new variable, you must specify the type of data it will contain, such as a string or an integer. Furthermore, you cannot concatenate a string with a nonstring: you must first convert the data in the nonstring variable to string data, and then you can concatenate it with another string. There are pros and cons to both methods, but for the beginning programmer, PHP is much easier to learn than some other languages.

LESSON 2 Using Includes

Includes are a very useful yet very simple function of PHP. They can be used to replace library items and are much more powerful than library items. Includes can contain static content, just like library items, or includes can contain programming code. ***Includes*** are files that exist outside of a page but, at the time of processing, they are included in the code of the page. They are also called "server-side includes" (SSI).

The weakness of library items is that if a change is made to a library item, all pages that use it must be updated and uploaded. Includes, like library items, are parcels of code, but the action of combining the included code with the main page occurs when a visitor requests the page, not when the include is created or modified. Because includes don't combine with the main pages until the visitor requests the page, whenever you make a change to the included file, you don't need to update multiple files. In many ways, you could compare an include with an external CSS style-sheet file: even though many pages can use the common CSS file, you don't need to update the pages when you modify a style in the style-sheet file. However, when you modify an include, just as when you modify a style-sheet file, you must remember to upload the revised include file to the Web server or the old version will still be on the Web server.

There is one issue that you must recognize when using includes: you must use absolute paths to links or images. The include file and the page that uses the include file may be at a different folder depths. Therefore although `../images/picture.jpg` may work in some pages, for other pages, the correct relative path to that image may be `images/picture.jpg` or `../../../images/picture.jpg`. However, because an include can't adjust the paths in its code for different pages, the paths may be correct for some files, but incorrect for others. On the other hand, when using library items, Dreamweaver automatically adjusts the paths, depending on where the pages are located relative to the Library folder. This is not the case with includes: you must use absolute paths to images in an include.

There are two general naming conventions for include files. Many developers assign the filename extension .inc to the include file. The .inc extension is fine if the content of the include is static, such as an image, but if the include has PHP programming code, the include must be given the .php extension. For example, one include contains the code for a single-celled table. In the cell, there is another include, a nested include, as it were, for an image. The image include can end with .inc, but the table include must end with .php because it must be processed to incorporate the image include. Some developers use .inc.php for all includes to identify them as includes (.inc) and to allow for PHP processing, if necessary.

The PHP code for the include function is `include("/path/filename");` (the parentheses are optional: you may alternatively use `include "/path/filename";`). The path to the include file must not be absolute, but any paths used in the include file must be absolute. Of course, the include function must be in a PHP block, either by itself, if that is all you need, or with other PHP code.

PHP developers can use includes for different purposes so there are four types of include functions: include();, include_once();, require();, and require_once();. The include pair of functions insert the identified file, as you just learned, but if there is a problem with the include file, such as an accidental deletion of the include file, the page still displays without the included content. The require pair of functions also includes the identified file, but if the file is not available, the page halts immediately and an error message appears in its place. The require functions are essential if you have important programming code in the required files.

The _once varieties of the include and require functions prevent any additional insertions of the same include file into the current page. At times, due to the complexity of some PHP programming code, a bug in the code can cause a file to be included (required) more than once. This is annoying if it simply creates a duplicate image but it could be disastrous if it is a duplicate of programming code. The require and include functions without the _once suffix allow multiple insertions of the same file.

Work with Includes

In this exercise, you add the include function to two pages that are located at different folder depths. In the include is text, which of course does not depend on paths, and an image, which will only be visible if the path is absolute.

1   **Open includes1.php from the TO-P8 site folder.**

2   **In line 9, type `<?php include("includes/example.inc.php"); ?>`.**

```
 8 <body>
 9 <?php include("includes/example.inc.php"); ?>
10 </body>
11 </html>
```

FIGURE 8.22

3   **Save the changes to includes1.php and preview it in your browser.**

This is an image

This is some text

Notice that you can see text and an image.

FIGURE 8.23

4   **Return to Dreamweaver and open folder1>folder2>includes2.php.**

5   **In line 9, type `<?php include("../../includes/example.inc.php"); ?>`.**

The path to the include must be relative to the site root. There is another method in which the path to the include may be absolute, but it is more complex.

6   **Save the changes to includes2.php and preview it in your browser.**

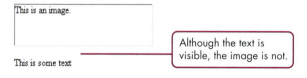

This is an image.

This is some text

Although the text is visible, the image is not.

FIGURE 8.24

7   **Return to Dreamweaver and open example.inc.php from the includes folder off the root folder of the TO-P8 site.**

8 Switch to the Design view and double-click the image.

9 Choose this_is_an_image.gif from the images folder. At the bottom of the Select Image Source dialog box, set the Relative to option to Site Root and click OK.

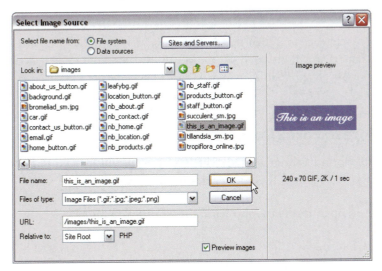

FIGURE 8.25

10 Close example.inc.php, saving your changes, and then upload example.inc.php to the server.

11 Refresh includes2.php in your browser again.

This time, the image is visible because the path to the image is an absolute path. Any page that uses this include will be able to see the image.

12 Return to Dreamweaver and close all open files.

LESSON 3 Working with Form Data

You learned in *Project 1: Collecting Information with Forms*, that form data is passed to the action URL as pairs of names and values, such as **firstName=Bob&lastName=Smith**. You learned that the form data is sent in the same format whether the form uses the get or post method, but when you use the get method, the name=value pairs are visible in the query-string portion of the URL in the address bar of your browser. Project 1 also explored how to create forms and how the form data is sent. In this lesson, you learn how to capture and process the form data.

To capture get or post data, you use virtually identical methods: **$_GET['fieldName']** for get data and **$_POST['fieldName']** for post data. Be careful to match the capture method with the form-delivery method; **$_POST** won't capture data sent via the get method and vice versa. You replace fieldName with the name of the field in the form (which is also visible in the query string if you use the get method).

You can use **$_GET** and **$_POST** to collect the data, but to use the data, you generally assign the contents of the **$_GET** or **$_POST** variables to a variable, such as **$firstName = $_GET['firstName'];**. In this example, **$firstName** would contain Bob in the earlier example given. You can then use the data from the form as content in the receiving page, such as **echo "<p>Good Morning " . $firstName . "!</p>";** which would display Good Morning Bob! in the page.

It can be confusing to see reference to **$_GET** and **$_POST** as variables. In fact, they are supervariables because they contain all of the data that is transferred via the get or post methods. They contain all name and value pairs sent by the form. However, although they may be variables, generally PHP developers assign their data to standard variables.

Capture and Process Form Data

For this exercise, a simple form has been created, which asks the visitor for first name, last name, and year of birth. You create the page that captures the form data and processes it.

1   In Dreamweaver, open formdata.php from the TO-P8 site folder.

2   Switch to the Code view.

3   In line 9, type **<?php**, press Enter/Return twice, then type **?>**.

4   Move the insertion point up one line and type the following code:

```
$firstName = $_GET['firstname'];

$lastName = $_GET['lastname'];

$birthYear = $_GET['birthyear'];

$age = date("Y") - $birthYear;
```

date('Y') is a special PHP date function that takes the date and time from the Web server and formats it according to the specifications between the parentheses, in this case just the year.

5   Locate **<p>Hello X!</p>**. Delete X and replace it with **<?php echo "$firstName $lastName"; ?>**.

6   Locate **Y years old.</p>**. Delete Y and replace it with **<?php echo "$age"; ?>**.

```
 9 <?php
10 $firstName = $_GET['firstname'];
11 $lastName = $_GET['lastname'];
12 $birthYear = $_GET['birthyear'];
13 $age = date("Y") - $birthYear;
14 ?>
15 <h1>Welcome to this Page</h1>
16 <p>Hello <?php echo "$firstName $lastName"; ?>!</p>
17 <p>This year, you will be <?php echo "$age"; ?> years old.   </p>
18 </body>
```

FIGURE 8.26

7 Close formdata.php, saving your changes.

8 Open form.php and preview the page in your browser. Complete the form and submit the information.

9 Return to Dreamweaver, but leave form.php open for the next exercise.

Capture Post Data

In this exercise, you learn that post data can be captured as easily as get data. All you need to do is ensure that the method specified in the **<form>** tag matches the method of capturing data sent by the form.

1 In the open file, form.php, switch to the Design view.

2 Click in the form, then click the **<form>** tag in the Tag selector, and set Method to Post in the Property inspector.

3 Save the changes but do not close form.php.

4 Open formdata.php and switch to the Code view.

5 Change the three occurrences of **$_GET** to **$_POST**.

```
10 $firstName = $_POST['firstname'];
11 $lastName = $_POST['lastname'];
12 $birthYear = $_POST['birthyear'];
```

FIGURE 8.27

6 Close formdata.php, saving your changes.

7 With form.php open, preview the page in your browser, enter data into the form, and click the Submit button.

FIGURE 8.28

8 Return to Dreamweaver and close form.php.

To Extend Your Knowledge

SECURITY OF FORM DATA

There are two reasons to validate form data — to ensure that visitors answer the forms correctly, such as typing "12" instead of "dozen" in the quantity field, and to make the data secure. Many forms display the form data to others, such as discussion forums in which members use forms to ask and answer questions. It is possible, assuming no security checks, to insert JavaScript into a reply form on a discussion-forum Web site and, when other visitors view the forum, their browsers are directed to another site. Forms, as you see in the next lesson, can be used to add data to a database. Although many discussion forums use a database to store the discussions, this issue is broader than discussion forums. Any time that a form uses the get method to pass data, unscrupulous users may add their own code to the query string that could be used to expose usernames and passwords (assuming they are not encrypted) or even delete tables or the database. If you are interested in learning more about PHP and MySQL, be sure to read up on security issues and how to prevent these types of activities.

LESSON 4   Creating a Database

A database is a collection of related data, such as your CD library. In it, you would likely record the name of the CD, the name of the band or musician, the year of release, and perhaps other data. *Fields* are the individual pieces of data, such as the CD name, and *records* are collections of fields, such as the complete description of a CD. Although it can seem, from this example, that a database consists of fields and records, in fact there is an intermediate level of organization within a database — the table. Technically, a *table* is made up fields and records, and a database is a collection of tables. In this example, there would be just one table in the database, but if your database was not just a catalog of your CDs but, instead, a catalog of all of your possessions, you might have a table for CDs, a table for books, and a table for videos, all within your database called "My Stuff."

The example of the My Stuff database has three tables that are not related to each other. For example, although you may have a book or two written by a musician and you may have a music video of a musician for which you also have a CD, these situations would probably be rare. However, in many business situations, you would have many more relationships between tables of data. For example, consider a sales invoice in which the customer, products, and salesperson are identified: this is a situation in which three tables are easily identified. In fact, there is a fourth — the invoice itself is a record of a particular sale and is part of the invoices table. Within the customer table, you would identify the customer's name, address, phone number, and other particulars. The product table would identify the product name, product category (film, camera, or photo frame), price, minimum stock level, and other details. The salesperson table would identify the name, employee id, address, and other particulars. Finally, the invoice table would list the invoice number, employee number, product numbers, and date of sale (the prices would be drawn from the product table). This example, not only explains why a database may consist of multiple tables, but also shows how relationships between tables may work together. Although MySQL is perfectly capable of handling relationships, in this lesson, we don't deal with related tables as it would considerably increase the complexity of the lesson.

When people are asked to list their CDs on a sheet of paper, they quite commonly also write numbers in the left column. Database designers do this, as well — they add a numerical ID to each record in a table. They do this to add a unique key to each record so that if you have two records with the same data, the unique number makes them unique. When designing a database, you add a field (besides the data you are most interested in collecting) in which this numerical ID will be recorded. Generally, this field uses a special feature, *auto_increment*: the database application, in this case MySQL, automatically *increments* (increases) the number in this field each time you add a new record. You see this in life all of the time: each invoice has an invoice number, each employee has an employee number, and each vehicle has a vehicle number. In database applications, it is not the contents of a record that identify a particular product or book but the record ID number. How many times have you driven around town and seen a car exactly like yours? If you have a popular model in a popular paint color, it is quite likely that (without the license plate), you could mistake someone else's car for yours. The vehicle identification number, however, properly identifies your car.

MySQL supports many *data types* (formats of data), such as text, integers, decimal numbers, and dates. When you extract data from the database into PHP variables, the data-type information is lost — the PHP variables simply contain string data, such as "Bill", "123", or "June 10, 1999". You set data types in MySQL to involve MySQL in the data validation. For instance, a year of birth can't be "1990A" so if the form validation does not pick up the "A" in the date, MySQL does and rejects the data entry. There are other functions that MySQL can provide, such as calculating the total sales for each salesperson, but if the data type of the sales column is set to

To Extend Your Knowledge

OPEN-SOURCE APPLICATIONS

Open source is a term associated with many computer applications that have been receiving much press recently. *Open-source* means that the source code of the application is available for anyone to download, view, and even modify, if they so choose. (By code, we do not mean the PHP code, such as you create in Dreamweaver. In PHP, the PHP interpreter takes the PHP code you create, processes it, and returns the results of the processing: the PHP interpreter is open-source.) Open-source applications are generally free, although, sometimes, there are restrictions on commercial use of the application.

Linux is an open-source operating system; Mozilla and Firefox are open-source browsers; PHP, Perl, and Python are open-source programming languages; Apache is an open-source Web server, and MySQL, PostgreSQL, and Firebird are open-source database servers. In fact, the acronym LAMP describes a popular package of open-source applications used for Web development: Linux, Apache, MySQL, and PHP.

Open-source applications are constantly compared with commercial applications (which are closed-source and, often, not free). MySQL, for example, does not have the feature set of Microsoft's SQL Server, but MySQL is constantly improving. On the other hand, the Firefox browser has much better support for HTML, CSS, and JavaScript than IE does. As a developer and designer of Web sites, especially if you are learning something new, such as Web databases and Web programming, free open-source applications are a great starting point, and many people make a living from PHP and MySQL Web development without having to learn or use similar commercial applications.

text, the mathematical calculation cannot be performed. MySQL also supports data subtypes, such as tinyint (an integer between 0 and 255), year (2- or 4-digit number), and char (text characters, for which you can specify how many, such as 15 for a firstname).

When you work with databases, except for desktop products, such as Paradox, Access, or FileMaker Pro, you must use a language called **SQL** (Structured Query Language). Access, FileMaker Pro, and Paradox can use SQL in the background, but this is not always obvious to the average user — like Dreamweaver, the visual interface of these programs hides the complexities of the code in the background. SQL is the standard database command language that performs all activities in a database, such as creating tables, displaying data, inserting data, or deleting (dropping) tables. Generally, when working with databases on the Web, you must learn to use SQL (in addition to PHP or other server-side language) so that you can display the products or correct an employee's name. However, in this lesson, you don't need to know how to use SQL to create the database, tables, and fields. It will be done using forms on your Web site. The SQL Manager function in the Site Administration area of your Control Panel is a Web form in which you can specify the name of the database you want to create.

Create a Database

There are several steps to creating a database. The first is to assign it a name, a username, and a password. The username and password prevents visitors from accessing your database and viewing data you don't want viewed, or worse, modifying or deleting data. If Web-hosting service expects the databases to be in high demand, the Web-server administrator can put the databases on another server (a database server). Therefore, you must also know the location of the database. This information is provided to you when you create your database.

1   **Open your browser and navigate to the Control-panel login page and, using your login name and password, log in in your Control panel.**

2   **Click the Manage SQL Databases link in the Site Manager group.**

FIGURE 8.29

3   Type `proj8` in the DataBase Name field and then type the same password in both
password fields.

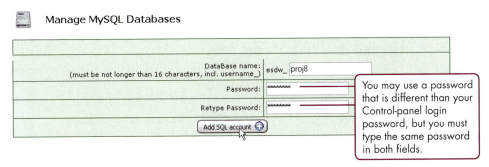

FIGURE 8.30

4   Click the Add SQL Account button at the bottom of the form.

5   From the table at the top of the page, record the full database name, your password, and the
database host name on a piece of paper.

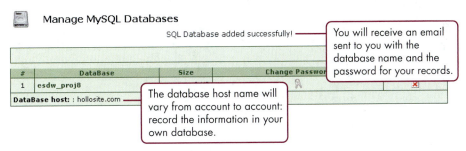

FIGURE 8.31

6   Keep your browser open to this page for the next exercise.

Create the Table and Set Up the Fields

After creating the database, the SQL Manager activates PHPMyAdmin, a very complex (in terms of the
programming) but very popular PHP application for managing databases. (This application is free. You can
download it from phpmyadmin.net and use it to create and maintain MySQL databases on your computer.)
Using this application, you create the tables and the fields.

1   Click the database name link in the top table.

#	DataBase	Size	Change Password	Delete
1	esdw_proj8	0 KB	𝓡	✖
DataBase host: : hollosite.com				

FIGURE 8.32

2 Type your username and password, then click the Login button.

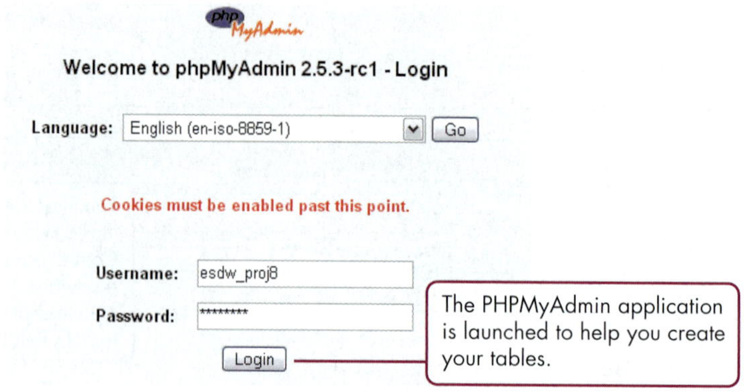

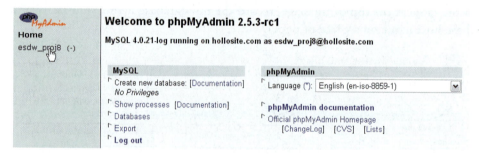

FIGURE 8.33

3 Under the Home link on the left side, click the name of your database (which is a link).

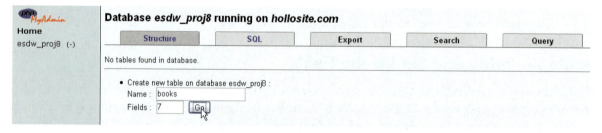

FIGURE 8.34

4 Type **books** in the Name field and **7** in the Fields field, and click Go.

FIGURE 8.35

5 In the first row, name the Field **book_id**, choose int from the Type list, choose auto_increment from the Extra list, and to the right, click the Primary radio button. Leave the Null field at not null.

6 In the second row, name the Field **title**, choose varchar from the Type list, type **100** in the Length/Values field, and choose null from the Null list.

7 In the third row, name the Field **pubyear**, choose year from the Type list, type **4** in the Length/Values field, and choose null from the Null list.

8   In the fourth row, name the Field `author`, choose varchar from the Type list, type **100** in the Length/Values field, and choose null from the Null list.

9   In the fifth row, name the Field `description`, choose varchar from the Type list, type **255** in the Length/Values field, and choose null from the Null list.

10   In the sixth row, name the Field `price`, choose decimal form the Type list, type **5,2** in the Length/Values field, and choose null from the Null list.

The length 5,2 means 5 numbers, 2 to the right of the decimal place. This allows a number up to 999.99.

11   In the seventh row, name the field `image`, choose varchar from the Type list, type **20** in the Length/Values field, and choose null from the Null list.

Database *esdw_proj8* - Table *books* running on *hollosite.com*

Field	Type [Documentation]	Length/Values*	Attributes	Null	Default**	Extra	
book_id	INT			not null		auto_increment	
title	VARCHAR	100		null			
pubyear	YEAR	4		null			
author	VARCHAR	100		null			
description	VARCHAR	255		null			
price	DECIMAL	5,2		null			
image	VARCHAR	20		null			

Setting Null to null means that you allow these fields to be blank. While this may not seem to make sense, if these fields were set to not null, you would have to create PHP form validation to catch any empty fields; otherwise, MySQL would reject the data entry.

FIGURE 8.36

12   Click Save but do not close your browser window.

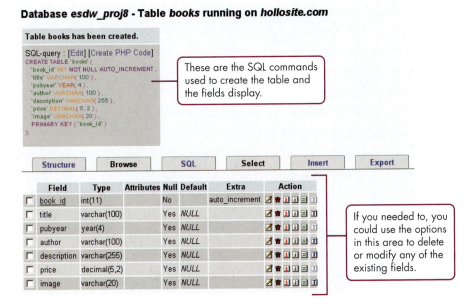

Database *esdw_proj8* - Table *books* running on *hollosite.com*

Table books has been created.

SQL-query : [Edit] [Create PHP Code]
```
CREATE TABLE `books` (
  `book_id` INT NOT NULL AUTO_INCREMENT ,
  `title` VARCHAR( 100 ) ,
  `pubyear` YEAR( 4 ) ,
  `author` VARCHAR( 100 ) ,
  `description` VARCHAR( 255 ) ,
  `price` DECIMAL( 5, 2 ) ,
  `image` VARCHAR( 20 ) ,
  PRIMARY KEY ( `book_id` )
);
```

These are the SQL commands used to create the table and the fields display.

	Structure	Browse	SQL	Select	Insert	Export

	Field	Type	Attributes	Null	Default	Extra	Action
☐	book_id	int(11)		No		auto_increment	
☐	title	varchar(100)		Yes	NULL		
☐	pubyear	year(4)		Yes	NULL		
☐	author	varchar(100)		Yes	NULL		
☐	description	varchar(255)		Yes	NULL		
☐	price	decimal(5,2)		Yes	NULL		
☐	image	varchar(20)		Yes	NULL		

If you needed to, you could use the options in this area to delete or modify any of the existing fields.

FIGURE 8.37

Add One Record to the Database

In this exercise, you add one record to the database to get you started. The description field is not wide enough to display all of the text. You need to scroll back and forth to verify your entry.

1 Click the Insert link near the top of the page.

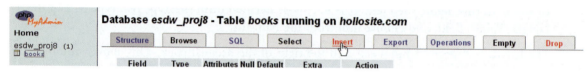

FIGURE 8.38

2 Do not enter anything in the book_id Value field, but type The Book of Bromeliads in the title Value field.

3 Press Tab and type 2002 in the pubyear Value field.

4 Press Tab and type Ronald W. Parkhurst in the author Value field.

5 Press Tab and type A stunningly beautiful, high quality, non technical coffee-table-style book with general information and over 650 outstanding large color identification photos. in the description Value field.

6 Press Tab and type 39.95 in the price Value field.

7 Press Tab and type book1.jpg in the image Value field.

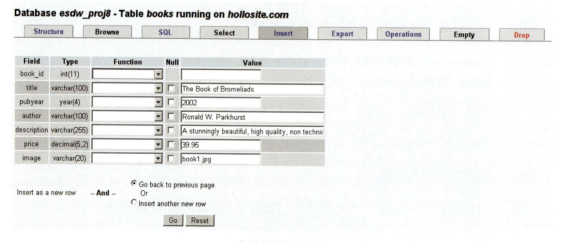

FIGURE 8.39

8   Leaving the radio button set to Go Back to Previous Page, click the Go button.

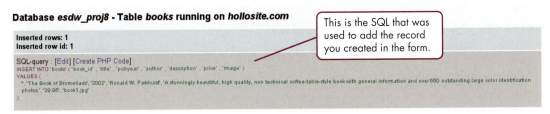

FIGURE 8.40

9   Click the Browse link to view the record you have entered.

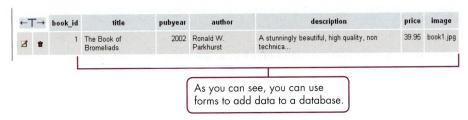

FIGURE 8.41

Use SQL to Add More Records to the Database

In this exercise, you add eight more records to the database but to simplify the procedure, you use SQL. You don't have to worry about creating the SQL (or, for this project, even understand the SQL); it is prepared for you. To insert the SQL, copy the SQL code from the books.sql.txt file into the SQL field of PHPMyAdmin and PHPMyAdmin executes the SQL. The books.sql.txt file contains an INSERT command that is very similar to what you saw in Step 8 of the preceding exercise except that it inserts several records at the same time.

1   In Dreamweaver, open books.sql.txt from the TO-P8 site.

2   Select all of the code in this file and copy it to the clipboard.

3   Close the file and switch to your browser.

4   Click the SQL link near the top of the page.

FIGURE 8.42

5 Delete any text (SQL commands) that exist in the large text field and paste the copied text into the field.

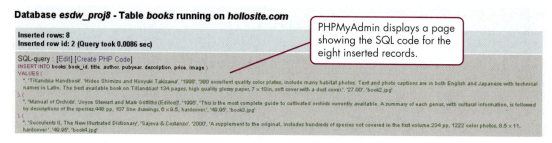

Database esdw_proj8 - Table books running on hollosite.com

| Structure | Browse | SQL | Select | Insert | Export | Operations | Empty | Drop |

Run SQL query/queries on database esdw_proj8 [Documentation]

Fields: book_id, title, pubyear, author

Insert

of Orchids', 'Pridgeon', '1992', 'A beautiful book that amateur and pro will like and find infinitely useful. 1,000 thousand color photos for easy identification and capsule information that is understandable to all.', '45.00', 'book8.jpg'), (', 'Agaves, Yuccas, and Related Plants: A Gardener\'s Guide', 'Irish & Irish', '2000', 'This new book outlines the gardening use of a wide variety of agaves and yuccas and some other related species. A must-have book for all those interested in this diverse ahd horticulturally important group of plants.', '49.95', 'book9.jpg'), (', 'Thai Orchid Species', 'Somsak', '1992', 'An extremely useful identification guide.', '27.50', 'book10.jpg');

☑ Show this query here again

Or Location of the textfile :

Browse...

Compression: ⦿ Autodetect ○ None ○ "gzipped" ○ "bzipped"

Go

FIGURE 8.43

6 Click the Go button.

Database esdw_proj8 - Table books running on hollosite.com

Inserted rows: 8
Inserted row id: 2 (Query took 0.0086 sec)

> PHPMyAdmin displays a page showing the SQL code for the eight inserted records.

SQL-query : [Edit] [Create PHP Code]
INSERT INTO books(book_id, title, author, pubyear, description, price, image)
VALUES (
'', 'Tillandsia Handbook', 'Hideo Shimizu and Hiroyuki Takizawa', '1998', '380 excellent quality color plates, include many habitat photos. Text and photo captions are in both English and Japanese with technical names in Latin. The best available book on Tillandsias! 134 pages, high quality glossy paper, 7 x 10in, soft cover with a dust cover.', '27.00', 'book2.jpg'
), (
'', 'Manual of Orchids', 'Joyce Stewart and Mark Griffiths (Editors)', '1995', 'This is the most complete guide to cultivated orchids currently available. A summary of each genus, with cultural information, is followed by descriptions of the species.448 pp, 107 line drawings, 6 x 9.5, hardcover.', '49.95', 'book3.jpg'
), (
'', 'Succulents II, The New Illustrated Dictionary', 'Sajeva & Costanzo', '2000', 'A supplement to the original, includes hundreds of species not covered in the first volume.234 pp, 1222 color photos, 8.5 x 11, hardcover.', '49.95', 'book4.jpg'

FIGURE 8.44

7 Click the Browse link to view the records.

←T→		book_id	title	pubyear	author	description	price	image
✎	🗑	1	The Book of Bromeliads	2002	Ronald W. Parkhurst	A stunningly beautiful, high quality, non technica...	39.95	book1.jpg
✎	🗑	2	Tillandsia Handbook	1998	Hideo Shimizu and Hiroyuki Takizawa	380 excellent quality color plates, include many h...	27.00	book2.jpg
✎	🗑	3	Manual of Orchids	1995	Joyce Stewart and Mark Griffiths (Editors)	This is the most complete guide to cultivated orch...	49.95	book3.jpg
✎	🗑	4	Succulents II, The New Illustrated Dictionary	2000	Sajeva & Costanzo	A supplement to the original, includes hundreds of...	49.95	book4.jpg
✎	🗑	5	Bromeliads, A Cultural Manual	1992	Rutka	This BSI handbook is a must for all beginners. A c...	3.50	book5.jpg

FIGURE 8.45

8 Close the browser window containing PHPMyAdmin.

9 In the Control-panel browser window, click the Logout link at the top right of the browser window.

10 Close your browser window.

To Extend Your Knowledge

OTHER SQL RESOURCES

In its Reference panel, Dreamweaver has the O'Reilly SQL Language reference, which is a great resource. Be aware, however, that if you are new to the language, it can be quite challenging to understand. Other resources for learning SQL include w3schools.com (not associated with the W3C) and sqlcourse.com.

LESSON 5   Displaying Records from a Database

Before you can display records from a database, your PHP code must connect to the database. This is one of the reasons you recorded the database information when the database was created. The other reason is to allow you to log in to PHPMyAdmin to manage your database. You need four pieces of information to connect to a database: username, password, database name, and database host. The connection takes two steps — one to connect the user to the database server, and the other to specify which database to use (even if you have only one). The first step uses the **mysql_connect()** function, which requires three parameters in the following order: host, username, and password. The second step specifies which database to use through the **mysql_select_db()** function.

The format of the **mysql_connect()** function is **$dbc = mysql_connect(host, username, password);**. Instead of **$dbc**, you can use any other variable name you like, but because the variable is storing the database connection information, dbc is an appropriate abbreviation. The selection of the database uses **mysql_select_db(database_name, $dbc)** — database_name is replaced with the actual name of the database and $dbc can be replaced with whatever variable name you used for the database connection.

In both cases, problems may occur with your Web-hosting account: the database server could be down, preventing you from connecting to it, or your database may be unavailable. We therefore recommend that you add error checking to the two previous functions. First of all, to prevent the MySQL error messages from displaying, you place the @ character before the two functions, such as **@mysql_connect** and **@mysql_select_db**. Secondly, you provide more meaningful error messages through the **die()** function. If either of the two functions fails, the database is unavailable and no queries can be run against the database. Therefore, you can use the **die()** function to cancel all other actions. Between the parentheses, you may add a comment, such as **die("The database server is unavailable.")**. Therefore, the database connection function becomes **$dbc = @mysql_connect(host, username, password) or die("The database server is unavailable.");**. A similar methodology is used with the **mysql_select_db** function.

Any PHP page that needs access to the database must use this connection information. In the lead-in to Lesson 2, we discussed the differences between **include()**, **include_once()**, **require()**, and **require_once()**. In Lesson 2, you used **include()** because the content in the include was not critical enough to require the **require()** function, nor did it really matter if the include was included more than once. However, when dealing with databases and database connections, we recommend that you use the **require_once()** method of including the connection information. The advantage of storing this information in an include is that you don't need to copy the connection information into every page that requires it, just the include code. Also, if your database connection information should change, all you need to do is change this one file and all pages that require access to the database will use the new information.

Create the Database Connection File

In this exercise, you create a PHP page (not an HTML page that you name with the .php extension). In this page, you insert only PHP code so the HTML code is unnecessary. You enter the database connection-information code into this page. Because each reader's host, username, and password are different, wherever you see host, username, or password in the following code, replace them with your own host, username, and password.

1   **Create a new Dynamic PHP page, switch to the Code view, and delete all of the HTML code.**

2   **Type `<?php` and press Enter/Return.**

3   **Type `$dbc = @mysql_connect("host", "username_proj8", "password") or die("The database server is unavailable.");` and press Enter/Return.**

Change "host", "username_proj8", and "password" to match your database settings. Keep the quotation marks around each parameter.

4   **Type `if (!@mysql_select_db("username_proj8", $dbc)) {` and press Enter/Return.**

Replace "username_proj8" with your database name.

5   **Type `die("The database is unavailable.");` and press Enter/Return.**

6   **Type `} else {` and press Enter/Return.**

7   **Type `echo "Connection established";` and press Enter/Return.**

8   **Type `}`, press Enter/Return and type `?>`.**

```
1  <?php
2  $dbc = @mysql_connect("hollosite.com", "esdw_proj8", "CaLlFOrnla") or die("The database server is unavailable.");
3  if(!@mysql_select_db("esdw_proj8", $dbc)) {
4      die("The database is unavailable.");
5  } else {
6      echo "Connection established";
7  }
8  ?>
```

The code in line 3 means that if the connection to username_proj8 database is not successful, then line 4 cancels any further processing and displays a message. If the connection is successful, the else clause runs and displays Connection established instead.

FIGURE 8.46

9   **Save the page as `db_connx.php` in the includes folder of your site, but leave it open.**

10   **Preview the page in your browser.**

Connection established

FIGURE 8.47

? **If you have problems**

If you see the error message stating that the database server is unavailable, check the code in line 2. If you see an error message stating that the database is unavailable, check the code in line 3. Be certain to replace host, username, and password in lines 2 and 3 with your own host, username, and password.

11   **Return to Dreamweaver and delete lines 5 and 6.**

```
1  <?php
2  $dbc = @mysql_connect("hollosite.com", "esdw_proj8", "cameroon") or die("The database server is unavailable.");
3  if(!@mysql_select_db("esdw_proj8", $dbc)) {
4     die("The database is unavailable.");
5  )
6  ?>
```

> Every connection should be successful from now on. You don't want that message in all of your Web pages, so it has been removed.

FIGURE 8.48

12   **Close db_connx.php, saving your changes, and then upload the changed file to the Web server.**

Query the Database

In this exercise, you use the database connection to display the list of books in the database. First, you need the db_connx.php file included in the page to connect you to the database. Second, you issue the SQL command to MySQL. Again, like the connection code, you add error-trapping code to display your own message when an error occurs. Finally, you loop through the results of the database query and display each record.

In this exercise, you use the SELECT command to identify records that meet the criteria. SQL commands are commonly written in all uppercase letters to clearly separate the commands from the field or table names. Following SELECT, you create a comma-separated list of the fields you want displayed. The next item is FROM to identify from which table the data is to be drawn. Therefore, the simplest SELECT command is **SELECT fieldname FROM tablename;**. All SQL commands must end with a semicolon.

Commonly, Web database developers store the SQL commands in a variable and then insert the variable into the **mysql_query()** function. It doesn't matter which method you use, but at times it is easier to debug any errors if the command is stored in a variable. In this exercise, you create a **$sql** variable and assign it with the SQL command. Then you run the command or query using the **mysql_query()** function and capture the results in the **$results** variable.

1   **Open books.php from the TO-P8 site and switch to the Design view.**

2   **Click to the right of the Books heading and press Enter/Return.**

3   From the Property inspector, insert an unordered list and type `title`.

FIGURE 8.49

4   Switch to the Code view, click to the left of the `<!DOCTYPE>` tag on line 1, and press Enter/Return.

5   Move the insertion point up to the blank line, type `<?php`, and press Enter/Return.

6   Type `require_once("includes/db_connx.php");` and press Enter/Return.

7   Type `$sql = "SELECT title FROM books;";` and press Enter/Return.

This code is so short that it doesn't really need to be assigned to a variable, but it is good practice to do so.

8   Type `$result = @mysql_query($sql) or die("Error performing query.");` and press Enter/Return.

The `mysql_query($sql)` code executes the SQL command and stores the results of the command in a variable called `$result`. If the SQL command should fail, the custom error message is displayed.

9   Type `?>`.

```
1  <?php
2  require_once("includes/db_connx.php");
3  $sql = "SELECT title FROM books;";
4  $result = @mysql_query($sql) or die("Error performing query.");
5  ?>
6  <!DOCTYPE HTML PUBLIC "-//W3C//DTD HTML 4.01 Transitional//EN">
7  <html>
8  <head>
```

FIGURE 8.50

10   Preview the page in your browser.

If you don't see the Error performing query message, it means that the query was successful, even though you don't see any results.

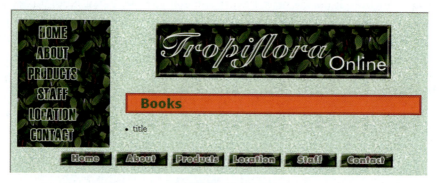

FIGURE 8.51

11   Return to Dreamweaver and leave books.php open for the next exercise.

Loop through the Results of the Query

As you know, there are nine books listed in the database. The **$result** variable has each returned record stored within it. This would be true whether one field (as in this lesson) or many fields, one record or many records were requested. Unlike the simple variables you used previously, the **$result** variable can contain a two-dimensional array. (An *array* is a collection of data, such as the title, author, year, and price for a single book. A *two-dimensional array* contains that data for multiple books. You could compare a one-dimensional array with a single database record and a two-dimensional array with multiple database records, all stored within one variable.)

To extract a row of data from the **$result** array, you use the **mysql_fetch_array($result)** function and assign the results to a variable. If you selected multiple fields with the SELECT command, **$row = mysql_fetch_array($result)** would assign an array of data to **$row**. In this exercise, only title is selected, so **$row** would contain just one piece of data. Even though a single piece of data in a variable does not make that variable an array, it is best to become accustomed to treating the **$row** variable as an array so that you can use the same code whether you have only one piece of data or many in **$row**. There are two ways you can access the data in **$row**: you can use the numerical index of the array or the name of the field. An array with four pieces of data is assigned data to the 0, 1, 2, and 3 indices (array indices always start at 0) such as **$row['0']**, **$row['1']**, **$row['2']**, and **$row['3']**. With only one piece of data in the array, you could access the data using **$row[0]**. However, it is much easier to use the field name as the array index, such as **$row['title']**. When you use a numerical index to access data in an array, you don't surround the number with quotes but if you use the associated name of the data to retrieve the data, it must be surrounded by either single or double quotation marks: most PHP developers use single quotes.

The next step is to loop through the rows of results. Although there are different types of loops in PHP, the **while** loop is simple to use and very appropriate for this type of situation. The format is:

```
while (condition) {

code goes here

}
```

The condition in this case is **$row = mysql_fetch_array($result)** which has two components. First. **$row** is assigned the next row of results. Second, while there are results, the expression is true, but after the last result, the expression is false. At that point, the **while** condition evaluates false and the **while** loop ends.

The code between the **{}** may be simple or complex, but for this exercise, it is quite simple. You create a simple unordered list of the titles of the books. You want every book title to appear between the opening and closing **<li>...</li>** tags, but you don't want to repeat the **<ul>** and **</ul>** tags. Therefore, the **<ul>** and **</ul>** tags are kept out of the while loop but the while loop generates the **<li>** tags along with the book title.

1   In the open file, books.php, locate the **<li>title</li>** code.

2   Click to the right of the **<ul>** tag above, press Enter/Return, and then type   <?php.

3   Click to the right of **</li>**, press Enter/Return, and type ?>.

FIGURE 8.52

4   Click to the right of **<?php**, press Enter/Return, and type `while ($row = mysql_fetch_array($result)) {`.

5   Change the **<li>** line to `echo "<li>" . $row['title'] . "</li>";` and press Enter/Return.

In this line, you echo the **<li>** and **</li>** tags, and you insert the book title from the current row of the result of the query between them. The while loop repeats this code until there are no more records in the result array variable.

6   Type **}**.

```
40      <ul>
41      <?php
42      while ($row = mysql_fetch_array($result)) {
43        echo "<li>" . $row['title'] . "</li>";
44        }
45      ?>
46      </ul></td>
```

FIGURE 8.53

7   Preview the page in your browser.

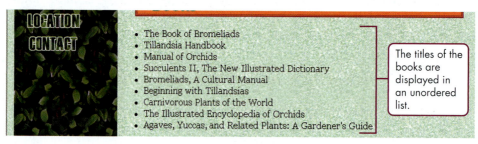

- The Book of Bromeliads
- Tillandsia Handbook
- Manual of Orchids
- Succulents II, The New Illustrated Dictionary
- Bromeliads, A Cultural Manual
- Beginning with Tillandsias
- Carnivorous Plants of the World
- The Illustrated Encyclopedia of Orchids
- Agaves, Yuccas, and Related Plants: A Gardener's Guide

The titles of the books are displayed in an unordered list.

FIGURE 8.54

8   Return to Dreamweaver and close books.php.

To Extend Your Knowledge

WHY YOU SHOULD NOT USE *

In a SELECT query, you may use the * to select all fields such as **SELECT * FROM books**. However, you must remember that the first field in your books table is the book_id number. The book_id number would make no sense to a visitor. It also means that your **$result** variable (or whatever you choose to name it) contains data that you will not use. Furthermore, when you use the * selector, the fields are gathered in the order in which the fields were created. If you create the fields out of order (it really doesn't matter to the database), then you may expect **$row['3']** to contain author data but, instead, it contains pubyear data.

It is best to name the fields in the SELECT query; this allows you to specify which fields to collect data from. If you want to select multiple fields, you must separate the fields with a comma, such as **SELECT pubyear, title, price FROM books**.

LESSON 6   Inserting a Record into a Database

Databases are great for storing data and you have seen how you may query the database to display the data in the database. However, you must also be able to insert new data into the database. You have already seen how you can use forms to insert data into a database, such as the forms in PHPMyAdmin. You also saw the details of the INSERT command in PHPMyAdmin. In this lesson, you create the SQL and PHP to insert a new book into the database.

The format of the INSERT command is **INSERT INTO tablename SET fieldname=fielddata, fieldname=fielddata, …;**. In the case of this database, as with many, the book_id field is an auto_increment field: it is not part of the INSERT command but MySQL knows to increment it automatically. Given that we have set all fields, excepting book_id, to allow null, which means that you are allowed to enter nothing into a null field, in any INSERTs we place into this database, it does not matter if a field has no data because the structure of the books table allows it. If you set any or all fields to not null, then you have two options. either you need to use form validation to ensure that the not null fields have data or you can employ a MySQL field option to provide a default value if the collected data is null, such as "No description is available" for the description field.

As you may recall, the SQL command is surrounded by quotation marks, too, such as **$sql = "INSERT … title="$title";"**, which means that the quotation mark to the left of **$title** would end the quoted block. There are two solutions to this problem. One solution is to escape the double quotes using the backslash (\), which is a special character that tells PHP to treat the following character literally (as a quotation mark, not as the end of a quoted snippet of code). Therefore, you would write **$sql = "INSERT … title=\"$title\";"**. The other is to use single quotes as in **$sql = "INSERT … title='$title';"**. However, in situations where quote characters may be part of the data, such as a book title that has a single quote character in it, like **Bob's Book on Succulents**, the single quote in the title would cause a problem. For that reason, you may want to use double quotes all of the time around the SQL command and escape any nested double quotes.

Capture the Post Data

In this exercise, you create the PHP code to gather the post variables from the form.

1   Open new_book.php in Dreamweaver in the Design view and examine the form.

2   Close new_book.php and open insert_book.php.

3   Click to the right of the heading New Book Inserted, press Enter/Return, and type `message`.

4   Press Enter/Return, type `View all books`, and link the word books to books.php.

5   Switch to the Code view, delete the word `message` (don't delete the <p> and </p> tags), and press Enter/Return twice.

   If you are not comfortable working with HTML, it is useful to type text that you can find easily in the code.

6   Move the insertion point up to the blank line, type `<?php`, and press Enter/Return.

7   Type `if (isset($_POST['title'])) {`, press Enter/Return, type `$title = $_POST['title'];`, press Enter/Return, type `} else {`, press Enter/Return, type `$title = "";`, press Enter/Return, type `}`, and type `>?`.

This code means that if there is content for the title, assign it to the $title variable, otherwise assign nothing to the $title variable. When you assign nothing to a variable, the variable exists even though it is empty. Later on in the code, we need to use the contents of $title, and if the $title variable did not exist, an error message would appear.

```
49      <p>
50      <?php
51      if (isset($_POST['title'])) {
52          $title = $_POST['title'];
53      } else {
54          $title = "";
55      }
```

FIGURE 8.55

8   Repeat Step 7 five more times, changing all four occurrences of title in each block to author, year, description, price, and image.

9   Save the changes but leave insert_book.php open.

Create the INSERT SQL Command

In this exercise, you add the code to connect to the database. You also create the INSERT SQL command and assign it to the $sql variable. The format of the INSERT command is **INSERT INTO tablename SET fieldname="data";**, where **fieldname="data"** may be repeated as many times as necessary. If your database has an auto_increment field, you may omit it from the list because it will be incremented automatically.

1   In the open file, insert_book.php and press Enter/Return after the last }.

2   Type `require_once("includes/db_connx.php");` and press Enter/Return.

3   Type `$sql = "INSERT INTO books SET title=\"$title\", author=\"$author\", pubyear=\"$pubyear\", description=\"$description\", price=\"$price\", image=\"$image\";";`.

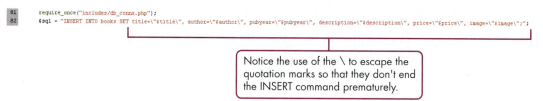

```
81   require_once("includes/db_connx.php");
82   $sql = "INSERT INTO books SET title=\"$title\", author=\"$author\", pubyear=\"$pubyear\", description=\"$description\", price=\"$price\", image=\"$image\";";
```

Notice the use of the \ to escape the quotation marks so that they don't end the INSERT command prematurely.

FIGURE 8.56

4   Save the changes but leave insert_book.php open.

Add the mysql_query() Function

In this exercise, you create the code to execute the SQL command using the **mysql_query()** function, in which you use an if clause to display a message stating whether or not the insert was successful. The if is written as **if (mysql_query($sql))** which accomplishes two purposes. The **mysql_query($sql)** function runs the SQL code stored in the **$sql** variable. If the execution is successful, **mysql_query($sql)** returns a true value, which results in **if (true)** and the code immediately following is executed. If the SQL execution is unsuccessful, then the if condition results in **if (false)** and the code in the **else** clause (if it exists) is run. This is a very efficient method of both running code and checking to see if it has run successfully at the same time.

1   In the open file, insert_book.php, at the end of the $sql assignment line, and press Enter/Return.

2   Type **if (@mysql_query($sql)) {**, press Enter/Return, type **echo "Your new book has been added to the database.";**, press Enter/Return, type **} else {**, press Enter/Return, type **echo "Error adding new book.";**, press Enter/Return, and type **}**.

```
83    if (@mysql_query($sql)) {
84      echo "Your new book has been added to the database.";
85      } else {
86      echo "Error adding new book.";
87    }
```

FIGURE 8.57

3   Close insert_book.php , saving your changes, and upload it to the server.

Test the Insert Form

In this exercise, you enter new book data into the form and observe the Your new book has been added message when the insert is successful. You also go to the books.php page and see that the new book has been added to the listing.

1   Open new_book.php in Dreamweaver and preview the page in your browser.

2   In the Title field type **Thai Orchid Species**.

3   In the Author field type **Somsak**.

4   In the Year field type **1992**.

5   In the Description field type **An extremely useful identification guide.**.

6   In the Price field type **27.50**.

7   In the Image field type `book10.jpg`.

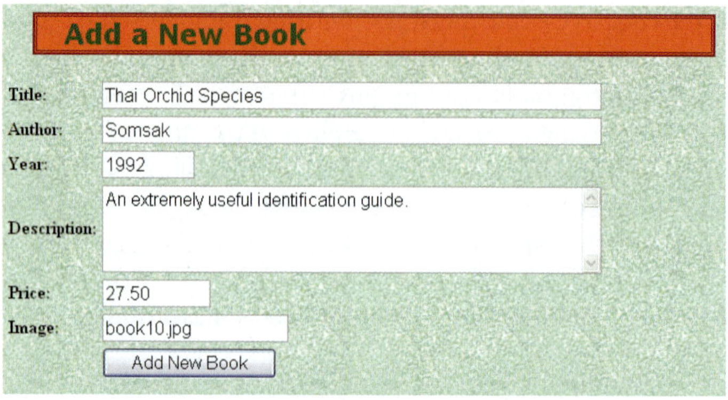

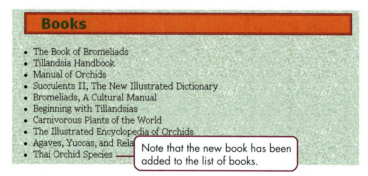

FIGURE 8.58

8   Click Add New Book.

9   Click the link to books.php.

FIGURE 8.59

To Extend Your Knowledge

DIFFERENT INSERT FORMATS

There are two formats of the INSERT command. The SQL command, employed by PHPMyAdmin to insert the eight additional books, used the format `INSERT INTO tablename (field1, field2, field3, …) VALUES ("data1", "data2", "data3", …);`. In this lesson, you use a slightly different format: `INSERT INTO tablename SET field1="data1", field2="data2", field3="data3", …;`. Either format may be used to insert a single record, but only the first format may be used to insert multiple records at the same time. You can use the second format to insert multiple records, but only if you repeat it for each record.

The first format is also a little more difficult to work with in that you must remember to list the data in the same order as the fields or you record the data into the wrong field. The second format is easier because the field name and data are paired with each other. In either case, it doesn't matter in what order the data are inserted. You don't need to insert the data in the same order that the fields were created in the table — as they are listed in PHPMyAdmin.

LESSON 7 Selecting and Sorting Database Records

In the exercises so far, you have learned to use the SELECT command but you have not selected specific records, just all of them. The records (books) are listed in the same order in which they were added, but you may want to change the order, such as making it alphabetical by author or title, or sorted by year or price. These options, too, are available using the SELECT command.

To select specific records, you use the WHERE clause, which always follows SELECT/FROM. There are many different conditions you may place in the WHERE clause. The most common condition uses the equality operator (=), such as `title="Tillandsia Handbook"` or `book_id="3"`. The condition is only true if the comparison is exact, including letter case, because "tillandsia handbook" does not equal "Tillandsia Handbook". A similar comparison uses the LIKE operator, which has the added benefit of allowing wildcards. For example, `title LIKE "till%"` would return the book with the title "Tillandsia Handbook" and "tillandsia handbook". The LIKE operator is not case sensitive so `"Till" LIKE "till"` is true. In many computer applications the * is used as a wildcard, but the `%` is its equivalent in SQL.

Another condition that may be placed in a WHERE clause is the BETWEEN/AND operator, such as year `pubyear BETWEEN 1998 AND 2000`. The BETWEEN/AND operator is inclusive — in the previous example, any books published in 1998, 1999, and 2000 would be selected using this condition. When using the BETWEEN/AND condition, you must state the number in ascending order: `pubyear BETWEEN 2000 AND 1998` returns no results. Other operators for numerical data include `pubyear<1995`, `pubyear>2000`, `price<=29.95`, and `price>=39.95`. You may combine conditions, such as `WHERE pubyear BETWEEN 1995 AND 2000 AND price<30`.

You cannot easily sort the results of a database query in PHP. It is much easier to get the database to sort the result of a query so that the `$result` variable in PHP contains sorted results. The sorting command is ORDER BY and must appear after WHERE (if it is used). Using ORDER BY is very simple — you simply identify the field name you want the data to be sorted by, such as `ORDER BY pubyear`. By default, sorting is in ascending order. You can reverse this by adding DESC (descending), such as `ORDER BY pubyear DESC`. You can sort by multiple fields, such as `ORDER BY pubyear, title`, which sorts by titles within sorted years.

Select Records Using WHERE Conditions

In this exercise, you modify the query in the books.php page to select books by year.

1   **Open books.php, switch to the Code view, and scroll to line 3 containing the $sql assignment.**

2   **Change SELECT title to** `SELECT title, pubyear`.

3   **In line 43, change the echo line, as follows, to insert the year surrounded by parentheses:**

```
echo "<li>" . $row["title"] . " (" . $row["pubyear"] . ")</li>";
```

```
41    <?php
42    while ($row = mysql_fetch_array($result)) {
43        echo "<li>" . $row["title"] . " (" . $row["pubyear"] . ")</li>";
44    }
45    ?>
```

FIGURE 8.60

4 Preview the page in your browser.

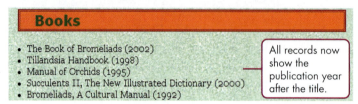

Books

- The Book of Bromeliads (2002)
- Tillandsia Handbook (1998)
- Manual of Orchids (1995)
- Succulents II, The New Illustrated Dictionary (2000)
- Bromeliads, A Cultural Manual (1992)

> All records now show the publication year after the title.

FIGURE 8.61

5 Return to Dreamweaver and go to line 3.

6 After books, type WHERE pubyear=2000.

```php
1 <?php
2 require_once("includes/db_connx.php");
3 $sql = "SELECT title, pubyear FROM books WHERE pubyear=2000";
4 $result = @mysql_query($sql) or die("Error performing query.");
5 ?>
```

FIGURE 8.62

7 Preview the page in your browser.

Books

- Succulents II, The New Illustrated Dictionary (2000)
- Agaves, Yuccas, and Related Plants: A Gardener's Guide (2000)

> Only two records meet the criteria of the query.

FIGURE 8.63

8 Return to Dreamweaver and go to line 3.

9 After 2000, press the Spacebar and type AND title LIKE \"%plants%\".

```php
1 <?php
2 require_once("includes/db_connx.php");
3 $sql = "SELECT title, pubyear FROM books WHERE pubyear=2000 AND title LIKE \"%plants%\"";
4 $result = @mysql_query($sql) or die("Error performing query.");
5 ?>
```

> The % both before and after plants means that plants can be anywhere within the title.

FIGURE 8.64

10 Preview the page in your browser.

Books

- Agaves, Yuccas, and Related Plants: A Gardener's Guide (2000)

> Only one record meets the criteria of the query.

FIGURE 8.65

11 Return to Dreamweaver, but keep books.php open for the next exercise.

Sorting Records Using the ORDER BY Clause

In this exercise, you sort records using the ORDER BY clause. You also learn to combine the ORDER BY clause with the WHERE clause. Remember to insert the WHERE clause before the ORDER BY clause.

1 In the open file, books.php, go to line 3 and delete `WHERE pubyear=2000 AND title LIKE \"%plants%\"`.

2 After FROM books, if necessary, press the Spacebar and then type `ORDER BY pubyear`.

3 Preview the page in your browser.

Books

- Bromeliads, A Cultural Manual (1992)
- The Illustrated Encyclopedia of Orchids (1992)
- Thai Orchid Species (1992)
- Manual of Orchids (1995)

All books are displayed from earliest to latest publication years: the default sort order is ascending.

FIGURE 8.66

4 Return to Dreamweaver.

5 After `ORDER BY pubyear`, press the Spacebar and type `DESC`.

6 Review the page in your browser.

Books

- The Book of Bromeliads (2002)
- Beginning with Tillandsias (2001)
- Succulents II, The New Illustrated Dictionary (2000)
- Agaves, Yuccas, and Related Plants: A Gardener's Guide (2000)
- Tillandsia Handbook (1998)

All books are displayed from most recent to earliest.

FIGURE 8.67

7 Return to Dreamweaver.

8 Before the ORDER BY clause, type `WHERE pubyear>1995`.

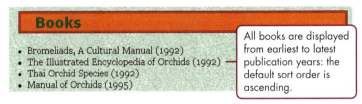

```php
1  <?php
2  require_once("includes/db_connx.php");
3  $sql = "SELECT title, pubyear FROM books WHERE pubyear>1995 ORDER BY pubyear DESC";
4  $result = @mysql_query($sql) or die("Error performing query.");
5  ?>
```

FIGURE 8.68

9   Preview the page in your browser.

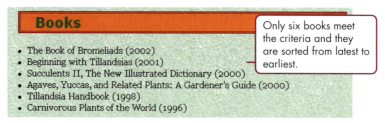

FIGURE 8.69

10   Return to Dreamweaver and close books.php.

To Extend Your Knowledge

DREAMWEAVER'S VISUAL INTERFACE TO MYSQL

Much of what you have learned to do by interacting with the MySQL database using PHP code could be done using functions from the Application Insert bar. However, using these functions depends on you having remote access to the database server, which 100webspace.com does not allow but some other Web-hosting providers do. We found the connection between Dreamweaver and 100web-space.com was irregular, at best, and some functions never worked for us, very possibly the result of disabled remote access.

If you have the opportunity to work with a database server either set up for you in class or installed on your computer, you may want to explore the options available through the Application Insert bar.

SUMMARY

In this project, you learned how to set up your site definition so that you can test your pages on a remote server. You learned to create Dynamic PHP pages using the New Document dialog box. You discovered how to create PHP tags and insert PHP code. You learned about strings, numerals, and variables, and how to concatenate strings and variables. You learned how to capture data sent from forms that use either the get or post method. You learned about includes and how they may be helpful to the maintenance of a Web site. You created a database and a table using PHPMyAdmin on your Web site. You learned how to use PHP to connect a PHP page to your database. You learned to use the SELECT command to get data from your database and you used PHP to insert the collected data between HTML tags. You also learned how to use the INSERT command to insert data into the database from data entered into a form.

C A R E E R S   I N   D E S I G N

WORKING AS A FREELANCE WEB DESIGNER

Web and graphic design are two professions that provide many freelance opportunities, and many people are attracted to the opportunities of working at home or in a small office space of their own. It is quite humorous to read some of the anecdotes of a freelancer whose day starts off with a coffee, a shower, and getting dressed in their work clothes (and fuzzy slippers). For Noah, it gives him an opportunity to spend time with his toddler daughter. For Terry, she can work through the night, as she prefers. There are many reasons why people like to work on their own, whether it be in a home office or in a small, rented office space, but you must remember that your work is your income and you must treat it with respect so that your clients will treat you with respect, as well.

There are many resources in your community that you may call upon for assistance, such as the Chamber of Commerce. In addition to meeting other members and perhaps expanding your client-base — which seems to be why many members join such groups — these types of organizations can provide you with contacts for other business members who may give you advice on managing your business, such as accounting, time management, client relations, and many other functions that a larger business would handle through the use of specialized personnel in different departments.

There also are many resources on the Internet that can help freelancers. Creativepublic.com is a site that specializes in providing supportive information for freelancers, including the design of a home-office. Brendon Sinclair is a regular contributor to sitepoint.com and has created a large book package (two binders plus CD-ROM) called *The Web Design Business Kit* (sitepoint.com/books/freelance1/) to assist freelance Web designers with many aspects of business management. Freelance work can be very enjoyable, but without a support system that you would normally find within a business organization, you must seek the support on your own.

KEY TERMS

array	includes	SELECT FROM
ASP	INSERT INTO	server-side
ASP.Net	JSP	SQL
auto_increment	LIKE	SQL Server
BETWEEN AND	MySQL	string
Coldfusion	numeral	table
concatenate	ORDER BY	testing server
data type	PHP	two-dimensional array
database	PHP tag	variable
dynamic pages	PostgreSQL	WHERE AND
field	query	
Firebird	record	

CHECKING CONCEPTS AND TERMS

SCREEN ID

Identify the indicated areas from the list below:

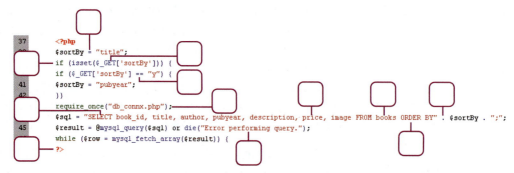

```
37    <?php
      $sortBy = "title";
      if (isset($_GET['sortBy'])) {
      if ($_GET['sortBy'] == "y") {
41    $sortBy = "pubyear";
42    }}
      require_once("db_connx.php");
      $sql = "SELECT book_id, title, author, pubyear, description, price, image FROM books ORDER BY" . $sortBy . ";";
45    $result = @mysql_query($sql) or die("Error performing query.");
      while ($row = mysql_fetch_array($result)) {
      ?>
```

FIGURE 8.70

a. Sort clause

b. Comparison of equality

c. Concatenation operator

d. Variable assignment

e. SQL command

f. Capture data from query string

g. Include a file

h. Table name

i. Message if query fails

j. Field name

k. If clause

l. Closing PHP tag

MULTIPLE CHOICE

Circle the letter of the correct answer for each of the following:

1. Which is not a programming language?

   a. PHP

   b. JavaScript

   c. ASP.Net

   d. None of the above

2. Which PHP code would you use to capture data sent via the query string of a URL?

   a. `Request.QueryString`

   b. `mysql_querystring()`

   c. `$_GET[]`

   d. All of the above

3. Which concatenation would fail?

   a. `"t-" . "shirt"`

   b. `"A" . 1`

   c. `2 + 5`

   d. None of the above

4. If $firstName has been assigned "Bob", which of the following would display Hello Bob in the Web page?

   a. `<?php echo "Hello" . $firstName; ?>`

   b. `<p>Hello <?php echo $firstName; ?></p>`

   c. `<?php echo "<p>" . $firstName . "</p>"; ?>`

   d. All of the above

5. If you want to include a file containing non-critical code that may be used multiple times, you would use _____.

a. `require_once()`

b. `include()`

c. `include_once()`

d. `require()`

6. A database contains collections of similar data known as _____.

a. fields

b. tables

c. records

d. rows

7. In the following block of code, which of the following options would display We have a winner!?

```
if ($condition) {
        echo "We have a winner!";
} else {
        echo "Sorry, try again!";
}
```

a. `$condition = 1 == 1;`

b. `$condition = "We have a winner!";`

c. `$condition = !(2<=3);`

d. All of the above

8. In order to display the full name of a client using `echo $row['firstName'] . " " . $row['lastName'];`, which SELECT command would provide the necessary data?

a. `SELECT lastName, firstName, client_id FROM clients`

b. `SELECT firstName, lastName FROM clients WHERE clientType="corporate"`

c. `SELECT client_id, clientType, firstName, lastName FROM clients ORDER BY client_id`

d. All of the above

9. Given the following results, which sorting method was used?

```
Brown, James, 1930
Brown, Sarah, 1932
Dolson, Carmen, 1929
Green, Jeff, 1931
```

a. `WHERE lastName<"H"`

b. `ORDER BY lastName, birthYear DESC`

c. `ORDER BY birthYear ASC, lastName DESC`

d. None of the above

10. In an order form in which visitors are to type the quantity (number) of products they want to purchase, if you want to prevent a nonnumeric entry (such as "dozen"), which components could you set to prevent invalid entries?

a. JavaScript

b. PHP

c. MySQL

d. All of the above

DISCUSSION QUESTIONS

1. It is easy to use databases to store very strictly defined data, such as name and phone number. Although the database field type varchar is limited to 255 characters, the text field type allows up to 65,535 characters, more than enough to store the HTML code of most Web pages. Even though you can store the highly variable content of a Web page within a database text field, what challenges would this present for the creation and maintenance of Web pages? Assume that the actual images, not the <img> tags that call them, are not stored in the database.

2. Large Web sites often have a database in the background to store the content of the pages and a Web programming language, such as PHP, to extract the appropriate data and display it in the pages. Does the fact that a database-driven Web site, which uses just a few page templates into which different content is inserted from the database, diminish the role of the Web designer? State your position with reasons.

SKILL DRILL

Skill Drills reinforce project skills. Each skill reinforced is the same, or nearly the same, as a skill presented in the lessons. Detailed instructions are provided in a step-by-step format. Work through these exercises in order.

1. Displaying Data in a Table

In this Skill Drill, you use a table to format the data available for a particular book. So far, you have created a simple list containing only the title and year of publication. In this exercise, you use almost all of the book data stored in the database, except the book_id field, and format it in cells of a table. A template table has been prepared for you. Your task is to incorporate the PHP and SQL code into the table code so that the table displays all of the data available for the books.

1. Open books2.php in the Design view, choose File>Save As, and name it **books.php**, overwriting the existing file.

   Notice that an image placeholder has been created to indicate the position of the book image and that text has been inserted into table cells, indicating where the data from the database will be inserted.

2. Click in the table, switch to the Code view, and locate the opening **<table>** tag for this nested table (approximately line 36).

3. On the following line, insert the opening PHP tag and the include code for the database connection by typing **<?php**, press Enter/Return, type **require_once("includes/db_connx.php");**, and press Enter/Return.

4. Type **$sql = "SELECT title, author, pubyear, description, price, image FROM books";**, press Enter/Return, type **$result = @mysql_query($sql) or die("Error performing query.");**, and press Enter/Return.

5. Type **while ($row = mysql_fetch_array($result)) {**, press Enter/Return, and type **?>**.

6. Scroll down to approximately line 56, the blank line between the **<tr>** and **</table>** tags, and type **<?php } ?>**.

    The while loop occurs within the table, which means that all of the books will be listed in one table, not one table per book.

7. Scroll up to line 44 with the **<img>** tag, and between the two quotation marks of **src=""**, type **<?php echo "books/" . $row['image']; ?>**, resulting in **src=" <?php echo "books/" . $row['image']; ?>"**. Remove the **width** and **height** attributes, as they vary from image to image.

8. On the next line, replace the word title with **<?php echo $row['title']; ?>**.

9. Locate the words pubyear, author, description, and price and, using the same pattern as in Step 8, replace these placeholder words with the PHP code to display their data collected from the database.

10. Concatenate the dollar sign in front of the price by typing **"$" .** to the left of $row.

```
36    <table align="center" cellpadding="2" cellspacing="0">
37    <?php
38    require_once("includes/db_connx.php");
39    $sql = "SELECT title, author, pubyear, description, price, image FROM books";
40    $result = @mysql_query($sql) or die("Error performing query.");
41    while ($row = mysql_fetch_array($result)) {
42    ?>
43      <tr>
44        <td rowspan="4"><img name="cover_image" src="<?php echo "books/" . $row['image']; ?>" alt=""></td>
45        <td><strong><?php echo $row['title']; ?> (<?php echo $row['pubyear']; ?>) </strong></td>
46      </tr>
47      <tr>
48        <td><?php echo $row['author']; ?></td>
49      </tr>
50      <tr>
51        <td><?php echo $row['description']; ?></td>
52      </tr>
53      <tr>
54        <td><?php echo "$" . $row['price']; ?></td>
55      </tr>
56      <?php } ?>
57    </table>
```

FIGURE 8.71

11. Preview the page in your browser.

12. Close your browser, return to Dreamweaver and close books.php.

2. Create and Populate a New Field in the Database Table

In this exercise, you add to the database table and populate a new field. This field is named category and will contain su, ti, br, or, or ot, which are abbreviations of succulents, tillandsias, bromeliads, orchids, and other. This field identifies the category of the book according to the type of plant for which it was written. (This category is used in the next Skill Drill.)

1. Open your browser and log in to the Control panel of your site.

2. Click the PHPMy Admin link in the Site Manager group, click the link to your database in the next page, then log in to the PHPMyAdmin application.

3. In the PHPMyAdmin application, click the books link under your database name at the top left.

4. In the main part of the page, below a horizontal line, set Add New Field to **1** and At End of Table, and click Go.

5. Type **category** under Field, choose CHAR from the Type list, type **2** under Length/Values, type **ot** under Default, and click Save.

6. Click the Browse link at the top of the page.

7. Click the edit icon in the left column of the top row of the table, change the category from **ot** to **br**, and click Go.

   In the area near the top of the page, note the new SQL command, UPDATE, that specifies which field to update, the new value of the field. The UPDATE command uses book_id to identify to which record to apply the update.

8. Repeat Step 7 changing the rest of the categories to **ti**, **or**, **su**, **br**, **ti**, **ot** (leave the Carnivorous Plants book unchanged), **or**, **su**, and **or**.

9. Close your browser window.

3. Create Book Lists According to Category

In this Skill Drill, you create lists of books in the bromeliads.php, succulents.php, and tillandsias.php pages that only display the books for that category of plants.

1. Open bromeliads.php and preview it in your browser.

   At the bottom of the page is the list of books but, despite the heading above it, the list contains more books than just those about bromeliads.

2. Return to Dreamweaver, switch to the Code view, and scroll down to line 46 with the SELECT command.

3. Click between **books** and the ", press Spacebar, and type **WHERE category=\"br\"**.

4. Preview the page in your browser.

   Only books about bromeliads appear.

5. To prepare this block of PHP code for reuse in the tillandsia.php and succulents.php pages, you store the category in a variable. Replace **\"br\"** with **\"" . $category . "\"**.

6. Click to the right of **<?php** on line 44, press Enter/Return, and type **$category = "br";**.

7. Select lines 44 to 52 inclusive, the complete PHP block, and copy it to the clipboard. Create a new Dynamic PHP page, select all of the code, delete it and paste in the copied code from the clipboard. Delete line 2 containing the **$category = "br";** code. Close, saving the file as **booklist.inc.php** in the includes folder, and then upload it to the server.

```
1   <?php
2   require_once("includes/db_connx.php");
3   $sql = "SELECT title FROM books WHERE category=\"" . $category . "\"";
4   $result = @mysql_query($sql) or die("Error performing query.");
5   while ($row = mysql_fetch_array($result)) {
6   echo "<li>" . $row['title'] . "</li>";
7   }
8   ?>
```

FIGURE 8.72

8. In bromeliads.php, delete lines 46 to 51. Click to the right of **"br";** on line 45, press Enter/Return, and type **require_once("includes/booklist.inc.php");**.

```
43    <ul>
44    <?php
45    $category = "br";
46    require_once("includes/booklist.inc.php");
47    ?>
48    </ul>
```

FIGURE 8.73

9. Select lines 44 to 47 inclusive and copy them to the clipboard. Close bromeliads.php, saving your changes.

10. Open tillandsias.php, scroll down to line 47, select the line, delete it, and paste the copied code. In line 48, replace **"br"** with **"ti"**. Close, saving the changes.

11. Open succulents.php, and repeat Step 10 except that you replace **"br"** with **"su"**.

12. One by one, open tillandsias.php and succulents.php, and preview them in your browser.

Note that each page displays only related books at the bottom of the page.

4. Create Links from Book Titles to Book Details

In this Skill Drill exercise, you enhance the listing of books on the Bromeliads, Tillandsias, and Succulents pages by making the title of the book a link to the specific book on the books.php page. There are only two snippets of code that need changing: the books.inc.php include, to insert the link, and the books.php page, to create anchors so the link from the title takes the visitor directly to the book of interest. This is a very elegant example of how, with relatively little effort, PHP and MySQL may be used to improve the usability of a Web site. Furthermore, if you add any more books to the database, you don't have to make any changes — the code just accommodates the new books as they are added.

1. Open books.php in the Code view.

2. On line 39 to the left of title in the SELECT list, type **book_id,** and press the Spacebar.

   The book_id will be used in the anchor link to identify the specific book.

3. On line 45, between the **<td>** and **<strong>** tags, type **<a name="book<?php echo $row['book_id']; ?>"></a>**.

   This code creates anchors for each book in the format of book# where the PHP code inserts the book_id number in place of the #. This is an example of how book_id may be used very simply to identify a particular book.

```
39    $sql = "SELECT book_id, title, author, pubyear, description, price, image FROM books";
40    $result = @mysql_query($sql) or die("Error performing query.");
41    while ($row = mysql_fetch_array($result)) {
42    ?>
43    <tr>
44      <td rowspan="4"><img name="cover_image" src="<?php echo "books/" . $row['image']; ?>" alt=""></td>
45      <td><a name="book<?php echo $row['book_id']; ?>"></a><strong><?php echo $row['title']; ?> (<?php echo $row['pubyear']; ?>) </strong></td>
```

FIGURE 8.74

4. Close books.php, saving your changes.

5. Open booklist.inc.php from the includes folder.

6. On line 3 to the left of title in the SELECT list, type **book_id,** and press the Spacebar.

7. On line 6, after **<li>**, type **<a href=\"books.php#book" . $row['book_id'] . "\">**. Near the end of line 6 between " and **</li>**, type **</a>**.

```
1    <?php
2    require_once("includes/db_connx.php");
3    $sql = "SELECT book_id, title FROM books WHERE category=\"" . $category . "\"";
4    $result = @mysql_query($sql) or die("Error performing query.");
5    while ($row = mysql_fetch_array($result)) {
6    echo "<li><a href=\"books.php#book" . $row['book_id'] . "\">" . $row['title'] . "</a></li>";
7    }
8    ?>
```

FIGURE 8.75

8. Close booklist.inc.php, saving your changes.

9. Upload booklist.inc.php to the server.

10. Open bromeliads.php and preview the page in your browser. Click any of the book links.

    The links take you to the specific book in the books page, and all of the books functionality is dynamic through the use of PHP and MySQL.

11. Close your browser and close all open files from Dreamweaver.

CHALLENGE

Challenge exercises expand on, or are somewhat related to, skills presented in the lessons. Each exercise provides a brief introduction, followed by instructions in a numbered-step format that are not as detailed as those in the Skill Drill exercises. Work through the exercises in order.

1. Generate a List from the Database

This is the first of three Challenge exercises that work towards a creating a system whereby an existing record may be changed. To insert a new record, you need two components: the form in which you may enter the data and the PHP script that captures the post variables and inserts the new record into the database. A system to modify an existing record requires three components: a means to choose which record to modify, a form that has been prefilled with the existing data, and a script that takes the revised form data and updates the record in the database.

In this Challenge exercise, you create a PHP script that populates a select list with the titles of the books in the database. Much like the last Skill Drill exercise in which the book_id data was used to match a link with a destination, the book_id data will be used to identify the record selected for modification. As you learned in the lessons, if you have two or more records that have the same data, the numerical id is the only means to isolate one from the others.

1. Open select_book.php in the Code view and scroll to line 37.

   Note that the name assigned to the select list is bookNumber. This is important to the next step.

2. In line 38, click to the right of **</option>**, press Enter/Return, type **<?php**, press Enter/Return twice, and type **?>**.

3. Move up to the empty line, type **require_once("includes/db_connx.php");**, and press Enter/Return.

   This is the standard method you have been using to connect to a database.

4. Type **$sql = "SELECT book_id, title FROM books";** and press Enter/Return.

   You need both the title and the book_id from the database so that you may choose which book to edit from its title. The book_id is also used in the SELECT command when querying the database for the details of the selected book.

5. Type **$result = @mysql_query($sql) or die("Error performing query.");** and press Enter/Return.

   This is the standard method you have been using to collect the data from the database.

6. In this next step, you create the while loop to create **<option>** tags in the form **<option value="book_id">title</option>**. Type **while ($row = mysql_fetch_array($result)) {**, press Enter/Return, type **echo "<option value=\"" . $row['book_id'] . "\">" . $row['title'] . "</option>";**, press Enter/Return, and type **}**.

```
37       <select name="bookNumber" id="bookNumber">
38         <option selected>Select a book</option>
39         <?php
40         require_once("includes/db_connx.php");
41         $sql = "SELECT book_id, title FROM books";
42         $result = @mysql_query($sql) or die("Error performing query.");
43         while ($row = mysql_fetch_array($result)) {
44           echo "<option value=\"" . $row['book_id'] . "\">" . $row['title'] . "</option>";
45         }
46         ?>
47       </select>
```

FIGURE 8.76

7. Preview the page in your browser and observe that the list is populated with the titles of the books.

   To select a record from a database with 100 or more entries, you would probably want to use a different method of selecting a record to edit, such as creating a searching capability to narrow the choices before presenting a final list.

8. Return to Dreamweaver and close select_book.php.

2. Populate a Form with Data from the Database

Using the book_id from the selected book from the select_book.php page, you populate the edit form with the data for that book. You also store the book_id in a hidden field of the form. This is used by the next script to ensure that when you select book 1, you don't update book 2's data. Although you don't see the hidden field's data on screen, it is passed via get or post to the page specified by the action URL.

1. Open edit_book.php in the Code view and scroll to line 50.

   As you can see from the code, some of the common code has already been created for you.

2. You must first identify the book_id of the selected book. In the empty line 50, type
   `$selectedBook = $_POST['bookNumber'];`.

   This code captures the book_id number of the selected book from the bookNumber select list.

3. Near the end of line 52, click between **books** and ", press the Spacebar, and type `WHERE book_id=\"" . $selectedBook . "\"`.

   This code adds a WHERE clause to the SELECT command, restricting the returned record to just that specific book. The next part of the code is to insert the current values for the book as the default values for the form.

4. On line 59, between the "" of **value=""**, type `<?php echo $row['title']; ?>`.

5. On line 63, between the "" of **value=""**, type `<?php echo $row['author']; ?>`.

6. On line 67, between the "" of **value=""**, type `<?php echo $row['pubyear']; ?>`.

7. On line 71, between > and **</textarea>**, type `<?php echo $row['description']; ?>`.

8. On line 75, between the "" of **value=""**, type `<?php echo $row['price']; ?>`.

9. On line 79, between the "" of **value=""**, type `<?php echo $row['image']; ?>`.

10. On line 83, between the "" of **value=""**, type `<?php echo $row['category']; ?>`.

11. On line 87, between the " " of **value=""**, type `<?php echo $row['book_id']; ?>`.

```php
49    <?php
50    $selectedBook = $_POST['bookNumber'];
51    require_once("includes/db_connx.php");
52    $sql = "SELECT book_id, title, author, pubyear, description, price, image, category FROM books WHERE book_id=\"" . $selectedBook . "\";";
53    $result = @mysql_query($sql) or die("Error performing query.");
54    $row = mysql_fetch_array($result);
55    ?>
56      <form action="update_book.php" method="post" enctype="application/x-www-form-urlencoded" name="editbook" class="style1" id="editbook">
57        <table>
58          <tr>
59            <th>Title:</th>
60            <td><input name="title" type="text" class="wide" id="title" size="60" maxlength="100" value="<?php echo $row['title']; ?>"></td>
61          </tr>
62          <tr>
63            <th>Author:</th>
64            <td><input name="author" type="text" class="wide" id="author" size="60" maxlength="100" value="<?php echo $row['author']; ?>"></td>
65          </tr>
66          <tr>
67            <th>Year:</th>
68            <td><input name="pubyear" type="text" id="pubyear" size="6" maxlength="4" value="<?php echo $row['pubyear']; ?>"></td>
69          </tr>
70          <tr>
71            <th>Description:</th>
72            <td><textarea name="description" cols="70" rows="4" class="wide" id="description"><?php echo $row['description']; ?></textarea></td>
73          </tr>
74          <tr>
75            <th>Price:</th>
76            <td><input name="price" type="text" id="price" size="8" maxlength="6" value="<?php echo $row['price']; ?>"></td>
77          </tr>
78          <tr>
79            <th>Image:</th>
80            <td><input name="image" type="text" id="image" size="18" maxlength="20" value="<?php echo $row['image']; ?>"></td>
81          </tr>
82          <tr>
83            <th>Category</th>
84            <td><input name="category" type="text" id="category" size="4" maxlength="2" value="<?php echo $row['category']; ?>"></td>
85          </tr>
86          <tr>
87            <th><input name="book_id" type="hidden" value="<?php echo $row['book_id']; ?>"></th>
88            <td><input name="Submit" type="submit" value="Submit Changes"></td>
89          </tr>
90        </table>
91      </form>
```

FIGURE 8.77

12. Close edit_book.php, saving your changes. Upload edit_book.php to the server.

13. Open select_book.php in Dreamweaver and preview it in your browser. Select a book and click Edit.

    The data for the book have been inserted into the fields of the form, and the book_id has been inserted into a hidden field.

14. Return to Dreamweaver and close select_book.php.

3. Create the Update Page

In this exercise, you add the final piece to the edit process — you create the page to update the database with the changed record. When you create a new record, you use the INSERT command, but when you update a record, you use the **UPDATE** command. It is used as **UPDATE tablename SET fieldname1=data1, fieldname2= data2, fieldname3=data3, … WHERE condition**. You can use the **UPDATE** command without the **WHERE** condition, but this replaces all records in the table with the data specified in the **fieldname=data** pairs. In this exercise, you use the book_id in the **WHERE** condition to identify which record you want to update with the changed data.

Although it would appear to be more efficient to update only those fields that have been changed, in fact, the savings, in terms of the demands on the database server, are smaller than the increased demands on PHP needed to compare the previous and current data and determine what data remained the same and what data changed. As a result, updating all fields in a record, except auto_increment fields, is quite acceptable.

1. Open update_book.php in the Code view and scroll to line 92.

   Most of the PHP code has been created for you. Lines 51 to 90 are very similar to those in the insert_book.php page, in that the data is collected from the post variables.

2. In the empty line 92, type `$sql = "UPDATE books SET title=\"$title\", author=\"$author\", pubyear=\"$pubyear\", description=\"$description\", price=\"$price\", image=\"$image\", category=\"$category\" WHERE book_id=\"" . $book_id . "\";";`.

3. Close update_book.php, saving your changes.

4. Upload update_book.php to the server.

5. Open select_book.php in Dreamweaver, select a book, and click Edit.

6. Make a change to the data about the book (but not the image data) and click Submit Changes.

7. Click the link to view all of the books and examine the page for your change.

8. Close your browser, return to Dreamweaver, and close all open files.

4. Create Sort Links

In this exercise, you create links in the books.php page that link back to the same page, but with a query string added to the URL. The query strings are **sortBy=y** and **sortBy=t**, which are used to sort by year or title, respectively. You know that forms using the get method pass the form data via the query string, and that the **$_GET** variable is used to collect the query-string variables. You can create your own links with query strings in them: query strings are not restricted to just get data from forms.

You use the **$_GET** variable to capture the data from the query string. Using the **if** clause, you set the **ORDER BY** clause in the **SELECT** command to either pubyear or title using **ORDER BY $sortBy**, where **$sortBy** is a variable containing either pubyear or title. When a visitor goes directly to the books.php page, there is no query string so you test for the existence of **$_GET['sortBy']**. If it exists, you assign **$sortBy** with the appropriate field. However, if **$_GET['sortBy']** does not exist, you set **$sortBy** to title as the default. Therefore, there are two types of checks that must be satisfied: does **$_GET['sortBy']** exist, and if so, what value does it hold?

1. Open books.php in the Code view and scroll to line 37.

2. Click to the right of **<?php** and press Enter/Return.

3. Type **$sortBy = "title";** and press Enter/Return.

   This sets a default value for the **$sortBy** variable in case there is no query string.

4. Type **if (isset($_GET['sortBy'])) {** and press Enter/Return.

5. Type **if ($_GET['sortBy'] == "y") {** and press Enter/Return.

   This line of code only runs if **sortBy** exists in the query string. If **sortBy** does not exist in the query string, the default sort order is used.

6. Type **$sortBy = "pubyear";** and press Enter/Return.

7. Type **}}**.

   There is no need to test for **sortBy** equaling anything else because only **sortBy=y** will change the sort order. By restricting the possible choices, there is no chance that a visitor could hijack the query string to perform some malicious activity because only **sortBy=y** is allowed. All other possibilities do not change the default sort order.

8. At the end of line 44 between **books** and ", press the Spacebar and type **ORDER BY $sortBy**.

9. Click in line 35, and type **Sort by: Title Year**.

```
34    <td align="left" valign="top"><h2>Books</h2>
35    Sort by: Title Year
36    <table align="center" cellpadding="2" cellspacing="0">
37    <?php
38    $sortBy = "title";
39    if (isset($_GET['sortBy'])) {
40    if ($_GET['sortBy'] == "y") {
41    $sortBy = "pubyear";
42    }}
43    require_once("includes/db_connx.php");
44    $sql = "SELECT book_id, title, author, pubyear, description, price, image FROM books ORDER BY $sortBy";
45    $result = @mysql_query($sql) or die("Error performing query.");
46    while ($row = mysql_fetch_array($result)) {
47    ?>
```

FIGURE 8.78

10. Switch to the Design view and set the format of this line to Paragraph from the Property inspector.

11. Select the word Title and, in the Link field, type **books.php?sortBy=t**. Select the word Year and, in the Link field, type **books.php?sortBy=y**.

    As you know, it doesn't matter what we set with **sortBy** in the Title link because the code only checks for **sortBy=y** and nothing else. However, in case you want to provide another sorting option later on, you should add **sortBy=t** to remind you of its purpose and to prepare you to check for the t.

12. Preview the page in your browser and test the two links.

13. Return to Dreamweaver and close books.php.

5. Send Comments via Form Mail

The basic **mail()** function is very simple and contains just four parameters: **mail($to, $subject, $comments, $from)**. You may use other variable names than the four shown here, but these indicate the purpose of the four parameters. The first parameter must contain the email address of the person to whom the email is being sent, generally yourself or your client. You could insert this email address in a hidden field in the form or you could capture it using **$_GET** or **$_POST** (whichever method is used in the form). As we discussed in *Project 1: Collecting Information with Forms*, however, hidden fields are exposed to anyone who wants to examine the HTML code of a page, including email-harvesting software used by spammers. Therefore, this address should be stored as a variable in the PHP code that is never exposed to visitors.

The fourth parameter may contain more than just the email address of the person who is sending the message. It can contain **CC:** (carbon copy or courtesy copy) and **BCC:** (blind carbon copy or blind courtesy copy) email addresses as well as other information. However, for the sake of simplicity in this Challenge exercise, this parameter will only contain the name of the sender and their email address.

There are two other caveats to the code you work with in this exercise — there is no form validation in the PHP, and the **mail()** function is disabled on the 100webspace.com Web site. Using PHP for form validation has, for the most part, been omitted in this project, especially email-address validation for which the code can become quite complex. There are many resources on the Internet on how to validate email addresses. Furthermore, 100webspace.com, like many other free Web-hosting services, does not provide email addresses for free accounts and, therefore, form-mail scripts fail. These form-mail scripts must be sent through a valid email address, so if you do not have a paid account with 100webspace.com, your form-mail scripts will fail. Nevertheless, you may use this script, with some form validation, when you have a paid account with 100webspace.com or any other Web-hosting provider.

1. Open contact_thankyou.php, switch to the Code view, and scroll down to line 49.

2. Type **<?php** and press Enter/Return.

3. Type **$to = "myEmail@address.com";** and press Enter/Return.

   To prevent email harvesters from harvesting your email address, it is stored here in the PHP code. To use this code properly, change the email address to your own.

4. Type **$subject = $_POST['subject'];** and press Enter/Return.
   Type **$comments = $_POST['comments'];** and press Enter/Return.

5. Type **$ from = "\"" . $_POST['name'] . "\" " . $_POST['email'];** and press Enter/Return.

   This code concatenates the name of the visitor to his or her email address.

6. Type `if(mail($to,$subject,$comments,$from))` `{` and press Enter/Return.
    Type `echo " <h3>Your Message</h3>";` and press Enter/Return.
    Type `echo " <p><strong>From:</strong> " . $from . "</p>";` and press Enter/Return.
    Type `echo " <p><strong>Subject:</strong> " . $subject . "</p>";` and press
    Enter/Return.
    Type `echo " <p><strong>Comments:</strong> " . $comments . "</p>";` and press
    Enter/Return.
    Type `echo "<p>We will contact you as soon as we can.</p>";` and press
    Enter/Return.
    Type `}` `else` `{` and press Enter/Return. Type `echo "<p>Email failed.</p>";` and press
    Enter/Return.
    Finally, type `}`.

    This block of code uses the **mail()** function. If the **mail()** function is successful, it returns a true
    value and, therefore, the email message displays with a message stating that you will contact the
    visitor. Otherwise, the Email failed message appears.

```
48   <td align="left" valign="top"><h2>Thank you for your message</h2>
49   <?php
50   $to = "myEmail@address.com";
51   $subject = $_POST['subject'];
52   $comments = $_POST['comments'];
53   $from = "\"" . $_POST['name'] . "\" " . $_POST['email'];
54   if(mail($to,$subject,$comments,$from)) {
55   echo "<h3>Your Message</h3>";
56   echo "<p><strong>From:</strong> " . $from . "</p>";
57   echo "<p><strong>Subject:</strong> " . $subject . "</p>";
58   echo "<p><strong>Comments:</strong> " . $comments . "</p>";
59   echo "<p>We will contact you as soon as we can.</p>";
60   } else {
61   echo "<p>Email failed.</p>";
62   }
63   ?>
```

FIGURE 8.79

7. Close contact_thankyou.php, saving your changes, and then upload it to your Web site.

8. Open contactus.php in Dreamweaver and preview it in your browser. Fill out the fields and click
    Send Message.

    This code, in a free account on 100webspace.com, will return a true value but, in fact, the message
    will never be sent. Nevertheless, you have learned how to create a form-mail script.

9. Close your browser, return to Dreamweaver, and close any open files.

P O R T F O L I O   B U I L D E R

Create a Database-Driven Portfolio

Databases are great for storing and categorizing data. Using the categories, you can query a database for all records that fall into a particular category. Your résumé or portfolio can be stored in a database and, when a visitor opens one of your pages, the database populates the page with the appropriate data.

1. Using the categories of Web design, graphic design, and animation, create a list of 15 projects you have (or would like to have) been part of — put 5 for each category. In the list, record the name of the company, the year of the project, and a description of your role, and assign it a category code.

2. Create a new database table called **portfolio** on your site with fields named **company**, **year**, **description**, and **category**. Set all fields as varchar type with lengths of **20**, **4**, **200**, and **3**, respectively.

3. Insert your data into your table.

4. Create a PHP page in which you require the db_connx.php page.

5. Create an SQL query using SELECT company, year, and description FROM portfolio.

6. Create an ordered list (**<ol>**) in which the list-item tag contains **<li>**company (year)**
description</li>**. Using **$row['fieldname']**, replace **fieldname** with **company**, **year**, and **description** to display the contents of the records.

7. When successful, add the WHERE clause to the SELECT command to display only records that fall into a particular category.

INTEGRATING PROJECT

This project reflects a real-world Web-site job, drawing on the skills you learned throughout this book. The files you need to complete this project are located in the RF_Dreamweaver_L2>IP folder.

From the Stovetop to the Tabletop Web Site

From the Stovetop to the Tabletop is a small business that sells food-preparation equipment to both the home and restaurant markets in your town. They have asked you to create their Web site that will, at first, simply promote their products. Ultimately, though, they would also like to sell their products online. In order to prepare the site for future expansion into online commerce, you realize that you must create a database of their products. They would also like their Web site to use current technologies. You interpret this to mean that the site should not use tables or frames for layout, but instead should use CSS. To demonstrate the working draft of the site to your clients, you create a subdomain on your Web site so you can use PHP and MySQL and your clients can view the site from their computers.

PART 1 | **Preparing the Site, the Server, and the Database**

In this first section, you create a subdomain, in which you will store your pages, in your account at 100web-space.com. You define a new site in Dreamweaver with the settings from your new subdomain. You configure cloaking to prevent some files from uploading to the site and upload the remaining files in your site folder. Finally, you create a new table in your database and populate it with data on the kitchen products.

Create the Subdomain

As you may remember, 100webspace.com allows free accounts to have up to five subdomains (including the original). When you have completed this integrating project, you may delete all (but the original) subdomains and use this account for your own personal use.

1   Open your browser and, following the instructions in the email from 100webspace.com, go to the login page for your Control panel, and log in with your username and password.

2   In the Site Manager group of links, click the Subdomain Manager link.

3   In the Subdomain field, type your username followed by **3**, such as esdw3.

4   Set the domain name to the same domain name as your two other subdomains.

5   Leave the rest of the settings as they are and click the Add Subdomain button.

FIGURE IP.1

Define the Site in Dreamweaver

1 Launch Dreamweaver and create a new site definition named **IP** from the RF_Dreamweaver_L2> IP folder.

2 In the Remote Info category, set Access to FTP. Type the IP address from Step 4 of the previous exercise into the FTP Host field.

3 Type the URL of the subdomain in the Host Directory field.

4 Type your username and password into the Login and Password fields, and click the Test button.

? If you have problems

If the test is not successful, open your email message from 100webspace.com and copy/paste your username and password from the message into the fields. The username and password are the same for all subdomains in your account.

5 In the Testing Server category, set Server Model to PHP MySQL, and Access to FTP.

6 If necessary, remove the IP address from the URL prefix field.

7 Click OK and then click Done.

Cloak Files and Folders

The Photoshop folder contains the original graphics for parts of this Web site. In the Documents folder are ip.sql.txt, aboutus.html, and policies.html files that also contain information for building the database and other pages so you do not need to upload then.

1 In the Files panel, Right/Control-click the Photoshop folder and choose Cloaking>Cloak.

2 Right/Control-click the Documents folder and choose Cloaking>Cloak.

3 Right/Control-click in the Files panel and choose Cloaking>Settings. Enable the Cloak Files Ending With option. Delete all of the existing filename extensions.

Files ending with .fla do not exist on this site but .png files do exist and should be uploaded.

4 Click OK, and then click OK again to re-create the site cache.

5 Click the name of the Site at the top of the list of files in the Files panel, and then click the Put button.

6 When asked if you wish to upload the entire site, click OK.

There are quite a few image files so the upload may take a few minutes, depending on the speed of your Internet connection.

7 When the upload has finished, click the Disconnect button to disconnect from your Web site.

Create the IP Table in the Database

Your free account with 100webspace.com allows only one MySQL database, but you may create as many tables as you like, as long as the total space taken by the database is no more than 5 MB, much more space than you need for this project.

1 Return to your browser. If you logged off from your Web-space account, log in to the Control panel again.

2 In the Site Manager group of links, click the PHPMy Admin link, and then click the link to your existing database.

3 Using your database login information (sent to you in another email message), log in to PHPMyAdmin.

4 Click the name of your database below Home, on the left.

5 Near the bottom of the page where it reads Create new table, type **ip** in the Name field, type **5** in the Fields field, and click Go.

6 Name the first field **prod_id**, choose Varchar as the Type, type **7** in the Length/Values field, and leave the rest of the options at their defaults.

7 Create the rest of the fields as follows:

Field	Type	Length/Values
name	Varchar	**50**
description	Varchar	**255**
price	Decimal	**5,2**
category	Char	**2**

Database *esdw_proj8* - Table *ip* running on *hollosite.com*

Field	Type [Documentation]	Length/Values*	Attributes
prod_id	VARCHAR	7	
name	VARCHAR	50	
description	VARCHAR	255	
price	DECIMAL	5,2	
category	CHAR	2	

FIGURE IP.2

8 Click Save.

9 After the ip table has been created, click the SQL link between the SQL code for creating the table and details of the new ip table.

10 Switch to Dreamweaver and open ip.sql.txt from the Documents folder. Select all of the content, copy it to the clipboard, and then close the file.

11 Return to your browser. Click in the large textarea field in the SQL page, delete the existing SQL command code, paste the copied text, and click Go.

12 Close your browser and return to Dreamweaver.

PART 2   Creating the Layout and Styles

While you create most of the styles for the site at this time, you don't create the styles for the form on the index.php page, as that form does not yet exist. You add other styles, as you need them, in later exercises.

Wrap the Contents in Div Containers

1 Open index.php from the IP site.

2 Click the top graphic and then click the **<a>** tag in the Tag selector.

3 From the Layout Insert bar, click the Insert Div Tag button, assign it an id of **header**, ensure that it is set to Wrap Around Selection, and click OK.

4 Select from Products to the Home link and, using the same procedures as in Step 3, wrap the selected content in a **<div>** tag with an id of **navbar**.

5 Select from Welcome to the right of the image (do not include the list of links at the bottom), and wrap the selected content in a **<div>** tag with an id of **content**.

6 Click in any of the links at the bottom of the page. Click the **<ul>** tag in the Tag selector and wrap the list of links at the bottom in a **<div>** tag with an id of **footer**.

7 Select all of the content. Wrap the selected content in a **<div>** tag with an id of **body**.

8 Save the changes to index.php and keep the page open.

Create the Body Styles and Layouts

1 With index.php file open in Dreamweaver, open the CSS Styles panel by selecting Window>CSS Styles, if it is not already open.

2 Right/Control-click in the CSS Styles panel and choose New. Choose Advanced as the Selector Type, type **body** in the Selector field, and ensure that Define in is set to New Style Sheet File. Click OK.

3 In the Save as field, type **styles.css** and click Save.

4 In the Type category, set the Font to Arial, Helvetica, Sans-serif, and type **#5369AC** in the Color field. In the Background category, set the Background Color to **#FFFFFF**, choose graphics/body-bg.png as the Background Image, set Attachment to Fixed, and set both Horizontal and Vertical positions to center. In the Box category, set the Top margin to **20** pixels and leave Same for All selected. Click OK.

5   Create a new CSS style for the **div#body** selector (Advanced type) to be defined in styles.css. In the Background category, set the Background Color to **#FFFFFF** and choose graphics/div-body-bg.png as the Background Image. In the Box category, set the Width to **750** pixels, uncheck Same for All for Margins, and set both Right and Left margins to auto. Click OK.

Although at times, it may be appropriate to change the Selector Type option in the New CSS Style dialog box from Class to Tag or Advanced, because you can create all types of selectors using the Advanced Selector Type, we only use the Advanced option in this project. Also, unless otherwise instructed, create all styles in the styles.css external style-sheet file.

6   Create a new CSS style for the **div#header** selector. In the Border category, just create a Bottom border and set the following properties: Style to solid, Width to **2** pixels, and Color to **#DCEDF8**. Click OK.

7   Create a new CSS style for the **div#navbar** selector. In the Background category, set the Background Color to **#FFFFFF**. In the Box category, set Width to **150** pixels, set Float to left, uncheck Same for All for Padding, and create a Left padding of **15** pixels. Click OK.

8   Create a new CSS style for the **div#content** selector. In the Box category, set Width to **555** pixels, and Float to left. Uncheck Same for All for Padding and create a **10**-pixel Left padding and a **15**-pixel Right padding. In the Border category, create a Right border that is solid, **2** pixels wide, with a color of **#DCEDF8**. Click OK.

9   Create a new CSS style for the **div#footer** selector. In the Background category, set the Background Color to **#FFFFFF**, choose graphics/div-footer-bg.png as the Background Image, set Horizontal position to center, and set Vertical position to bottom. In the Block category, set Text Align to center. In the Box category, set Width to **750** pixels, Height to **35** pixels, and Float to left. Uncheck Same for All for Padding and set the Top padding to **15** pixels. In the Border category, create a Top border only that is solid, **2** pixels wide, with a color of **#DCEDF8**. Click OK.

FIGURE IP.3

10   Save the changes to index.php and keep it open.

Create the Basic Navbar Styles

1 In the open file, index.php, create a new CSS style for the **div#navbar h2** selector. In the Type category, set Size to **1.2** em. In the Box category, set all paddings and margins to **0** pixels. Click OK.

2 Create a new CSS style for the **div#navbar ul** selector. In the Box category, set all paddings and margins to **0** pixels. In the List category, set Type to none. Click OK.

3 Create a new CSS style for the **div#navbar li** selector. In the Box category, set Height to **1.2** ems and click OK.

4 Create a new CSS style for the **div#navbar p** selector. In the Background category, set Background Color to **#DCEDF8** and click OK.

5 Create a new CSS style for the **div#navbar a** selector. In the Type category, set Color to **#5369AC**, and from the Decoration options, check none. In the Block category, choose block from the Display list. In the Box category, set Height to **1.2** ems. Click OK.

6 Create a new CSS style for the **div#navbar a:hover** selector. In the Type category, set Weight to bold and click OK.

7 Create a new CSS style for the **div#navbar p a:hover** selector. In the Background category, choose graphics/home-arrow.png as the Background Image, set Repeat to no-repeat, set Horizontal position to right, and set Vertical position to center. Click OK.

8 From the Files panel, upload styles.css to the server.

9 Preview this page in your browser. If prompted to save the file first, click Yes.

FIGURE IP.4

? If you have problems

If your browser displays the code of styles.css, it means that the focus was still on styles.css in the Files panel when you activated the browser preview function. Return to Dreamweaver, click in the index.php page, and then preview the page in your browser again.

10 Return to Dreamweaver and keep index.php open.

Create Color-Coded Links in the Navigation Bar

In the code of the five links in the left navigation bar, the links each have their own ids so you can create individual color styles for each link. These color styles identify the product group. In the products.php page, the colors in the page for each product group will match the color of the link in the left navigation bar.

1 In the open file, index.php, Right/Control-click in the CSS Styles panel and choose Attach Style Sheet.

2 In the Attach External Style Sheet dialog box, click the Browse button, choose navbar.css from the root folder of the IP site, click OK/Choose, and then click OK again.

3 Preview the page in your browser and move your mouse pointer over the navbar links.

Notice that the left borders and backgrounds change colors and arrows appear to the right. The basic concept is the same for them all, but the colors and specific arrow images differ.

4 Return to Dreamweaver.

5 In the CSS Styles panel, expand navbar.css.

6 Right/Control-click in the group of styles from the navbar.css file, and create a new CSS style for the `div#navbar a#se` selector. Ensure that Define in is set to navbar.css. Click OK.

7 In the Box category, create a Left padding of **3** pixels. In the Border category, create a Left border that is solid, **15** pixels wide, with a Color of **#E7DCF8**. Click OK.

8 Create a new CSS style for the `div#navbar a#se:hover` selector in the navbar.css file. In the Background category, set the Background Color to **#E7DCF8**, choose graphics/navbar-se-arrow.png for the Background Image, set Repeat to no-repeat, set Horizontal position to right, and set Vertical position to center. In the Border category, create a Left border that is solid, **15** pixels wide, with a Color **#C2A7ED**. Click OK.

9 Upload navbar.css to the server.

10 Preview the page in your browser and move your mouse pointer over the Serving link.

FIGURE IP.5

11 Return to Dreamweaver and keep index.php open.

Create the Content Styles

1 Create a new CSS style for the `div#content h1` selector. Ensure that Define in is set to styles.css. In the Type category, set Size to `1.4` ems, and Weight to normal. In the Box category, uncheck Same for All for Margins, and create a Top margin of `0` pixels and a Bottom margin of `15` pixels. Click OK.

In this exercise, until you are told otherwise, create the new styles in the styles.css file.

2 Create a new CSS style for the `div#content p.animation` selector. In the Block category, set Text Align to center and click OK.

3 Click the large image in the Document window. Right/Control-click the `<p>` tag in the Tag selector and set the Class to animation.

4 Keep index.php open.

Create the Footer Styles

1 In the open file, index.php, create a new CSS style for the `div#footer ul` selector. In the Box category, set Width to `600` pixels, and set all paddings to `0` pixels. Uncheck Same for All for Margins, set Top and Bottom margins to `0` pixels, and set both Left and Right margins to auto. In the List category, set Type to None, and click OK.

2 Create a new CSS style for the `div#footer li` selector. In the Box category, set Width to `150` pixels and Float to left. Click OK.

3 Create a new CSS style for the `div#footer a` selector. In the Type category, set Size to `0.9` ems and set Color to `#5369AC`. In the Box category, set Width to `150` pixels and Float to left. Click OK.

4 Create a new CSS style for the `div#footer a:hover` selector. In the Background category, set the Background Color to `#DCEDF8` and click OK.

5 Upload styles.css to the server.

6 Preview index.php in your browser and move your mouse pointer over the footer links.

FIGURE IP.6

7 Return to Dreamweaver and disconnect from the server. Keep index.php open.

PART 3   Creating Library Items and a Template

In the next series of exercises, you create library items from the header, navbar, and footer divs. From index.php you also create a template from which you create the other pages.

Create Library Items

1   In the open file, index.php, click the top graphic and then click the **`<div#header>`** tag in the Tag selector.

2   Switch to the Assets panel and click the Library icon down the left side of the Assets panel.

3   Click the New Library Item button at the bottom of the Assets panel and name the new library item **Header**.

4   Click in the navbar in the Document window, and then click the **`<div#navbar>`** tag in the Tag selector. Click the New Library Item button at the bottom of the Assets panel, and name the new library item **Navbar**.

5   Click in the footer and then click the **`<div#footer>`** tag in the Tag selector. Click the New Library Item button at the bottom of the Assets panel and name the new library item **Footer**.

6   Save the changes to index.php and keep it open.

Create a Template from Index.php

1   In the open file, index.php, choose File>Save as Template.

2   In the Save as field, type **common** and click Save.

3   When prompted to Update Links, and click Yes.

4   Click to the left of Welcome and then shift-click at the right of the photograph.

5   From the Common Insert bar, choose Editable Region from the Templates drop-down menu.

6   Type **content** in the Name field and click OK.

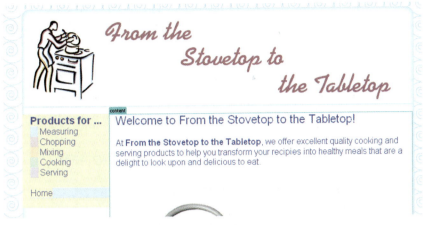

FIGURE IP.7

7   Close common.dwt.php, saving your changes.

Create Two Pages from the Template

1   Choose File>New. Click the Templates tab at the top of the New Document dialog box, and choose common from the IP site. Click Create.

2   Select all of the content in the editable region and delete it.

3   Open aboutus.html from the Documents folder. Select all of the content and copy it to the clipboard. Close aboutus.html.

4   Paste the content into the content editable region.

5   In the Document title, delete all of the text to the right of Stovetop to Tabletop: and type **About Us**.

6   Close aboutus.php, saving your changes in the root folder of the IP site folder.

7   Create a new page from the common template. Select all of the content in the editable region and delete it.

8   Open policies.html from the Documents folder. Select all of the content and copy it to the clipboard. Close policies.html.

9   Paste the content into the content editable region.

10   In the Document title, delete all text to the right of Stovetop to Tabletop: and type **Warranty, Shipping and Delivery Policies**.

11   Create a new CSS style for the **div#content h2** selector. In the Type category, set Size to **1.2** ems and Weight to normal. Click OK.

12   Close policies.php, saving your changes to the root folder of the IP site folder.

PART 4   Creating Timed Image Swaps

In this exercise, you create a timed image-swap animation, which shows potential customers the type of products they can purchase from this Web site.

Prepare the Timelines Panel

1 Open index.php.

2 Click the photograph and, in the Property inspector, name the image **swap**.

3 Choose Window>Timelines to open the Timelines panel.

4 Drag the swap image into the first animation channel starting at frame 1.

Many times during this exercise, various warnings may pop up unless you or another person using your computer has disabled them. If they do pop up, click OK to acknowledge them.

5 Drag the last keyframe to frame 51.

6 Change the frames per second (FPS) field to **5**.

7 Save your changes to index.php and leave it open.

Add Swap-Image Behaviors to the Timeline

1 In the open file, index.php, click frame 11 in the Behaviors channel of the Timelines panel.

2 If necessary, choose Window>Behaviors to open the Behaviors panel.

3 Click the plus-symbol/down-arrow to open the Behaviors drop-down menu and choose Swap Image.

4 From the Images list, select Image swap. You may have to click it a second time.

5 Using the Browse button, choose 0480025.jpg from the photos folder, click Choose/OK, and then click OK.

6 Click frame 21 in the Behavior channel.

7 Repeat Steps 3 to 5 and choose 0480048.jpg.

8 At frame 31, set the swap behavior to open 0480063.jpg. At frame 41, set the swap behavior to open 0480071.jpg. At frame 51, set the swap behavior to open 0280009.jpg. Enable both Autoplay and Loop.

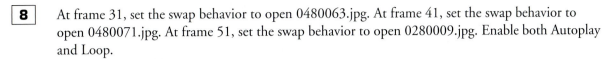

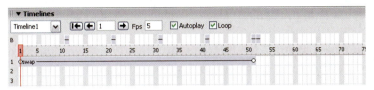

FIGURE IP.8

9 Close the Timelines panel by selecting Window>Timelines.

10 Preview the page in your browser.

? If you have problems

When you preview a remote page in your browser, sometimes the browser doesn't display the changes to the page. If you don't see a change, click the Refresh or Reload button in your browser.

---

11 Return to Dreamweaver and close index.php.

PART 5 Creating a Contact-Form Application

In this series of exercises, you create a contact form from the common template. In addition to name, email address, and comments, you ask the visitor to choose the product they are enquiring about from a list of the products sold through this Web site. The list will be dynamically generated from the database. You add JavaScript validation to the page to require the visitor to complete the name, email address, and comments field. Finally, you create a thank-you page to collect the data sent by the form, display the visitors' message, and send an email to the recipient address in the PHP code of the thank-you page. Remember, 100webspace.com does not allow the **mail()** function to work if you don't have a paid account with them, but the rest of the form works.

Create the Contact Form from the Template

1 Create a new page from the common template of the IP site.

2 Select all content in the content div and delete it.

3 Type **Contact Us** and, if necessary, format the line as a Heading-1 block.

4   Type **If you are enquiring about a product you had purchased, select the product name and provide the date of purchase. If you are simply enquiring about a product, please select it from the list. Otherwise, you may leave both fields unchanged.**. Press Enter/Return. Type **Please complete the Fullname, Email, and Comments fields.**.

5   Press Enter/Return and insert a form from the Form Insert bar. Name the form **contactus**, set the Action URL to **thankyou.php**, set the Method to Post, and set the Enctype to application/x-www-urlencoded.

6   Click in the form, type **Fullname:**, and press the Spacebar. Insert a text field from the Form Insert bar. In the Property inspector, name the field **fullname**, set the Char Width to **35**, and set Max Chars to **40**. Click to the right of the text field and press Enter/Return.

7   Type **Email Address:** and press the Spacebar. Insert a text field from the Form Insert bar. In the Property inspector, name the field **email**, set the Char Width to **35**, and set Max Chars to **40**. Click to the right of the text field and press Enter/Return.

8   Type **Product Name:** and press the Spacebar. Insert a List/Menu field and name it **productname**. In the Property inspector, click the List Values button. Under Item Label, type **Select a product** and press Tab twice. Type **name** and click OK. In the Property inspector, set Select a Product as the Initially Selected Value. Click to the right of the List/Menu field in the Document window and press Enter/Return.

9   Type **Purchase Date:** and press the Spacebar. Insert a text field from the Form Insert bar. In the Property inspector, name the field **purchasedate**, set the Char Width to **35**, and set Max Chars to **40**. Click to the right of the text field and press Enter/Return.

10   Type **Comments:** and press the Spacebar. Insert a textarea field from the Form Insert bar. In the Property inspector, name the field **comments**, set the Char Width to **30**, and set Num Lines to **4**. Click to the right of the textarea field and press Enter/Return.

11   Insert a submit button and, in the Property inspector, type **Send us your comments** in the value field.

12   Save the file as contactus.php and keep the page open.

Create the Field Labels

1 In the open file, contactus.php, select Full Name.

2 Right/Control-click the selected text and choose Wrap Tag from the contextual menu. Press **1** and press Enter/Return to accept the **<label>** tag. Press the Spacebar. Press **f**, press Enter/Return to accept the **for** attribute, type **fullname** between the quotation marks, and press Enter/Return.

3 Repeat Steps 1 and 2 for the remaining labels, assigning them the **for** attributes of **email**, **productname**, **purchasedate**, and **comments**, respectively.

4 Save the changes to contactus.php and keep it open.

Create Layout and Styles

1 In the open file, contactus.php, Right/Control-click in the CSS Styles panel and create a new CSS style for the **form label** selector. In the Box category, set the Width to **150** pixels and Float to left. Click OK.

2 Create a new CSS style for the **form input, form select, form textarea** selector. In the Type category, choose Arial, Helvetica, sans-serif for the Font; set Color to **#5369AC**. In the Box category, set Width to **250** pixels. Click OK.

3 Create a new CSS style for the **form input#submit** selector. In the Box category, set Width to **180** pixels. Uncheck the Same for All option for Margins, and set the Left margin to **150** pixels. Click OK.

4 Create a new CSS style for the **form input:focus, form textarea:focus** selector. In the Background category, set the Background Color to **#DCEDF8**. Leave contactus.php open.

FIGURE IP.9

Add JavaScript Validation

1 In the open file, contactus.php, click within the red dashed boundary of the form, and then click the **<form#contactus>** tag in the Tag selector.

2 If the Behaviors panel is not open, choose Window>Behaviors to open it.

3 From the Behaviors drop-down menu, choose Validate Form. Choose the fullname field in the Named Fields list. Check the Required option and choose Accept Anything.

4 Choose the email field in the Named Fields list. Check the Required option and choose Accept Email Address.

5 Choose the comments field in the Named Fields list. Check the Required option and choose Accept Anything. Click OK.

6 Save the changes and keep contactus.php open.

Create the Database Connection File

In order for the visitor to choose a product name from the list, the list must be populated with the names of the products. Given that the product list may often change and that the list is stored in a MySQL database table, the list will be populated dynamically from the database table. Because the database connection is used in different pages, you create a database connection file that is included by any page that needs to connect to the database.

1 Choose File>New, click the General tab, choose the Dynamic Page category, choose PHP, and click Create.

2 Switch to the Code view, select all of the code, and delete it.

3 Type **<?php** and press Enter/Return.

4 Type **$dbc = @mysql_connect("host", "login", "password") or die("The database server is unavailable.");**, replacing host with the URL of the database server, login with your database login, and password with your database password. Press Enter/Return.

Refer to the email you received when you created your database in Project 8.

5 Type **if (!@mysql_select_db("dbname", $dbc)) {** and press Enter/Return.

Replace dbname with the name of your database on 100webspace.com.

6 Type **die("The database is unavailable.");**, press Enter/Return, type **}**, press Enter/Return, and type **?>**.

```
1  <?php
2  $dbc = @mysql_connect("host", "login", "password") or die("The database server is unavailable.");
3  if (!@mysql_select_db("dbname", $dbc)) {
4  die("The database is unavailable.");
5  }
6  ?>
```

FIGURE IP.10

7   Close, saving the file as **db_connx.php**.

8   Upload db_connx.php to the server.

Query the Database for the Product Names

In this exercise, you query the database for the product names and create the select list. To do this, you must include the db_connx.php file, create the SQL, and loop through the rows of product names.

1   In the open file, contactus.php, scroll down to approximately line 68 and locate the **<option selected>Select a product</option>** code.

2   Click to the right of this line, press Enter/Return, type **<?php**, and press Enter/Return.

3   Click to the right of the following line containing **<option>name</option>**, press Enter/Return, type **}**, press Enter/Return, and type **?>**.

4   In the empty line above, type **require_once "db_connx.php";** and press Enter/Return.

5   Type **$sql = "SELECT name FROM ip ORDER BY prod_id";** and press Enter/Return.

6   Type **$result = @mysql_query($sql) or die("Error performing query.");** and press Enter/Return.

7   Type **while ($row = mysql_fetch_array($result)) {**.

8   Replace **<option>name</option>** with **echo "<option>" . $row['name'] . "</option>";**.

```
67        <select name="productname" id="productname">
68          <option selected>Select a product</option>
69          <?php
70          require_once "db_connx.php";
71          $sql = "SELECT name FROM ip ORDER BY prod_id";
72          $result = @mysql_query($sql) or die("Error performing query.");
73          while ($row = mysql_fetch_array($result)) {
74          echo "<option>" . $row['name'] . "</option>";
75          }
76          ?>
77        </select>
78    </p>
```

FIGURE IP.11

9   Switch to the Design view, preview the page in your browser, and test the select list.

10   Return to Dreamweaver and close contactus.php.

Create the Thank-You Page

In this exercise, you use the common template to create a page thanking the visitor for taking the time to contact you. You also show the message that the visitor sent.

1 Create a new page from the common template from the IP site.

2 Change the Document title to `Stovetop to Tabletop: Thank you for your comments`.

3 Select the content in the content div and delete it.

4 Open thankyou.html from the Documents folder. Select all of the content and copy it to the clipboard. Close thankyou.html.

5 Paste the copied content into the empty content div.

6 Save the file as `thankyou.php` and keep it open.

Capture the Form Data

In this exercise, you create the PHP code to capture the form data entered into the contact form and passed to this page via the post method. To capture post data, remember that you must use the $_POST variable.

1 In the open file, thankyou.php, switch to the Code view.

2 Scroll down to the code `<h1>Thank you for your message!</h1>` at approximately line 26, click to the right of this line, and press Enter/Return.

3 Type `<?php`, press Enter/Return twice, and type `?>`.

4 Move up to the empty line and type `if (isset($_POST['fullname'])) {`. Press Enter/Return and type `$fullname = $_POST['fullname'];`. Press Enter/Return and type `} else {`. Press Enter/Return and type `$fullname = "Nothing entered";`. Press Enter/Return and type `}`.

This block of code tests whether anything was entered into the fullname field. If there was, it is assigned to the $fullname variable; otherwise the text, Nothing entered, is assigned to the $fullname variable.

5 Select the five lines of code typed in Step 4 and copy them. Paste the block four times so that you have five identical blocks.

6 In the second block, the first pasted block, replace all occurrences of fullname with `email`, as in `$email` and `$_POST['email']`. In the third block, replace all occurrences of fullname with `comments`.

7 In the fourth block, replace all occurrences of fullname with `purchasedate`. In the fourth block delete Nothing entered from between the quotations leaving `$fullname = "";`.

8 In the last block, replace all occurrences of fullname with **productname** and delete Nothing entered from between the quotation marks. Also replace the first line of the block with **if ($_POST['productname'] != "Select a product") {**.

```
26   <h1>Thank you for your message!</h1>
27   <?php
28   if (isset($_POST['fullname'])) {
29   $fullname = $_POST['fullname'];
30   } else {
31   $fullname = "Nothing entered";
32   }
33   if (isset($_POST['email'])) {
34   $email = $_POST['email'];
35   } else {
36   $email = "Nothing entered";
37   }
38   if (isset($_POST['comments'])) {
39   $comments = $_POST['comments'];
40   } else {
41   $comments = "Nothing entered";
42   }
43   if (isset($_POST['purchasedate'])) {
44   $purchasedate = $_POST['purchasedate'];
45   } else {
46   $purchasedate = "";
47   }
48   if ($_POST['productname'] != "Select a product") {
49   $productname = $_POST['productname'];
50   } else {
51   $productname = "";
52   }
53   ?>
54   <p><strong>Full Name:</strong> fullname</p>
```

> A select list is always isset() so you must change the if condition to look for the Select a product data, which means that the visitor did not select a product.

FIGURE IP.12

9 Save the changes to thankyou.php and keep it open.

Display the Form Data in the Page

In this exercise, you display the data that was sent from the form in this page so that the visitor may view what he or she has written.

1 In the open file, thankyou.php, locate the code **<p>Full Name: fullname</p>** at approximately line 54.

2 Replace fullname with **<?php echo $fullname; ?>**.

3 In the next line, replace email with **<?php echo $email; ?>**.

4 In the next line, replace **<p>Product Name: productname</p>** with **<?php if (!$productname == "") {echo "<p>Product Name : $productname</p>"; } ?>**.

Because this field is optional, if nothing has been sent from the field, the thankyou.php page hides the heading.

5 In the next line, replace **<p>Purchase Date: purchasedate</p>** with **<?php if (!$purchasedate == "") {echo "<p>Puchase Date : $purchasedate</p>"; } ?>**.

6 In the next line, replace comments with **<?php echo $comments; ?>**.

```
54    <p><strong>Full Name:</strong> <?php echo $fullname; ?></p>
55    <p><strong>Email Address:</strong> <?php echo $email; ?> </p>
56    <?php if (!$productname == "") {echo "<p><strong>Product Name :</strong> $productname</p>"; } ?>
57    <?php if (!$purchasedate == "") {echo "<p><strong>Purchase Date :</strong> $purchasedate</p>"; } ?>
58    <p><strong>Your Comments Were:</strong> <?php echo $comments; ?></p>
59    </div>
```

FIGURE IP.13

7 Save the changes to thankyou.php and keep it open.

Send the Message via Email

1 In the open file, thankyou.php, click to the right of the **<?php echo $comments; ?></p>** at approximately line 58 and press Enter/Return.

2 Type **<?php** and press Enter/Return.

3 Type **$to = "myemail@domain.com";** replacing the email address with your own and press Enter/Return.

4 Type **if ($productname == "") {**, press Enter/Return, type **$subject = "Message from Contact Form";**, press Enter/Return, type **} else {**, press Enter/Return, type **$subject = "Regarding: " . $productname;**, press Enter/Return, type **}**, and press Enter/Return.

This block of code checks to see if a product name had been selected. If so, then the subject line of the message is Regarding: productname; otherwise the subject line is just Message from Contact Form. Because your free account does not allow you to send email, you can't verify this.

5 Type **if (mail($to, $subject, $comments)) {**, press Enter/Return, type **echo "<p>Your message was sent.</p>";**, press Enter/Return, type **} else {**, press Enter/Return, type **echo "<p>Email failed.</p>";**, press Enter/Return, type **}**, press Enter/Return, and type **?>**.

```
58    <p><strong>Your Comments Were:</strong> <?php echo $comments; ?></p>
59    <?php
60    $to = "myemail@domain.com";
61    if ($productname == "") {
62    $subject = "Message from Contact Form";
63    } else {
64    $subject = "Regarding: " . $productname;
65    }
66    if (mail($to, $subject, $comments)) {
67    echo "<p>Your message was sent.</p>";
68    } else {
69    echo "<p>Email failed.</p>";
70    }
71    ?>
72    </div>
```

FIGURE IP.14

6 Switch to the Design view.

7 Close thankyou.php, saving your changes. Upload the page to the server.

8 Open contactus.php and preview it in your browser. Experiment with the form to see how it works from a visitor's perspective.

9 Return to Dreamweaver and close contactus.php.

PART 6   Creating a Dynamic Products Page

In this lesson, you create a dynamic page that displays an individually selected product, offers a JavaScript pop-up window to view a larger photo of the image, and provides a list of products in the selected category. This page is dynamic in that when a visitor selects a different category of products or a different individual product, the page content changes in response to these factors.

Create the Basic Products Page

In this lesson, you create the basic products.php page. Unlike the previous pages, you won't be using the template, because part of the dynamics of this page is to change a couple of the colors in this page and Dreamweaver does not allow you to create embedded styles in a page built from a template, unless you modify the template itself.

1 Create a new Dynamic PHP page, save it as **products.php**, and leave it open.

2 In the Document title, type **Stovetop to Tabletop: Products**.

3 Open the Assets panel and click the Library icon.

4 Click the Header library item and click the Insert button at the bottom of the Assets panel.

5 In the Document window, click below the Header library item and, using the same procedures as in Step 4, insert the Navbar library item.

6 Click below the Navbar library item in the Document window and insert the Footer library item from the Assets panel.

7 Right/Control-click in the CSS Styles panel, choose Attach Style Sheet, and choose styles.css. Right/Control-click in the CSS Styles panel and attach navbar.css.

8 Click to the right of the Navbar and, from the Layout Insert bar, insert a div with an id of **content**.

9 In the Document window, select all of the content and wrap the selected content in a div with the id of **body**.

10 Open products.html from the Documents folder. Select all of the content and copy it to the clipboard. Close products.html.

11 Select the text Content for id "content" Goes Here and paste the copied content from products.html.

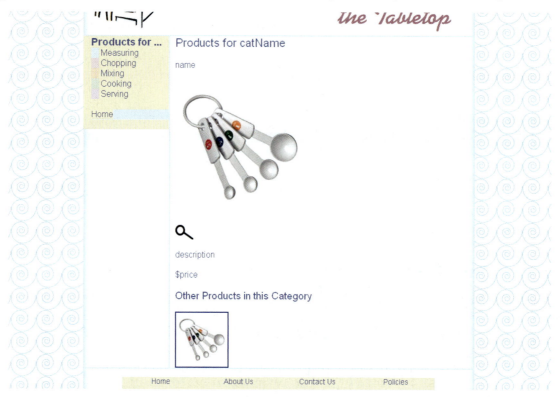

FIGURE IP.15

12 Save the changes to products.php and keep it open.

Create the Layout for the Products Page

1 In the open file, products.php, click to the left of Name, just above the large photo, and then Shift-click to the right of $price.

2 Wrap the selected content with a **<div>** tag and assign it the id of **prod_details**.

3 Click to the left of Other Products (below $price) and Shift-click to the right of the small photo. Wrap the selected content with a **<div>** tag and assign it the id of **cat_list**.

You won't be creating the styles for this section so it is important that you type prod_details and cat_list properly so that the CSS can use these ids in the selectors.

4 Right/Control-click in the CSS Styles panel and attach the style-sheet file, products.css.

FIGURE IP.16

5 Save the changes and keep products.php open.

Create the JavaScript Pop-Up Window

1 In the open file, products.php, click the magnifying-glass graphic below the large photo.

2 If the Behaviors panel is not open, choose Window>Behaviors to open it. From the Behavior drop-down menu, choose Open Browser Window.

3 Click the Browse button, choose 0280009.jpg from the photos album, and click Choose/OK.

4 Set both Window Width and Window Height to **500** and click OK.

5 In the Behaviors panel, from the list of events, change the event from onLoad to <A> onClick.

6 Preview the page in your browser and click the magnifying-glass graphic.

7 Close the pop-up browser window and return to Dreamweaver.

8 Save the changes to products.php and keep it open.

Capture and Use the Get Data

You now have a working template for this page. Unlike Dreamweaver templates, however, the page will not be used to create other static pages but will change in response to data sent via the query string. Recall that the five product links in the left navigation bar each have a query string, such as **products.php?cat=me**, which is used to display the products for measuring. You use the **$_GET** variable to capture the data in the query string and change the contents in the page, accordingly.

1 In the open file, products.php, switch to the Code view, scroll to line 1, and click to the left of **<!DOCTYPE**.

2 Type **<?php**, press Enter/Return twice, type **?>**, and press Enter/Return.

3   Move up to the blank line, type `if(isset($_GET['cat'])) { $category = $_GET['cat'];`, press Enter/Return, type `} else {`, press Enter/Return, type `$category = "me";`, press Enter/Return, type `}`, and press Enter/Return.

This block of code tests to see if the query string contains the cat variable. If it does exist, the data is assigned to the $category variable. If it does not exist, $category is assigned me as a default.

4   Type `if ($category == "me") { $catName = "Measuring"; }` and press Enter/Return.

The $catName will be used to display the name of the product category on the page.

5   Repeat Step 4 another four times (copy and paste is simplest), replacing me and Measuring with `ch` and `Chopping`, `mx` and `Mixing`, `co` and `Cooking`, and `se` and `Serving`.

6   Type `if (!($category == "me" || $category == "ch" || $category == "mx" || $category == "co" || $category == "se")) { $category = "me"; $catName = "Measuring"; }`.

```
 1  <?php
 2  if(isset($_GET['cat'])) { $category = $_GET['cat']; }
 3  if ($category == "me") { $catName = "Measuring"; }
 4  if ($category == "ch") { $catName = "Chopping"; }
 5  if ($category == "mx") { $catName = "Mixing"; }
 6  if ($category == "co") { $catName = "Cooking"; }
 7  if ($category == "se") { $catName = "Serving"; }
 8  if (!($category == "me" || $category == "ch" || $category == "mx" || $category == "co" || $category == "se")) { $category = "me"; $catName = "Measuring"; }
 9  ?>
10  <!DOCTYPE HTML PUBLIC "-//W3C//DTD HTML 4.01 Transitional//EN" "http://www.w3.org/TR/html4/loose.dtd">
```

FIGURE IP.17

The problem with the code in Step 3 is that a person could modify the query string to ?cat=xx, which does not match any of the categories. In Step 6, the code checks to see if $category=xx matches any of the existing categories and, if not, assigns $category and $catName with the default values for the measuring products.

7   Scroll down to approximately line 43, `<div id="content" class="xx">`. Replace `xx` with `<?php echo $category; ?>`.

8   On the next line, replace `catName` with `<?php echo $catName; ?>`.

```
43  <div id="content" class="<?php echo $category; ?>">
44    <h1>Products for <?php echo $catName; ?></h1>
45    <div id="prod_details">
```

FIGURE IP.18

9 Preview the page in your browser and click the left navigation-bar links.

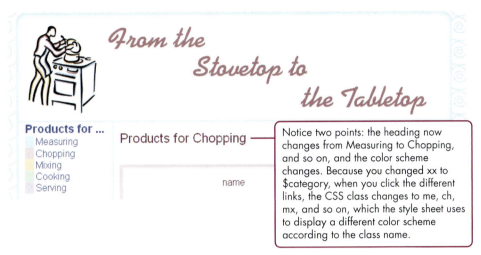

Notice two points: the heading now changes from Measuring to Chopping, and so on, and the color scheme changes. Because you changed xx to $category, when you click the different links, the CSS class changes to me, ch, mx, and so on, which the style sheet uses to display a different color scheme according to the class name.

FIGURE IP.19

10 Return to Dreamweaver but keep products.php open.

Display a List of Products for the Category

In this exercise, you query the database for the product ids and product names for the selected category, such as all of the measuring products. The cat_list div on the right will be populated with a column of photos of the products in the current category that was set by the $category variable from the $_GET data.

1 In the open file, products.php, scroll up to line 1, click to the right of **<?php**, and press Enter/Return.

2 Type **require_once "db_connx.php";**.

This code does not necessarily need to appear at the top of the page, but placing it there means that it always appears before any database queries.

3 Scroll down to approximately line 55, **<h2>Other Products in this Category</h2>**. Click to the right of this line and press Enter/Return.

4 Type **<?php**, press Enter/Return, type **$sql = "SELECT prod_id, name FROM ip WHERE category=\"$category\" ORDER BY prod_id;";**, and press Enter/Return.

5 Type **$result = @mysql_query($sql) or die("Error performing query.");** and press Enter/Return.

6 Type **while ($row = mysql_fetch_array($result)) {**, press Enter/Return, and type **?>**.

7 Scroll down two lines, click to the left of **</div>**, type **<?php } ?>**, and press Enter/Return.

These lines of code query the database for the product ids and names of the products for all products in the currently selected category.

8 On line 61, change **prodid=prod_id** to **prodid=<?php echo $row['prod_id']; ?>**.

This code, used later, modifies the query-string portion of the link to add the product id for the current product item.

9 On line 61, change **0280009_sm.jpg** to **<?php echo $row['prod_id']; ?>_sm.jpg**. Change **alt="name"** to **alt="<?php echo $row['name']; ?>"**.

```
54    <h2>Other Products in this Category</h2>
55    <?php
56    $sql = "SELECT prod_id, name FROM ip WHERE category=\"$category\" ORDER BY prod_id;";
57    $result = @MySQL_query($sql) or die("Error performing query.");
58    while ($row = MySQL_fetch_array($result)) {
59    ?>
60    <p><a href="products.php?prodid=<?php echo $row['prod_id']; ?>"><img src="/photos/<?php echo $row['prod_id']; ?>_sm.jpg" alt="<?php echo $row['name']; ?>" width="100" h
61    <?php } ?>
62    </div>
```

FIGURE IP.20

This code dynamically creates the image name and alt text from the product id and product name. All of the images are 100 × 100 pixels so you don't need to worry about varying sizes.

10 Preview the page in your browser. Click the links in the left navigation bar.

Notice that the images on the left change to reflect just those products in the current category. Notice also the use of the **overflow: auto** CSS property to create a frame-like appearance of the column of product photos.

11 Return to Dreamweaver and keep products.php open.

Display the First Product of the Select Category

Currently, no matter which category you choose, the same photo of the plastic measuring spoons is visible in the main portion of the content. In this exercise, you query the database for the first product (as sorted by product id) of each category and display its details.

1 In the open file, products.php, scroll up to approximately line 47, where you find **<div id="prod_details">**. Click to the right of this line and press Enter/Return.

2 Type **<?php**, press Enter/Return twice, type **?>**, and press Enter/Return.

3 Move up one line, type **$sql = "SELECT prod_id, name, description, price FROM ip WHERE category=\"$category\" ORDER BY prod_id;";**, and press Enter/Return.

4 Type **$result = @mysql_query($sql) or die("Error performing query.");**, and press Enter/Return.

5 Type `$row = mysql_fetch_array($result);`.

This line of code is a little different from the way you used it before, when you inserted it into a while loop. In this instance, you want only the first row of the results array so you don't insert this code into a loop.

6 On line 53, change `<p>name</p>` to `<p><?php echo $row['name']; ?></p>`.

7 On line 54, change `0280009_md.jpg` to `<?php echo $row['prod_id']; ?>_md.jpg`.

8 On line 55, change `0280009.jpg` to `<?php echo $row['prod_id']; ?>.jpg`.

9 On line 56, change `description` to `<?php echo $row['description']; ?>`.

10 On line 57, change `$price` to `$<?php echo $row['price']; ?>`.

```
46    <div id="prod_details">
47    <?php
48    $sql = "SELECT prod_id, name, description, price FROM ip WHERE category=\"$category\" ORDER BY prod_id;";
49    $result = @mysql_query($sql) or die("Error performing query.");
50    $row = mysql_fetch_array($result);
51    ?>
52      <p><?php echo $row['name']; ?></p>
53      <p><img src="/photos/<?php echo $row['prod_id']; ?>_md.jpg" alt="" width="250" height="250"></p>
54      <p><a href="javascript:;" onClick="MM_openBrWindow('photos/<?php echo $row['prod_id']; ?>.jpg','','width=500,height=500')"><img src="/graph
55      <p><?php echo $row['description']; ?></p>
56      <p>$<?php echo $row['price']; ?></p>
57    </div>
58    <div id="cat_list">
```

FIGURE IP.21

11 Preview the page in your browser. Click any of the links in the left navigation bar and notice that the highlighted product is the first one in the list on the right. Click the magnifying-glass graphic and notice that the pop-up window displays an enlarged image of the same product.

12 Return to Dreamweaver and keep products.php open.

Display the Selected Product

You completed part of this exercise earlier when you added the product id to the link from the product images on the left, such as **product.php?prodid=0280009**. Now, you add code that checks for the existence of the prodid variable in the query string.

1 In the open file, products.php, scroll up to line 2, click to the right of the line, press Enter/Return, type `if (isset($_GET['prodid'])) {`, press Enter/Return, type `$sql = "SELECT prod_id, category FROM ip WHERE prod_id=" . $_GET['prodid'] . ";";`, and press Enter/Return.

The purpose of using the prodid query-string data to select prod_id from the table is to verify its existence. If someone were to change products.php?prodid=0280009 to products.php?prodid=0280090 and that product id did not exist, then the page would display an error.

2 Type `if($result = @mysql_query($sql)) { $row = mysql_fetch_array($result); $prodid = $row['prod_id']; $category = $row['category']; }`, press Enter/Return, and type `}`.

This code queries the database, and if $result is not empty, then `$_GET['prodid']` is valid and $prodid and $category are assigned their data from the database.

3 Type `} else { $prodid = ""; }` and press Enter/Return.

```
1  <?php
2  require_once "db_connx.php";
3  if (isset($_GET['prodid'])) {
4  $sql = "SELECT prod_id, category FROM ip WHERE prod_id=" . $_GET['prodid'] . ";";
5  if ($result = @mysql_query($sql)) { $row = mysql_fetch_array($result); $prodid = $row['prod_id']; $category = $row['category']; }
6  }
7  } else { $prodid = ""; }
```

FIGURE IP.22

4 Scroll down to line 51 and change **ORDER BY** to **$prodid ORDER BY**.

Although not yet complete, this code modifies the WHERE clause to search on both the category and product id, which narrows the search to just that particular product. You must add AND to the WHERE clause, but because AND is not always needed, as you saw in the most recent browser preview, AND will be added to $prodid.

5 Click to the right of **<?php** in the previous line, press Enter/Return, and type `if (!($prodid == "")) { $prodid = "AND prod_id=\"$prodid\""; }`.

> If $prodid does not equal "" (empty), then reassign $prodid with AND prodid=$prodid. Therefore, in the following line, either $prodid contains nothing and won't be used in the SELECT query or it contains AND prodid="product number" and will narrow the search to just that product id.

```
49  <h1>Products for <?php echo $catName; ?></h1>
50  <div id="prod_details">
51  <?php
52  if (!($prodid == "")) { $prodid = "AND prod_id=\"$prodid\""; }
53  $sql = "SELECT prod_id, name, description, price FROM ip WHERE category=\"$category\" $prodid ORDER BY prod_id;";
54  $result = @mysql_query($sql) or die("Error performing query.");
```

FIGURE IP.23

6 Preview the page in your browser. Click any of the product categories, and change the query string to any fictitious category or product id (all of the product ids are 7-digit numbers beginning with 0).

Notice that using this single page, 5 categories and 25 products can be displayed. It would be very easy to add some new records to the database and new images; without a single change to the code (assuming no new categories), you could add and display new products. With relatively little effort, you could also add new categories.

7 Close your browser, return to Dreamweaver, and close the application.

TASK GUIDE

Task	Windows	Macintosh

Managing Files

New document	Control-N	Command-N
Open an HTML file	Control-O	Command-O
Open in frame	Control-Shift-O	Command-Shift-O
Close	Control-W	Command-W
Save	Control-S	Command-S
Save as	Control-Shift-S	Command-Shift-S
Exit/Quit	Alt-F4 or Control-Q	Option-F4 or Command-Q

Opening and Closing Panels

Insert bar	Control-F2	Command-F2
Properties	Control-F3	Command-F3
CSS Styles	Shift-F11	Shift-F11
Tag Inspector	F9	F9
Reference	Shift-F1	Shift-F1
Site	F8	F8
Assets	F11	F11
Show/Hide panels	F4	F4

Viewing Page Elements

Page Properties	Control-J	Command-J
Selection Properties	Control-Shift-J	Command-Shift-J

Previewing and Debugging in Browsers

Preview in primary browser	F12	F12
Preview in secondary browser	Shift-F12	Shift-F12

Task	Windows	Macintosh

General Editing

Task	Windows	Macintosh
Undo	Control-Z	Command-Z
Redo	Control-Y or Control-Shift-Z	Command-Y or Command-Shift-Z
Cut	Cut Control-X or Shift-Delete	Cut Command-X or Shift-Delete
Copy	Control-C	Command-C
Paste	Control-V or Shift-Insert	Command-V or Shift-Insert
Clear	Delete	Delete
Bold	Control-B	Command-B
Italic	Control-I	Command-I
Select All	Control-A	Command-A
Move to page up	Page Up	Page Up
Move to page down	Page Down	Page Down
Select to page up	Shift-Page Up	Shift-Page Up
Select to page down	Shift-Page Down	Shift-Page Down
Select line up/down	Shift-Up/Down	Shift-Up/Down
Move to start of line	Home	Home
Move to end of line	End	End
Select to start of line	Shift-Home	Shift-Home
Select to end of line	Shift-End	Shift-End
Go to previous/next paragraph	Control-Up/Down	Command-Up/Down
Go to next/previous word	Control-Right/Left	Command-Right/Left
Delete word left	Control-Backspace	Command-Backspace
Delete word right	Control-Delete	Command-Delete
Select character left/right	Shift-Left/Right	Shift-Left/Right
Find and Replace	Control-F	Command-F
Find next/find again	F3	Command-G
Replace	Control-H	Command-H
Preferences	Control-U	Command-U

Task	Windows	Macintosh

Code Editing

Print code	Control-P	Command-P
Open Quick Tag Editor	Control-T	Command-T
Insert tag	Control-E	Command-E
Edit tag (in Design view)	Control-F5	Command-F5
Go to line	Control-G	Control-,
Move to top of code	Control-Home	Command-Home
Move to end of code	Control-End	Command-End
Select to top of code	Control-Shift-Home	Command-Shift-Home
Select to end of code	Control-Shift-End	Command-Shift-End

Text Editing

Create a new paragraph	Enter	Return
Insert a line break 	Shift-Enter	Shift-Return
Insert a nonbreaking space	Control-Shift-Spacebar	Command-Shift-Spacebar
Move text or object to another place in the page	Drag selected item	Drag selected item
Copy text or object to another place in the page	Control-drag selected item	Option-drag selected item
Open and close the Property inspector	Control-Shift-J	Command-Shift-J
Check spelling	Shift-F7	Shift-F7

Opening and Closing Panels

Insert bar	Control-F2	Command-F2
Properties	Control-F3	Command-F3
CSS Styles	Shift-F11	Shift-F11
Behaviors	Shift-F4	Shift-F4
Snippets	Shift-F9	Shift-F9
Reference	Shift-F1	Shift-F1
Files	F8	F8
Assets	F11	F11
Results	F7	F7
Timelines	Alt-F9	Option-F9
Show/Hide panels	F4	F4

Task	Windows	Macintosh

Getting Help

Using Dreamweaver Help Topics	F1	F1
Using ColdFusion Help Topics	Control-F1	Command-F1
Reference	Shift-F1	Shift-F1

Site Map

View site files	F8	F8
Refresh Local pane	Shift-F5	Shift-F5
View as root	Control-Shift-R	
Show page titles	Control-Shift-T	Command-Shift-T
Zoom in site map	Control-Plus (+)	Command-Plus (+)
Zoom out site map	Control-Hyphen (-)	Command-Hyphen (-)

Site Management and FTP

Connect/Disconnect	Control-Alt-Shift-F5	Command-Option-Shift-F5
Refresh	F5	F5
Create new file	Control-Shift-N	Command-Shift-N
Create new folder	Control-Alt-Shift-N	Command-Option-Shift-N
Cut file	Control-X	Command-X
Delete file	Del	Command-Delete
Copy file	Control-C	Command-C
Paste file	Control-V	Command-V
Duplicate file	Control-D	Command-D
Rename file	F2	F2
Get selected files or folders from remote site	Control-Shift-D	Command-Shift-D
Put selected files or folders to remote site	Control-Shift-U	Command-Shift-U
View site map	Alt-F8	Option-F8
Refresh Local pane	Shift-F5	Shift-F5
Refresh Remote pane	Alt-F5	Option-F5

GLOSSARY

* The universal selector, used to create a style that applies to all content.

above the fold The area of a Web page that a user can view without scrolling either vertically or horizontally.

absolute path The location of a file or Web page beginning with the root. Includes all necessary information to find the file or page. In the case of a Web page, called "absolute URL." See *relative path*.

absolute positioning Specifying the position of a div using the upper-left corner of the page as a fixed reference point. See also *div* and *relative positioning*.

accessibility The ability for a disabled viewer to use a Web site.

action The URL that receives data from a form.

alert box A pop-up box with a message for the user to acknowledge.

alt text Alternate Text. Text that can be displayed in lieu of an image.

animation The technique of simulating movement by creating slight changes to an object or objects over time.

anonymous FTP FTP protocol that allows users access to files for downloading. The user ID is anonymous, and the password is any valid email address.

ASP Active Server Pages. A specification for a dynamically created Web page that contains either Visual Basic or JavaScript code. When a browser requests an ASP page, the Web server generates a page with HTML code. Only available on Windows servers.

asset An image, sound, video, or other file that may be in use in a Web page.

assistive device Hardware enabling a disabled viewer to use a Web site.

attribute An option that augments the element in which it appears; it also provide additional information about the element. Attributes appear as name-value pairs in the element's start-tag.

background A static object or color that lies behind all other objects.

bandwidth The transmission capacity, usually measured in bits per second, of a network connection.

behavior A JavaScript action or reaction to an event.

browser Software program that allows you to surf the Web. The most popular browsers are Microsoft Internet Explorer and Netscape Navigator. The very first browsers, such as Lynx, only allowed users to see text. Also called "Web browser."

browser compatibility A term that compares the way a Web page functions on different browsers. Incompatibilities often exist due to the way a browser interprets the HTML. The differences may be very slight or significant.

bullet A marker preceding text, usually a solid dot, generally indicating the text is part of a list.

button An element a user can click to cause an effect, such as submitting a form.

button state A visual version of a button. For example, when clicked, the button is in its down state; when dormant, it is in its up state. When the mouse is hovered over the button, the button is in its over state.

CFML Cold Fusion Markup Language. A proprietary markup language, owned by Macromedia, that is mixed in HTML. Cold Fusion may perform functions and interact with databases. It only runs on a Cold Fusion Server.

CGI Common Gateway Interface. Interface that allows scripts to run on a Web server. CGI scripts can be used to put the content of a form into an email message, to perform a database query, or to generate HTML pages on the fly.

CGI script A CGI program used to process a form or provide other dynamic content.

cgi-bin The most common name of a directory on a Web server in which CGI scripts are stored.

checkbox A square that can be clicked to cause the form to send a name-value pair to the action; a form element that allows a user to choose zero or other choices.

class A style designation that can be added to multiple elements.

click-through rate A measure that reflects the percentage of users who clicked through to a Web site divided by the total number of messages that were delivered, inviting them to do so.

client A computer system or application that requests a service of another computer system on the network. See *server*.

client-side Scripting or other actions that take place within the browser, as opposed to the server.

code hint A pop-up menu that presents code options for HTML tags, attributes, options, CSS, and some programming languages. Code hints are only available when working with the code directly.

co-location Most often used to refer to having a server that belongs to one person or group that is physically located on an Internet-connected network that belongs to another person or group.

comment   A line in a piece of programming code that is intended to be read, not executed.

conditional statement   A statement that evaluates as either true or false. Conditional statements are used in if-then and while clauses that must evaluate whether or not the condition is true before proceeding or repeating.

contextual menu   A menu containing options relative only to the object for which the menu is activated.

cookie   Information a Web server writes to your computer hard disk via your browser, containing data such as login information and user preferences. This data can be retrieved so Web pages can be customized before they are sent to the visiting browser.

CSS   Cascading Style Sheets. Part of a Web-page file listing properties that affect the appearance of selectors, the content to which those properties apply, and their values.

dead link   A link whose destination has been changed or removed. Also called "broken links."

default   A specification for a mode of computer operation that occurs if no other is selected. The default font size might be 12 point, or a default color for an object might be white with a black border.

deprecated   The status of a tag or attribute that can still be used, but will eventually be removed, and so should be avoided, if possible.

development server   A server that houses a Web site while it is still being created and tested. (See *server*.)

DHTML   Dynamic HTML. JavaScript programs that dynamically change cascading-style-sheet properties, allowing parts of your Web page to be hidden, shown, or animated.

div   A block of content that can be positioned on the page. See *absolute positioning* and *relative positioning*.

DNS   Domain Name Server or Domain Name System. A service that maps IP numbers to a more easily remembered name. When you type http://www.somedomain.com into a browser, the DNS searches for a matching IP address (228.28.202.95).

document root   The main directory for a Web site.

domain name   A unique name that is used to identify a Web site, FTP site, and/or email server. A domain name always points to one specific server, even though the server may host many domain names.

domain-name registrar   A company that may sell domain names. Some provide hosting and other related services as well.

down state   A state that occurs when the user clicks a button.

drag   To position the pointer on an object, press and hold the mouse button, move the mouse and release the button.

drop-down menu   A selection list.

DSN   Data Source Name. Used to access a database.

DTD   Document Type Definition. A separate document that contains formal definitions of all of the data elements in a particular type of HTML, SGML, or XML document. By consulting the DTD for a document, a program called a "parser" can work with the markup codes that document contains.

dynamic   Content that changes according to client-side or server-side scripting.

ECMA   European Computer Manufacturers Association. A non-profit international industry association founded in 1961 dedicated to the worldwide standardization of information and communication systems.

ECMAScript   An official, standardized version of JavaScript maintained by the ECMA.

e-commerce   Electronic Commerce. Conducting business online, including product display, online ordering, and inventory management. The software, which works in conjunction with online payment systems to process payments, resides on a commerce server.

element   The portion of an HTML tag between the angle brackets. <p> is the paragraph tag whereas p is the paragraph element.

em   A printers measurement; the height, in points, of the font size.

email address   An electronic mail address. Email addresses are in the form of: user@domain.com (for example, chris@webguest.net).

embedded style sheet   Style information included within a Web page.

empty tag   A tag that has no closing element tag.

event   An action or occurrence detected by JavaScript. Events can be user actions (such as clicking a mouse button or pressing a key), timed events, or the loading and unloading of a Web page.

event handler   A function or method containing program statements that are executed in response to an event.

export   To save a file generated in one application into a format that is readable in another.

external style sheet   Style information included in a separate file referenced by a Web page.

folder   The digital equivalent of a paper file folder, used to organize files in the Macintosh and Windows operating systems. Double-clicking the icon opens it to reveal the files stored inside.

font   A font is the complete collection of all of the characters (numbers, uppercase and lowercase letters, and in some cases, small caps and symbols) of a given typeface in a specific style; for example, Helvetica Bold.

font class   In Web design, the type of font (serif, sans serif, monospace, cursive, or fantasy) that will be used if the user's computer does not have any of the font-family members. See *CSS*.

font family   In Web design, a grouping of (supposedly) similar fonts, which will be used to display text in the Web page.

form   A page that enables a user to type information and send it to a site via form elements such as text boxes and pull-down lists.

form validation   The process of making certain a Web form contains all required data and no invalid data.

frame rate   The number of successive images that are displayed in one second. Designated fps (frames per second).

frame-by-frame animation   Animation using a series of keyframes with no tweening; it creates a flipbook type of animation.

FTP   File Transfer Protocol. Internet method to transfer files through the Internet from one computer to another. FTP is used to download files from another computer, as well as to upload files from your computer to a remote computer.

function   A script that can be referenced by name.

get   A method for sending form data by appending it to the action URL. See *post*.

graceful degradation   A technique that ensures content remains usable, even if all features are not available. Graceful degradation is the goal when designing pages using standards that may not be supported in older browsers.

grayed out   Any option (menu selection, button, etc.) that is not available.

grayscale   An image composed in grays ranging from black to white, usually using 256 different tones.

header information   Information at the beginning of a Web-page file that defines the contents and characteristics of the page.

hex values   Numbers specified in the hexadecimal system, commonly used for specifying colors on Web pages.

home page   Main page of a Web site.

HTML   Hypertext Mark-Up Language. A tagging language that allows content to be delivered over the World Wide Web and viewed by a browser.

HTTP   Hypertext Transfer Protocol. The method used by browsers and Web servers to communicate, such as to request and deliver content, respectively.

ID   An identifier for a particular tag, added as an attribute and typically used to add style information.

if-then statement   A programming construction that executes one section of code if a conditional statement is true, and a second section if it is not.

IIS   Internet Information Server. Microsoft's Web server that runs on Windows NT platforms. IIS comes bundled with Windows NT 4.0. IIS is tightly integrated with the operating system, so it is relatively easy to administer.

information architecture   The structure and organization of the information on a Web site.

input   An element, such as a text box, that receives information from the user.

Internet   A global system of interconnected computers.

Internet Explorer   A common Web browser from Microsoft.

intranet   A small network dedicated to information and resources about and for the corporation or organization that maintains it. Enables a company to share resources with employees without confidential information being made available across the Internet.

IP address   A unique, 32-bit Internet address consisting of four numbers, separated by dots and sometimes called a "dotted quad" (90.0.0.95).

ISP   Internet Service Provider. An organization that provides access to the Internet for such things as electronic mail, bulletin boards, chat rooms, or use of the World Wide Web.

JavaScript   A scripting language, designed by Netscape, which can be embedded into HTML documents.

Jscript   Microsoft's version of JavaScript.

JSP   Java Servlet Pages. Web pages created using the Java programming language run on a Web server.

keyframe   An individual frame in a sequence of animation, from which other frames are extrapolated. For instance, a linear movement can be extrapolated from two keyframes, one at the beginning and one at the end of the movement.

keywords   Words that identify the content of a Web page and can be used by search engines as part of their process of determining the results of searches.

layout   The arrangement of text and graphics on a page.

leading   Space added between lines of type. Named after the strips of lead that used to be inserted between lines of metal type. In specifying type, lines of 12-pt type separated by a 14-pt space is abbreviated "12/14," or "12 over 14." The CSS property for leading is line-height.

left alignment   Text having a straight left edge and a ragged right edge.

letter spacing   The insertion or addition of white space between the letters of words.

Linux   The UNIX-based operating system for personal computers that is available for little or no cost, and offers developers free access to the uncompiled code.

list A series of items.

LiveScript The original name for JavaScript.

log in Enter into a computer system. Also the account name (or user ID) that you must enter before you can have access to some computer systems.

looping The process of continually returning to a location until another action occurs, such as the movement of the mouse pointer or the selection of a button.

mail server Server that handles incoming and outgoing email.

meta tag An optional HTML tag that is used to specify information about a Web document. Some search engines index Web pages by reading the information contained within the meta tags.

mouseover The event triggered at the moment the user rolls the mouse pointer over an area or item on a Web page. Typically used to tell the browser to do something, such as execute a rollover script.

Mozilla The organization created when Netscape Corporation decided to open source the code of their Netscape browser. Mozilla.org has released the powerful and sophisticated Mozilla, Firefox, and Camino browsers. Netscape version 6+ is based on Mozilla code. All Mozilla-based browsers are free to download.

MySQL A fast, free, open-source database suitable for Web database functionality.

nested tag A tag contained within another tag.

no-frames section Content provided for browsers that do not support frames; contained within a noframes element.

ODBC connectivity A standard database access method developed by Microsoft. The goal of ODBC is to make it possible to access any data from any application, regardless of which database management system (DBMS) is handling the data.

Opera Popular, advanced browser for Windows, Macintosh, Linux/Unix and cell phones from Opera.com. The free version is supported by advertising which may be removed for a fee.

orphaned files Files that exist below the root of the site but are not linked or used in any pages in the Web site.

over state A button state that occurs when the user passes the mouse pointer over a button.

page title Text that appears in the Title bar of the user's browser when the page is viewed. Also called the "document title."

page weight The total number of bytes required to download the HTML document and all associated assets, such as images, CSS, and JavaScript files. Dreamweaver's Download indicator identifies the page weight. Try to keep the page weight below 60 KB.

panel In Macromedia's workspace, the name given to palettes of tools and options.

parameter In programming, the term parameter is a synonym of argument, a value that is passed to a routine or function.

password Secret code you must enter after your user ID (login name) in order to log on to a computer.

password box A text box that replaces all characters with a bullet or asterisk to hide their identity.

Perl Practical Extraction and Report Language. A powerful computer language, especially used for writing CGI scripts that handle input/output actions on Web pages.

PHP An open-source server-side Web programming language capable of running on Unix, Linux, Windows, and Macintosh Web servers. Not only easy to learn but also capable of powerful and sophisticated functionality.

pixel Picture Element. One of the tiny rectangular areas or dots generated by a computer or output device to constitute images. A greater number of pixels per inch results in higher resolution on screen or in print.

point A unit of measurement used to specify type size and rule weight; equal to approximately 1/72 inch.

post A method for sending form data using headers. See *get*.

preloading Causing the browser to download images or other items before they are needed, so when they are needed, they are already in the browser cache; improves the speed with which they appear.

presentational HTML HTML tags and attributes that only provide style. The <b> (bold) tag and the align attribute are examples of presentational HTML. When designing a Web page, avoid using presentational HTML and use CSS instead.

protocol A set of rules and conventions that describe the behavior computers must follow in order to understand each other.

pt Abbreviation for point.

pull quote An excerpt from the body of a story; used to emphasize an idea, draw readers' attention, or generate interest.

PWS Personal Web Server. A feature-limited free version of IIS, available for Windows 98, enabling new developers to experiment with ASP and SQL Server database.

query Request for specific information from a database.

radio button   A single round button that can be clicked to cause the form to send a name-value pair to the action.

radio group   A group of radio buttons with the same name. Only one radio button may be selected at a time within a radio group.

redirect   To cause the browser to load a different page without intervention from the user.

refresh   To reload.

relative positioning   Specifying the position of a section of content, such as a div, based on the original location of the content. (See *div* and *absolute positioning*.)

resample   Resizing an image to decrease the physical size of the file, not just change the appearance on the page.

reset button   A button that, when clicked, causes a form to return to the state it was in when the page was first loaded.

rollover   The act of rolling the cursor over a given element on the screen.

root   Top-level directory from which all other directories branch out.

scripting   The process of adding programming capabilities to a program (e.g., AppleScript), file (e.g., ActionScript), or Web page (e.g., JavaScript).

search engine   A Web site that allows users to search for Web pages using keywords. Every search engine has its own strategy for collecting data.

search-engine optimization (SEO) Judicious incorporation of keywords and alt text in Web sites to maximize the likelihood that those sites are found by search engines.

select   Place the cursor on an object and click the mouse button to make the object active.

select list   A list of potential choices that can be displayed as a menu that appears when the user clicks on it, or as a box with its own scroll bar.

select option   A potential choice listed in a select list.

selector   Information used to determine the content to which style changes should apply.

server   A computer that has a permanent connection to the Internet. A Web site is stored on a Web server.

server-side   Pertaining to functions that are run at the computer that operates as a server before the results are sent to the client.

shopping cart   A piece of software that acts as the interface between a company's Web site and its deeper infrastructure, allowing consumers to select merchandise, review what they have selected, make necessary modifications or additions, and purchase the merchandise.

SHTTP   Secure HyperText Transfer Protocol. An encrypted version of HTTP used to transfer private information, such as credit-card information.

site map   A list of pages in a Web site. Commonly, the page names are links to the pages.

site root directory   The parent folder that contains all other files and directories for a Web site.

spam   To send identical and irrelevant postings to many different newsgroups or mailing lists. The name comes from a Monty Python song and is considered to be a serious violation of netiquette.

spamming a search engine   Providing false or repetitive information in the hope of improving search-engine rankings.

span   A section of inline content that can be styled.

spider   Program, also known as a "bot", used by some search engines to index Web sites. Spiders search the Web to find URLs that match the given query string.

SQL   Structured Query Language. A standardized query language for requesting information from a database. SQL also supports database updates, inserts and deletes, and user management.

string   A unit of text.

style   A defined set of formatting instructions for font and paragraph attributes, and other properties.

style sheet   A defined set of formatting instructions for font and paragraph attributes, tabs, and other properties of text.

syntax highlighting   A method of distinguishing different components of code (such as tags, attributes, comments, and text) by using text or background differently, or applying bold or italic styling.

template   A Web page containing layout, styles, and repeating elements (such as logos) by which a series of documents can maintain the same look and feel. A model page you can use as the basis for creating a new page.

text box   A box into which users can type.

this   Keyword that refers to the object that generated an event.

thumbnails   Small versions of larger images.

tweening   A process by which the in-between frames of an animation are automatically generated by the developing application.

UNIX   Multi-user computer operating system. The Internet and the Web matured on UNIX, and these days UNIX is still the most common operating system for servers on the Internet.

up state   Normally a button's default state, which occurs when the user has not clicked or passed over the button with the mouse pointer.

uploading   The process of sending a file from one computer to a remote server.

URL   Uniform Resource Locator. Address of any resource on the Web.

usability   The ease with which a user can access, navigate, and achieve goals on a Web site.

user ID   Unique identifier you must enter every time you want to access a particular service on the Internet. The user ID is always accompanied by a password.

validate   To analyze a file to ensure the structure, tag names, and attributes are correct, according to the DTD selected.

variable   A unit of information that can be referred to by name.

variable-width page   A characteristic of Web pages that allows the page to expand or contract horizontally, displaying as a percentage of the user's browser window. Also known as a "liquid layout."

VBScript   A Microsoft scripting language used for client-side scripting.

W3C   An acronym for the World Wide Web Consortium.

Web designer   An individual who is the aesthetic and navigational architect of a Web site, determining how the site looks, how it is laid out, and what components it contains.

Web developer   A person who builds the technical architecture of Web sites, providing the programming required for a particular Web product to work.

Web host   A company that provides access to a server on which you can place your Web-site content. This server is connected to the Internet, allowing the general public to access your Web site.

webmaster   The person who is responsible for the Web server (usually the sysadmin).

Web page   A single file or Web address containing HTML or XHTML information. Web pages typically include text and images, but may include links to other pages and other media.

Web-safe color   A color palette used for images that will be displayed on the Internet. The Web-safe color palette is a specific set that can be displayed by most computer-operating systems and monitors.

Web site   A collection of HTML files and other content that visitors can access by means of a URL and view with a Web browser.

World Wide Web   Client/server hypertext system for passing information across the Internet.

World Wide Web Consortium (W3C)   The group responsible for defining HTML Standards (http://www.w3.org).

XForms   An emerging specification defining advanced functionality for Web forms.

z-index   Value used for determining which of a set of overlapping layers will be displayed.

INDEX